Marriages and Deaths from Mississippi Newspapers

Volume 3
1813–1850

Compiled by
Betty Couch Wiltshire

HERITAGE BOOKS
2012

HERITAGE BOOKS
AN IMPRINT OF HERITAGE BOOKS, INC.

Books, CDs, and more—Worldwide

For our listing of thousands of titles see our website
at
www.HeritageBooks.com

Published 2012 by
HERITAGE BOOKS, INC.
Publishing Division
100 Railroad Ave. #104
Westminster, Maryland 21157

Copyright © 1989 Betty Couch Wiltshire

Other Heritage Books by the author:
CD: *Early Mississippi Records*
CD: *Early Mississippi Records: Volume 2*
Holmes County, Mississippi, Pioneers
Marriages and Deaths from Mississippi Newspapers: Volume 2, 1801–1850
Marriages and Deaths from Mississippi Newspapers: Volume 3, 1813–1850
Marriages and Deaths from Mississippi Newspapers: Volume 4, 1850–1861
Mississippi Index of Wills, 1800–1900

All rights reserved. No part of this book may be reproduced or transmitted in any form or by any means, electronic or mechanical, including photocopying, recording or by any information storage and retrieval system without written permission from the author, except for the inclusion of brief quotations in a review.

International Standard Book Numbers
Paperbound: 978-1-55613-198-1
Clothbound: 978-0-7884-9259-4

TABLE OF CONTENTS

Introduction	v
Sentinel & Expositor	1
Southern Galaxy	12
Southern Luminary	19
Southern Marksman	23
Southern Reformer	24
The Southern Star	51
The Southern Sun	60
Southern Telegraph	64
The Southron	71
State Rights Banner	90
State Telegraph	90
Statesman	90
Statesman & Gazette	90
Tri-Weekly Mississippian	93
The Tri-Weekly Sentinel	93
True Democrat	95
Vicksburg Daily Sentinel	97
Vicksburg Daily Whig	98
Vicksburg Register	168
Vicksburg Sentinel	187
Vicksburg Weekly Sentinel	188
Washington Republican	193
Washington Republican & Natchez Intelligencer	196
The Weekly Chronicle	200
Weekly Sentinel	202
The Woodville Republican	207
Woodville Republican & Wilkinson Weekly Advertiser	262
Index	267

INTRODUCTION

The Mississippi Territory (M.T.) was established by an act of the United States Congress in 1798. In 1801, Washington, a little town six miles east of Natchez, was made the capital. In 1802, there were only four counties: Adams, Claiborne, Jefferson, and Wilkinson, and settlements were primarily along the Gulf Coast and the Mississippi River. Mississippi became a state in 1817.

Volume I of Marriages and Deaths From Mississippi Newspapers extracted notices for the northern half of the state. Volumes II and III are concerned with the southern half, and because of the settlement pattern most newspapers included in volumes II and III are for the southwestern area of Mississippi. There are many notices of marriages and deaths in Louisiana, the neighboring states in this vicinity, as well as some northern counties and other states. All notices were copied from newspapers on microfilm at the Mississippi Department of Archives and History.

An effort was made to avoid duplication of notices, unless each contributed differing information. I've also tried to be as accurate as humanly possible. To the best of my knowledge, I abstracted all notices from newspapers available at the Archives for the southern part of Mississippi for this time period. The Archives continues to add newspapers to their microfilm collection, so even though your ancestor may not be listed in this book, you may find an obituary or marriage notice in the future.

Genealogy has given me many hours of pleasure, and I hope this book will add pleasure to the research of others.

Betty Couch Wiltshire

NEWSPAPER ABSTRACTS 1813 - 1850

SENTINEL AND EXPOSITOR (Vicksburg, Miss.)
By Green & Hagan

January 3, 1837
Married on Thursday last, by E. H. Maxey, Esq., Nathaniel Robinson, Esq., to Miss Margarett Raney.

Died at Mont Albon, Miss., of pulmonary consumption, on the 24th ult., Mr. Luther S. Creecy, late acting midshipman aboard the U. S. Frigate Constellation.

January 24, 1837
Died on Thursday morning last, Dr. Thomas C. Kenney, in the 22d year of his age, late of Baltimore, but for the last 18 years a resident of this county. He practised during the last summer in Tuscumbia, Louisiana.

February 21, 1837
Died in this city, on the 16th, of phthisis pulmonalis, Mr. Elisha B. Adams, a native of Philadelphia.

April 4, 1837
Died, 26th of March, Mrs. Martha C. Ward, consort of P. W. Ward, Esq., of this city.

May 2, 1837
Married on the 23d, by the Rev. Thomas Hutchison, Mr. John B. Small to Miss Lavinia E. Vinton, both of this city.

Married in Washington county, on the 27th, by the Rev. T. C. Brown, Rev. W. H. Hamer, of Virginia, to Mrs. E. Metcalfe, of Washington county, Miss.

Married on the 6th ultimo, by Rev. Mr. Downing, Mr. Joseph H. Arthur, formerly of Virginia, to Miss E. A. W. Sydnor, daughter of Mr. Thomas Sydnor, also formerly of Virginia, now all of Lincoln county, Mississippi.

June 20, 1837
Died of paralysis, in this city, on Wednesday last, Dr. James M.

Crump, formerly of Fredericksburg, Va. The deceased graduated in the University of Pennsylvania about two years ago, and in the fall of 1835 he emigrated to this city.

Died on Wednesday last, of small pox, P. W. Ward, Esq., late Post-Master of this city.

August 1, 1837

Died at Clinton, on the 23d ult., James Hamilton, Esq., commander of the Clinton Guards, and late editor of the Clinton Gazette.

Died at Rodney, 25th July, Thomas B. Palmer, Esq., Editor of the Rodney Telegraph and commander of the Rodney Guards.

August 8, 1837

Married at Fredricksburg, Va., 10th July, by the Rev. E. C. McGuire, Mr. A. M. Paxton, of Vicksburg, to Miss M. L. Ellis, daughter of Robt. Ellis, Esq., of the former place.

September 12, 1837

Married at Norfolk, Va., on the 15th ult., in the Methodist Episcopal Church, by the Rev. D. S. Doggett, E. W. Moore, merchant of this place, to Miss Mary A. O. Tabb, of the former place.

September 23, 1837

Married on Thursday evening last, by E. H. Maxey, Esq., Harvey Jenkins, Esq., to Miss Virginia Royall.

Died at Benton, in Yazoo county, on the 6th, Joseph Christy, Esq., formerly of Fredricksburg, Va. Mr. C. was a native of the county of Derry, Ireland, but had resided from his boyhood in Virginia.

Died on the 12th, in this city, of yellow fever, James Raney, Esq., aged 28 years, a native of Ireland.

Died on the 13th, in this city, of yellow fever, Mr. Hamilton Hosack, aged 34, a native of New York. Mr. H. was the husband of the distinguished melo-dramatic actress, Mrs. Pritchard.

Died in this city on Thursday night, Mr. Jeremiah Donovan, aged about 25 years, a native of the county Cork, Ireland.

Died at Natchez, on the 13th, the Rev. O. S. Hinckly, professor of Oakland College, in this State.

September 28, 1837

We regret to announce the death by the prevailing epidemic of G. C. Kring, Esq., assistant Postmaster of New Orleans. Mr. Kring was a native of Rockingham Co., Va., but had resided from his boyhood in Alexandria, D. C.

Died in New Orleans, of the same disease, Mr. Wm. H. Thompson, also of Alexandria, D. C.

Died in New Orleans, of yellow fever, on the 13th, Mr. H. M. Ratcliff, formerly of Fairfax county, Virginia.

Died in New Orleans, on the 17th, Wm. E. Watkins, of Virginia.

Died in the same place, on the 16th, John A. Kirk, formerly of Alexandria, D. C.

Died in the same place, on the 19th, John D. Lindenburger, of Baltimore.

November 7, 1837
Married in Cincinnati, on the 28th ult., by the Rev. Adam Hurdus, Mr. L. W. Stephenson, of Vicksburg, to Miss E. M. Simpson, recently of Baltimore.

November 14, 1837
Married on the 25th ultimo, by the Rev. Mr. Fox, Doctor James W. Barnett to Miss Mary T. Randolph, all of Warren county.

December 3, 1837
Died in Louisville, Ky., on the 17th ult., Ann Eliza, daughter of Wm. Hale of Vicksburg, Miss., aged 7 years.

December 26, 1837
Married on the 20th, by the Rev. J. R. Hutchison, Thomas J. Goodman, Esq., to Miss Elizabeth B. Manlove, all of this city.

February 1, 1842
Died at Montalban, on the 25th, Julia Ann Dart, in the 11th year of her age.

Died on the 23d, at the residence of his brother, in this county, Wm. Purvis, Esq., late merchant of Mobile, aged 30 years.

Our fellow citizen, Mr. Alexander Peale, died yesterday, of tetanus, by the accidental discharge of his gun while on a hunting expedition about 3 weeks ago. His hand and arm were severely shattered, and in a few days tetanus appeared. Mr. Peale was, we believe, a native of Pennsylvania, and had been a resident of this city for several years.

February 15, 1842
Died on the 7th, Mrs. Emily Jane Sexton, consort of Mr. John M. Sexton, and eldest daughter of the late Benjamin Harris, of this city, in the 31st year of her age.

May 3, 1842
Died on the 16th, of consumption, in Greenville, Louisiana, Mr. George W. Simpson, printer, formerly a resident of this city.

Died on the 24th, Florence, infant daughter of H. & E. C. Hendren.

May 31, 1842
Married in this city, on the 28th, by Richard Barnett, Esq., Justice of the Peace, Mr. Moses Blackstock to Miss Martha Winslow, both of Madison parish, Louisiana.

Report of the Sexton of the City of Vicksburg:
Henrietta Kent, aged 2 years, drowned.
Louisa Davis, aged 21 years, chronic gastritis, resident of Vicksburg.

June 14, 1842
Died at his residence, Livingston, Miss., on the 5th, Mr. Daniel Rice.

July 26, 1842
Married on Tuesday evening last, near Clinton, by the Rev. Mr. Comfort, Mr. Daniel Morgan, of the firm of Bruner & Morgan, of this city, to Miss Narcissa Harvey, daughter of the late Evan Harvey, dec'd.

August 16, 1842
Died in this city, on the 4th, of inflammatory bilious fever, in the 28th year of his age, Mr. William Aldwell, a native of Clonmel, Ireland, and for the last six months a resident of Vicksburg.

Died at Grand Lake, Arkansas, of bilious fever, on the 6th, Mrs. Mary Jane Gillespy, consort of A. M. Sterrett, Esq., formerly of this city, aged 17 years.

August 30, 1842
Died at the residence of W. H. Paxton, Esq., in Springfield, on the 24th August, Charles L. Bowyer, Esq., a native of Botetourt county, Virginia.

October 11, 1842
Died at the residence of his brother, Dr. Geo. W. McElrath, in Warrenton, Warren county, Miss., on 3d October, 1842, of congestive fever, E. D. Cutler McElrath, Esq., in the 25th year of his age. His remains were followed to the family burial ground at Bethel, by sorrowing friends.

October 25, 1842
Died at his residence near Red Bone, John B. Stevens, Esq., aged 63 years. Mr. Stevens was a native of Columbus county, North Carolina and emigrated to this county about 1810.

November 10, 1842
Died at Cairo, on the steamboat Gen. Pike, on the 24th October, Mrs. Eliza Rocket, aged 29 years.

November 22, 1842
Married on November 8th, by the Rev. C. K. Marshall, Mr. John A. Klein to Miss Elizabeth B. Day, both of this city.

December 13, 1842
Died on the 8th December, of inflammation of the brain, John M. Shannon, son of Marmaduke and Levina Shannon, aged 6 years and 18 days.

December 27, 1842
Died Dec. 11, at his residence on Mulberry Street, Mr. Edward Gallaher. Mr. G. was a native of Ireland.

January 3, 1843
Died on Wednesday evening last, Thaddeus Stith, eldest son of Captian Stith, of this city.

February 21, 1843
Died on the 6th, at the residence of Dr. E. Hansford, in this place, his daughter, Malvina Hansford, of scarlet fever, aged 6 years and 10 months.

April 18, 1843
Married on the 12th, by the Rev. Mr. Wood, Mr. Andrew Gamble to Miss Patience Potticary, all of this city.

April 25, 1843
Died the 20th, Michael, only son of Michael and Mary Donovan, aged 4 months and 5 days.

May 9, 1843
Died in this city yesterday, Mr. Basil Aldwell, printer, aged about 30 years. The deceased was a native of Clonmel, Ireland.

August 1, 1843
Report of Sexton for week ending July 29th, 1843:
John Raferty, 38 years, intemperance.
John Tuoley, 35 years, resident of Vicksburg.
Michael Kortz, 29 years, resident of Vicksburg, fever.
Jacob Gullock, 30 years, bilious fever.
Mrs. Briggs, inflammation of bowels.

August 15, 1843
Died on 12th, Margaretta Virginia, daughter of Jno. R. and Margaretta A. Davis, aged 7 months and 11 days.

October 31, 1843
Died yesterday a.m. in this city, Mr. William Stevens, of New York.

Died at his residence in this county, on the 28th, A. N. Warren, Esq.

Sextons report ending the week of October 31st:
John V. Cruser, 35 years.
William Gray, 38 years, yellow fever.
Elizabeth Cruser, 8 days.
L. W. Whittington, 2 years, yellow fever.
Lucinda Brown, 14 years, yellow fever.
William Pollock, 25 years, yellow fever.
William N. Wood, 36 years, bilious fever.

March 26, 1843
Died on the 16th, at Warrenton, Miss., Elizabeth E. Tompkins, aged about 18 years.

April 9, 1844
Mrs. Julia Gartley, wife of Wm. Gartley, Esq., breathed her last on the 31st ult., in the 42d year of her age. She was for many years a member of the Mound Bluff Baptist Church.

April 16, 1844
Married by the Rev. M. D. O'Reily, on the 11th, in Yazoo county, Frederick W. Whelees, Esq., of Yazoo City, to Miss Elizabeth Anne, oldest daughter of Doctor Richard S. Dorsey.

May 14, 1844
Died in this city, on the 2d, Capt. Joel Paul.

May 21, 1844
Married May 5th, by John Townsend, Esq., Mr. Thomas Kidd to Mrs. Sarah Bolls, all of Warren county.

Died on Sunday last, in the 12th month of his age, Brooke, infant son of James R. and Henrietta B. Creecy.

June 1, 1844
Died at his residence, opposite this city, on Wednesday evening last, Col. Lewis.

July 23, 1844
Died on the 2d of July, 1844, at his residence in Warren County, Jesse Evans, Esq. He was born in Marion District, South Carolina, on the 1st October, 1804. He emigrated to Warren county, Miss., with his parents, in 1807. He left a widow and three sons.

August 20, 1844
Died on Wed. a.m. last, at the residence of his mother, in this city, John R. Armstrong, only son of Mrs. Charles Armstrong, aged 15 yrs.

Died in Madison parish, La., on the 10th, Capt. John M. Perry, formerly of Albermarle Co., Va., aged about 60 years.

Died on the 17th, Dr. John M. Perry, formerly of Albermarle Co., Va., aged about 23 years.

August 27, 1844
Sextons report ending week of Aug. 17th, 1844:
James Cummens, aged 42, intemperance.
James Macnis, aged 30, consumption.
William Trumbull, aged 34, general debility.
Patrick Heiting, aged 36, congestive fever.
William White, aged 26.
John S. Watrous, aged 34, stabbed.

September 3, 1844
Died in this city, on the 28th, at the residence of Dr. Lightcap, Miss Ann Brisban, aged about 23 years. She was a native of Ireland, county of Tyrone, parish of Killdress.

February 4, 1845
James R. Black, aged 44 years, of Vicksburg, died January 27th.

February 25, 1845
Died, Patrick Carroll, 28 years, on the 5th of February.

March 4, 1845
D. G. Gere, 44 years of age, died of dropsy in Covington county, February 8th.

Elizabeth M. Carter, aged 24 years, died of enteritis, in Hinds county, on Feb. 28th.

Married on the 25th, by the Rev. A. W. Chapman, Mr. Eugene Newman to Miss Eliza Mitchell, both of this city.

Sextons report for week ending March 1st, 1845:
Infant of T. J. Hanna, 6 days, convulsions.
Infant of T. Bert, 3 months, convulsions.

March 11, 1845
Sextons report:
Feb. 16th - John Wease, 35 years, mania a portu.
Feb. 18th - Timothy Davine, 33 years, mania a portu.
Feb. 21st - Infant of William Porterfield, congestion of brain.

John S. Winn departed this life at his residence in Zinesville, Ohio, on the 26th February, 1845. aged 68 years and 9 months. He was a native of Prince George county, Maryland, and had been a resident of Muskingum County, Ohio for 26 years. He leaves a widow and 16 children; of these Col. A. M. Winn, of this city is the eldest.

April 8, 1845

Married on the 12th, by Rev. John Lane, Mr. W. J. Cowan to Miss S. R. Spann, both of this county.

Married in Natchez, on the 26th February, by the Rev. Mr. Page, Jefferson Davis, Esq., of Warren, to Miss Varia B., daughter of Wm. B. Howell, Esq., of Adams county.

Married on the 26th ult., by the Rev. S. M. Montgomery, Capt. H. B. Balch to Mrs. A. B. W. Christian, both of this city.

Sextons report:
March 23 - Felix Carroll, 41 years, dropsy.
March 24 - Jane Ford, of Missouri.
March 24 - Hugh Memarin, 25 years, intemperance.
March 28 - T. W. Bancks, 30 years, enlargement of the heart.

$250 Reward -- William G. Beard, did on the 21st day of January, 1845, at Raleigh, in Smith county, in this state, inflict several mortal wounds on the body of Peter G. Campbell, with a pocket knife, and the said Beard did escape from jail and is now at large.

April 22, 1845

$250 Reward -- George W. Burton, did on the 26th day of March last, in the county of Washington, in this state, kill one W. B. Rucker, and he has fled from justice.

Died on the 14th, Margaret Virginia, daughter of W. H. Paxton, of this place.

Died at the residence of J. Philip Stewart, of Warren county, Miss., April 16th, Frances Adeline Stewart, fifth child of J. Philip and Mary C. Stewart, aged 2 years, 5 months and 18 days.

April 29, 1845

Departed this life the 19th day of April, at his residence in this county, of malignant erysipelas, in the 36th year of his age, Dr. William B. Smith, a native of Brunswick county, Va., and for the last 10 years a resident of this county. He left a wife and five children.

Sextons report:
Apr. 13 - Susan McElroy, 5 years, scarlet fever.
Apr. 13 - Mrs. Hammer, congestion of the lungs.
Apr. 14 - William Pate, 24 years, congestion of the lungs.
Apr. 15 - Margaret V. Paxton, 8 months, scarlet fever.
Apr. 16 - Ellen S. Bruner, 7 years, scarlet fever.
Apr. 18 - Mary A. C. Herring, 8 years, scarlet fever.
Apr. 19 - Osman C. Hall, 7 years, pertassis.

May 21, 1845
Died on Tuesday last, the Rev. Robert Smith, aged about 40 years. The deceased was a clergyman of the Methodist Church.

June 24, 1845
Married on the 18th, at the residence of Dr. Wm. L. Balfour, in Madison county, Miss., by the Rev. D. R. Campbell, Dr. H. Golden Blackman to Miss Mary Jane Balfour.

July 29, 1845
Died on the 17th, W. L. Searls, infant son of C. J. and C. R. Searls, of this city.

August 12, 1845
Married on the 7th, at the Catholic Church in this city, by the Rev. M. D. O'Reily, James E. Stewart, Esq., to Miss Honora Scannell.

September 9, 1845
Died of disease of the heart, on Saturday last, in the 73d year of his age, at the residence of Dr. J. P. Parker, near this town, Maj. John Milliken, late of Louisiana. Major Milliken emigrated from North Carolina more than forty years ago. (*Port Gibson Herald*).

Sextons report:
Aug. 26 - Samuel M. Boylen, 34 years, chronic diarrhea, of Yazoo Co.
Aug. 27 - J. W. Brown, 25 years, suicide.

September 23, 1845
Died at Lake Providence, La., on the 1st day of September, S. Fredonia V., infant daughter of William R. and Mary E. Jones, aged 1 year, 4 months and 22 days.

September 30, 1845
Died at the residence of John W. Jones, Esq., Leander S., only son of D. G. H. Goodwin, of this city, aged 7 years and 5 months.

Died, Margaret A. Kiger, of Warren co., aged 52 yrs., of bilious fever.

October 28, 1845
Died October 12th, H. H. Stite, of Yazoo county, aged 31 years, swamp fever.

Died October 13th, Henry Garnett, of Yazoo county.

December 2, 1845
Died Nov. 24th, Mary G. White, of Vicksburg, of perpetual fever.

December 9, 1845
Married on the 20th Nov., by Rev. Montgomery, G. L. Potter and Miss Cynthia, daughter of D. Mayes -- all of Hinds county.

Married on the 6th of November, at Pontotoc, Miss., by Rev. T. C. Stewart, Hon. Stephen Adams and Mrs. Mary Ann Parish.

Died December 1, Capt. Wm. Shrodes, of Louisville, Ky., caused by explosion of steamboat boiler.

December 23, 1845

Married at Raymond, on Wednesday last, by Judge Johnston, Mr. Samuel Guthrie to Miss Clarissa Owen, all of that place.

December 30, 1845

Sextons report:
Dec. 22 - Isabella A. Hay, aged 20 months, scarlet fever.
Dec. 23 - Honora Stewart, aged 22, chronic inflammation of stomach.
Dec. 25 - Owen O'Brien, aged 35, pneumonia.
Dec. 25 - E. R. Strickland, aged 28, consumption.

January 6, 1846

Died on be 30th of scarlet fever, Laura W., daughter of J. J. and Ann Jane Hall, aged 8 years and 11 months.

February 3, 1846

Sextons report:
Jan. 18 - John King, of Pennsylvania, aged 32, bleeding at the nose.
Jan. 20 - Thomas Harrington, aged 35 years.
Jan. 21 - Joseph Carson, Ala., aged 21 years, consumption.
Jan. 30 - William F. Stites, aged 14 months, scarlet fever.

Died Friday a.m., William Folwell, son of Girard and Mary L. Stites.

February 17, 1846

Married February 12th, 1846, by Samuel B. Harwood, Esq., Mr. Thomas Mason to Miss Elizabeth Collins, all of this county.

Married on the 10th of Feb., in the vicinity of Raymond, by Rev. L. Wiley, Col. David Gordon, of Hinds County, Miss., to Mrs. Susan E. Fisher, formerly of Fauquier county, Virginia.

Married on the 10th, by the Rev. R. Wiley, at the residence of A. Grafton, Mr. George Grafton, of Natchez, to Miss Emma Harlan, of Danville, Ky.

March 3, 1846

Died on the 14th, of pulmonary consumption, Mrs. Ann Jane Hall, consort of Col. J. J. Hall, Esq., and daughter of Joseph N. Graddick, Esq., of this place.

Died Feb. 11th, Henry Divine, aged 40 years, of dropsy.

Died on the 24th, Mr. Wm. J. Estes, long a resident of this city.

Died in this city, on the 25th, the Rev. Wm. C. Payne, formerly pastor of the M. E. Church.

Married Feb. 23d, 1846, by S. B. Harwood, Esq., Mr. John Doan to Miss Jane King, all of this county.
Sextons report:
Feb. 23 - Emma Elizabeth Reading, died in N. Orleans, 18 months, scarlet fever.
Feb. 25 - Wm. J. Estes, 35 years, inflammation of the bowels.
Feb. 28 - James Keenan.

March 10, 1846
Died on the 6th, Laura C., only daughter of Robert and Teresa Hammet, aged 2 years, 1 month and 20 days.

Died on the 6th, Tama Houesman, aged 37 years, scalded.

March 17, 1846
Died March 13th, Wm. H. Arrison, aged 36 years, of pneumonia.

April 7, 1846
Died in Yazoo City, on Wednesday morning, Miss Maria A. Barnett.

Died March 30th, of consumption, at the residence of the Rt. Rev. Dr. Blane, Catholic Bishop of this Diocese, the Rev. Michael D. O'Rielly, aged 56 years. The deceased was the son of John O'Rielly, Esq., of Groin, County Cork, Ireland.

Died in Madison county, on the 24th ult., of pulmonary consumption, Mrs. Emily, wife of Mr. R. M. Martin, and daughter of the late Dr. William Balfour, at the age of 19 years.

April 21, 1846
Mr. P. T. Hubbell, the senior partner of the firm of Hubbell & Wheeler, died yesterday morning.

May 5, 1846
Married in Carroll County, on the 21st ult., by the Rev. Mr. Austin, Mr. Hugh Barefield, of this county, to Mrs. Susanna Shamburger.

May 12, 1846
Married the 10th, by Samuel B. Harwood, Esq., Mr. John Grandonna to Mrs. E. Williams, all of this place.

Died, John Adair, aged 24 years, of pneumonia.

May 19, 1846
Married on the 12th, at the residence of the Hon. C. R. Clifton, of Jackson, by the Rt. Rev. Bishop Otey, Mr. Wm. Parker Scott, Esq., of Vicksburg, to Miss Fanny May, daughter of the late Dr. Joseph Bibb, of Alabama.

Married recently, at Fort Washita, E.E. Galloway, Esq., of Winchester, Virginia, to Miss Eugenia Coffee, of Jackson.

July 14, 1846

Departed this life, the 12th, Mr. Thomas L. Jones, a member of the Lafayette Volunteers. Mr. Jones died of congestive fever. He was born in Georgia and a brother-in-law of our Congressman, Jacob Thompson. He was in the 24th year of his age.

Sextons report:
June 28 - Margaret Ann McGarvin, of New Orleans, age 21 years, by violence.
July 1 - William Barrickenin, of Indiana, aged 40 years, consumption.
July 2 - John I. Henderson, of Marshall Co., aged 41 years.

July 21, 1846

Married on the 11th, by S. B. Harwood, Esq., Mr. John King to Miss Nancy Stout, both of this county.

Sextons report:
July 5 - Hugh Dicert, aged 25 years, congestive fever.
July 11 - Bridget McGraim, aged 33 years.

September 15, 1846

Died on the 6th, at the residence of his father, in this county, Mr. Samuel H. Porter, aged 32 years, 6 months, and 4 days.

September 22, 1846

Married on the 17th, Mr. David G. Hardiway to Miss Adaline W. Neely, both of this county.

SOUTHERN GALAXY (Natchez, Miss.)
Published by William C. Grissam & Co.

June 12, 1828

Died in this city on Sunday morning last, Mrs. Mary Bloxton, aged 60 years, formerly of Philadelphia Theatre, and for the last 6 years attached to the New Orleans and Nashville Theatres.

June 26, 1828

Died on the 31st ult., at his residence in Marion County, George F. Norton, Esq., father of our highly respected fellow citizen and Marshal of the State, aged 77.

July 24, 1828

Died in this town, Joseph Augustus Peabody, Esq., aged 31.

Died at the Mansion House, on yesterday morning, the Honorable Joshua G. Clark, Chancellor of the State of Mississippi.

November 27, 1828

Died this morning, very suddenly, Mr. John Campbell, grocer.

Married on the 20th, by the Rev. Mr. Muller, the Honorable Peter Randolph, Judge of the District Court of the U. States for the District of Mississippi, to Miss Elizabeth Leatherberry.

January 1, 1829

Married at Cantonment Jessup, near Natchitoches, La., on the 22d, by the Reverend Rector of Trinity Church, Natchez, Major George Birch, of the United States Army, to Miss Anne Remson Boream, of Brooklyn, New York.

January 15, 1829

Married on Thursday evening, the 8th, by the Rev. James A. Fox, B. M. Covington, Esq., of this city, to Miss Louisa C. Newman, daughter of Mr. John Newman, of Jefferson County.

Married on Thursday evening last, by Wm. B. Fowls, Esq., Mr. Henry Luse to Miss Sarah Holiday, daughter of John Holiday, Esq., all of this county.

January 29, 1829

Married in Alexandria, La., on Monday evening last, by the Rev. G. A. Iron, Mr. Thomas J. Wells to Miss Martha L. Dent.

Died on Friday, the 9th, of consumption, at the residence of her aunt, Mrs. Robinson, Susan, the wife of Thomas W. Beck, of Rodney, J. C., aged 24 years.

February 5, 1829

Married last evening, by the Rev. Mr. Muller, Mr. Angus McNeill to Miss Rebecca Jane, daughter of Robert H. Adams, Esq., all of this city.

February 12, 1829

Married on the 10th, by the Rev. Mr. Muller, Felix Huston, Esq., to Miss Mary E. Dangerfield.

Died on the 7th, Mrs. Martha, wife of Richmond Bledsoe, Esq., of this city.

Died on the 9th, Mrs. Theodosia L. Griffith, widow of the late William B. Griffith, and daughter of the Hon. Edward Turner.

March 5, 1829

Married on the 5th, by the Rev. D. Cooper, Mr. James Ballance, of Yazoo, to Miss Eliza Adams, of this county.

A most horrid murder was committed in this county this evening. A man by the name of Daniel Easley shot a rifle ball through a constable by the name of Wilson, when in discharge of his duty as an officer. (Woodville, Miss.)

March 19, 1829
Died on the 22d, Miss Harriett, daughter of Gray Briggs, Esq., of Amite County, in her 15th year.

April 2, 1829
Died on the 24th, at the residence of Judge McGehee, in Wilkinson County, Mrs. Elizabeth, wife of the Rev. John C. Burress.

Died on the 28th, Lauretta Antionette, daughter of Mr. A. G. Edstrom, aged 13 months.

May 7, 1829
Deaths in Natchez:
Apr. 27 - Frederick Cotton, aged about 2 years, inflammation of the bowels due to measles.
Apr. 28 - James Cecil, aged about 20 months, measles & whooping cough.
Apr. 30 - Fenton Cartwright, aged 7 months, whooping cough.
May 2 - Mrs. Polly Heany, aged about 28 years, gastritis.
May 3 - Charles R. Cobb, aged about 35 years, small pox.
May 3 - W. P. Noland, aged about 2 years, measles.

May 14, 1829
Died on board the steamboat General Hamilton, on her passage from Louisville to Cincinnati, on Monday morning last, Mr. Clark Aldridge, formerly of this place. It is not known whether he had any relations other than a brother, who resides in or about Natchez, Miss. (Lawrenceburgh "Indiana" Palladium).

Died in Natchez, Washington Germany, on the 8th, of intemperance.

June 4, 1829
Married at China Grove, on Thursday evening, 28th ult., by the Rev. Mr. Chaise, Jno. Baynton, Esq., to Miss Cornelia Sessions.

Married at the same time and place, the Hon. John M. Maury to Miss Caroline L. Sessions, all of this county.

Departed this life on Thursday last, at his residence near this place, Mr. Tacitus G. Calvit, planter of this parish.

Died in Natchez, May 29th, B. F. Weigart, aged about 27 years, of consumption.

June 11, 1829
Married in Burlington, N. J., on the 13th, by the Rev. Dr. Wharton, James Dinsmore, Esq., of Natchez, to Martha K., daughter of Alexander Macomb, Esq.

June 25, 1829
Died on Tuesday, the 23d, Mr. Peter Black, a native of Manchester, Vermont, and for a number of years a merchant of our city. Mr. Black

emigrated to this city in 1820. He left in his native town a wife and an aged mother.

July 2, 1829
Deaths in Natchez:
June 23 - Peter Black, aged 37 years, of bilious fever.
June 23 - Reuben Bourden, died in jail.
June 27 - Elizabeth Ferney, aged 77 years.

July 9, 1829
Married Tues. eve. last, by the Rev. Mr. Walker, Mr. John Sterling, Cashier of the Branch Bank of Louisiana at St. Francisville, to Miss Susan B. Miller, daughter of Christopher Miller, Esq.. of this city.

July 16, 1829
Died in Natchez, July 7th, J. Sedgwick, aged about 34 years.

July 23, 1829
Married on Thursday evening last, by the Rev. George Potts, John T. Griffith, Esq., Postmaster of the city, to Miss Eliza, daughter of the late Peter Walker, Esq.

August 6, 1829
Married in Philadelphia, on the 7th ultimo, by the Rev. Mr. Sandford, Wm. J. Minor, of Natchez, Miss., to Rebecca A., daughter of the late Dr. James Gustine, of the same place.

Died August 1st, Jas. Underwood, of steamboat North America, of visceral inflammation, consequent to drinking a quantity of ice water when much heated and fatigued.

August 13, 1829
Died in Natchez, August 9th, Frederick Bartlow, aged about 40 years, of derangement of body and mind, occasioned by intemperance.

September 3, 1829
Died on the 31st ult., at his residence in this county, Peter Bisland, Esq. Mr. Bisland was suffering under a severe attack of bilious fever, but was considered convalescent. He went to the cistern for water and it is supposed that, through extreme weakness, he was seized with a vertigo and fell. A servant at a distance, seeing his master fall, gave the alarm. The body was immediately taken from the water, but all attempts at resucitation were fruitless.

September 10, 1829
Died on the 11th ult., at the Bay of St. Louis, John Forsyth, Esq., formerly of this place.

Died on the 6th, in Natchez, Mr. Murray, a printer, aged 24 years, of bilious congestive fever.

September 17, 1829
Deaths in Natchez:
Sept. 8 - Mr. Hall, a native of Pennsylvania, aged about 25 years, of congestive bilious fever.
Sept. 8 - Giles Bledsoe, aged about 35 years, of bilious fever.
Sept. 9 - Jacob Winkler, about 14 years, of fever.
Sept. 9 - Mr. Wilcox, about 28 years, of malignant bilious fever.
Sept. 10 - Mr. Russell, about 35 years, malignant fever.
Sept. 11 - Sally May.
Sept. 12 - Susan Masalettexia, about 35 years.
Sept. 12 - John Barlow, of yellow fever.

September 24, 1829
Died on Friday last, at Hunter's Hall, a residence of George D. Bankes, Esq., Mr. Aaron Stanton, junior, a partner of the firm F & A Stanton, of this city.

Died at Mountpleasant, the residence of the late Robert Moore, near Natchez, on Monday the 21st, Mr. James Mitchell, a native of Richmond, Virginia, in the 20th year of his age.

Died on the 2d, at Benton, Yazoo County, the Rev. Joseph Slocumb, in the 57th year of his age. He was of the Baptist order.

October 1, 1829
Died in Harrisonburgh, Louisiana, on Saturday, Sept. 26th, Turpin Kilby Sargent, in his 14th year.

Deaths in Natchez:
Sept. 25 - Jesse Trahern, about 36 years, bilious fever.
Sept. 25 - Andrew Selkirk, about 26 years, fever.
Sept. 25 - Mr. Barry, fever.
Sept. 26 - Fred. Belsinger, aged 19 years, congestive fever.
Sept. 28 - John Ferry, aged 40 years, consumption.

October 8, 1829
Married at Hartford, Conn., on Monday, the 3d of August, Mr. Thomas C. Coit, of the house of Coit and Whittemore, of this city, to Miss Mary Ann Morgan, of the former place.

Died on Thursday, the 1st Oct., at the residence of Mr. Wm. Ferriday, Second Creek, Mr. Richard Walsh, born in Dublin, and aged 30 years. Mr. Walsh had not been two years in this country.

Deaths in Natchez:
Oct. 2 - James Serdith.
Oct. 4 - J. T. Richards, of fever.
Oct. 5 - Mrs. Bruce.

October 15, 1829
Died this morning, John W. Grubbs, a native of Virginia.

Deaths in Natchez:
Oct. 8 - Mr. Thompson, aged 28 years, malignant fever.
Oct. 10 - Mr. Hutchison, aged about 26 years, malignant fever.
Oct. 10 - Mr. Carol, about 27 years, fever.

October 22, 1829
Deaths in Natchez:
Oct. 14 - John Acor, 47 years, fever.
Oct. 15 - John W. Grubbs, 23 years, congestive typhus fever.
Oct. 15 - Mrs. H. C. Hamilton, 23 years, relapse of bilious fever.
Oct. 16 - John Gowan, 27 years, malignant fever.
Oct. 16 - E. D. Fields, 20 years, bilious fever.
Oct. 17 - Batlett Gamble, 12 years, whooping cough.
Oct. 18 - Edward T. Lion, malignant fever.

October 29, 1829
Died in Natchez, October 22d, A. Daniel, aged about 35 years, of hepatic abcess.

November 5, 1829
Deaths in Natchez:
Oct. 30 - Miss Catherine McGraw, aged 9 years, dropsy.

November 12, 1829
Married on Thursday last, by the Rev. Mr. Vancourt, Mr. A. T. McMurtry to Mrs. Rebecca M. Moss, all of this county.

Died, George D. Bankes.

November 19, 1829
Married on Thursday, the 12th, by the Rev. Benj. M. Drake, Mr. Ambrose J. White to Miss Mary Munce, both of this city.

Married on Tuesday, the 17th, by the Rev. Mr. Burrows, Mr. John P. Walworth, of the city of Natchez, to Miss Sarah, daughter of Dr. W. Wren, of the same place.

Died on Tuesday, the 17th, at Washington, Mr. Andrew Dunlap, a native of Boston, and formerly of this place, son of the late Andrew Dunlap, Esq.

Died on Sunday, the 15th, Mr. Edmond Dangerfield, at the residence of his mother, Mrs. E. M. Dangerfield.

Died Tuesday evening, the 17th, Dr. W. J. Scott, at the same place.

November 26, 1829
Died in Natchez, on the 22d, Wm. Shannon, aged about 25 years, of abcess of the lungs, a consequence of measles.

Married on Wednesday evening last, by the Rev. Mr. Walker, Mr. David Miller to Miss Mary Bathis, all of this city.

December 3, 1829
Deaths in Natchez:
Nov. 26 - Mr. McAdora, fever.
Nov. 28 - Jacob Foushte, 27 years, visiral inflammation.
Nov. 30 - Capt. Mouchette, 37 years.

December 10, 1829
Married in this city, on Tuesday evening last, by the Rev. Mr. Fox, Mr. Thomas Barnard to Miss Eliza Jane Wood.

Died in Jefferson County on the night of the 27th of November last, Mrs. Emily Green, aged 30 years, wife of Mr. Filmer W. Green.

December 17, 1829
Married on the 8th, by the Rev. John C. Burrus, Mr. John Newman, for many years a resident of Washington, Adams County, aged 55, to Miss Martha Sanders, aged 49, of Wilkinson County.

December 24, 1829
Married on the 10th, by the Rev. George Potts, Dr. G. Colhoun, recently of Philadelphia, to Miss E. Jane, daughter of the late Adam Bingaman, Esq., of this county.

December 31, 1829
Deaths in Natchez:
Dec. 25 - Andrew Ross, aged 30 years, died of beating.
Dec. 27 - James Kenny, aged about 30 years, pulmonary consumption.

January 21, 1830
Died on Sunday evening last, Samuel Duncan, Esquire, formerly of Pennsylvania.

Deaths in Natchez:
Jan. 13 - Charles L. Lee, green jaundice.
Jan. 15 - Edward Salters, aged 6 years.
Jan. 17 - Samuel P. Duncan, dysentary.

Married on Wednesday, the 13th, at Neale Park, the residence of Dr. Samuel Metcalfe, by the Rev. John C. Burrus, Mr. Calvin Stephen Smith, of this county, to Miss Martha Keary, eldest daughter of the late Mr. Keary, of Louisiana.

Married on Thursday, the 21st, by Samuel Postlethwaite, Esq., Mr. Berry Shaw to Miss Caroline Keys, both of this city.

February 18, 1830
Married on Thursday evening, by the Rev. George Potts, D. D., Mr. Cyrus Marsh to Miss Isabella Munce, all of this city.

March 4, 1830
Killed in the explosion of the steamboat Helen McGregor, at Memphis: Richard Hancock, Louisville, Ky., A. VanMeter, Hardin Co., Tenn.,

---- Talbot, Long Reach, Ohio, James Bledsoe, Kentucky, ---- Carroll, Cincinnati, Ohio, Ed. P. Beadles, Clark Co., Ind., J. Dunn, East Tennessee, G. B. Giles, Cincinnati, Ephraim Goble, Brookville, Ind., William Stockwell, Salem, Ind., Delany, a free black, Wm. Ewing, Clark Co., Ind., J. Reaves, Harrison Co., Ind., Lewis Young, a black fireman.

Deaths in Natchez,
Feb. 23 - Jno. Gage, aged 4 years.
Feb. 24 - Mrs. Phillips, cancer.
Feb. 25 - Susannah Shannon, aged 33 years.
Feb. 26 - C. Gage, aged 14 months.

March 18, 1830

Died in Natchez, on the 14th, Geo. H. Fithian, aged 25 years.

April 1, 1830

Married on Tuesday evening, the 30th ult., by the Rev. Mr. Potts, Mr. Sion G. Rowan to Miss Elizabeth B. Dunlap, daughter of Mrs. Elizabeth H. Dunlap, all of this city.

April 8, 1830

Died in Natchez, March 31st, Henry Murtha, aged about 21 years.

April 15, 1830

Died at Worcester, Mass., Charles Griffin, brother of the Editor of this paper.

Died on Friday, the 2d of April, at the residence of her son, the Hon. Peter Randolph, Mrs. Sally Randolph, in her 69th year.

April 29, 1830

Died in Natchez, April 23d, Mrs. Varina Stanton, aged about 70 years, of chronic diarrhea.

May 20, 1830

Died in Cincinnati, on the 28th April last, Miss Elizabeth G. Riley, in the 19th year of her age. She was just returned from Natchez where she had been spending the winter season.

SOUTHERN LUMINARY (Jackson, Miss.)
Printed & published by Silas Brown & Co.

August 24, 1824

Yesterday the sentence of the law was executed on the body of Campbell Carlisle, for the murder of Dr. Drahan, on the 26th Dec. last.

August 31, 1824

Departed this life, on Friday night, the 20th, at his residence near Washington, the Honorable Louis Winston, Judge of the 2d Judicial District.

September 7, 1824
Departed this life on the 28th August, Mrs. Elizabeth Degen, of Marion County. She has left a numerous family of orphans.

September 14, 1824
Died at the residence of Wesley Trahern, near this place, on Sunday the 12th, James Trahern, Jr., late of Henry County, Virginia.

September 21, 1824
Died at the residence of his brother 9 miles west of Jackson, Mr. Silenus O. Sadler, son of Isaac Sadler, of Green County, Alabama, in the 25th year of his age.

Died at his residence in Monroe County, on the 31st ult., Dr. Wm. T. Henderson.

October 5, 1824
Married on Wednesday evening, the 29th ult., by the Rev. Randal Gibson, Mr. Abram Bridges to Miss Margaret Humphreys, daughter of Captain Geo. W. Humphreys, all of Claiborne County.

General George H. Nixon died at Pearlington on the 19th day of August last. General Nixon was a native of the State of Virginia, but emigrated amongst the first settlers to the Pearl River, in the year 1809.

Died on the 22d ult., at the residence of Mr. James Cowdon, in Jefferson Co., Mr. James Mackey, of the house of Bedford & Mackey, of New Orleans.

Died on the 24th ult., Mrs. Agness Ann Burnett, consort of Col. Daniel Burnett, of Claiborne County.

October 12, 1824
Married on Thursday evening, the 7th, by the Rev. Mr. Potts, Mr. Miller Stewart to Miss Jane Elenora Marschalk, daughter of Andrew Marschalk, editor of the *Mississippi State Gazette*, all of Natchez.

October 19, 1824
Married on Thursday last, by Silas Brown, Esq., Mr. Oliver R. Ingram, of Pike County, to Miss Anna Housley, of this county.

October 26, 1824
Died, John Smith, Esq., of Monroe County. Mr. Smith was a respectable planter.

Died on the night of the 18th, in Port Gibson, Sophia Jones, infant daughter of Doctor David Dickson, of that place, aged 1 year, 6 months and 21 days.

Died in the town of Columbus, Miss., on the 4th day of October, 1824, on his way from New Orleans, a man about 30 or 35 years of age.

From papers found in his possession his name was supposed to be William Minigar or Minigan.

We learn by a letter from a gentleman in Cotton-Gin Port, that a most shocking murder was committed in the neighborhood of that place a few weeks since, by Henry and Robert Bickerstaff, upon a certain James Mullens.

November 9, 1824

Died in Jefferson County, Miss., on the 16th ultimo, Mr. G. K. Caswell, in the 30th year of his age. He was a native of Taunton, Mass., and emigrated to this county in 1819.

November 16, 1824

Married on Thursday last, by John W. N. A. Smith, Esq., Mr. James Osborn to Miss Mary G. Lackey, daughter of Mr. Archibald Lackey, all of this county.

Married at Fayetteville, Tenn., on the 14th Oct., by the Rev. John McLin, Thos. B. Mullin, of Moorfield, Virginia, to Miss Melinda M. Weaver, daughter of Major Jesse Weaver, of Monroe County, Miss.

Our venerable neighbor, the virtuous Indian, the friend of the whites, the Mingo Puckshenubee, is no more! At Maysville, Ky., on his way with a deputation of Choctaw Chiefs and Warriors from the Nation to Washington City, this aged warrior and chief fell from the abutments of the road to the landing, upon the stone pavement below, and received such injury that his soul soon winged its way to that Great Spirit. His remains were interred at the Methodist Church.

November 30, 1824

Married on Tuesday, the 23rd, by J. W. N. Smith, Mr. Samuel Young to Miss Amanda H. Lackey, daughter of Archibald Lackey, all of this county.

Died at New York, Jonathan Battelle, Esq., Editor of the *Mobile Commercial Register*.

December 7, 1824

Died on yesterday, at the residence of Wm. J. Austin, Esq., one mile south of this place, Rolly Thomas, disease - epistaxis.

Died, Col. Wm. Yerby, of Wilkinson County, a member of the House of Representatives.

Died at his father's residence near Winchester, on the 22d of November, in the 26th year of his age, James B. McRae, Esq.

December 28, 1824

Died on Saturday, the 11th, at his residence near Monticello, Alexander Hall, Esq., of lingering fever. He has left a wife and ten children.

January 29, 1825
Married on Thursday, the 20th, by the Rev. Miles Harper, Wm. Mellon, Esq., to Miss Caroline Stovall, both of the town of Columbia, in Marion County.

February 2, 1825
Married on Sunday evening last, by Robert Steen, Esqr., Mr. John Smith, to Miss Mary Smith, all of this county.

July 19, 1825
Died at the residence of her father, in this county, on Sunday, the 17th, Mrs. Martha Lawson, consort of Charles M. Lawson, Esqr., of Warren County.

August 16, 1825
Married on Sunday last, the 14th, by Landy Lindsey, Esq., Mr. Martin Stricklin to Miss Penelope Fisher, of this county.

August 23, 1825
Last night's mail brought us the melancholy tidings of the death of Dr. Bartley C. Barry, of Monroe County. He died on Wednesday, the 17th, of bilious fever.

Died about the same time, his brother-in-law, John B. Razer, merchant at Columbus, and Postmaster.

August 30, 1825
It is our painful duty to record the death of William B. Long, Esqr., well known as the senior editor of the *Huntsville Democrat*.

September 13, 1825
Died on Wednesday, the 31st of August, Charles Nafe, Esqr., late Coroner of Adams County. He has left a wife and three small children.

September 27, 1825
Married on the 6th, by James Ainsworth, Esqr., Robert C. Blount, Post Master in Gallatin, and Clerk of the Circuit Court of Copiah County, to Miss Malinda Keller, of Wilkinson County.

Died in Monticello, Miss., on the 19th, Mr. William Bracey, in the 77th year of his age. He was a native of South Carolina.

Died on the 9th, at his father's residence in Warren County, Wm. F. Cook, in the 12th year of his age.

October 18, 1825
We are called to announce the loss of a very respectable minister of the Gospel, the Reverend James Gilleland, of Copiah county.

Died at Oakley (the seat of Beverly R. Grayson, Esq.) on the 27th of September, Mrs. Ellen M. G. Old, wife of Mr. William A. Old, late of Tennessee, in the 20th year of her age.

Died on the 29th September, Mr. Wm. Murray, printer, a native of this place, but late from Chambersburgh, Pennsylvania.

October 25, 1825

Married at Pearlington, Miss., on the 20th ultimo, Mr. Samuel White, merchant, to Miss Beatina M. Nixon, daughter of the late Gen. George A. Nixon.

November 8, 1825

Died at Natchez on the 18th, of malignant fever, Samuel Postlethwaite, Esq., President of the Bank of the State of Mississippi.

Died in Natchez, on Monday last, of the prevailing fever, Mrs. Mary Forsyth, wife of John Forsyth, Esquire, Sheriff of Adams County.

Died on Saturday week, Dr. John S. Cornell.

Died on Thursday morning last, of malignant fever, Dr. Thomas Jewell, a native of the State of Kentucky, and late a practitioner of medicine in the town of St. Francisville, Louisiana.

Died on Monday, the 17th, at the residence of his grandfather, Mr. Robert Dunbar, Senr., Doctor George Cochran Ferguson, in the 23d year of his age. Dr. Ferguson was a native of Adams County, Miss.

November 15, 1825

Married last evening, by Silas Brown, Esq., Mr. James Jones to Miss Sarah Smith.

SOUTHERN MARKSMAN (Clinton, Miss.)
C. P. McDaniel, Editor; G. D. Gere, Publisher & Proprietor.

December 4, 1838

Married in Covington County, Miss., on the 15th Nov., by Jesse Burkhalter, Esq., Mr. Wiley W. Williamson to Miss Rebecca Norris, all of this county.

Married in Gallatin, Tenn., by the Rev. J. W. Hall, Maj. William H. Hall to Miss Catherine D. Barry, all of that county.

January 1, 1839

Married in Vicksburg the 27th ult., Samuel A. Brodhead, Esq., of N. Y., to Miss Mary Wyatt Clarke, daughter of the late James B. Clarke, of Richmond, Va.

February 13, 1839

Married on the 5th of February, by S. W. Humphreys, Esq., Mr. Willis Champion to Miss Martha Ellis, both of this county.

February 27, 1839
Died on the 12th, in the 35th year of his age, near Clinton, Hinds County, Miss., Mr. Sumner M. Sharp, of Williamson Co., Tenn.

SOUTHERN REFORMER (Jackson, Miss.)
W. M. Smyth

September 25, 1843
Married in Yazoo County, on the 17th, Wm. C. Hays to Miss Elizabeth Stephens.

Married in Lowndes County, 14th, Benjamin Halstead to Miss Emily A. Huddleston.

Married in Natchez, 7th, John B. Quegles to Miss Margaret M. McGraw.

Married in Grand Gulf, 20th ult., Nicholas C. Howard to Mrs. Missouri Tarpley.

Married in Wilkinson County, 30th ult., Isaac Alexander to Miss Martha Langford.

Married on the 31st ult., Jesse M. Netterville to Miss Catharine R. Lanehart.

Married in Hinds County, 5th, Samuel M. Phelps to Miss Elizabeth Sparrow.

Married in Holmesville, 31st ult., T. D. Paddleford to Miss Sarah M. Burton.

Married in Lawrence County, 24th ult., James E. Harper to Miss Ancyvilia Campbell.

Married in Adams County, 8th ult., Augustus H. Bradley to Miss Sarah A. E. Brown.

Married in Covington County, 7th, Joseph Graves to Miss Sarah Ann Allen.

Married in Smith County, 6th, Thomas J. Coleman to Miss Martha Caroline Rawls.

Married at Barra Tarria Bay, 27th ult., M. H. Abrams to Miss Susan Nephthali Levoy.

Died on the 10th, in Hinds County, John Cochran. On the 7th, Miss Eliza Dickson. On the 21st ult., Charles Campbell.

Died in the city of Jackson, on the 3d, Mrs. Mary Ann Richards. On the 14th ult., William Johnson. On the 17th ult., Hon. James C. Mitchell. On the same day, Mrs. F. A. Whitehead.

Died on the 5th, in Claiborne County, Henry W. Calhoun. On the 29th Aug., Adam Gordon Calhoun. On the 6th Aug., E. W. Pollett. On the 16th Aug., James P. Scisson. On the 30th Aug., Mrs. E. Duncan.

Died on the 24th Aug., in the city of Natchez, Isabella Jane Caldwell. On the 9th, Hamilton Wilson.

Died on the 13th Aug., near Little Rock, Ark., F. G. Hopkins, of Jackson, Miss.

Died on the 20th Aug., in Newton County, Mrs. A. Graham.

Died on the 27th Aug., in Winston Co., Mrs. Eliza H. Lucas.

Died on the 29th Aug., in W. B. Rouge, La., Felix Bernard.

October 2, 1843

Married on the 3d, in the parish of St. Tammany, La., Dr. John V. Wren, of Liberty, Miss., to Miss Van Allen.

Married in Jasper County, 3d ultimo, Isaac Anderson to Miss Sarah Morse.

Married in Covington County, 7th ult., J. P. Stewart to Mrs. Rhoda L. Watts.

Married in Jackson, 28th ult., George Southerland to Miss Amanda Dawson.

Married in Warren County, 14th ult., D. B. Gardner to Miss Moore, of Warrenton.

Died in Amite County, Levi Dreyfus, Jonas Causey and Stephen Wilkinson.

Died in the parish of Concordia, La., Jas. M. Norwood, formerly of this state.

Died on the 13th ult., at Rodney, Harrison Logan. On the 15th, Robert Logan. On the 17th, Mary Andrews.

Died on the 6th ult., at Fayette, Washington S. Burch. Died on the 9th ult., at Holly Springs, Mrs. Catharine Talliferro. Died on the 8th ult., in Lafayette County, Samuel M. Gill. Died on the 15th ult., at Houston, Miss., B. T. Dibrell.

Died on the 8th ult., at St. Louis, G. Earl Martin, of Rodney.

Died on the 24th ult., at Concordia, La., Mrs. A. C. H. Wood.

Died on the 19th ult., at Richmond, La., Mary Jane Dortch. On the 25th, Albert Gallatin Dortch.

Died on the 14th ult.. at Little Rock, Ark., Jefferson Smith, of Natchez.

Died on the 6th ult., at Oxford, George S. Smith.

Died on the 20th ult., at Columbia, Armstrong Irving Blackburn.

Died on the 3d ult., in Wilkinson County, Hiram Antoine.

Died in Yazoo County, 10th ult., Mrs. Sarah Grayson.

Died in Monroe County, 4th July, Miss S. L. J. Sims.

Died at his grandmother's in Jefferson County, Miss., 15th day of Sept., 1843, of congestion of the brain, William Mortimer Smyth, junior, only son of Wm. M. and Elizabeth J. Smyth, aged 5 years, 8 months and 4 days.

October 9, 1843

Married in this city, 3d, William G. Blake to Miss Martha Ann Scott.

Married in Clarke Co., 28th Sept., William E. Jones to Miss Mary Bowen.

Married at Vicksburg, 26th ult., Henry McFarland to Miss Julia Harvy.

Married at Port Gibson, 21st ult., John H. St. John to Mrs. Ellen Davis.

Married at Vidalia, La., 27th ult., John Dunigan to Miss Armenia Arnold.

Died at Louisville, Ky., 14th ult., Dr. Andrew Macrery.

Died at Port Gibson, 15th ult., Theodore Allen, infant son of Moses and Amelia Clarke.

Died in Claiborne County, 19th ult., Mr. Chunn.

Died in Jasper County, 27th ult., Henry Clay, youngest son of W. A. Hicks.

Died in Washington County, 19th ult., Thomas Ingram.

Died at Raymond, 6th, Mary, infant daughter of Hasting Epperson. On the 2d, Rebecca Elizabeth Elder, daughter of Col. Jordan Elder. On the 1st, Mrs. Sarah W. Thomas.

October 16, 1843

Married in this city, on Thursday evening last, by the Rev. Mr. Halsey, J. H. Boyd, Esq., Mayor of the city of Jackson, to Eliza Ellis.

Married in Grand Gulf, 11th, George M. Dickerson to Miss Mary E. Burford.

Died in this county, 9th, Joseph Madden.

Died at Vicksburg, 3d, E. D. Conklin.

Died at Bay of St. Louis, 29th ult., Richard W. Webber, late of Mendville, in this state.

October 23, 1843

Married in Vicksburg, W. P. Anderson, of this place, to Miss Martha Anderson, of Vicksburg.

Married in West Feliciana parish, La., 9th, G. W. Purnell to Miss Mary Ann Smith.

Died at Benton, 17th, James R. Clark. On the 19th, J. W. Scruggs.

Died in Holmes County, 15th, Miss Nancy Watson.

Died in Hinds County, 11th, Nathan Bryant.

Died in Jefferson County, 3d, Giles H. Clark.

Died in Wilkinson County, 30th Sept., Francis William McGehee, son of Judge Edward McGehee.

Died in Copiah County, 3d, George R. Miller.

Died in Warren County, 5th, Miss Elizabeth Yates Stuart. On the 16th, N. S. Dunningham.

Died in Adams County, 14th, Miss Sinah Holliday.

Died at New Orleans, 14th, Mrs. Jane P. Gherard, daughter of the late Rev. Aaron Bancroft, of Worchester, Mass. On the 12th, Wm. M. Bell, member of the firm of J. Bell & Son, late of Pontotoc, Miss.

October 30, 1843

Departed this life on Friday, the 6th October, in Monroe, John Sidney Hamblin, only son of Eliza W. Warfield and Dr. John M. A. Hamblin, deceased, aged 15 years and 10 months.

November 4, 1843

Departed this life on Monday, the 30th of October last, in the 14th year of her age, Elizabeth Courtney Cohea, daughter of Maj. Perry Cohea, of this city.

Married in this city, on Thursday evening last, Dr. A. B. Cabaniss to Miss Susan Lindsay.

Married in Kosciusko, 17th October, A. Crane, to Miss Jane Williams.

Married in Vicksburg, 28th Oct., Bsnjamin R. Wilkinson, of Benton, Yazoo County, to Miss Eliza C. Smith, of Madison County. On the 26th Oct., Antonia Genella to Miss Louisa Harris.

Married in Louisville, Ky., 3d Oct., P. S. Kennard, of Milliken's Bend, La., to Miss Helen E. Keene, of Scott County, Ky.

Married in Baltimore, Md., 4th Oct., Worthington G. Sneathen, of New Orleans, to Miss Virginia Polk, of the former place.

Died in Smith County, 24th Oct., John Ross.

December 12, 1843

Married near Brownsville, Hinds County, on the 7th, by the Hon. H. G. Johnson, Dr. E. W. Eckles to Miss Mary A. Reynolds.

Married in Yazoo County, 30th ult., Gibson Barnes to Miss Frances H. Keeble.

Married at Natchez, 20th ult., John B. Dixon to Mrs. Mary L. Brown.

Married at Vicksburg, 7th, Stephen R. Melven to Miss Mary James.

Married in Warren County, 9th, William Briggs to Miss Susan A. Flowers.

Married at Paulding, Dr. Samuel P. Ferrell to Miss Zelena Dupree. On the 15th ult., H. C. Chambers to Miss Lucretia J. Petty.

Died in Yazoo County, 15th ult., Miss Rebecca F. Chew.

Died in Washington County, 27th ult., Jas. McCrutchen.

Died in Madison Parish, La., 16th ult., Mrs. S. Wilkinson.

Died near Natchez, 6th ult., Mrs. Elizabeth J. Marrero.

Died in sight of Natchez, on board steamboat, 15th ult., James Wemple.

January 9, 1844

Married on Monday evening, 1st, near Clinton, Hinds County, by the Rev. W. R. Nicholson, Samuel Ford to Miss Cornelia V. Nicholson, daughter of Judge I. R. Nicholson.

Married on Thursday, the 28th ult., by the Rev. Mr. Jones, Daniel Loftin, Esq., to Miss Rosanna Lowe, daughter of Col. Aaron Lowe, all of Covington County.

Married on the same day, in the same county, by Gilbert D. Gere, Esq., John Burkhalter to Miss Ruth Stewart.

February 19, 1844

Married on Thursday, the 15th, at the residence of Dr. H. J. Holmes, by the Rev. Thomas Ford, Mr. Jacob R. Funches to Miss Virginia A. Wych, both of Hinds County.

Died at his residence, near Vernon, Madison County, Miss., on Sunday, 28th January, Maj. Robert V. Davis, in the 23d year of his age, leaving a wife and four children.

March 11, 1844

Married at Woodville, 14th ult., David Woods to Miss Ann B. Gibson. On the 8th ult., Ferdinand C. Ford to Miss Jane Jeter.

Married in Jefferson County, 24th ult., George Wilson Humphreys to Miss Balissa Prince. On the 21st ult., John Cobun Humphreys to Miss Sarah A. G. Stewart.

Married in Lafayette County, 21st ult., Walter J. Douglass to Miss Elizabeth A. Couger. On the 29th ult., Milton Irby to Lovey Tens.

Married in Yazoo County, 27th ult., Wm. Battaile to Miss M. J. Hendricks.

Married in Kemper County, 27th ult., R. J. Edmonds to Miss M. A. Mitchell.

Died on the 12th ult., in Adams County, Col. Henry A. Garnett.

Died on the 4th, at Vicksburg, Mrs. Euphemia H. Spitzer.

Died on the 24th ult., James Forsks, of Pittsfield, Indiana.

Died on the 11th ult., at Columbus, Isaac B. Jones.

Died on the 23d ult., in Concordia Parish, La., Mrs. Levisa Bradley.

March 30, 1844

Departed this life on the 18th March, at his father's residence in Madison County, Miss., John C. B. Mabry, youngest son of Col. Jesse and Nancy Mabry, aged 14 years, 1 month and 21 days.

Died at Concordia, La., 18th March, Captain James M. Grice.

Married in Covington County, 14th, Col. William R. Eaton to Miss Nancy Louisa Harper, both of that county.

Married at Monticello, 19th, Dr. J. W. Pendleton to Mrs. Frances Knight.

Married in Lawrence County, 20th, J. Ross to Miss Martha Hargroves.

Married in Hinds County, 17th, John Hansel to Mrs. Elizabeth Sibby.

April 6, 1844

Died in Jackson, Miss., on Sunday night last, 31st March, Mr. J. H. North.

Died in Claiborne County, Miss., 24th ult., Mrs. Delia S., relict of the late Francis W. Turpin, of Grand Gulf.

Died in St. Francisville, La., 19th March, Ann Frances and Sarah Eliza, daughters of the late John Barclay.

Married at Edenton, N. C., 13th March, George D. Dixon, of Mississippi, to Mary B., daughter of Gen. Duncan McDonald, of the former place.

Married near Clinton, La., 20th March, James H. Muse to Miss Martha Ann Ketlet, both of East Feliciana parish.

Married in Wilkinson County, Miss., 21st ultimo, Hampton D. Scott, to Mrs. Mahalet Bet, both of that county.

Married in Clinton, La., 21st ult., M. Kobler to Nancy McClendon.

April 13, 1844

Married in Yazoo County, 29th ult., Torrence Trainer to Mrs. Mariah Ann Sibbley.

Married in Rankin County, 28th ult., Jesse Lee to Miss Sarah Cooper. On the same evening, Isaac White to Miss Joice Ann Forf. On the same evening, Napoleon Bonapart Speed to Miss Flora Ann Watkins,

Married in Madison Parish, La., 31st ultimo, John Briscoe to Miss Martha Mason.

Married in Yalobusha County, 4th April, Mr. McMath to Miss M. Spann.

Died at Monticello, 6th, James Reed.

April 27, 1844

Married in Adams County, 16th, John McDonald to Emiline Tipton.

Married at Paulding, 12th, Henry F. Miller to Miss Mary A. Dease.

Married in Wilkinson County, 22d, L. K. Barber to Miss Eliza Hester.

Married in Jefferson Co., 10th, J. O. Rundell to Miss M. A. Griffing.

Died in Clinton, 14th, William R. Dearing.

Died in Marshall County, 9th, Leander Grey. On the 20th ult., Heneretta Davidson. On the 5th, Charles R. Morgan.

Died at Alexandria, La., 3d, Mrs. Laura H. Brent.

Died in Fayette, 18th, Thomas, infant son of Daniel and M. Sullivan.

May 10, 1844

Married in the city of Jackson, on Thursday morning, 9th, by the Rev. James E. Matthews, Mr. George W. Boddie to Mrs. Louisa A. Forbes, daughter of Gen. William Clark, all of Jackson.

Married on the 21st April, at Hopahka, Leake County, D. R. Russell, of Carrollton, to Miss Julia Hall, of Hopoahka.

Married on the 24th ult., in Dallas County, Ala., Leroy J. Halsey, of Jackson, Miss., to Miss C. A. Anderson.

Married on the 11th ult., at Port Gibson, N. Bennedict, of Ohio, to Mrs. E. Hondon, of the former place.

Married on the 21st ult., in Vicksburg, William Hogan to Miss Isabella Baird, all of Hinds County.

Married on the 11th ult., at Monticello, Wm. H. Hendricks to Miss Amelia Langston.

Married on the 26th ult., in Warren County, C. Schierholz to Mrs. Julian Kropf.

Married on the 2d, in Jasper County, Wm. J. Husbands to Miss Sebra Overstreet.

Married on the 24th ult., in Lowndes County, Alex. Cobb to Miss Caroline A. Wallace.

Married on the 11th ult., in Copiah County, James M. Lyon to Mrs. Matissa Speed.

Married on the 8th ult., in Wilkinson Co., L. K. Barber to Miss Eliza Hester. On the 7th ult., H. J. Powell to Mrs. Eliza Ann Hammond.

Died in the city of Jackson, 7th, Dr. Thos. Glaskins.

Died in Warren County, on the 4th, Mrs. E. Berry.

Died in Marshall County, on the 7th, Miss Rebecca Dowdle. On the 6th, Robert Crawford.

Died in Jasper County, 11th ult., M. C. Williams.

Died in Grand Gulf, 29th ult., Lewis Matthews. On the 25th ult., Dr. T. C. Cropper. On the 22d ult., James Hunter, of Madison County. On the 28th ult., John W. Benton. On the 10th ult., John W. John.

Died in Natchez, Margaret Jane Snyder.

Died in Carroll County, 31st March, James Kelly.

Died in Winston County, Amzi Godden.

May 18, 1844

Married on Thursday evening, May 16, 1844, by the Rev. L. B. Holloway, Richard P. Winslow to Miss Minerva O. Benson, both of Hinds County, Miss.

June 8, 1844

Married in Hinds County, on Thursday, May 23d, at the residence of Nathan S. White, Esq., by Rev. Mr. Barnes, Elisha B. Lemon, of Hinds, to Miss Frances Marble, of Claiborne County.

June 15, 1844

Died in this city, on the 12th June, Laura Dade, eldest daughter of A. E. and Emily H. Smoot, aged 6 years, 1 month and 15 days.

Died at Philadelphia, Neshoba county, on the 2nd June, Charles, son of John J. and Mary A. McRae, aged 7 years and 9 months.

June 22, 1844

Died at Hopahka, Leake Co., on the 20th June, Delia Ann, infant dau. of John B. and Elizabeth E. Forrester, aged 2 years & 1 month.

June 29, 1844

Married near Brownsville, on the 18th June, by the Rev. D. Comfort, Mr. James B. Cox to Miss Cornelia F., only daughter of Dr. O. D. Langston, all of Hinds County.

July 6, 1844

Married at Natchez, 20th June, William L. Harrison to Miss Maria Louisa Wade.

Married in Columbus, 28th June, Isham Harrison to Miss Julia A. Whitfield.

Married in Hinds County, 28th June, Nathaniel M. Taylor, of Madison County, to Miss Catherine J. McGehee.

Married at Ripley, 13th June, William F. Stearns, of Holly Springs, to Miss Emeline A. Rutherford, of Ripley.

Died in Cincinnati, Ohio, 19th June, John P. Morris, formerly of Natchez.

Died in Wilkinson County, 9th ult., Mrs. Rachael N., wife of Judge Joseph Johnson, aged 73.

Died in Jefferson County, 3d June, Mrs. A. L. Baldwin.

Died at Natchez, 24th June, Thomas Barnard.

July 20, 1844

Died at Philadelphia, Neshoba County, Miss., on the 29th June, 1844, infant and only daughter of John J. and Mary A. McRae, aged 5 weeks and 3 days.

July 27, 1844

Died in this city on Sunday last, 21st July, Eliza Winslow, infant daughter of Benjamin and Louisa Albertson, aged 2 years, 7 months and 10 days.

Died in Lawrence County, on the 18th July, John Warren, recently of Jackson, Miss.

August 17, 1844

Died at his residence near Brandon, Rankin County, Miss., on Saturday, 10th August, Bynum Howell, Esq., in the 30th year of his age. He emigrated to this state from Morgan County, Georgia, some four or five years ago.

Funeral services occasioned by the recent decease of the Rev. John Whitfield Buie, Pastor elect of the Baptist Church of this city, will be conducted on Sabbath morning next, 18th.

August 31, 1844

The Hon. Isaac R. Nicholson, who has long been a citizen of Hinds County, departed this life on Wednesday evening, the 28th.

September 21, 1844

Departed this life on Wednesday morning, the 4th September, 1844, at the residence of Daniel Yates, near Utica, Miss., Ambrose Howell, aged about 40 years. He died of consumption.

Died in Jackson, on the 15th day of Sept., 1844, Mrs. B. Dixon, consort of Henry St. John Dixon, in the 59th year of her age.

September 28, 1844

Married in Warren County, on the 22d September, Thos. W. Tompkins, Esq., merchant, of Warrenton, to Miss Sarah Jane McArthur.

October 19, 1844

Married on Tuesday, September 12, 1844, at Caseyville, Union Co., Ky., by the Rev. Mr. Wall, M. O. Hopkins, of Port Gibson, Miss., to Miss Enfield, daughter of Rev. B. W. Johnston, of the former place.

Married on the 26th September, 1844, at the residence of Mr. Jesse Cage, in Sumner County, Tennessee, by the Rev. J. T. Wheat, Daniel W. Adams, of Jackson, Miss., to Miss Ann M. Bullus, of the former place.

October 26, 1844

Departed this life on the night of October 13, 1844, Roderick McLeod, aged about 80 years. Being an orphan at an early age he did not know precisely the time of his birth. A native of Scotland, he emigrated to this country when a child, was raised in South and North Carolina.

November 2, 1844

Died in Smith Co., Miss., on Thursday night, the 10th October, 1844, Mr. Ithiel Town Lemley, son of Col. Saml. Lemley, in his 21st year.

November 9, 1844

Married in Clinton, La., Oct. 3, Peyton Cook Chapman to Miss Samantha Jane Nettles. At the same time and place, Richard Jacobs, proprietor of the Macon, Miss., Jeffersonian, to Miss Elvira E. Nettles, of Clinton.

Died in Wilkinson County on the 17th, Thomas L. Johnson. On the 14th, B. C. Bryant, son of D. Bryant.

Died in Benton, 21st Oct., Mrs. Elmira Ross.

Died in Adams County, Nov. 3, J. D. Proctor, M. D.

November 19, 1844

Married in Port Gibson, Claiborne County, 7th November, James N. Harding to Miss Elizabeth Maury, both of said town.

Married in Caroline County, Virginia, 29th Sept., Fleming Wood, of Natchez, Miss., to Miss Lucy Ann Tompkins.

Married at Patria, near Columbia, Chicot County, Arkansas, on the 10th of November, 1844, by the Rev. J. M. Taylor, of the above place, Doctor Oscar Hamilton, of Clinton, Miss., to Miss Sigismunda Mary, daughter of the Hon. John M. Taylor.

Married in Chickasaw County, 5th November, Rev. Thomas J. Lowery to Miss Rebecca H. Farr.

Married in Pike County, 5th Nov., W. M. Quin to Maria Jane McKay.

Married in Vicksburg, 13th Nov., Jacob Sartorious to Magdalena Ross.

Married in Warren County, 14th, Martin Kroes, of the city of Jackson, to Miss Louisa Berkenfent, of Vicksburg.

Died in Pike Co., 6th Nov., Mrs. Martha Elizabeth Pearson, aged 36.

Died in Memphis, Tenn., 11th Nov., Andrew Armstrong, of Ala.

Died in Choctaw County, 9th October, Miss Emily N. Fowler. At the same time, Miss Mary Harvey.

Died at Rodney, 6th November, Ellen Hammond Wilcox, aged 2 months.

Died at Fayette, 12th Nov., Alice Gertrude Hopkins, aged 11 months.

Died in Canton, on 10th Nov., Catherine Sophia Cordts, aged 6 months.

Died in Port Gibson, 6th Nov., Henry Devine, aged 30.

Died in Wilcox County, Ala., John Knox, aged 64.

Died in Lafayette County, 6th October, Mrs. Martha Ann Leeton. On the 21st October, Julia Ann, dau. of J. D. and Mary Palmer, aged 7.

Died in Rapids Parish, La., October 14th, Mrs. Emeline Ann Weaver.

Died in Sumter Co., Ala., 7th October, Martha Jane McGee, aged 17.

Died in Claiborne Co., on the 14th Oct., the wife of David McCaleb.

Died in Jefferson Co., 21st October, Miss Prescilla Jeffries, aged 25.

Died in Copiah County, 24th Oct., Mrs. Emily Dillard, aged 28.

November 29, 1844
Married in this city, on the 21st, by Rev. James E. Matthews, Col. J. H. Kilpatrick, editor of the Holly Springs Guard, to Miss Caroline, daughter of Gen. Wm. Clark, Treasurer of the State of Mississippi.

Died in Lawrence Co., Oct. 24, James P. Sheppard, late of Virginia.

December 6, 1844
Married in Lawrence County, 27th Nov., G. W. Douglass to Miss Virginia Francis.

Married in Columbus, 11th Nov., Henry Buchanan to S. A. Sullivan.

Married in Madison Co., 3d Dec., Rev. J. B. Walker to R. J. Ridley.

Died in Raymond, Hinds County, Miss., on the 20th November, 1844, Robert Williams Briggs, aged 25 years.

Died in Marion, Lauderdale County, 16th Oct., Mrs. Eleanor Smith.

Died in Jasper County, Ga., Mrs. Nancy Falkner, wife of Z. Falkner.

December 13, 1844

Married in this city, on the 12th, by the Rev. L. J. Halsey, Daniel H. Otto to Miss Sophia Sawkins, all of Jackson.

Married in Paulding, 1st, Daniel McLeod, of Green Co., to Miss Jane M'Lauren, of Jasper County. On the 3d, Wm. M. Williams to Miss Louisa Depriest, both of Jasper County.

Died in Hinds County, on Sunday evening, 1st, at the residence of her brother, Alexander K. Montgomery, Mrs. Sarah Gibbes, wife of Wilmet R. Gibbes, of this county.

Died in Woodville, 4th, John W. Leatherman, aged about 25.

December 23, 1844

Married in Dallas Co., Alabama, on the 25th Nov., Hon. A. H. Pegues, Senator from Lafayette County, Miss., to Miss Rebecca Ann Pegues.

Married in Jefferson County, on the 3d December, Samuel C. Montgomery to Miss Jane Kinnison. On the 4th, John Whitney to Melissa Ann Coleman.

Married in Giles County, Tenn., 1st Dec., Robert H. Laird, of Yalobusha County, to Miss Nancy M. Gordon, of the former place.

Married in Carroll Co., Miss., on the 5th Dec., Rufus M. Dillahunty to Miss Isabella Leflore.

Married in Yazoo Co., W. A. Moles to Nancy Plant, of Chickasaw.

January 3, 1845

Married in the city of Jackson, on Wednesday evening, January 1st, 1845, by Rev. Norman W. Camp, Mr. David N. Barrows to Miss Mary E. Langley, all of the city of Jackson.

Married at Lexington, Miss., on the 19th December, 1844, by the Rev. D. L. Russell, William Boyle to Miss Charlotte A., daughter of Dr. William Wilson, all of Holmes County.

Died in Madison County, Miss., the 26th Dec., of pulmonary consumption, Mrs. Denson, consort of William Denson.

January 10, 1845

Married in Warren Co., Dec. 24, Raleigh Folkes to Levina R. Owen.

Married at Lamar, John C. Hardwick to Miss Jane Elizabeth Boyd.

Married in Adams Co., Dec. 26, Joseph Cordell to Mary J. Harman.

Married at Nashville, Tenn., December 10, Dr. John R. Chapman, of Miss., to Miss Sarah Cheatham, of Nashville.

Married at Versailles, Ky., December 16, R. A. Watkinson, of Vicksburg, Miss., to Miss Sophia Tilley, of Versailles.

Married in DeSoto Co., Dec. 16, Rev. A. T. Scruggs to Sarah Dyer.

Married in Lowndes Co., Jan. 1, Jackson Massey to Suletta Wallace.

Married at Kingston, Dec. 28, Chas. N. Vanghen to Ann Eliza Farrar.

Married in Hinds County, Dec. 24, John R. Hall to Miss Sophia S. Dillard, all of Carroll County.

Married in Choctaw County, Dec. 19. Henry Yelvington to Miss Catharine Lee.

Married in Aberdeen, James F. Wilson to Mrs. Nancy A. Peugh.

Married in Lawrence County, David J. Herring to Miss Amanda H. Cannon; Leonard Smith to Miss Leonora Maxwell; Absalom H. Jayne, of Liberty, to Miss Emily Smith, of Lawrence County.

Married on the 17th Dec., Pryor Lee to Mrs. Mary M. B. Perkins.

Married in Smith Co., Dec. 19, Henry P. Hickman to Mary Galivant.

Married in Newton Co., Dec. 31, Jas. E. Carraway to Eliza B. Wall.

Died in the city of Jackson, Dec. 20, Mrs. Martha Ann Blake, consort of Wm. J. Blake. On the 23d Dec., Miss Mary Thomas.

Died in Lauderdale County, November 3d, Jacob Carter, aged 65 years.

Died in Leake County, December 20, George G. Hicks. On the 23d Dec., Canaan, son of John and Rebecca Bynum.

Died in Adams County, December 6, David Lea, aged 66 years.

Died in Wilkinson County, John W. Leatherman, aged 35 years.

Died in Madison Parish, La., Dec. 16, Thomas Jefferson Gilbert.

Died in Tensas Parish, La., Dec. 23, Charlotte Augusta Mandeville.

Died at Milliken's Bend, La., Dec. 17, Richard J. Lyons.

Died in Hinds County, January 1, David Dickson Farr. On the 31st Dec., Laura V., daughter of George T. and Ann E. Birdsong.

January 17, 1845

Married on Tuesday, the 7th Jan., in Jefferson Co., by Rev. William Montgomery, Miss Minerva Jane, eldest daughter of G. M. Buie, Esq., (of the latter place), to Mr. John N. Alsworth, of Madison County.

Married in Grand Gulf, 2d Jan., James Murrell to Elizabeth H. Bacon.

Married in Raymond, 7th Jan., B. G. Bankston to Miss Lucinda Kane.

Married in Holmes Co., Dec. 26, Salatine Covington to Mary Sproles.

Married in Lowndes Co., Dec. 26, J. L. G. Davis to Margt. J. Wright.

Married in Lafayette County, Dec. 29, John Wheeler to Miss M. W. Billingsley.

Married in Yalobusha Co., Dec. 29, James Smith to Jane Morrison.

Married in Warrenton, Jan. 1, Wm. A. Stockton to Ann H. McElruth.

Married in Natchez, Jan. 5, J. L. Sterry, of N. O., to Mary H. Parker.

January (no date given)

Married in Green County, Ala., January, Charlie Dowling, late of Macon, Miss., to Miss Nancy Holbrook, of the former place.

Married in Lawrence Co., Dec. 19, Anselin H. Jayne to Emily Smith.

Married in Jasper County, January 2d, John McAllum, of Perry County, to Miss Anna Hartfield, of Jasper County.

Married in Smith County, Jan. 2, Jefferson Windham to Miss Delila A. Jernagen.

Married in Warren County, Jan. 1, J. A. Richardson to Miss Frances A. Newman.

Married in Harrisonburg, Louisiana, December 24th, Catlette Tifle to Miss Prescilla Arnold, all of the parish of Catahoula.

Married in Chickasaw County, Dec. 26, Wm. Langham to Miss Hannah S. Clark.

Married in Warren County, Jan. 14, Sidney Conger to Miss Mary Bolls.

Married in Lowndes County, Dec. 31, James H. Smith to Mrs. Charlotte Tate.

Departed this life, on Wednesday evening, 11th December, 1844, at the house of Dr. Baugh, Port Gibson, Miss., Mrs. Mary Hassan Green, wife of Abram A. Green, of the house of Green & McDougall, New Orleans. She was the only child of Orville and Ann Carpenter and was born at the residence of her maternal grandfather, on 5th September, 1822, at Charleston, eastern shore of Maryland. Before the 2d year of her age her father was lost at sea. Her mother died soon after, of consumption, and she was adopted and raised by her uncle, Horace Carpenter.

Died in Grand Gulf, Jan. 8, George M. Dickinson, formerly of Virginia.

Died in Claiborne County, January 1st, Peter McIntyre, aged 65.

Died in Grand Gulf, on 4th Jan., Alexander Miller, aged 37.

Died at Oakland College, Dec. 25, Mrs. Frances Merwin Black.

Died in Yazoo County, Jan. 2, Allen Moore, aged 50.

Died in Yalobusha County, Jan. 8, A. G. McNutt, infant son of E. P. Howe.

Died in Claiborne County, Dec. 26, of consumption, John Stowers, aged 22.

Died in Adams County, Dec. 24, Mrs. Helen D., wife of H. W. Huntington, of La.

January 24, 1845

Married on the 9th Jan., in Copiah County, E. B. Taylor to Miss D. V. Green. On the 15th Jan., William Vardaman to Miss Rhoda Gustavus.

Married on the 14th Jan., Chas. C. Jacobs to Mrs. Lucinda M. Bush, of Yazoo.

Married on the 14th Jan., at Jackson, La., Jachiel Feligman to Miss J. Dryfuss.

Married on the 7th Jan., Ch. Trotter to Rebecca Edwards, of West Feliciana.

Married on the 5th Jan., in Lowndes County, Col. N. Davis to Mrs. Cynthia Kerr.

Married on 14th January, F. G. Bazille, of Mobile, to Miss Polly Breeland, of Green County, Mississippi.

Married in Jasper County, Jan. 6, W. G. Condift to Miss Eliza Street. 8th Jan., Thomas Millsaps to Miss Martha McCormick. 8th, E. Rush Buckner to Mrs. Georgiana Hann.

Departed this life, at his residence in Hinds County, on the 2d January, 1845. Mr. Alfred B. Cates, in the 27th year of his age.

Died in Port Gibson, 16th Jan., Edward Redding. On the 14th, Cyrus C. Mancaster.

Died in Claiborne County, 4th Jan., Franklin H. Dorsey.

Died in Warren County, 15th Jan., N. W. Hatch. 15th, Fanny, daughter of Mrs. Pinching.

Died in Natchez, 10th Jan., Thomas L. Evans.

Died in Columbus, Jan. 17, John Estes. 19th, Mrs. Sarah Spears.

Died in Baton Rouge, 28th Dec., William H. Eaton.

Died in New Orleans, 13th Jan., Mrs. Ann C., wife of Hon. Balie Peyton.

February 8, 1845

Married in Copiah County, Jan. 9, E. B. Taylor to Miss V. D. Green.

Married in Madison County, Jan. 29, Charles Sheppard to Miss Rebecca Cole.

Married in Wilkinson County, Jan. 21, Ferdinand Bensinger to Miss E. Standret.

Married in Lawrence County, 21st Jan., Dr. John H. Arrington to Miss Patience A., daughter of Gen. Arthur Fox.

Married in Lafayette County, Jan. 29, Thos. B. Allen to Miss Sarah Wilson.

Married in Jefferson County, Jan. 23, Wm. S. Beckley to Miss Mary Jane Scriber.

Died on the 7th Jan., at Macon, Noxubee County, Mrs. Martha A. Freeman.

February 22, 1845

Married in Monroe Co., 29th Jan., H. B. Meacham to Mary Riddle.

Married in Wilkinson Co., Jan. 28, George J. Dicks to Eliza Collins.

Married in Holmes Co., Jan. 31, Henry Brown to Mrs. Cath. Parker.

Married at Macon, Noxubee County, Jan. 22, Edmund W. Ferris to Miss Ann M. Marschalk.

Married in Canton, Jan. 11, Charles F. Bell to Miss Mary C. Kennedy.

Married in Paulding, Miss., 16th Jan., Jan. E. F. Bouchelle to Miss Maria T. Minor.

Married in Holmes County, 6th Feb., Jeff. Jones to Martha Morris.

Died on the 6th February, 1845, at the residence of Samuel A. Griffith, Esq., near the White Sulphur Springs, Lauderdale County, Mr. Richard Bush, about 24 years of age, a native of the State of Pennsylvania, and lately from Cincinnati, Ohio.

Died on the 10th Feb., at Nashville, Tenn., James Wand, aged 79 years.

Died on the 7th Feb., at Lexington, Miss., Susan L., daughter of W. B. Hines.

March 1, 1845
Married in St. Clair County, Ala., Dec. 10, George W. Sellers, of Jasper County, Miss., to Mrs. Nancy A. Bradford, of former place.

Married in Columbus, Feb. 13, L. L. Lincecum to Sarah Lauderdale.

Married in Benton, Feb. 20, John Lindheim to Miss Clara Sartorious.

Married in Natchez, Feb. 20, Moses Reim to Miss Sophia Ulman.

Married in Monticello, Feb. 19, Wm. Nairne to Elizabeth T. Hargis.

March 15, 1845
Died at Utica, Hinds County, Miss., on Thursday, the 27th February, Austin Bennett Woolley, son of Thomas R. Woolley, aged 4 years.

Died in Yazoo County, Mrs. A. A. Michie, wife of Maj. J. J. Michie.

March 29, 1845
Departed this life, in this city, on the 15th, Mrs. Amanda M., consort of D. W. Wilkinson, Esq., in the 31st year of her age.

April 5, 1845
Married on Monday, 21st March, at the residence of Doc. J. S. Copes, by the Rev. L. S. Halsey, Benj. F. Tankersley, of Houston, Texas, to Miss Gertrude Eliza Arick, of this city.

Married on Monday evening, the 31st March, by the Rev. Norman W. Camp, Willis W. Langley to Elizabeth A. Brown, all of this city.

Married on Thursday evening last, by the Rev. L. B. Holloway, Joseph H. Hutson to Miss Mary Ann Saterfield, daughter of Jonathan Saterfield, all of Hinds County.

April 12, 1845
Married on Tuesday March 18th, John A. Hunter to Miss Nancy Wilkinson, all of Jefferson County.

Married on Sunday, March 2d, Hugh Kelly to Miss Euphemia Gilchrist, all of Jefferson County.

Married on Tuesday, March 13, Mr. John Dunbar, of Brandy Wine Springs, to Miss Clarinda Short, all of Jefferson County.

Married on Thursday, February 27th, John Prichard to Miss Celia Ann Stringer, both of Franklin County.

Married in Clark Co., Mar. 22, William Clark to Harriet Williams.

Married in Vicksburg, March 20, J. W. Edwards to Elizabeth D. Riley.

Married in Hinds Co., March 27, Jarret R. Cook to Minerva L. Hines.

Married in Monroe County, March 6, Francis Decatur Inge to Miss Julia Bass.

Married in Noxubee Co., March 16, Wm. S. McMurry to Jane Weeks.

Married in Gainesville, March 16, B. D. Mitchell to Ellinder Wood.

Married in Lafayette County, March 20, U. S. Williams to Miss Maryann Wood.

Married in Wilkinson Co., March 21, Wm. Coon to Christina Inman.

Married in Adams County, February 26, Jefferson Davis to Miss Varion B. Howell.

Married in Port Gibson, Feb. 27, Peter Winn to Margaret McComb.

Married in Grand Gulf, Feb. 27, Horace Fulkerson to Charlotte B. McBryde.

Married in Holmes Co., March 22, Daniel L. Russell to Mrs. Sarah Blount.

Married in Lowndes Co., March 23, William Bean to Eliza Carouthers.

Married in Amite County, March 6, Wm. H. Rider to Catherine Gordon.

Married in Natchez, March 14, Jacques F. Lelievre to Olympa F. Mougeaun.

Died in Columbus, 24th February, Ewing F. Calhoun, aged 35.

Died in Adams Co., 3d March, Mrs. Sarah Fowler.

Died in Vicksburg, March 5th, Robert Stanard, aged 7.

Died in Adams County, March 17, George Newman.

Died in Monroe County, February 27, Mrs. Mary Beatty.

Died in Rankin County, March 18, Mrs. Nancy Rainwater, aged 56.

Died in Port Gibson, March 20, Margaret A. Hay, aged 3.

Died in Natchez, Jan. 28, Gustave Adolphe Holt, aged 5 and 6 months.

Died in Noxubee Co., Miss., March 29, James Jenkins, aged 48 years.

Died in Columbia, Tenn., March 3, Russell M. Williamson, aged 40.

Died in Canton, recently, Samuel T. Feamster.

Died in Columbus, March 15, Armsted Jones, aged 16.

April 19, 1845

Married in this city, on Wednesday evening last, Mr. Howell Hobbs to Miss Elizabeth Ellis, both of Jackson.

Married at Woodville, 27th March, Dr. A. Powell to Adelaide Evans.

Married at Richland, Holmes County, 23d March, John Morrow to Mrs. N. N. Johnson, both of Richland.

Departed this life on the 18th, near Madisonville, Madison Co., Mrs. Sophia Ann Galloway, consort of Mr. Alfred Galloway, of congestive fever. She has left a husband and five children.

Died in Canton, Thursday, 10th, the infant daughter of Wesley and Matilda Drane.

Died in Vicksburg, 9th, Miss Fanny Cook, aged 17. On the 8th, Sarah E., daughter of Daniel Sweet, aged 2 years.

Died in Warren County, 5th, Maj. A. G. Creath. On the 8th, Thomas R. Newman.

Died in Memphis, Tenn., 31 March, Mrs. Mary Roane, daughter of Maj. James and Mrs. Agnes Ruffin, of Panola County, Miss.

Died in Raleigh, Smith Co., 2d April, Aurelius, infant son of T. J. and Martha C. Coleman.

May 3, 1845

Married at Carrollton, 23d, George W. Mabry, of Madison, to Miss Mary E. Davis, of Holmes County.

Married in Copiah County, on the 24th April, Col. Robert E. Barris to Miss Nancy E., daughter of Hon. Buckner Harris.

Married near this city, on the 23d April, Mr. David Shelton to Miss Lavinia, eldest daughter of Pryor Lea.

$250 Reward, by Governor Albert G. Brown, for Christopher J. Davis, who killed T. S. Mackleroy on the 19th day of April, in Lauderdale County. Davis is about 28 years of age, 5 feet 10 inches high; trim built well set man, weighs about 140 pounds, keen blue eyes and dark hair, a scar on one cheek, intelligent countanance and speaks quick.

$200 Reward for Christopher J. Davis, who did on the 19th day of April, 1845, commit a most atrocious and unprovoked murder on the body of Zacheus S. McElroy. Signed: W. V. White, Jno. M. D. W. McElroy, Allen Christian, R. McElroy.

June 7, 1845

Married at Little Rock, Ark., Tuesday, 27th May, by Rev. A. Hunter, Gen. Solon Borland to Mary Isabel, only dau. of George Melbourne.

June 14, 1845

Andrew Jackson is no more. He died on Sunday evening last.

Married at Clinton, Thursday, May 22d, by the Rev. Thomas Ford, James J. Shirley to Miss Harriet J. Dunton.

June 28, 1845

Married in Vicksburg, June 10, James O'Neill to Mrs. Sarah Gill.

Married in Lexington, June 3, E. G. McKee to Miss Maria B. Arnold.

Married in Clinton, June 17, J. C. Lanier to Miss Mary J. McRaven.

Married in Madison County, June 18, Dr. H. Goldin Blackman to Miss Mary Jane Balfour.

Married in Washington City, June 7, Francis Hume to Miss Ann M. Donohoo.

Married in Port Gibson, June 17, James A. Gage to Rosannah Hogg.

Died in Jefferson County, June 8, James G. Wood.

Died in Warren County, June 10, Archibald Cameron.

Died at Vicksburg, May 31, John W. Miller.

Died in Yazoo County, June 4, Algernon S. Duvall.

Died at Grenada, June 4, Mrs. Elizabeth R. McRae.

July 12, 1845

Died in Jefferson County, Miss., on the 15th June, at his mother's, of congestive fever, Reuben Newman.

July 19, 1845

Married in Jackson, Monday morning, July 7th, by John P. Oldham, Esq., Heyman Hilzheim to Miss Martha M., daughter of Gen. T. C. McMackin, all of Jackson.

Married in Hinds County, July 10, Silas J. Carey to Miss Harriet J. Gillespie.

Married in Vicksburg, July 1st, John McKenzie Monroe, of New Orleans, to Miss Mary Artimise Gillespie.

Married in Tensas Parish, La., John F. Harper to Miss Ann Bieller.

Married in the parish of West Feliciana, La., June 8, 1845, Roger D. Woodward, of East Feliciana (after an engagement of seven years), to Miss Olivia Adaline, daughter of the Hon. Cyrus Ratliff, of former parish.

Died in Hinds County, July 7th, Sarah Ann Gold, dau. of Jas. Bush.

Died in Lowndes County, on June 29th, Henry A. Timberlake.

Died in Wilkinson County, June 28, Reuben Weed, a soldier of the Revolution, aged 81.

August 2, 1845

Died in Louisville, Ky., July 14th, Geo. J. Sneed, of Lafayette Co., Miss.

August 16, 1845

Married on Tuesday last, 12th August, by Rev. Robert Ross, Dr. J. L. M'Cool, and Miss Eliza Ross, both of Madison County, Miss.

Married in Hinds Co., 1st Aug., James D. Burney and Mary Clower.

Died in Holmes County, Aug. 2, Morgan, son of Morgan McAfee.

Died in Wilkinson County, July 23, Mrs. Mary P. Campbell.

Died in Clark Co., July 18, James K. Polk, infant son of J. M. Scale.

August 23, 1845

Married in Lauderdale County, July 28, Caleb Hill and Miss Elizabeth Stafford. Same day - Wm. Ooton and Miss Margaret Snowdon.

Married in Yazoo County, July 31, John B. Arnold and Medoria Bailey.

Married in Union Parish, La., July 20, G. W. Copley and Miss M. A. Larkins.

Married in Clark Co., July 20, M. Atkinson and Miss Elizabeth Williford. On July 3d, James Proctor and Miss Rachel Ellons.

Married in Lexington, July 13, Wm. E. Holley and Miss Adriann Laughlin.

Married in Lowndes County, 24th, Silas Lile and Catharine Morris.

Married in Nashville, Tenn., Robert S. Currin and Sophronia Williams.

Married in Adams County, William H. Fox and Miss Virginia E. Bass.

Married in Warren County, 7th, Vincent A. Wilkinson and Mrs. Julia Seviet. Same day, James E. Stewart and Miss Honora Scannell.

Married in Panola County, David Butts and Miss Angelina E. Hunt.

Married in Jefferson County, July 31, James H. McCoy and Helen Skinner.

Died in Wilkinson County, at the mansion of her father, on Saturday, the 2d August, of inflammation of the brain, Alacia Maria, daughter of D. L. and M. A. Phares, aged 7 years.

Died in Adams County, July 12, being drowned, Daniel S. McIntosh.

Died in Madison County, 18th August, William Moore, aged 63 years, and the oldest settler of this county.

Died in Greensboro, 8th, Francis R. Gregory, aged 34 years.

Died in Bolivar County, 6th, George Alexander, aged 89 years.

Died in Yazoo County, 4th, Mrs. Elizabeth Slade, aged 28 years.

Died on the 14th July, on Black River, La., Mrs. Ann H. Catlin.

Died in Tensas, La., 15th July, Elijah R. Paul, aged about 80 years.

Died in Yazoo City, on the 19th July, Wm. M'Cormack, aged 23 years.

August 30, 1845

Married in Jefferson Co., July 31, James H. McCoy and Helen Skinner, daughter of the late Major Richard Skinner.

Married in Marshall County, Aug. 12, B. R. Melton and Olevia Coopwood. On the 5th August, Robert C. Harwell and Harriet W. Erwin.

Married in Lowndes Co., 14th, Dr. A. V. Winter and Isabella S. Crute.

Married in Noxubee, 13th, Augustus H. Roby and Mary C. Brooks.

Married in Holmes County, 6th, A. M. West and Caroline O. Glover.

Married in Lawrence County, 14th, R. S. Moore and Caroline Vance.

Married in Covington Co., July 24, Philip McCrainey, of Rankin, and Miss Mary Leggett, of former county. John Fowlett, aged 75 years, and Mrs. Elizabeth Snow, aged 90 years, both of Jones County.

Died in Choctaw County, Miss., on the 6th August, 1845, Mrs. Elizabeth F. Peeples, consort of Col. Allen Peeples, aged 41 years.

Died in Winston County, 3d, Miss Susan Berry.

September 6, 1845

Married in Madison County, 19th ult., Thomas R. Green and Miss Rosanna E. York.

Married in Winston County, 24th ult., Saml. Pierson and Miss Martha J. Bradford.

Died in Lafayette County, Mrs. Margaret Caroline Meaders. On the 19th ult., Capt. Samuel M. Caruthers. On the 18th ult., Christian, daughter of Capt. C. G. and Mrs. B. Butler.

Died in Claiborne County, 22d ult., son of J. A. and Sarah M. Maxwell. On the 24th ult., Elia Amelia, infant daughter of Moses Clark.

Died in Vicksburg, 25th ult., Samuel M. Boylan, aged about 34 years.

September 13, 1845

Died on the 6th Sept., at the residence of Joseph Carson, in Yazoo Co., Abraham McAfee, youngest son of Morgan McAfee, aged 10 mos.

September 20, 1845

Married in Jefferson County, Miss., 2d September, by Hon. Judge Duncan, Levi Bromgogle, of Madison, to Miss Zenobia A. Bullen.

Married in Buffalo, New York, August 31, F. C. Wadsworth, of Vicksburg, and Miss Cytheria E. Bivens, of the former place.

Married in Polkville, Smith County, Aug. 27, J. W. Crook and Miss A. E. Myers.

Died in Madison County, the 14th September, Mrs. Elizabeth Ross, consort of Reverend Robert Ross.

Died in Brownsville, Hinds County, 10th September, John L. Doxey, aged 32. He was a member of the Masonic Society.

September 27, 1845

Died on the 23d of August, 1845, in Bowie County, Texas, Jethro Orren Battle, son of Orren Datus Battle, and Sarah F., his wife. He was born the 10th of June, 1824, in Robertson County, Tennessee, and raised principally in Hinds County, Miss. He was a student at Centenary College from February 1843 until March 1845, when he left this state for Texas.

October 4, 1845

Married on Wednesday last, 1st October, at the residence of Judge Cooper, near the city of Jackson, by the Rev. N. W. Carp, John T. Hull and Anna M. Blair, both of this city.

Married in Holmes Co., Sept. 10, Andrew Weeks and Maria Ellis.

Married in Yazoo County, Sept. 7, James Blundell and D. F. Graves.

Married in Jefferson Co., Sept. 15th, J. G. G. Garrett and Mrs. A. M. McCaleb.

Married in Carroll Co., Sept. 18, D. W. Price and Mary G. Arnold.

Married in Noxubee Co., Sept. 21, Thos. S. Freeman and Miss Sarah Cornelia Shipman, daughter of Jacob Shipman, Esq.

October 25, 1845

Married in Lowndes County, Sept. 11th, John N. Spears and Mrs. Julia Ann Ham; Thomas B. Lock and Miss Mary Ann Clayton; 10th Sept., James B. Lyon to Mrs. Sarah Word.

Married in Tippah Co., Sept. 4, Jos. C. Spight and Nancy K. Chapman.

Married in Frederick Co., Va., recently, Isaac Hite Hay, of Vicksburg, Miss., and Miss Ann Maury, of former place.

Married September 2d, Lysander Wiley and Miss Adeline A. Hammett, of Raymond.

Married in Pike Co., Sept. 1, John M. Girtman and Serenia L. Spence.

Married in Vidalia, La., Sept. 16, Reynold Quarl and Miss Feliciana Calvert.

Married in Jefferson County, Sept. 14, Wm. S. Rundell and Miss Eunice Griffing.

Married in Oktibbeha Co., Sept. 18, B. T. Taylor and Mary L. Reese.

Married in Jackson, Tennessee, Sept. 20, John P. Pryor, of Hernando, Miss., and Miss Eliza J. Long, of Marshall County, Miss.

Married in Madison Co., -- 9th Sept., James M. Jones and Mrs. Elizabeth Crawley -- 23d Aug., P. H. Luckett and Miss C. E. Melton -- 29th Sept., John L. Pratt and Miss Helen M. Marble, of Satartia.

Married in Marshall Co., September 1, Alexander M. Lucas and Miss Sarah Jane Robinson.

Married September 2d, J. L. W. Bullock, of Pike county, and Miss E. J. Catchings, of Simpson County.

Died in Lexington, Kentucky, on the 23d September, 1845, Thomas S. Walton, of Holmes County, Miss., aged 39 years.

Died in Holmes County, Sept. 18, William Wyatt -- Sept. 16, George Thomas Baughn, aged 3 years -- Sept. 12, an infant daughter of J. M. and Malissa Dyer -- Sept. 16, Henry Noble.

Died in Madison Co., Sept. 14, Wm. C. Hale, of Carrollton.

Died in Union Parish, La., Sept. 7, A. B. Nash.

Died in Jefferson County, Sept. 13, Mrs. Mary P. Allen, aged 28.

Died in Lawrence Co., August 28, William Jones Jayne.

Died in Tippah County, Sept. 16, Mrs. Margaret E. Baird, aged 40.

Died in Yazoo Co., Sept. 28, Thomas Montgomery, aged 45 -- Oct. 2, Washington Dorsey.

Died in Marshall County, 4th Sept., John A. Lausett.

Died in Smith Co., October 1, B. Crawford, aged 43 years.

Died in DeSoto Co., Sept. 29, Martha Massee Mimms, aged 18 mos.

Died in Pontotoc Co., Sept. 12, Mrs. Martha Dandridge.

Died in Washington Co., lately, Shalane Yerger, 19 months.

Died in Pontotoc Co., 19th Sept., Peter Sweeney.

Died in Newton Co., Sept. 15. Watson Evans, aged 39.

Died in Jasper Co., recently, John Dyess, aged 45 -- Sept. 17, C. L. Powell, aged 47 -- Sept. 12, Hanson Snell, aged 18.

Died in Adams Co., Miss Frances Farrar, aged 20.

November 8, 1845
Died at Columbus, Oct. 28, Mrs. Martha E. Humphries.

Died at Paulding, Oct. 24, James E. Hart, aged 18 years.

November 22, 1845
Died near Jackson, Miss., November 14th, 1845, Mrs. Sarah Morris, wife of Capt. John J. Morris, in the 33d year of her age. She was the daughter of Wm. H. Hobbs, of Greenville Co., Va. With her husband and family she moved to Mississippi in 1836.

November 29, 1845
Married on the 19th November, in the city of Jackson, by Rev. Hollaway, Judge J. B. Reese, of Texas, and Mrs. Ann B. Robinson.

Married on the 20th Nov., by Rev. Montgomery, George L. Potter and Miss Cynthia, daughter of D. Mayes -- all of Hinds County.

December 27, 1845
Married Dec. 9th, Major G. A. Ware, of Jackson, and Miss Sarah Rebecca Jones, formerly of North Carolina.

Married Dec. 16, Doctor H. C. McLaurin, of Simpson County, and Miss Harriet E. Love, of Madison County.

Married Dec. 18, C. S. Spann and Miss W. H. Lanier, both of Hinds Co.

Married Dec. 17, Samuel Guthrie and Clarissa M. Owen, both of Hinds.

Married Dec. 18, C. W. Simmons and Annes McLendon, of Newton Co.

Married Dec. 4, Benjamin Williams and Miss Sophronia A. Pope, of Hinds County.

Married Dec. 7, William McBride and Mrs. Ann E. Feamster, of Madison County.

Married in Copiah County, Dec. 17, Elijah Spell and Miss Sarah A. Beesly. Dec. 18, George W. L. Green and Miss Amanda Wilson. December 4, A. Moody and Mrs. Painela Thomas. December 5, C. D. Norman and Miss Delia Ann Randall.

Married in Wilkinson County, Dec. 18, Thomas E. Ogden and Isabella Virginia Morris. Nov. 20, Thomas M. Land and Miss Louisa Roach. Dec. 6, Thomas S. Dawson and Miss Mary Jane Black.

Married Dec. 15, John Noonan and Keziah M. Bryan, both of Attala Co.

Died at Grand Caillou, Louisiana, on the 28th of November, Captain Albert J. Quitman, brother of John A. Quitman.

Died in Warren Co., Dec. 20, Uriah Flowers, aged 54.

Died in Yazoo, Dec. 11, Doctor Richard B. Dorsey, aged 46.

Died in Noxubee Co., December 10, Mrs. Nancy R. Bryan.

February 2, 1846
Married by the Rev. H. Leavel, the 27th January, James A. Groves, of Kosciusko, Miss., and Mrs. Ann Mitchell, of the vicinity of Jackson, Miss.

March 9, 1846
Died at the residence of Mr. M. E. Thomas, in this city, on the 7th March, 1846, Mrs. P. W. Dawe, in the 46th year of her age. She was the daughter of Mr. Jas. S. Pickett, of Fauquier County, Virginia, and came to the south in the fall of '44.

THE SOUTHERN STAR (Gallatin, Miss.)
George R. Kiger, Editor & Proprietor.

December 23, 1837
Married in this county, on the 19th, by Geo. Rea, Esq., Mr. Jepththa Furr to Miss Arena Coleman, all of this county.

January 13, 1838
Married on Thursday evening last, by H. W. Bishop, Esq., Mr. Hugh J. Price to Miss Martha Ann, daughter of William Robinson, Esq., all of this county.

Married at Oakland, Claiborne County, Miss., on Monday, the 1st of January, by the Rev. R. H. Ranny, Mr. Francis Hume, of this place, to Miss Mary, youngest daughter of John Rail, Esq., of the former place.

January 20, 1838
Married in this county, on Thursday evening last, by B. Gresham, Esq., Mr. Felix W. Magee, to Miss Martha C. Dickson, daughter of the late Wm. Dickson, dec'd., all of this county.

Died in this county, on Thursday evening last, Mr. John J. Holliday, aged about 35 years. The deceased left a wife and three children.

February 17, 1838
Married in Franklin County, on the 1st, Mr. William W. Cook, of this place, to Miss Isabella Finley, of Franklin County.

Died in this county, at his residence, of bilious pleurisy, Mr. Thomas Shamburger, aged about 37 years. The deceased has left a wife and five small children.

March 3, 1838
Married in this county, on Sunday, the 20th ultimo, by George Rea, Esq., David Milton Massie, Esq., formerly of Winchester, Virginia, to Miss Margaret, second daughter of the Hon. Thomas A. Willis.

Died in this county, at the residence of her father, on Tuesday last, Miss Sarah Rembert, daughter of John Rembert, Esq.

March 24, 1838

Died in the city of Vicksburg, on Wednesday, 14th, in her 21st year, Mrs. Adeline Louisa Harris, the wife of James R. Harris, Esq., and eldest daughter of Joseph Brown, Esq., of this county. She left a daughter in her 3d year.

April 14, 1838

Married on Tuesday evening last, by the Hon. S. H. Johnson, Mr. William R. Blake to Miss Nancy H. Thompson, all of this county.

June 9, 1838

Married in this county, on Tuesday evening last, by H. W. Bishop, Esq., Mr. Oliver Haley, Esq., to Miss Elizabeth, daughter of William C. Wroten, Esq., all of this county.

Died in this county on the 24th ult., Mrs. Nancy H. West, consort of James M. West, in the 37th year of her age. She has left a husband and five small children.

July 7, 1838

Married in this county, on the 4th, by George Rea, Esq., Mr. Needham Patrick to Miss Jane Ainsworth, all of this county.

Married in Claiborne County, on the same day, Mr. Love Shelby to Miss Martha Barnes.

Married in Monticello, Lawrence County, on the evening of the 3d, by Wm. Peebles, Esq., Mr. Joseph Neylans, merchant, to Miss Amanda Bell, of Louisiana.

July 13, 1838

Died in this county, on Tuesday, the 10th, Mrs. Susan Burnley, consort of Edwin Burnley, Esq., of this county.

September 7, 1838

Married in the city of New York, on the 4th August, by the Rev. Thos. DeWitt, Mr. Robert Hume, of Grand Gulf, Miss., to Miss Nancy C. P. Brown, daughter of Joseph Brown, Esq., near Mount Washington, Miss.

Died in this place, on Sunday the 26th ult., Mr. Charles K. Brown, a resident of Rankin County.

Died near this place, on Monday evening last, Mr. Abraham A. Harvey. The deceased emigrated from Tennessee to this county about ten years ago.

September 28, 1838

Died in this county on the 26th, at the residence of her grandfather, Jos. Brown, Esq., Francina, aged 3 years, only daughter of James R. Harris, Esq., of Vicksburg.

October 19, 1838
Married on Tuesday evening, 9th, by E. L. Bowen, Esq., Major Joseph G. Anderson, of Copiah County, to Miss Martha J. Mangum, eldest daughter of Mrs. Elizabeth Mangum, of Monticello.

November 2, 1838
Died at his residence in this co., on Wed. a.m. last, Mr. John Coor.

November 9, 1838
Married in the city of Natchez, on Thursday evening, 25th, by the Rev. Mr. Page, John Sims, Esq., Cashier of the Branch of the Mississippi Rail Road Bank, at Gallatin, to Miss Ellen L. Clay, daughter of the late Curtis Clay, Esq., of Philadelphia.

Married in Lawrence County, on the 25th ult., by Wm. Peebles, Esq., the Hon. Arthur Smith, Senator from that county, to Miss Eliza Neylans, of Lawrence County.

Departed this life in this place, on the 31st Oct. last, Mr. Wm. McDonald, in the 34th year of his age.

December 7, 1837
(Out of place, or probably should read 1838)
Married in this county, on Sunday the 3d, by George Rea, Esq., Mr. Nathaniel W. Lattimer to Miss Martha B. Stubbs, all of this county.

Died at his residence in this county, on Sunday, the 3d, of bilious pleurisy, Mr. David W. Vaughn, aged about 50 years.

Died on Wednesday evening, of bilious pleurisy, Mr. Benson Walker, aged about 30 years.

January 4, 1839
Married in Pike County, on the 15th ult., by the Hon. C. Hoover, Phillip Scott Catching, Esq., Att'y. at Law of this place, to Miss Nancy Burton, of that county.

January 12, 1839
Married on Wednesday evening last, by Roland Johnson, Esq., Mr. Arthur Scott, of Hinds County, to Mrs. Sarah Ann Reynolds, of this place.

Died in this county, Celia Ann, daughter of Thomas and Nancey Stewart, aged 6 years.

January 26, 1839
Married in this county, on the 17th, by the Rev. Mr. Johnson, Mr. John Broomfield to Miss Ann Stubbs.

Married in this county, on Thursday evening last, by Geo. Rea, Esq., Mr. Asa Potter to Miss Matilda, daughter of Wm. Alexander, Esq., all of this county.

Petition for Divorce -- John Twoney -vs- Bridget Twoney.

February 9, 1839
Married on the 26th ult., by the Rev. John G. Lee, Lewis Kenneday, Esq., to Miss Artalissa B. Harrison, eldest daughter of Benjamin Harrison, Esq., all of Copiah County, Miss.

March 30, 1839
Died in this county, on Sunday morning last, at the residence of Mrs. Vaughns, Dr. Henry Potter, formerly of Kentucky, aged about 25 years.

Died in Lawrence County, on the 12th, Mrs. Sarah Johnson, in her 47th year, consort of Jordan Johnson, Esq., of that county.

April 5, 1839
Married on Tuesday evening last, by George Rea, Esq., Thomas Tillman to Miss Elizabeth Ellis, all of this county.

May 4, 1839
Died on the 28th of April last, Mr. William Tombs, aged 53 years.

June 1, 1839
Died at Forest Grove, in Copiah Co., on the 22d of May, Mrs. Caroline Matilda, consort of Duncan McRae, and 2nd dau. of the late W. W. Lloyd, Esq., of this co. She died aged 29, of consumption.

June 3, 1839
Died Gen. Silas Brown, State Treasurer. He died on Monday last.

Died at his residence near Mississippi Springs, in this co., on the 25th May, Col. Philip Dixon, formerly of Jefferson Co., aged about 45 yrs.

Died in this city, on Monday last, Benajmin Quitman, son of Col. T. B. J. Hadley, in the 3d year of his age.

June 22, 1839
Departed this life suddenly, in this place, on Wednesday last, Mrs. Frances Brown, aged 78 years and 3 months. She was a native of North Carolina but had been a resident of this state several years.

Mrs. Elizabeth Hargis, wife of Aaron Hargis, Esq., of Monticello, is no more. She died on the 11th, in the sixtieth year of her age.

July 6, 1839
Married on Thursday evening, the 27th, by Benjamin Gresham, Esq., Dr. David C. Dickson, of Georgetown, to Miss Nancey E. Magee, daughter of David Magee, all of this county.

July 20, 1839
Died on Wednesday, the 10th, at the residence of her husband, six miles west of Gallatin, Mrs. Nancy Blake, wife of Mr. William R. Blake, aged about 17 years, leaving a husband and infant son.

August 10, 1839
Married on Sunday evening, 4th, by William A. Wade, Esq., Mr. Robert P. Evans to Miss Assenith Willis.

Married on Tuesday, 6th, by the same, Henry Lewis to Miss Mariane Jackson, all of this county.

August 24, 1839
Married on Thursday, the 15th, in this county, by Roland Johnson, Esq., Mr. Wiley B. Vaughn to Miss Mary R. Wiggins.

Married in this county, on Sunday evening last, by the Hon. Buckner Harris, James S. Fairly, Esq., of this place, to Miss Effy Fairly, of Jefferson County.

Married in this county, on Wednesday last, by W. A. Wade, Esq., Mr. J. F. P. Franklin to Miss Elizabeth Null.

Married in this place, on Wednesday last, by Roland Johnson, Esq., John Campbell to Miss Elizabeth Ann Smith.

September 7, 1839
Died in this county, on Friday, the 30th ult., Mrs. Mary Fairbanks, aged seventy-two years, and consort of W. Fairbanks, Esq. She was a pious member of the Presbytarian Church.

September 28, 1839
Married in this county, on the 11th, by Roland Johnson, Esq., Mr. J. W. Coor to Miss Harriet Hawzey, all of this county.

October 26, 1839
Died at Mount Washington, on Tuesday, the 15th October, Henry Nahum, infant son of T. J. and Mary B. Thompson, aged 8 days.

November 9, 1839
Died in this county, on Friday, the 24th ult., Narcissa Ann, aged 19 months and 4 days, youngest daughter of Judge Barnabus Allen.

November 23, 1839
Married in this county, on Sunday last, Mr. John Sims to Miss Harriett A. Cassity, both of this county.

Died in this place, on Wednesday evening last, Jacob Lafayette, infant son of W. E. Tomlinson.

November 30, 1839
Married in this county, on Thursday evening last, by the Rev. Mr. Harveston, Mr. Samuel Hillburn to Miss Emily Bishop, both of this county.

Married in this county, on Wednesday evening last, by Roland Johnson, Esq., Mr. John J. Wise to Miss Sarah Ann D. Lambright.

December 7, 1839
Married in Lawrence County, at the residence of Gen. A. Fox, on Wednesday, the 20th ult., by the Hon. W. B. Cannon, Capt. D. J. Hill, of New Orleans, to Miss Elizabeth Lark, eldest daughter of Gen. Arthur Fox.

Married in this county, on Tuesday evening last, the 3d, by John Terry, Esq., Mr. Wm. Alexander to Miss Lanora Peevy, eldest daughter of Archibald Peevy, Esq.

Married in this co., on Thursday last, by Jno. Terry, Esq., Mr. James M. Goode, of Hinds County, to Miss Mary Ann Matinly, of this county.

December 21, 1839
Died suddenly, at the residence of his mother, in Lawrence County, a few days since, Mr. Peter Bridges, aged about 25 years.

Married last evening, 15th, by the Rev. Mr. Drake, Mr. Isaac Hoof, of Winchester, Virginia, to Mrs. Sarah Wood, of this city.

February 1, 1840
Married on the evening of the 15th, at the residence of Richard Flowers, Esqr., in Covington County, by George D. Patterson, Esqr., Mr. Duncan McRae, of Copiah, to Mrs. Nancy J. Dove, of the former place.

February 8, 1840
Married in this county, on Wednesday evening last, by Wm. A. Wade, Esq., Mr. William McCallister to Miss Margaret Mathews, all of this county.

February 29, 1840
Married in this county, on Sunday last, by Rowland Johnson, Esqr., Mr. Turney Alford to Miss Asenith Vick, of this county.

Died in Monticello, on Saturday, the 22d, after a protracted illness of pulmonary nature, Mrs. Elizabeth Lark Hill, consort of Capt. D. Hill, and eldest daughter of Gen. Arthur Fox, of Lawrence County.

March 7, 1840
Married in this town, on Thursday morning last, by Wm. A. Wade, Esq., Mr. John Perkins to Elizabeth Berry, all of this county.

Died at the residence of her nephew, the Rev. Thomas B. Adams, Copiah County, Miss., Miss Mary Peachy Gilmer, of Rockingham County, Virginia, in the 72d year of her age.

Died in this county, at his residence on Wednesday evening last, Col. John Barfield, aged about 45 years. The deceased was an old and respected resident of this county.

March 14, 1840

Died at his residence in the county of Lawrence, on Friday, the 6th, Mr. James Freelock, formerly of North Carolina.

Married in Vicksburg, on the 5th, at the residence of Dr. Gwin, by the Rev. C. K. Marshall, Dr. Wm. P. King to Mrs. Frances A. Clarke, both of that city.

Married on the same day, at Hendren's Hotel, Vicksburg, by the Rev. C. K. Marshall, Dr. John H. Lawson to Mrs. Ann H. P. Noble, both of Louisiana.

March 21, 1840

Died in this county, on Monday morning last, at the residence of his father, Mr. Gideon Buffkin, aged about 17 years.

May 23, 1840

The tral of Richard M. Jones for the murder of Col. James M. Hulett, at this place in June, 1838, took place at the regular May term of Jefferson County circuit court last week. The argument closed on the evening of the 2d day, when the jury retired and after being out about two hours returned a verdict of guilty of manslaughter.

May 30, 1840

Married on Thursday, the 14th, by R. Johnson, Esq., Mr. John K. Mooney, of Hinds County, to Miss Mary W., daughter of J. W. Legrand, of this county.

Married on Sunday, the 24th, Mr. Alexander King, of this place, to Miss Nancy Edwards, of Hinds County.

June 20, 1840

Married in Lawrence County, on Wednesday evening last, at the residence of Wm. Neylans, Esq., by E. L. Bowen, Esq., Samuel Smith, Esq., Att'y. at Law of Monticello, to Miss Nancy Neylans.

Died in Edgar Co., Illinois, on the 23d May, 1840, Delilah Delay, infant and only, until then, surviving child of J. R. Loveless, junior editor of this paper.

July 11, 1840

Died at his residence in this co., a few days since, Mr. John Barlow, aged about 30 years. Mr. B. was for a long time afflicted with scrofu.

Died at his residence in Hinds County, on the 8th, of pulmonary consumption, William Beesley, in the 37th year of his age. The deceased left a wife and four children.

Died in this county, on Thursday last, Mrs. Judith Webb, consort of Wm. R. Webb, Esq., of this county.

Died suddenly, in this county, on Friday morning, the 11th, at the residence of her father, Mr. James Smith, Mrs. Sarah Evans.

Died in Grand Gulf, Claiborne Co., Miss., on Sunday, the 28th ult., Joseph Napoleon, infant son of Robert C. and Nancy C. P. Hume, aged 11 months.

Died on the same day, Margaret Matilda, only daughter of Dr. Trawack, of this county, aged 1 year and 10 months, at the residence of her father, near Georgetown.

August 8, 1840

Died at the residence of Thomas J. Thompson, at Washington, Copiah County, on the 30th ult., Robert Wm. Thompson, in the 20th year of his age. He left an aged and widowed mother and several brothers and sisters. He was born in Stafford Co., Va.

Died in Yazoo City, Yazoo Co., on the 30th ult., John Harris, printer, aged 33 years, a native of Chambersburg, Penn.

Died near Clinton, Hinds Co., on the 29th ult., at the residence of Gen. Mead, Miss Sarah B. Mead, aged 29 years.

Died at Monticello, Lawrence Co., on the 3d ult., Mrs. Delilah Pendleton, aged 35 years.

August 22, 1840

Died on Saturday last, Mr. Goins, for a long time a citizen of this county, aged 65 years.

Died on Tuesday last, Mr. Wm. R. Webb, aged about 30 years.

Died on the same day, Mrs. Mary Ellis.

August 29, 1840

It is with painful regret that we announce the demise of General Thomas Hinds, of Jefferson County. He died at his residence on Sunday morning last, 23d. The general was thrown from his horse a few days before, which ruptured a blood vessel and terminated his existence. He was aged about 56 years.

Died in this county, at his residence, on Thursday morning, 27th, Mr. Berry Ellzy, aged 69 years and 5 months. Mr. Ellzy was one of the oldest and most respected citizens of Copiah Co.

Died in this county, on the 22d, Mrs. Mary Malone, aged about 40, and consort of David Malone, Esq., of this county.

Died on the same day, at the residence of her father, Miss Jane Cassidy, aged 18.

Died in the county, at the residence of his father, T. W. Ellis, Esq., Thomas Ellis, aged 11 years.

Died in this county, at Georgetown, Bej. Franklin Catching, son of B. Catching, Esq., of that place, aged 2 years and 3 months.

Died on the 23d, Miss Eliza Barfield, aged 14 years.

Died on the 25th, at the residence of his father, Norvill, infant son of Wm. R. Gresham, Esq.

September 11, 1840

Died last week, the Rev. Jas. Thigpen, Jr., of this county, minister of the Baptist Church. (*Raymond Times*)

Died on Friday last, Mr. Stephen Granberry, of this county, aged about 50 years.

September 18, 1840

Married in this county, on Tuesday, the 8th, by John T. More, Esq., Mr. John Maxwell to Miss Eveline Cassity, all of this county.

Died on Tuesday last, Mrs. Sarah Stackhouse, consort of Wm. Stackhouse, Esq., aged about 60 years.

Died on Saturday, the 5th, Silas, second son of B. H. Catching, Esq., of Georgetown, aged 9 years.

Died in Lowndes Co., on the 27th ult., Dr. John H. Harrison, aged 27.

October 30, 1840

Married on Tuesday evening, the 20th, by Hon. S. H. Johnson, Samuel J. Morehead, Esq., Attorney at Law of this place, to Miss Amanthus L., daughter of Gen. Wiley P. Harris, of this county.

September 28, 1841

Married in New Liberty, Owen County, Ky., on the 31st August, Rankin R. Revile, Attorney at Law, formerly of Gallatin, Copiah County, Miss., to Miss Eliza Jane Gale, daughter of Dr. Gale, of that place.

Departed this life, on Friday last, Albert G. Brown, the only son of Edwin R. and Sarah Brown, in the fifth year of his age.

Died in Vicksburg, on Tuesday night last, Col. John L. Irwing, an old and highly esteemed citizen of that place.

THE SOUTHERN SUN (Jackson, Miss.)
Dobson, Dickey & Elliott - Publishers & Proprietors

June 16, 1838
Died in Clinton, Miss., on the morning of the 11th, Mr. Addison L. Shackelford, a native of Virginia.

June 23, 1838
Died in this place, on Sunday morning, John W. Gildart, Esq. The deceased was an eloquent lawyer.

Died in Vicksburg, Miss., on the 8th, in his 19th year, Mr. Henry M. Dilliard, son of Merrit Dilliard, Esq., of Hinds County, Miss., late of Raleigh, North Carolina.

July 28, 1838
Departed this life on the morning of the 25th of July, Mrs. Catharine Payne, consort of Dr. Nathaniel W. Payne, in the 44th year of her age.

August 11, 1838
Married in Leake County, on Tuesday, the 31st ultimo, by the Rev. John McCauley, Dr. James McKeith, late of Kentucky, to Miss Elizabeth, daughter of Colonel Jas. Perry, all of Leake County.

Died on Society Ridge, Hinds County, on the morning of the 15th ultimo, in the 21st year of her age, Mrs. Elizabeth Jane Lewis, wife of Exum Lewis, Esq. The deceased has left a husband and two children.

September 22, 1838
Died at the residence of her brother, Dr. W. H. Young, in the county of Rankin, on the 17th, Mrs. Letitia Harris, wife of Mr. Harris, a merchant of Carroll County, Miss. Mrs. Harris was a native of Ireland, aged 21 years. She has left her husband and a child, aged two years.

Married on Sunday, the 16th, by David H. Dickson, Esqr., Mr. Selah Judd to Mrs. Louisa C. W. Learned, all of this city. .

Married on Thursday evening, the 20th, by the same, Mr. Thomas Gordon to Miss Julia Moore, all of this place.

Married in Clinton, Miss., on the 5th, by Rev. Daniel Comfort, Mr. William S. Caball to Miss Elvia K. Payne.

September 29, 1838
Married on Thursday, the 18th, by the Rev. Thos. Ford, Mr. Daniel Greenleaf to Miss Emily Lindsey, all of this place.

October 6, 1838
Died at the residence of her husband, on the 24th September, Mrs. Sarah L. Ludlow, aged 38 years, wife of B. A. Ludlow.

November 10, 1838
Married on Sunday morning, the 3d, by the Rev'd. Daniel Comfort, of the Presbyterian Church, Col. E. M. Laurence, of Clinton, Miss., formerly of Fayetteville, Tenn., to Mrs. Martha Diles, of Clinton, Miss., formerly of Maury County, Tenn.

November 17, 1838
Married on Thursday, 25th Oct., at the residence of Mr. Samuel Norred, by the Rev. Mr. Jones, of Sharon, Robert E. Halford, Esq., to Miss Martha Ann Childress, eldest daughter of Mrs. Martha Childress, all of Leake County.

Married at the Mississippi Springs, on Thursday evening last, by the Rev. P. Donan, Mr. William P. Stone, of this city, to Miss Amanda Ragan, daughter of Jesse B. Ragan, Esq., of this county.

Died in this city, on Sunday evening last, Miss Louisa Mayson, eldest daughter of the late Charles C. Mayson, Esq., aged 14 years.

Died in Philadelphia, recently, Doctor Coningham Crawford, a native of Ireland, but for some years past a resident of Clinton, Miss.

November 24, 1838
Died in Clinton, Miss., on the 23d of October last, Mr. George P. Mayo, aged about 22 years.

Died in Clinton, Miss., on the 17th, Major G. W. Wyche.

December 8, 1838
The trial of William S. Parham, Esq., for the murder of Mr. A. L. Shackelford, on the 11th June last, came to be heard during the present term of the Circuit Court. The jury returned a verdict of "Not Guilty".

January 15, 1839
Married in Carthage, Miss., on Thurs., 27th ult., by Rev. Isaac Wells, Hon. Edwin Fox to Miss Caroline M. Childress, all of Leake Co.

February 12, 1839
Doctor James L. Forsyth, of Westville, committed suicide by cutting his throat, on the morning of the 5th. Dr. Forsyth was formerly from the State of New York.

March 5, 1839
Married on the 28th February, at the residence of Mrs. Forts, by the Rev. George W. Stewart, Mr. Wm. A. Simmons, of Livingston, Madison County, to Miss Morning Williams, of Hinds County.

March 12, 1839
Married in Rankin County, on Monday evening last, by Rev. Mr. Porter, Maj. Joseph E. Miller, of this city, to Mrs. Elizabeth Purvis.

Died in this county, on Wednesday evening last, Maj. William Trahern, an old and respectable citizen of Hinds.

June 11, 1839

Died at the residence of Rev. P. Donan, in this county, on Tuesday, the 28th ult., of an affection of the lungs, Jannett Gemmell, the only surviving child of Ann P. Gemmell, aged 2 years and 9 months.

Married in this county, on the 29th ult., by Rev. L. B. Holloway, Dr. George Stokes, formerly of Greenville, N. C., to Miss Charlotte C. Greaves, formerly of Marion, S. Carolina.

Married in Mount Sterling, Ky., on the 30th May, by the Rev. Mr. Marcy, Mr. James H. Massey to Miss Ann Eliza, eldest daughter of Jas. Rainey, Esq., all of Mississippi.

July 2, 1839

Married in this city, on Tuesday evening last, by the Rev. L. B. Holloway, Col. A. B. Saunders, Auditor of Public Accounts, to Mrs. Margaret E. Mayson, relict of the late Charles C. Mayson.

Died at Clinton, Miss., on the 13th ult., Mr. R. C. Williams, aged 26 years. The deceased was a native of Wilson County, Tennessee.

Married in Elizabeth City, N. C., on Sunday evening, the 16th ult., by the Rev. Mr. Stanley, of the Episcopal Church, Dr. William S. Langley, of this city, to Miss Sophia D., daughter of Col. Lemuel C. Moore, formerly of that place.

Died in this place, on the 5th, Margaret Reed Dickson, daughter of the Hon'l. David Dickson, late of this city, aged 6 years and 11 months.

July 23, 1839

Died in this place, on yesterday evening, Col. Nathan Lester, editor of the *Mississippian*. He had only taken charge of the *Mississippian* a few days preceeding his death.

July 30, 1839

Died in Clinton, Miss., on the 26th, Mr. James Askew.

Married in Winchester, Tennessee, on the 16th of May last, by the Rev. J. A. Bumpass, Mr. Richard Sharpe, of Winchester, to Miss Indiana Cordelia M. Spann, of Raymond, Miss.

Married in Raymond, on Tuesday, the 23d, by the Rev. T. Ford, Dr. G. G. Barnes to Miss Lucy, daughter of Maj. G. H. Gray, all of Clinton.

No Date

Died on Sunday, the 4th, Samuel, infant son of Wm. J. Wells, Esq., aged 16 months.

Married in Clinton, on Tuesday, the 23d ultimo, by the Rev. T. Ford, Dr. G. G. Banks to Miss Lucy, daughter of Maj. G. H. Gray, all of Clinton.

August 13, 1839

Died at his residence near Benton, on the 1st, Maj. Spence M. Grayson, in the 39th year of his age -- for the past two years a Senator in the Legislature from Yazoo County.

August 20, 1839

Married in the Methodist E. Church, on Sunday evening last, by Rev. Mr. Porter, Mr. Noble M. Goode to Miss Harriet E. Swanson, all of this county.

September 10, 1839

Died in this city, on the 30th ult., Mrs. Harriet L. St. Clair, consort of Mr. Walter St. Clair.

Died at Mississippi City, on the 29th ult., Mr. James T. Phillips, of this place, in the 31st year of his age.

October 1, 1839

Died in Covington Co., Miss., on the 15th, Mrs. Elizabeth Stewart, consort of Mr. Allan Stewart, in the 65th year of her age. The deceased was, for about 40 yrs., a member of the Presbytarian Church.

October 8, 1839

Married in Yazoo City, on Friday, the 20th Sept., by his Honor the Mayor of Benton, Mr. John Hamilton, commedian, to Mrs. Caroline Robinson, Dansicure.

Died of consumption, on Thursday, the 26th, at the residence of Mr. Edwin Shumway, in Brownsville, in this county, Dr. John H. Bailey, aged 26 years. Mr. Bailey was born in Virginia where his mother is still living. He was a graduate of the University of Virginia.

Died in this city, on Thursday last, Sarah, infant daughter of Fairfax Washington, aged about one year.

October 22, 1839

Died in this city, on Saturday evening last, Mr. B. B. Dillard, aged about 30 years.

Died in Gallatin, Copiah County, on Sunday last, Mr. John Shields, of this city, aged about 45 years.

October 29, 1839

Died at the residence of Dr. Mark Snow, in this county, Dr. Ezra G. Snow, in the 24th year of his age. Dr. Snow was a native of Cheshire Co., N. Hampshire, but for the last three years a resident of this co.

December 3, 1839
Died in this city last night, Margaret E., daughter of Mr. J. J. H. Morris, aged 6 years, 5 months and 19 days.

February 4, 1840
Died at her residence near this city, on Tuesday morning last, Mrs. Minerva Ann Lea, consort of Pryor Lea, Esq.

February 25, 1840
Died on the night of the 21st, Laura Ann, daughter of S. W. and Elizabeth Humphreys, of Clinton, aged 1 year, 9 months and 21 days.

April 21, 1840
Died on the 3d, near Mt. Carmel, Covington County, in her 18th year, Mrs. Lethy Ann Robertson, consort of M. A. Robertson, Esq. Mrs. R. left a husband and an infant daughter.

April 28, 1840
Married at Gallatin, Copiah County, on Wednesday last, by R. Johnston, Esq., Maj. James K. Whelan, of this city, to Mrs. Matilda Jane Speer, of the latter place.

Died at his residence in Lowndes County, Miss., on the 13th, Dr. John H. Brownrigg, formerly of Edenton, N. C.

Died in this city, on Saturday evening last, Mary, infant daughter of H. K. Moss, aged 18 months.

May 12, 1840
Married near this city, on Wednesday last, by the Rev. Mr. Speer, Mr. John J. Poindexter to Miss Mary Cohea, daughter of Mr. Perry Cohea.

May 20, 1840
Married on Thursday evening last, at Cold Springs, Claiborne County, Miss., by the Rev. John Lane, William H. McCardle, Esq., senior Editor of the Vicksburg Whig, to Miss Emily Caroline Byrnes, only daughter of the late Robert Ralston Byrnes, Esq.

June 9, 1840
Married in this vicinity, on Tuesday evening, the 26th ult., by Rev. P. Donan, William H. Garland, Esq., to Miss Frances Ann Eubank.

SOUTHERN TELEGRAPH (Rodney, Miss.)
Published by Thomas B. Palmer & Co.

July 30, 1834
Died at the residence of Israel Coleman, Esq., in Claiborne County, Miss., of congestive fever, Mr. Robert B. Robinson, of Pickens County, Alabama, aged 27 years and 3 months.

August 13, 1834
Died on the 11th, of congestive fever, Alfred Metcalfe, aged 35 years.

Died in this county, on Wednesday last, the 6th, Daniel McKay, Esq.

Died this morning, in this place, Joseph Rockman, aged 22 years, late of Tuscarawas County, Ohio.

August 20, 1834

Died in this place, on the 14th, of congestive fever, John Hamilton, aged about 25 years.

Died on the 1st, of fever, at the residence of John E. Hall, Esq., in this county, Mr. Joseph Smith.

Died on Monday evening, of congestive fever, in this county, W. T. Hodge, aged about 35 years.

Died on Sunday evening last, of congestive fever, at her residence near Rodney, Mrs. P. Coleman, aged about 62 years.

Died on Sat. evening last, Mrs. Sarah Griffin, consort of B. C. Griffin.

August 27, 1834

Died at his rsidence near Greenville, in this county, on the 31st ult., Mr. Abner Pipes, in the 62d year of his age. He was born near Louisville, Kentucky, and in his eighth year came to Natchez (in 1780).

September 3, 1834

Married on Sunday last, by John Ducker, J. P., Mr. James Clayton and Mrs. Martha K. Andrews, both of this place.

Married on Sunday last, by the Rev. Mr. Murray, Dr. A. P. Jones and Miss Olivia Watson.

September 10, 1834

Died at Natchez, 30th August, of congestive fever, James G. Brooks, aged about 20 years, and recently of this burrough.

Died on Sept. 4, Rev. J. Burch, for many years a resident of this co.

Died on the 15th ult., of congestive fever, on the Roundaway Bayou, La., Mr. Jacob Cable, aged 24 years.

Married on the 15th June last, by the Rev. Mr. Wiley, Turman Jones to Margaret W. Jones, both of Somerset County, Md.

Married on Thursday last, by the Rev. Mr. Murray, Mr. Asa Coleman to Miss Mary Divine, both of this county.

October 22, 1834

Married on the 17th, at Baton Rouge, La., Col. Samuel Gwin, of Chocchuma, Miss., to Mrs. E. Hampton, of Springfield, parish of East Baton Rouge.

Died on Monday night last, Mrs. Parthena Hubbard, relict of the late Asa Hubbard.

Died at Washington, Miss., on the 10th, Thomas Lewis, Esq., Receiver of Public Moneys, aged 33 years.

October 29, 1834

Died in this place, on Saturday afternoon, William Henry, youngest son of David Bone, Esq., aged six years.

Died at the house of Moses Groves, near New Carthage, La., on the 15th, John H. Dunscomb, a house carpenter by trade, late from Trumbull, Ohio.

November 5, 1834

Died this morning, Mr. N. M. Henderson, merchant of this place.

November 19, 1834

Married, Nov. 13, by the Rev. Mr. Murray, Mr. David C. Griffin to Miss Theresa Frisby, both of this county.

December 3, 1834

Died in Madison County, on the 7th, Mr. Thomas Y. Berry, in the 69th year of his age. The deceased was a soldier of the Revolution.

December 10, 1834

Died in Natchez, on Monday morning last, the Hon. Fountain Winston, late Lt. Governor of Mississippi, and Senator at the time of his death, in the State Legislature, from Adams County.

December 17, 1834

Married on last evening, by the Rev. Dr. Chamberlain, Capt. Samuel D. Walker to Miss Frances Minerva, daughter of Jeremiah Watson, of La.

Married on the 10th, by the Rev. Abraham Hagaman, Mr. Charles H. Rochester, of Danville, Kentucky, to Mary McCaleb, of Adams County.

January 14, 1835

Married on the 8th, by G. T. Martin, Esq., Daniel Greenleaf, Esq., to Miss Eliza R. Watson, both of Claiborne County.

January 21, 1835

Married in the city of Natchez, on the 18th, B. M. Stedman, of this place, to Miss Balinda A. Clapp, of that city.

The funeral sermon of Mrs. Sabra R. Odom, who was so cruelly and inhumanely murdered by one of her servants, in this neighborhood, some time in November last, will be delivered by Rev. Jno. C. Johnson, on the 25th.

January 28, 1835
Married on Wednesday evening last, by the Rev. J. Chamberlain, Richard Valentine to Mrs. Adeline Hunt, eldest daughter of Stephen Compton, Esq., of this vicinity.

Died in Carroll Parish, La., on the 5th, at the residence of her father, Mr. H. Ledbetter, Mrs. Mary Jones, consort of B. F. Jones, Esq., of Jefferson County, Miss. She was in the 20th year of her age.

February 4, 1835
Died in this place on Sun. a.m. last, Alfred Fuller, aged about 25 yrs.

February 18, 1835
Died in this place, on Monday last, of a lingering pulmonary disease, William Barrett, aged about 21 years, formerly of Lexington, Ky.

March 4, 1835
Married on the 19th, by the Rev. Jere. Chamberlain, James Watson to Miss Mary Jane Bolls.

Died at his residence in Louisiana, on Monday morning last, Elijah Bass, aged about 45 years.

April 1, 1835
Died on Saturday night last, at the residence of his son-in-law, A. G. Bowen, in Concordia Parish, La., Job Bass, at an advanced age.

Died on the same night, Mrs. Mary Montgomery, Esq., of this neighborhood.

Died in this place, of measles, on Sunday night last, Joseph Carouth, aged about 28 years. He had graduated but a short time since from the University at Nashville.

April 15, 1835
Married on the 1st, at the residence of Mr. Thomas Vaughn, Jefferson Co., by Rev. Z. Butler, Edward Bradford to Miss Virginia Campbell.

April 22, 1835
Died this afternoon, in this place, Lucinda, daughter of Mrs. Ann Clayton, in the 11th year of her age.

Died at Grand Gulf, on Sunday morning last, of congestive fever, Benjamin Flowers, late of this place, aged 19 years.

April 29, 1835
Married on the 23d, by the Rev. Jeremiah Chamberlain, Green T. Martin, Esq., of this place, to Miss Margaret S. Logan, of Claiborne County.

Married on the 28th, at the residence of Mr. D. K. Galtney, by the Rev. Mr. Murray, Mr. Joseph Tillburn to Theodosia Barefield, all of this co.

July 24, 1835
Married on the 21st, by the Rev. Mr. Bertron, Joshua B. Long, of this place, to Miss Sarah Berry, daughter of Thomas Berry, Esq., of Claiborne County.

Died at Jackson, on the 10th, of congestive fever, Putnam T. Williams, Esq., of Fayette, aged about 30 years.

October 30, 1835
Died on board the Chief Justice Marshall, on October 24th, 1835, Miss Mary Briscoe, daughter of Wm. Briscoe, Esq., of Claiborne County. Her remains were interred at the family burial ground.

November 12, 1835
Died on the 20th ultimo, in Lexington, Ky., Mrs. Sarah Campbell, aged 59 years.

Died on the 5th, at the residence of Dr. Keen, Tompkin's Bend, La., Miss Sarah Ann Ely, aged 18 years.

December 25, 1835
Married on the 13th, near Fayette, by Rev. Christopher Murray, Alexander Willis to Miss Katharine Sillers, all of this county.

Died in this place, on Tuesday night last, Thomas Culberson, aged about 52 years.

January 1, 1836
Died on the 26th, James, only child of J. B. Warren, aged 2 years, 1 month and 13 days.

January 8, 1836
Married on the 7th, by the Rev. Mr. Potter, Mr. John G. James to Miss Ann Skinner, daughter of Richard Skinner, Esq., all of this county.

February 5, 1836
Married on Tuesday evening last, by the Rev. Jno. C. Johnson, Mr. Nathan C. Hall to Miss Maranda Raney, all of this county.

Died in Fayette, on Thursday last, Mr. Norman Squires, aged about 30 years. The deceased was a member of the Presbyterian denomination.

March 4, 1836
Died on the 5th ultimo, near Matanzas, Cuba, James W. Taylor, aged 25 years, a native of Lincoln County, Ky. Mr. T. has been a resident of our town for several years.

March 18, 1836
Married on Thursday evening last, by the Rev. R. Smith, Mr. V. M. Stuart to Miss Martha E. Cogan.

Married on Tuesday evening last, by the Rev. Christopher Murray, Mr. Preston W. Netherry to Miss Elizabeth Hawk, all of this vicinity.

March 25, 1836

Married on Sunday evening last, Mr. John J. Griffing, of this county, to Miss Harriet Frisby, of Claiborne County.

April 22, 1836

Married on the 14th, by the Rev. J. C. Johnson, Mr. Lewis F. Norris to Miss Sarah Cloud, daughter of Dr. Cloud, of this vicinity.

May 6, 1836

Died on the 27th, Horace Carpenter, at his residence in Port Gibson.

May 20, 1836

Married on Tuesday evening last, by the Rev. J. Chamberlain, Mr. James Archer to Miss Mary Ann Hunt, daughter of David Hunt, Esq., of this vicinity.

Married yesterday evening, by the Rev. J. C. Johnson, Mr. S. A. Cochran to Miss Jane N. Ferguson.

May 27, 1836

Died at his residence in this co., on Sun. night last, Thomas A. Elam.

July 8, 1836

Died this morning at his residence, Smith C. Daniels.

Died in this place, of congestive fever, on the 5th, W. R. Monroe, saddler, aged about 35 years.

July 15, 1836

Died in Claiborne County, near Oakland, on the 8th, of congestive fever, Mrs. Martha Jane Watson, consort of James M. Watson, Jr., and daughter of Matthew Bolls, Esq.

Died on the 5th, at his residence in this county, Abner Marble.

August 9, 1836

Departed this life at the residence of her mother in this co., on the 29th ult., Jane P. M'Cormick, consort of B. Cormick, formerly of Va.

August 23, 1836

Died in this town, on the 17th, Lucretia Payne, wife of John Payne.

Died in this county, on the 13th, at the residence of her mother, Miss Hester Ann R. Marble, aged 24 years. She has left an aged mother, three brothers and two sisters.

September 6, 1836

Died on Saturday evening last, of congestive fever, at his residence in this county, Mr. A. E. Mills, aged about 30 years.

Died in this place, on Saturday evening last, Mr. Olds, a native of Kentucky.

Died in Fayette, on Wednesday morning last, Elizabeth, infant daughter of Thomas H. and Elizabeth Duggan, aged 11 months.

September 27, 1836

Departed this life at Capt. Samuel Bullen's residence, on Tuesday evening last, Mordecai Dudley Bullen, in the 17th year of his age.

Died on the 18th ult., Mrs. Elizabeth Floyd, late consort of Dr. Samuel Floyd, deceased. Mrs. F. left behind an only child, yet an infant.

Died in Claiborne County, on the 31st day of August, Miss Sarah Logan, daughter of Samuel Logan, Sen., Dec'd., of Richmond, Ky.

Died at Columbia, Texas, on the 3d, Mr. Samuel Logan, in the 31st year of his age.

January 24, 1837

Married on the 21st, by the Rev. John A. Cotton, Mr. Walter Smith, to Miss Louisa M. Folkes, all of this county.

January 31, 1837

Married in Natchez, on the 26th, by the Rev. O. S. Hinckley, Professor of Languages at Oakland College, William H. Pearce, Esq., to Miss Ann E. Gillett, daughter of the Rev. Eliphalet Gillett, D. D., of Hallowell, Maine.

Died of consumption, on the 30th, 20 miles below Natchez, Samuel C. Green, Esq., in the 28th year of his age, a citizen of Jefferson Co.

February 28, 1837

Departed this life, on the 11th, in Warren County, Mrs. Hannah Brown Harrison, aged about 38 years, the late consort of Richard Harrison, formerly of Jefferson County.

April 18, 1837

Died at her residence on Cole's Creek, Jefferson County, Mrs. Julian Stamply, consort of Mr. Solomon B. Stamply. She has left a husband and several children.

April 25, 1837

Married at Veristaw, Indiana, on the 16th March, by the Rev. Thomas Curtis, Mr. Israel C. Curtis, of Grand Gulf, Miss., to Miss Lucy M., daughter of the Hon. J. L. Holman.

May 2, 1837

Died near this place, on the 17th, of small pox, Henry Vose, Esq. The deceased was educated at West Point, N. Y. (*Woodville Republican*)

June 6, 1837
Died recently at Louisville, Ky., Mr. Samuel A. Mason, of the firm of Mason, Kelly & Co., of this city. (*Natchez Courier*)

Died on the 31st ult., Mr. Gabriel Osteen, an aged citizen of this neighborhood.

Married on the 30th ult., by the Rev. Mr. Drake, Mr. Thomas Carothers, of Sharon, Madison County, (formerly of this place), to Miss Lydia O. Coleman, of Jefferson County.

July 18, 1837
Died in Claiborne County, on the 29th, Mrs. Martha Burns, consort of ---insley Burns, in the 30th year of her age.

Died in this town, on Friday last, of congestive fever, Mr. James S. Watson, aged about 30 years.

THE SOUTHRON (Jackson, Miss.)
Published by Benjamin Albertson

February 20, 1841
Married in this city on Saturday evening last, by the Rev. C. K. Marshall, Mr. J. H. Ledbetter to Miss Susan Ellis, all of this city.

May 4, 1841
Died near this city, on Thursday last, Mr. Lewis Whitesides, an old and respectable citizen of this county.

May 25, 1841
Died in this city, on Friday last, Mr. William B. Woodley. He was interred on Saturday, with military and masonic honors.

Died on Sunday last, Mr. Michael Findley, a native of Ireland.

June 1, 1841
Married on the 22d ult., by John P. Oldham, Esq., Mr. Robert Jack to Miss Hester Smith, all of this city.

June 29, 1841
Married on the 22d, by John P. Oldham, Esq., Dr. L. S. Evans to Miss Eliza Jane Davis, all of this county.

July 20, 1841
Married in Vicksburg, on the 13th, by the Rev. Dr. Weller, Loyd R. Coleman, Esq., to Miss Harriet L. Moore, all of that city.

August 26, 1841
Died in this city, on the 20th, Dr. James J. Allen, of consumption. Dr. Allen was the son of Gen. Allen of Greensburg, Ky., and was born on the 29th of March, 1811.

September 9, 1841
Married at 23 Duke St., Edinburgh, Scotland, on the 28th of July, by the Rev. William Glover, of Greenside, James Smith, Ts., of Jackson, Miss., eldest son of James Smith, Jr., of Edinburgh, to Anne W., eldest daughter of Robert Brown, Esq., Duke St. Edinburgh.

September 23, 1841
Died this morning, Mrs. Elizabeth Bigger.

September 30, 1841
Died on the evening of the 23d, from the effects of a fall, Mr. Lewis L. Parker, aged 24 years and 9 months, a native of Sterling, Mass.

Died at her residence in this county, on Sunday last, Mrs. Rebecca M'Manus, aged 53 years. It was only last week that we announced the decease of her husband.

October 7, 1841
Married in this city, on Tuesday evening last, by the Rev. Mr. Holloway, Mr. Daniel H. Otto, formerly of Pennsylvania, to Miss Sarah Ann, daughter of Dr. M'Cluer, late of Indiana.

Departed this life in this city, on the 27th ult., Mrs. Louisa P. Clark, in the 44th year of her age, consort of Gen. William Clark, formerly of Greenville, North Carolina.

November 9, 1841
Died in this town, on the 6th, of a short and violent attack of croup, Julia, aged 4 years, 4 months and 15 days, daughter of Mr. Dickman.

November 18, 1841
Died in this city, on Wednesday last, Mrs. Mary H. Learned, consort of Mr. C. D. Learned, and daughter of Isaac Hamlin, of Livermore, Maine, aged 36 years, leaving a husband and two daughters.

December 16, 1841
Married in Vicksburg, on Thursday, the 9th, by the Rev. Mr. Lawrence, L. V. Dixon, Esq., and Miss Sarah J. Foster, both of this city.

December 23, 1841
Married at Pine Springs, in this county, on Tuesday morning, the 21st, Irvine M. Quin, M. D., of Holmesville, and Miss Elizabeth F. Percyman, of the former place.

January 13, 1842
Died at the residence of Major Peyton, in Raymond, on the 4th, Archibald, only son of Gen. Wm. Lewis, aged 1 year and 7 months.

January 20, 1842
Married at Brandon, on Thursday, the 13th, by the Rev. S. H. Hazard, Mr. Lemuel M. Petrie to Miss Rosa M., daughter of Dr. Farrar.

January 27, 1842

Married in this city, on Thursday last, by the Rev. Mr. Houghton, Mr. John C. M'Allister and Miss Elmira Judd, all of this place.

Married in Clinton, on Wednesday last, by Seneca Pratt, Esq., Captain Robert M'Aleer and Miss Caroline Gregory, all of Hinds County.

Died in this city, on Wednesday last, Mr. George B. Traweek.

February 10, 1842

Died on Saturday, the 5th, Margaret L. Hall, daughter of Mrs. Lucinda Hall, aged 6 years, 6 months and 4 days.

On the same day, Henry Young, son of Wm. H. and Louisa Young, aged 1 year, 1 month and 7 days.

Died on Monday, the 7th, James F., son of Mr. Sam'l. P. Beasley, aged 1 year and 9 months.

Died on Tuesday last, in this city, Mr. Daniel Walton, formerly of Tennessee, aged about 40 years.

Died on Sat. last, Sarah Jane, infant daughter of Mrs. Louisa Forbes.

March 3, 1842

Married at the house of Saleb Judd, by the Rev. Mr. Houghton, Hon. Gardner Holcomb, member of the House of Representatives, to Mrs. Sophia M. Robinson, of London, England. Immediately after the ceremony the happy couple set off for their residence in Marion Co.

Died in this city, on Friday night last, Col. Augustus B. Saunders, Auditor of Public Accounts, aged 51, leaving a widow and several children.

March 10, 1842

Married in Natchez, on the 3d, the Hon'l. Sargeant S. Prentiss to Miss Mary Jane, daughter of Mrs. J. C. Williams.

Married in this city, on the 7th, by A. Morgan, Esq., Mr. John Settle to Mrs. Margaret Bullington.

Married in this city, on the 8th, by James H. Boyd, Esq., Mr. John Wessel to Miss Elizabeth Caroline Williams.

Departed this life at the residence of Maj. Perry Cohea, on the 26th ult., John Blair, Esq., a native of Ireland, but for nearly half century a resident of the United States, and about half that time a citizen of this state.

March 17, 1842

Died in this city, on Wednesday, the 16th, of consumption of the lungs, Mr. George Hartford, in the 20th year of his age.

April 7, 1842
Married on Thursday last, by J. H. Boyd, Esq., Mr. Augustin Mezell and Miss Ann Gibbons, both of this city.

April 14, 1842
Married in this vicinity, on Tuesday evening last, by the Rev. C. K. Marshall, of Vicksburg, John D. Freeman, Esq., of this city, Attorney General for the State of Mississippi, to Miss Eliza Ardine, daughter of the Hon. George Adams.

Died in Vicksburg, on the 6th, Mr. William Moore, a native of Newport, R. I., but for several years a citizen and merchant of Vicksburg, and formerly of Norfolk, Va.

April 21, 1842
Married on Tuesday, the 19th, by the Rev. Peter Donan, Wm. H. Stewart, Esq., of Natchez, to Margaret N., daughter of Richard N. Eubank, Esq., of Madison County.

Died in this city, on Sunday morning last, Dr. J. M. Sitler, formerly of Brandon, aged about 40 years.

May 5, 1842
Died in Louisville, Ky., on the 22d ult., on her way to Virginia for the benefit of her health, Mrs. Susan Henry, consort of Robert W. Henry, Esq., of Raymond.

May 26, 1842
Died on Friday last, Jane Henry, infant daughter of Col. Wm. H. and Frances Ann Garland.

Died on Monday, the 23d, at the age of 15 months, James D., only son of Charles H. and Adeline Manship.

Died last night, William Martin, son of Dr. William S. and Sophia D. Langley, aged 2 years and 2 months.

June 23, 1842
Married in this city, on Thurs. eve. last, by the Rev. P. Donan, Henry C. Daniel to Miss Mary Hart, eldest daughter of Maj. C. M. Hart.

July 28, 1842
Married in Washington, Texas, on the 7th, Maj. D. D. Crumpler, formerly of this county, to Miss Myra E. Lusk.

Married Tues. eve., 26th, by J. H. Boyd, Esq., J. W. Brien to Mrs. Eveline T. Owen, dau. of James Jackson, all of vicinity of Jackson.

September 22, 1842
Married on Thursday evening last, by the Rev. Dr. Cropper, Mr. George Stillman to Mrs. Elizabeth S. Head, all of this city.

September 29, 1842
Died in this city, on Friday morning last, Mrs. Mary E. Blake, consort of Mr. Wm. G. Blake.

November 10, 1842
Died this morning, at the Mansion-house, in this city, Mr. P. M. Ledbetter, a native of Virginia, and for many years a resident of Jackson.

December 8, 1842
Married on Thursday evening last, by the Rev. Bishop Andrew, the Rev. James Maclennan, of the Mississippi Conference, to Miss Lucy Ann Frances, daughter of Samuel P. Beasley, Esq., of Jackson.

January 5, 1843
Married at the residence of Gov. Lynch, near this city, on Tuesday evening last, Dr. William A. Ware to Mrs. Sarah M. Land.

Married in Noxubee County, on the 20th ult., by Bishop Andrew, Rev. Joshua T. Heard, of the Alabama Conference, to Miss Martha Matilda, daughter of Major Joseph Koger, formerly of South Carolina.

January 19, 1843
Departed this life on the 15th ult., at the residence of her husband, in Rankin County, Mrs. Caroline White, consort of T. S. White, Esq., in the 27th year of her age.

February 23, 1843
Married on Tuesday evening, the 14th, by Rev. P. Donan, at the residence of Dr. Hemingway, in this county, Dr. Thomas J. Catchings to Miss Nancy M. J. Glendennen.

Married on the 1st, by Seneca Pratt, Esq., Mr. Calvin Bray to Miss Angelitha Gregory, all of Hinds County.

Died near Clinton, Miss., on the 23d January, Mrs. Louisa King, consort of Capt. Charles B. King, aged 27 years.

March 16, 1843
Married on Tuesday evening, the 2d, by the Rev. Silas H. Hazard, Mr. George W. Gibbs to Miss Susan Elder, daughter of Col. Jordan Elder, both of Raymond.

March 23, 1843
Married in this city, on the 19th, by the Mayor, J. H. Boyd, Esq., Mr. Rhesa Hatcher to Miss Eliza J. P. Coggin.

Died on Tuesday morning last, Mr. Selah Judd, a resident of this town.

Died on the 17th, at the residence of his son, Daniel Mann, Esq., of this county, Captain William Mann, in the 85th year of his age.

May 3, 1843
Died at the Centenary College, on Tuesday evening, the 25th, of abcess of the liver, Mr. William R. King, of Yazoo County, formerly of Franklin County, Miss., aged 17 years and 1 day.

May 10, 1843
Married in this city, on the 3d, by J. H. Boyd, Mayor, Mr. Charles Bordwell to Miss Ann Pace.

May 17, 1843
Married on the evening of the 11th, at the residence of Mrs. Elizabeth Cabell, in Clinton, by the Rev. James S. Green, Mr. Benjamin E. Roper, of Hinds County, to Miss Catharine W. Payne, daughter of Dr. Nathaniel W. Payne, of Lynchburg, Va.

May 24, 1843
Married on Sunday, 21st, by Hon. J. M. Taylor, Mr. H. Keating to Mrs. S. C. Robertson.

June 7, 1843
Died at Indianapolis, Illinois, on the 25th ult., at the residence of her parents, Mrs. Sarah Ann, consort of our townsman, Mr. Daniel H. Otto, just as the 17th summer of her life had passed away, leaving an infant to the care of a devoted husband and affectionate father.

June 14, 1843
Married on Thursday evening, the 8th, by the Rev. James Maclennan, Mr. F. A. Whiting to Miss Elizabeth G. Beazley, daughter of Samuel P. Beazley, Esq., of this city.

July 12, 1843
Married on Thursday morning last, at the residence of her father, James R. Russell, Esq., in Madisonville, Madison County, by the Rev. P. Cooper, George Finucane, Esq., of Jackson, to Mrs. Ann Carty, of the former place.

Died on the 25th June, 1843, at the residence of Vincent Murphy, Esq., Hinds County, Miss., his consort, Mrs. Susan F. Murphy, in the 42d year of her age. Mrs. Murphy was a native of Columbus County, N. C. She has left a husband and 5 children.

July 19, 1843
Died on Tuesday morning, the 27th day of June last, at China Grove, her late residence in Hinds County, Mrs. Mary O. Smith, a native of South Carolina. Mrs. Smith settled in the territory composing this county while it was occupied by the Choctaw indians, before its organization. Four small children have been left behind.

July 26, 1843
Married on the 21st June last, in Essex County, Virginia, by the Rev. Ferguson, Mr. Henry E. Sizse, of Jackson, Miss., to Miss A. E. Pil-

cher, of the former place. The happy young couple arrived in this city, their future home, on Sunday evening last.

August 9, 1843
Died on Tuesday morning, in the 9th year of his age, George W., son of J. S. Gooch, Esq., of this city.

August 23, 1843
Departed this life the 17th, at her residence in this city, Mrs. F. A. Whitehead, in her 45th year.

August 30, 1843
Died in Kentucky, on the 10th of June last, Mr. J. D. Ross, of the firm of Manship & Ross, of this city. He on a visit to Ky. for his health.

September 13, 1843
Married on Wednesday, the 20th August, by J. H. Boyd, Esq., Mr. A. B. Weeks to Miss Nancy Grant, all of Hinds County.

Died on the 27th August, 1843, Mary O. Ferry, daughter of John C. Ferry, aged 2 years, 7 months and 16 days.

Died on Sunday morning, 10th, Col. Andrew Hays, formerly of Tennessee, but for many years a resident of this city.

September 27, 1843
Married on Thursday, the 21st, by J. H. Boyd, Esq., Mr. Lewis Reno to Miss Sarah Ann Jackson, all of Hinds County.

October 4, 1843
Married on Tuesday evening, the 3d, by the Rev. Preston Cooper, Mr. William G. Blake to Miss Martha Ann Scott, all of this city.

Died on Monday morning, the 2d, Jerelene, youngest daughter of Col. James Dupree, aged 14 months.

October 11, 1843
Died at his residence, Spring Ridge, Hinds County, Miss., of congestive fever, on the 6th, in the 49th year of his age, Leroy H. Tatom.

November 15, 1843
Died Tues. p.m., the 7th, of pleurisy, Luke Kent, of Hinds Co., 57 yrs.

November 29, 1843
Died in Carthage, Miss., on the 5th of October, Virginia Caledonia, and on the 11th, William Harrison, only son and daughter of R. E. and Martha Ann Halford.

December 27, 1843
Married on the 21st, by the Rev. Washington Ford, Mr. Samuel D. Terry, to Miss Emeline R., daughter of Mr. Samuel Skinner, the former of Madison County, the latter of Leake.

January 10, 1844
Married in Leake County, on the 27th December, 1843, by S. S. Pender, Esq., Mr. Green H. Leapard to Miss Celo Sanders, the former 24 years and the latter, 37 years of age, all of this county.

Married in the same county, on the 29th of December last, by S. S. Pender, Esq., Mr. Isaac Sanders to Miss Nancy Ellison, the former a Revolutionary soldier, 95 years old, the latter 25 years old, all of Leake County.

Married in the same county, on the 1st day of January, 1844, by S. S. Pender, Esq., Mr. W. Masey to Miss Nancy Bunch, the former of Leake and the latter of Attala County.

January 31, 1844
Died on the 16th, at his residence near this city, in the 45th year of his age, James Elliot, Esq., a native of Scotland, for many years a citizen of this state.

March 13, 1844
Married on Tuesday, the 5th, by the Rev. F. W. Boyd, Pastor of Christ's Church, Mr. Thomas A. Marshall, of Vicksburg, to Miss Letitia, daughter of Major Anderson Miller.

Married at the residence of Mrs. Catherine Prince, on the 24th ult., by the Rev. B. M. Drake, Mr. George Wilson Humphreys, of Claiborne County, to Miss Balissa Prince, of Jefferson County.

March 15, 1844
Married on the morning of the 9th, by the Rev. James E. Matthews, Mr. George W. Boddie to Mrs. Louisa A. Forbes, daughter of Genl. William Clark, all of this county.

Died in this county, at the residence of her husband, Mr. William Hester, on Sunday, the 12th, Mrs. Theresa Hester, aged 25 years. She was the daughter of Hugh Montgomery, Esq., of Jefferson County.

August 6, 1845
Married on Thursday evening last, by the Rev. Mr. Leavel, Mr. Hargrove to Mrs. Mary North, all of Jackson.

Drowned on Sunday last, in Pearl River below this city, William S., son of Saml. P. Beazley, aged about 9 years.

Died at the residence of her father, near Clinton, Miss., on Monday, July 21st, Ella, only child of Benjamin E. and Catharine W. Roper, aged 4 months and 18 days.

October 15, 1845
Died in this city, on the 12th, Alexander G. Shaw, aged 29 years.

October 22, 1845
Died in Brandon, on the 9th, Mrs. Elizabeth P. Woodfolk, aged 63 years. Mrs. W. was a native of Virginia and emigrated to this state with her children in the summer of 1837. She had been a member of the Baptist Church for 17 years.

November 5, 1845
Married on Thursday evening, 30th Oct., by the Rev. Francis Walker, Col. G. W. Williams to Miss Matilda, daughter of Willis Walker, all of Simpson County.

Married on the 23d ult., at the residence of A. R. Green, Esq., by the Rev. N. W. Camp, D. D., Wm. Steed, M. D., of this city, to Miss Laura M. Perryman, of Hinds County.

Married at the same place, on the 30th ult., by the same, Mr. Wm. Hester, of Hinds County, to Miss Caroline Steed, of Norfolk, Va.

Married at Paradise, La., by the Rev. Mr. Patterson, John F. Walker, Esq., to Martha Almedia Williamson, eldest daughter of the late Col. R. M. Williamson.

November 12, 1845
We are called upon to record the death of the Hon. Vantromp Crawford, who departed this life at his residence near Liberty, on the morning of the 31st October, in the 43d year of his age. The deceased had been a resident of this county since the year 1825. He was by profession a lawyer, and was for a number of years Judge of the Probate Court of this county, and for the last 6 years Judge of the Circuit Court of the Eleventh Judicial District. (*Liberty Advocate*)

November 19, 1845
Married in DeSoto county, on the 30th of October, by the Rev. R. T. Gatewood, Asa Chambers, Esq., to Miss Margaret M., daughter of Judge George J. Keahey, all of DeSoto County.

Died in Attala co., Miss., Oct. 16th, 1845, Martha E. Simmons, infant dau. of Mary A. and W. W. Simmons, aged 11 months and 28 days.

November 26, 1845
Married on Thursday evening, 20th Nov., by Rev. Thomas Ford, S. Alexander, M. D. to Miss Elizabeth Ann Comfort, daughter of Rev. Daniel Comfort, D. D., all of Clinton, Miss.

Married on Wed. eve., 19th, by the Rev. Mr. Holloway, Judge J. B. Reese, of Brazoria Co., Texas, to Mrs. Ann B. Robinson, of this city.

Married on the 20th, by the Rev. Mr. Montgomery, of Vicksburg, Geo. L. Potter, Esq., to Miss Cynthia Mayes, eldest daughter of the Hon. Daniel Mayes, all of this city.

Died on Friday morning, the 21st, Henry Edwin, infant son of Henry E. Van Winkle, aged 5 months and 16 days.

Died on Saturday night, Mr. Thos. K. Gibbons, for several years a resident of Jackson. His remains were interred by the Masonic fraternity of which he was a member.

December 3, 1845

Married in this city, on the 25th ult., by the Rev. L. J. Halsey, Alexander Yerger, Esq., to Miss Elizabeth B., daughter of the Hon. James Rucks.

Married on Thursday evening, the 20th ult., by the Rev. Wm. Riddle, Mr. R. McNair to Miss Christian Priscilla Wilkinson, all of Simpson County, Miss.

Married on Wednesday, the 26th ult., at the residence of Talbot H. Parsons, Esq., in Clinton, Miss., by the Rev. Thomas Ford, Warren Eustace Pleasants, Esq., of Vicksburg, to Miss Anna E. Velvin, of the former place.

Married on Thursday evening last, by the Rev. John Lane, Hon. John W. King, of Coahoma County, to Miss Mary E., only daughter of Aaron Wicklitle, Esq., of Washington County, Miss.

Died at the residence of Mrs. R. Canley, in Rankin County, on the 26th November, Julia E., eldest daughter of Thomas S. White, Esq., aged 6 years, 11 months and 26 days.

December 24, 1845

Married on the 9th, by the Rev. Mr. Gray, Maj. G. A. Ware, of this place, to Miss Sarah Rebecca, daughter of Rev. Hill Jones, formerly of North Carolina.

Married on the 16th, by the Rev. Robert Ross, Dr. H. C. McLaurin, of Simpson County, to Miss Harriet E., daughter of Judge Robert Love, of Madison County, Miss.

Married on Thurs. eve., the 18th of Dec., by the Hon. George W. Shelton, of Newton County, Miss., Charles W. Simmons to Miss Annes M'Clendon, eldest daughter of L. B. M'Clendon, all of Newton Co.

Married on Thursday, the 18th, at Brownsville, Hinds County, by the Rev. N. R. Granberry, C. S. Spann, Esq., to Miss Henrietta W. Lanier.

Married at Raymond, on the eve. of Wed. last, by Judge Johnston, Mr. Samuel Guthrie to Miss Clarissa M. Owen, all of that place.

January 14, 1846

Married in Westville, on the 6th, by Green Fenn, Esq., the Rev. James Powell, aged 75 years, to Miss Mary Palmer, aged 17 years, daughter of the Rev. John Palmer, of Copiah County.

February 4, 1846
Married by the Rev. H. Leavel, on the 27th ult., James A. Groves, of Kosciusko, Miss., to Mrs. Ann Mitchell, of the vicinity of Jackson.

February 18, 1846
Died on Saturday night last, at his residence in Raymond, N. W. Vallandingham, M. D., aged 36 years.

Died on Sunday morning last, at St. Francisville, La., Mrs. Elizabeth M., consort of the Hon. Robert Hughes, of this city.

February 25, 1846
Died here, on Mon. last, Mr. E. T. Hart, formerly of Halifax Co., Va.

March 11, 1846
Died in this city, of scarlet fever, on the 8th, Selah J., only child of John C. and Almyra J. McAllister, aged 16 months and 14 days.

April 1, 1846
Married by Rev. H. Leavel, at residence of Mr. King, in Rankin Co., on 24th ult., Geo. W. Dougharty, of Benton, Miss., to Prudence King.

April 8, 1846
Married at the residence of Dr. J. S. Copes, of this city, by Rev. L. J. Halsey, on Tuesday evening, 31st ult., Mr. E. Crisswell, of Warsaw, Ala., to Miss Janes H. Copes, of Madison County, Miss.

May 13, 1846
Married on the 12th, at the residence of the Hon. C. R. Clifton, of this city, by the Rt. Rev. Bishop Otey, William Parker Scott, Esq., of Vicksburg, to Miss Fannie May, daughter of the late Dr. Joseph Bibb, of Alabama.

Married recently, at Fort Washitaw, E. E. Galloway, Esq., of Winchester, Virginia, to Miss Eugenia Coffee, of this city.

Married in Yazoo City, April 30th, by Rev. A. Newton, of Clinton, Mr. Alfred Murdock, of Sunflower Co., to Miss Mary Catharine Holt, daughter of Maj. Holt, of Louisiana.

Died in Hinds County, on the 4th, in the 27th year of her age, Mrs. Margaret S. Dulaney, consort of Dr. William J. Dulaney.

June 3, 1846
Married on Wednesday morning last, by the Rev. D. C. Page, Mr. Edward W. Upshaw to Miss Mary L. Bradford, all of Holly Springs.

July 1, 1846
Married on Sunday, the 21st June, at the residence of Dr. Wm. J. Dulaney, on Society Ridge, by the Rev. James E. Matthews, Gen. William Clark to Mrs. Sarah G. Sutton, all of Hinds County.

July 22, 1846
Died on the 15th, at his residence in Adams County, Jo. Dunbar, Esq.

Died at Grenada, on the 14th, Nancy Steel Morton, consort of Col. G. K. Morton.

Died in this city, on Thursday last, Harrison Wigfield W., infant son of George W. and Ailspey K. Johnson, aged 18 months and 19 days.

August 5, 1846
Married in Simpson Co., on Thursday, the 23d of July, by Green Fenn, Esq., Mr. Edwin Harper to Miss Harriet Jones, all of Simpson Co.

Married in Brandon, on the 27th ult., by His Honor Judge Finley, Hon. F. E. Plummer to Mrs. Mary C. Coffee, both of Jackson.

September 16, 1846
Died in Columbus, Miss., on the 27th of July, Mrs. Georgeanna, wife of Enos Rush Buckner, Esq.

September 23, 1846
Married in Grenada, on Thursday, the 10th, at the residence of James Sims, Esq., by Rev. Charles Morgan, Mr. James H. Mitchell to Miss Velina L. Ganong.

Died on Thursday last, in this city, at the residence of Judge Hughes, Mr. T. Gorman, late of Texas. The deceased came to his death from injuries received on board the ill-fated steamer New York, which was wrecked on her passage from Galveston to New Orleans.

September 30, 1846
Married in Bowlinggreen, Ky., on the 10th, by the Rev. Mr. South, Mr. J. M. White, of this city, to Miss Maria J. M'Allister, of Kentucky.

Died at the residence of his father, in Rankin County, the Hon. Mr. Farrar, George H. Farrar, late member of the State Fencibles.

October 14, 1846
Died on Wednesday, the 30th of Sept., at the residence of Mr. William Hamilton, in Clinton, C. W. Lewis, Esq., in the 36th year of his age.

Died near Moon Lake, in Coahoma County, on the 11th of August last, Mary Margaret, daughter of Jacob and Mary Jane Magee, aged 5 years, 3 months and 15 days.

November 19, 1846
Died on the 15th, at the residence of his son, R. L. Dixon, Esq., near this city, Henry St. John Dixon, aged 73 years. The deceased was born in Williamsburg, Virginia, and at the age of 21 removed to the south-western part of this state, where he engaged in the practice of law. In the year 1843 he removed to this county.

December 3, 1846
Married on Thursday evening, Nov. 26th, at "Rural Felicity", near Jackson, by the Rev. S. H. Montgomery, of Vicksburg, David Fisher, Esq., to Miss Margaret, daughter of Wm. and Ann Gahan, late of Washington, D. C.

Died in Jackson, on the 28th November, Amanda Olitipa, infant dau. of Amanda and William H. Terrett, aged 14 months and 12 days.

December 10, 1846
Married in Holly Springs, on Thursday evening, 26th November, by the Rev. A. C. Page, D. C. Glenn, Esq., of Jackson, Miss., to Miss Patience B. Wilkinson, daughter of the late Dr. Wilkinson, of Petersburg, Va.

January 8, 1847
Married in Wetumpka, Ala., on the 22d ult., by the Rev. M. Sparks, Mr. Wilie Cherry, of this county, to Miss Jane M. Carson, of the former place.

February 5, 1847
Married at Jaynesville, Covington County, by the Rev. Wm. Riddle, on the 28th ult., James McNair, Esq., of Simpson Co., to Miss Harriet Jane, daughter of Joshua R. White, of Jaynesville.

February 12, 1847
Died in this city, on the 26th ult., at the residence of Col. R. M. Hobson, his infant son, Richard M., aged 10 months and 22 days.

May 28, 1847
Died on Sunday night, the 16th, at the residence of Mrs. Conant, near Raymond, Mr. Gabriel F. Henry, in the 28th year of his age. Mr. Henry was the son of the Hon. Robert P. Henry of Kentucky. He has left a widow and an infant daughter.

July 30, 1847
Died in this city, on Friday, the 23d of July, Mary Amelia, eldest dau. of Amanda and W. H. Terrett, aged 4 years, 7 months and 29 days.

Departed this life on the 22d, in the town of Brandon, Mr. Thomas V. Wilkinson, formerly of Pittsylvania Co., Va., aged 36 yrs. and 9 mos.

August 6, 1847
Died on Monday, the 14th of June, at Mississippi City, of apoplexy, Dr. D. Peyton Harrison, formerly of Stafford County, Va., age 47 years and 2 months.

August 20, 1847
Died near Livingston, Madison County, Miss., on the 10th of August, 1847, Mrs. Catharine A. Tucker, consort of Mr. Robert Tucker, sister

of Dr. G. W. Stewart, and daughter of Andrew and Margaret Stewart, formerly of Anderson County, East Tennessee, aged 31 years.

September 10, 1847
Married at Oasis, Rankin County, the residence of Dr. Jas. H. Belt, on the 7th, by the Rev. James W. Hoskins, Mr. D. W. Wilkinson, of Brandon (formerly of Danville, Va.), to Miss Jane M. Belt, third daughter of the late Capt. T. J. Belt, of Baltimore, Maryland.

October 29, 1847
Married on Thursday evening last, by the Rev. J. B. Walker, Miss Hannah, daughter of Sam'l. P. Beazley, Esq., to Andrew Paxton, Esq., all of the city of Jackson.

Died on Saturday last, Robert J. Patrick, Esq., for many years a resident of this city.

Departed this life, on the 14th of September, in the 33d year of her age, at the residence of her husband, Dr. Ed. H. Stiles, in Port Gibson, Claiborne County, Mrs. Mary Osborn Stiles, a native of Philadelphia.

November 12, 1847
Died in Madison County, on the 22d of October last, Mrs. Sarah E. Barrow, consort of Seth L. Barrow, aged 26 years and 5 days, leaving a husband and 3 infant children.

The friends and acquaintances of Gen. William Lewis are invited to attend his funeral this evening, to proceed from his late residence.

December 3, 1847
Married on Thursday evening last, at the residence of Col. J. F. Foute, by Rev. Rob't. McLain, Gen. Cornelius McLauren, of Covington County, to Miss Martha Elizabeth, only daughter of Col. J. F. Foute, of Hinds County.

Died on the 13th ult., of wounds received by an accidental fall from his gin house, Hugh C. Stewart, Esq., of Covington County, but formerly a resident of this county. He has left one brother and 2 sisters.

Died on Wednesday, 24th ult., at his residence in Clinton, Peter Sanders, Esq., aged about 48 years.

December 10, 1847
Married at D'Estoteville, near Lake Washington, Miss., on Wed., 1st of December, by the Rev. Dr. MacLeod, Rector of St. John's Church, Green P. Foute, Esq., of the city of Jackson, to Miss Jenny Cary Skipworth, daughter of George G. Skipworth, Esq., of Isaquena Co.

December 31, 1847
Married on Thursday evening, the 9th, at Rose Hill, the residence of the Hon. S. H. Johnson, by the Rev. Thomas B. Adams, Mr. Benjamin K. Hawkins to Miss Mary E. Brown, all of Copiah County.

January 21, 1848
Died on Sunday last, in this city, in the 31st year of her age, Mrs. Anne Virden, wife of Thomas Virden, formerly of the city of New York.

Departed this life, at his residence in Jackson, on the 14th, in the 57th year of his age, Colonel Samuel Lemly, Sr. He was a native of Rowan County, North Carolina.

January 28, 1848
Died in Carroll Parish, La., on the 17th, by injuries from a fall from his horse, Joseph J. Dunklin, in the 28th year of his age. He has left a wife, a widowed mother, and a sister.

February 4, 1848
Died on the 22d ult., aged 64 years, at his residence in this city, John Crary, a native of Vermont, and for 40 years a resident of Ohio.

March 10, 1848
Married on the 7th, by Rev. Mr. Frazee, B. T. Cleveland, of Yalobusha County, to Miss Anna E. Edwards, of this city.

Died in this city, on the 6th, Mary Ann Catharine, youngest daughter of John and Martha Kerns, aged 6 years.

Died in this city, on the 7th, Orlando, infant son of Joshua and Elizabeth J. Green, aged 8 months and 23 days.

Died in this city, on the 8th, Perry Corea/Cohea, aged about 65 years. Disease: consumption.

March 17, 1848
Died on Sunday evening, March 12th, Mary Wortland, youngest daughter of Charles and Harriet Dudley, aged 2 yrs., 6 mos., 5 days.

March 31, 1848
Married on the 9th, at "Elmwood" the residence of Col. T. M. Nash, of Coahoma County, by the Rev. Aaron Shelby, Capt. B. F. Saunders to Miss H. C. Creighton, of Jefferson County.

Died in this city, on Thursday morning last, Mrs. Susannah, wife of S. P. Beazley, Esq., and on Friday afternoon, Mrs. Lucy A. F. Maclennan, daughter of Mr. & Mrs. Beazley.

Died on the 11th, of measles, Laura, youngest daughter, and on the 20th, Albert Gallatin, youngest son of Gen. T. L. Lemly, of Harrison County, Miss. The mother of these children died last fall.

April 14, 1848
Died at the residence of Marcus Hemphill, Esq., near Newtown, Hinds County, on the 9th, Mrs. Nancy, wife of Dr. L. B. Hemphill, in the

35th year of her age. The deceased was a native of Morgan County, Georgia.

June 2, 1848

Died at Bladon Springs, Alabama, on the 7th of May, of consumption, Samuel Frisbie, Sr., in the 64th year of his age, leaving a wife and nine children.

Died in this city, on Friday morning, 26th ult., Lewis Moseley, aged 22 years, of Oktibbeha County, on his return home from Mexico whither he had gone as a member of the Mississippi Battalion. He died of pulmonary consumption.

June 9, 1848

Married on the 29th ult., in Hillsborough, by Asa Chambers, Esq., Mr. Solomon Hurst, of Jackson, to Miss Teresa Rees, of Scott County.

Married in Woodville, Wilkinson County, on Monday, 29th ultimo, by the Rev. Mr. Buch, Hon. J. A. Ventress and Miss Charlotte Pinchen, both of that place.

July 7, 1848

Married in Kemper County, on the 22d June, by the Rev. F. Fincher, Mr. James M'Donald, of Neshoba County, to Miss Mary Ann M'Bride, of Kemper County.

July 14, 1848

Married on the 4th, by the Rev. Mr. Frazee, Mr. John W. Crary, to Miss Louisa Maria, daughter of Thomas J. Hawkins, Esq., all of the city of Jackson.

Died near Jackson, Miss., July 5, 1848, Mrs. Ann E. Morris, wife of Maj. J. J. Morris, in the 22d year of her age. She was the daughter of Col. B. D. Chapman, of Brownsville, Hinds County, Miss.

March 9, 1849

Died on Wednesday evening, the 28th of February, Horace Keating, youngest son of Col. Sidney S. and Caroline R. Erwin, of this county, aged 16 months and 16 days.

Died in Rankin County, Miss., on the 25th of February, John Zachary Taylor, infant son of John B. and Nancy J. Lewis, aged 5 months and 20 days.

March 30, 1849

Married in Washington City, on the 13th of March, by the Rev. Thos. M. Reese, Thomas Palmer, Proprietor of the Southron, to Miss Julia D., dau. of the late Capt. John Hunter Terrett, of Fairfax Co., Virginia.

Married in Hannibal, Mo., Dr. Lloyd Selby, of the "Jacksonian", to Miss Jane Cunningham.

Married in Woodville, on the 15th ult., by the Rev. Mr. Blenkinsop, Gen. Carnot Posey to Miss Jane White, of Wilkinson County.

Died in this city, on Wednesday night last, of consumption, Dr. Miller Wilson, in about the 40th year of his age. He was a native of Kentucky, but had long been a resident of Jackson.

September 7, 1849

Died at Cooper's Well, in Hinds County, of chronic diarrhea, on Saturday, the 25th of August, Robert Clark, a native of County Sligo, Ireland, in about the 35th year of his age. Mr. Clark was a carpenter by trade and had lived in this country since 1838.

September 14, 1849

Died in this city, on the 8th, of inflammation of the lungs, Mrs. Mary A. J. Collins, at the residence of her husband, Thomas F. Collins.

Died on Sunday night, the 9th, William Augustus, second son of John and Viola E. Voight, aged 9 years and 5 months.

October 12, 1849

Died in this city, on Wednesday afternoon, William Burns, Clerk of the U. S. District Court, in the 60th year of his age.

Died in Cumberland, Maryland, on the 24th of September, Clifton M'Leod, aged 6 years, son of George M'Leod, formerly of this city.

October 26, 1849

Died of cholera, in Lexington, Ky., on the 3d of July last, Stephen Manship, brother of C. H. Manship, of this city, in 25th yr. of his age.

November 2, 1849

Married on Wednesday eve. last, at Cully's Well, Hinds County, Mr. John Hooker, of Clinton, to Miss Elizabeth Fondren, all of Hinds Co.

It has pleased the all wise Creator to remove from among us John G. Lewis, who departed this life on Tuesday, 23d October, 1849.

November 30, 1849

Died near Victoria, Texas, on the 15th day of October last, Margaret, eldest daughter of Isaac N. and Isabell Mitchell, formerly of Raymond, aged 10 years, 2 months and 12 days.

December 28, 1849

Mrs. Lucy Dinkins breathed her last in Madison County, on the 21st, in the 73d year of her age. Mrs. D. was a native of Virginia, but reared her family in Mecklingburg County, North Carolina.

Died of consumption, on the 10th of December, 1849, in Madison County, in the 21st year of her age, Miss Annie S. Hinton. She was the daughter of N. B. and C. Hinton, and was born in Bertie County, N. Carolina, February 23, 1829.

January 11, 1850
Died at his residence in Yazoo County, Miss., on Thursday, the 25th of October, 1849, of pneumonia, Mr. Cowles Meade, only son of the late Gen. Cowles Meade, of Clinton, Miss., in the 32d year of his age.

March 15, 1850
Died in this city, on the 8th, Lucy Virginia, daughter of L. V. and Sarah J. Dixon, aged 2 years and 50 days.

March 29, 1850
Married on Thursday evening, March 21st, 1850, by W. H. Taylor, Esq., Mr. T. J. Mann, of this city, to Miss Martha Jane Dunklin, of Louisiana.

Died in this city, on the 22d, of tubercular consumption, Samuel Stamps, aged about 54 years, Secretary of the State of Mississippi. Mr. Stamps was the eldest of five children of William and Franky Stamps, of Lawrence County, Miss., all of whom survive him. William Stamps removed to this state from Georgia, in 1813 (where the subject of this notice was born).

April 26, 1850
On Monday evening last, the Masonic brotherhood of this place attended the remains of Gordon D. Boyd to their final resting place. They were brought by a friend from about forty miles below New Orleans where he died on the 8th, with cholera. Col. Boyd was born in Mason County, Kentucky, in 1801.

May 31, 1850
Jefferson Walker and Andrew Foreman had a street fight today. Walker killed Foreman by stabbing him with a knife and is now undergoing an examining trial. (Holly Springs)

July 12, 1850
Married on the 4th of July, at the residence of her father, by Thomas S. White, Esq., Mr. James McNair, of Simpson County, to Miss Sarah, daughter of Mr. Daniel Allen, of Rankin County.

July 26, 1850
Died in this city, on the 22d, John G. Young, a native of Pennsylvania, but for several years a citizen of this place.

August 9, 1850
Died on the 28th day of July, at the residence of her mother near this city, Sarah Ann, dau. of Mrs. Elizabeth Patrick, aged 10 yrs., 3 mos.

August 16, 1850
Married on the 15th, at the residence of Mrs. Alexander, by the Rev. Jo. Bell, Judge John R. Enochs, of Rankin County, to Mrs. Louisa H. Burk, of this city.

Died at the residence of her brother-in-law, Gen. Wm. R. Miles, in this city, on Tuesday morning, the 6th of August, in the 30th year of her age, Mrs. Isabella Norvelle Taylor, consort of Dr. J. Theus Taylor.

September 13, 1850

Died on Monday evening, the 9th, Joshua Joseph, eldest son of Joshua and Elizabeth J. Green, aged 10 years, 11 months and 25 days.

September 20, 1850

Died at his residence in the city of Jackson, on Friday, the 13th day of September, 1850, of congestive fever, Warren E. Pleasants. He was born in Richmond, Virginia on the 11th of March, 1820. He removed to the state of Mississippi and settled in Vicksburg in 1835.

Departed this life on the 17th, in her 26th year, Martha, consort of H. Hilzheim, Esq., and daughter of Gen. T. C. McMakin.

September 27, 1850

Died in this city, on Sunday, the 22d, Major Gustavus A. Ware, long a resident of this place.

Ann G. Velvin was born in the county of Sussex, Va., in the year 1809, and departed this life on the 23d, in her 51st year.

October 4, 1850

Married in New Orleans, on the 22d August, by the Rev. Mr. Gulheim, Mr. John Myers, merchant of this city, to Miss Barbette Schwartz, of Covington, La.

Died in this city, on the 22d, Jeannie P., daughter of W. A. and Anne E. Lake, aged 4 years and 9 months.

October 11, 1850

Married on the 8th, by the Rev. Amos Cleaver, Rector of St. Luke's Church, Brandon, Wm. H. Kirkland, Esq., to Miss Virginia Shelton.

October 25, 1850

Died in her 18th year, Medora, eldest dau. of the late Robert Patrick.

November 15, 1850

Married on the 31st day of October, by Wm. H. Taylor, Esq., Wm. Tucker Holland to Mrs. Euriticity Cook, both of Hinds County.

Married on the 17th ult., at the residence of ex-Gov. Jos. W. Matthews, by the Rev. Samuel Lambert, Wm. L. Davis to Miss Maria Frances Cohea, late of this city.

Married on Sunday, 29th, by the Rev. D. W. Pollock, Thomas J. Hanna, Esq., to Miss Sarah W. Price, both of Mississippi.

Married at Belmont, Pine Ridge, Adams County, Miss., on Wednesday morning, the 6th, by the Rev. Mr. Drake, Francis Girault Green (son of

Gen. D. B. Green), to Miss Caroline, youngest daughter of the late James Dunbar.

STATE RIGHTS BANNER (Jackson, Miss.)
Edited & Published by Charles C. Mayson

June 13, 1833
On Thursday last, the 6th, Mr. Thomas Hardwick was drowned in the Pearl River. Mr. Hardwick was a young man just entering into life, about 21 years old.

Died at his residence near village of Georgetown, Copiah Co., on the 1st, William Dickson, Esq., third son of the late Gen'l. David Dickson, of Ga., in 44th year of his age. He was for many years a member of the General Assembly and presiding officer of Pike Co. Court.

STATE TELEGRAPH (Jackson, Miss.)

September 7, 1842
Married on the evening of the 7th, at the residence of Mrs. Susan Hodge, in Madison Co., Elijah Graves, of this city, to Miss E. Hodge.

October 12, 1842
Married on the 11th, by the Rev. J. H. Johnson, Mr. Samuel E. S---- to Miss Caroline, daughter of Dr. D. O. Williams, all of this county.

STATESMAN (Jackson, Miss.)
B. D. Howard, Editor

August 19, 1843
Died on Thurs. last, the 17th, at his residence near this city, the Hon. James C. Mitchell, formerly a member of Congress from Tennessee.

Died on Friday, the 18th, at the Mansion House, Capt. J. A. Shipley.

Died on Monday last, at the Eagle Hotel, Mr. William Johnson, a native of Williamson County, Tenn.

October 14, 1843
Married in this city, on Wednesday, the 11th ult., by the Rev. L. J. Halsey, James H. Boyd, Esq., to Miss Eliza Ellis.

STATESMAN & GAZETTE (Natchez, Miss.)
Published by Andrew Marschalk

January 17, 1828
Died on Saturday last, 12th, Mrs. Althea Gaines, consort of Wm. H. Gaines, of Kentucky.

January 24, 1828
Married on Sunday, the 20th, by F. Wood, Esq., Mr. John Miller to Mrs. Sarah A. Davis, all of Adams County.

March 13, 1828
Departed this life on Sunday last, at his residence near the old court house, Mr. William Dunbar, Sen.

May 15, 1828
Died on Saturday last, at Petit Gulf, Charles H. Jourdan, Sheriff of Jefferson County. He was a native of the county in which he died.

Died on the 8th, at Walnut Hills, Warren County, Mr. James Swing, of Cincinnati, Ohio.

May 29, 1828
Married on the 25th in Claiborne Co., at residence of Hon. Joshua G. Clarke, by the Rev. Rector of Trinity Church, Natchez, John Perkens, Esq., of the Briars, to Mrs. Zilpha Seloon, of the former place.

June 19, 1828
Died at the house of her father, near Port Gibson, on Wednesday morning last, Sarah Ross, daughter of P. A. Vandorn, Esq., aged 3 years and 6 months.

Died in Port Gibson, on Friday morning last, of paralysis, Capt. Jn. Campbell, in the 56th year of his age. He was born in Philadelphia and spent many of the last years of his life in this country.

July 24, 1828
Married on Wednesday evening, by the Rev. Dr. Cooper, Ferdinand L. Claiborne, Esq., to Miss Courtney Ann, eldest daughter of the late Archibald Terrell, all of this county.

January 31, 1829
Married on Thursday, 8th, in Amite County, by Rev. John Patterson, Mr. Joseph Montgomery, of Jefferson County, to Miss Amelia F., daughter of Rev. James Smylie, of Amite County.

Married on Thursday evening last, by Rev. George Potts, Richard S. Williams, Esq., of Nashville, Tenn., to Miss Agnes W. Hoggatt, eldest daughter of Mr. Nathaniel Hoggatt, of this county.

February 7, 1829
Married on the 29th ultimo, by the Rev. Mr. Drake, Mr. George W. Flower, to Miss Elizabeth Clark, both of this place.

Died on the 18th ultimo, Mr. Joseph Leonard, a planter of this county, aged 37 years. A widow, five children, and an aged father (whose only descendant he was), mourn his departure.

March 21, 1829
Married on Wednesday evening, the 11th, by the Rev. J. C. Burriss, Charles M. Sheppard, Esq., of Golden Grove, La., to Miss Margaret A. Hooke, of Salisbury Hill, Miss.

April 4, 1829
Died on Friday, the 27th ult., William Mathewson, 7 years of age, and on the following Thursday, Catherine Carson, 14 years of age. William was the grandson and Catherine the daughter of James Carson, Esq., of this city.

April 25, 1829
Married at the residence of Thomas Batchelor, Esq., Amite County, on Thursday evening, the 7th, by the Rev. Mr. Patterson, Rev. James Smylie to Mrs. Mary Ann H. Lea, both of Amite County.

Married on Thursday evening, the 16th, by the Rev. James A. Fox, at the residence of John Foster, Esq., in Jefferson County, Mr. Benjamin West to Miss Paulina Meng, of Louisville, Ky.

Married on Thursday evening, the 23d, by the Rev. Mr. Ganial, Mr. John Ahern to Mrs. Hannah Murphy, both of this city.

June 13, 1829
Died on the 6th, at the residence of the late Prosper King, in Jefferson County, Miss. A. E. King.

August 29, 1829
Mr. Abraham G. Claypoole, Esq., was a native of the city of Philadelphia, whence he removed to Chilicothe, Ohio, some years since, with his highly respected father, Abraham Claypoole, late Cashier of the Branch Bank of the United States at Chilicothe. From Ohio the subject of this notice emigrated to Natchez in January, 1826, and commenced the practice of law. Mr. Claypoole died in his 27th year, on the night of the 24th, of a bilious congestive fever.

September 26, 1829
Married at Philadelphia, on the 24th of Aug., by the Right Rev. Bishop White, Rev. James A. Fox, of Natchez, to Miss Emma Louisa Seguin, of New Orleans.

Deaths in Natchez:
Sept. 14 - Michael Ferrand, aged 23 years, bilious fever.
Sept. 14 - Samuel H. West, aged 25 years, yellow fever.
Sept. 14 - ---- Lake, aged 25 years, fever.
Sept. 14 - ---- Hustin, aged 25 years.
Sept. 19 - Mary Eaton.
Sept. 20 - Eli Muse, aged 25 years, malignant bilious fever.

October 3, 1829
Married in Jefferson County, on the 1st, by the Rev. Mr. Muller, Howell Hinds, Esq., to Miss Drusilla Cocks.

Died at his residence in Bellafontaine, on Wednesday evening last, Major John Whistler, of the United States Army.

October 17, 1829
Died on Tuesday, the 6th, at his plantation on the opposite side of the river, Peter Derbigny, late governor of this state. His death was occasioned by a wound in the head conceived from the trunk of a tree, while in the act of leaping out of his carriage to avoid the danger of its being overturned. (*Louisiana Advertiser*)

November 7, 1829
Died on the 31st ult., William Lyle, a native of Ireland, in the 18th year of his age.

Deaths in Natchez:
Oct. 26 - H. Deviline, of colica pictonum.
Oct. 27 - Daniel Rabb, aged 27 years, fever.
Oct. 27 - Mrs. Ursery, aged 35 years, fever.
Oct. 28 - Mr. Crowel, aged 38 years, malignant fever.
Oct. 29 - Mr. Taylor, aged 23 years, fever.
Oct. 30 - Miss Catherine M'Graw, aged 60 years, dropsy.
Oct. 31 - Wm. Lyle, aged 18 years, remittent fever.
Nov. 1 - John Jones.
Nov. 2 - Catherine Hearsey, aged 50 years, malignant fever.

TRI-WEEKLY MISSISSIPPIAN (Jackson, Miss.)
Bainbridge D. Howard, Editor

January 8, 1839
Died on the 21st December last, at St. Francisville, Col. Joseph E. Johnson, late president of the Senate of Louisiana.

February 16, 1839
Died at his residence in Clarke County, Mississippi, on the 26th ultimo, of chronic diarrhea, the Hon. Thomas S. Sterling, Judge of the Fifth Judicial District of the State of Mississippi. He left a widow and three small children.

THE TRI-WEEKLY SENTINEL (Vicksburg, Miss.)

May 16, 1849
Died of cholera, at Milliken's Bend, parish of Madison, La., May 7th, N. T. Williams, aged 42.

May 23, 1849
Died here, Sun. p.m. last, Mr. J. H. Masters, congestion of the brain.

May 30, 1849
Married in this city, on the 23d, at the Lagora House, by Simeon L. George, Esq., Mr. James Austin to Miss Catharine Ferguson, both of Madison Parish, La.

August 7, 1849
Died in this city, on the 31st of July, Ann Bruner, aged 43 years, consort of E. E. Bruner. Mrs. B. was a member of the Catholic Church.

September 19, 1849
Died in the city of Vicksburg, on the 10th, Francis Sohn, aged 19 years, of typhus fever.

September 25, 1849
Died, 18th, in Vicksburg, Peter Crouch, aged 26 yrs., of swamp fever.

Died on the 20th, in Vicksburg, Sydney Peterson, from Indiana, aged 22 years, of diarrhea.

October 9, 1849
Died, 5th, in Vicksburg, Wm. Porter, aged 62 yrs., of swamp fever.

Died recently, near Knoxville, Tenn., Micajah T. Purnell, Esq., of Carroll Co., Miss.

October 24, 1849
Died in Raymond, on Monday, the 15th, Mary, only child of Geo. W. and Susan Gibbs, aged 2 years, 4 months and 23 days.

Deaths within the city of Vicksburg:
Oct. 15 - L. M. Scogin, 23 years, general debility, of Vicksburg.
Oct. 18 - Sarah Williamson, 22 years, inflammation of bowels, of Vicksburg.

January 3, 1850
Married on the 20th ultimo, at the residence of Mrs. Ann Jackson, Bachelor's Bend, Washington County, by Rev. Dr. Dunn, Mr. Robert McConnell and Miss Elizabeth Barham, all of that county.

January 15, 1850
Married in this city, on the 8th, Mr. Abraham L. Roux, of Hinds County, to Miss Marietta Kendall, of this city.

Died at Plainsville, in Yazoo County, on the 2d, Louis Harrison, son of William and Elizabeth C. Gartley.

January 29, 1850
Died on the 24th, Rosana Owings, in the 89th year of her age, a native of Hanover County, Pennsylvania, and for many years a resident of Warren County, near this place.

February 13, 1850
Married by the Rev. Carter Jones, at the residence of Col. A. Russell, on the 7th, Joseph W. Maben, M. D., of Yazoo County, to Miss Lauretta, daughter of Col. Arnold and Mrs. B. Russell, of Warren Co.

February 27, 1850
Married by the Rev. S. C. Perrin, in Grant County, Ky., on the 14th of February, Mr. Wm. H. Sparke, of Vicksburg, to Miss Eliza W. Perrin, daughter of Green R. Perrin, of the former place.

March 12, 1850
Died in Vicksburg, on the 4th, Charles Luber, aged 35 years, from an accidental fall. He was a resident of Vicksburg.

April 2, 1850
Deaths within the city of Vicksburg:
March 24 - John Powell, 33 years, quinsy, of Vicksburg.
March 26 - Eliza Rabb, 35 years, measles.

April 3, 1850
Married on the 14th, by Hon. Christopher C. Scott, Mr. John M. Butler to Miss Martha Jane Coltharp, both of Little Rock, Arkansas.

April 11, 1850
Departed this life at the residence of Mrs. Lanier, of this county, on April 10th, her daughter, Mrs. Henrietta Spann, consort of Charles S. Spann, Esq., of Brownsville, in the 22d year of her age.

Died on Mon., the 8th, in this city, Dr. Robert Allen, in the 55th year of his age. He was a resident of this city for the past fifteen years.

TRUE DEMOCRAT (Paulding, Miss.)
By O. C. Dease

August 13, 1845
John Dozier, son of Dr. W. B. and Mrs. Lavinia Dozier, died on the 7th, of congestive fever, near this place, aged 6 years.

September 3, 1845
Died in the Prairies, Clark County, Miss., on the 19th, Mrs. Faith Trotter, consort of Col. Alexander Trotter.

September 10, 1845
Died at the residence of his father, last Friday evening, William Millsaps, aged about 22 years.

Died on the 6th of September, Joseph Harmon, infant son of Howel and Kitsey Hargrove, of Jasper County.

September 24, 1845
Died at his father's residence in this county, on the 20th, Mr. Morgan Bridges, son of Mr. Wm. Bridges, aged about 20 years.

Died in this co., on the 19th, Mr. Jesse M'Alpin. He leaves a family.

October 8, 1845
Married in Newton County, on the 24th ult., by Samuel Walker, Esq., Mr. Solomon Myer, of Decatur, to Miss Amanda Alexander.

November 12, 1845
Married on the 15th ult., at the residence of Mr. W. Carter, in Jackson county, by the Rev. J. Foster, Mr. Alexander A. M'Kay, of Green Co., to Miss Elizabeth Carter, of Jackson County.

January 21, 1846
Married on the 14th, by W. H. Edmonson, Esq., Mr. Hiram Sherman to Miss Mary Lewis.

Married on the 20th, by W. H. Edmonson, Esq., Mr. Samuel Parker to Miss Margaret F. Bingham.

February 18, 1846
Married in Quitman, Clark County, on the 29th ult., by Hon. William Covington, Col. William B. Trotter, of Clark County, to Miss Elizabeth Lee Terrell, late of Virginia.

The funeral sermon of the late Malcolm McNeill will be preached on the 5th Sabbath in March next, by the Rev. Duncan A. Campbell.

April 1, 1846
Married on the 26th ult., James N. Norsworthy to Miss Caroline Williams, daughter of William Williams, both of Wayne County.

April 6, 1846
Died on the 30th ult., Mr. Willis Holder, of this county, aged about 57 years.

Died on 16th ult., Mrs. Mary, wife of McCullom Metcalf, of Perry Co.

June 17, 1846
Married in Smith County, on Thursday last, by Rev. John P. Martin, Mr. W. T. Ward to Miss Hester Elizabeth Anderson, all of said co.

July 22, 1846
Married at the residence of Captain Jesse Hyde, by the Rev. J. N. Waddell, Dr. E. L. Sharman to Miss Sophronia E. Hyde.

Married on Thursday last, A. L. Farley, Esq., to Mrs. Margaret Moody, by Laban Caraway, Esq.

Died on the 4th, Rev. William Morris, at his residence in this county.

August 5, 1846
Died on the 1st, Mrs. Ellen Owens, aged about 24 years, wife of James Owens -- also their infant child. Mrs. Owens has left a husband and two little children.

It becomes our painful duty to record the death of Abner Carter, of Perry County, Miss. The deceased recently went to Kentucky to restore his health and died in a strange land. His remains were brought back and interred at his former residence. He died of congestive fever, aged 50 years and 23 days.

August 12, 1846
Died in Columbus, Miss., on the 27th of July ult., Mrs. Georgeana, wife of Enos Rush Buckner, Esq.

September 9, 1846
Died at his residence near Quitman, Clark County, Miss., on the 4th, Rev. Joseph B. Platt, aged about 35 years. He was a member of the Methodist Episcopal Church.

October 21, 1846
Died near Claiborne, of congestive fever, Mr. James Owens.

October 28, 1846
Died at his residence, near Paulding, Absolam Reid, about 60 yrs.

Married on Thursday last, at the residence of Col. J. Johnson, Sr., in Garlandsville, Dr. A. J. Cotton to Miss Agnes Johnston.

November 4, 1846
Married on the 29th, by Rev. Drury Sumrall, Mr. Thomas Bailiff, of Perry County, to Mrs. Mary C. Worral, of Jasper County.

Married on the same day, by W. H. Edmondson, Esq., Mr. John S. Murphy to Miss Eunice Ann Bingham.

November 11, 1846
Died on Wednesday, 28th October, at the residence of his mother, near Quitman, Miss., Mr. John H. Williford, aged 25 years.

Died on the 24th of October, at her residence in Perry County, Miss., Mrs. Elizabeth Jones, in the 73d year of her age. Mrs. J. was born and raised in Anson County, North Carolina, but she married and emigrated to this state at an early age.

December 30, 1846
Married on the 9th, in Baldwin County, Ala., at the residence of Capt. Joseph Booth, Mr. Alfred Brown, of this county, to Miss Mattha B. Hodgens, of Baldwin.

August 18, 1847
Died on the 10th, Mr. Ezekiel Land, of this county. On the same day, his daughter, Nancy; and on the 13th, Miss Martha Land.

VICKSBURG DAILY SENTINEL (Vicksburg, Miss.)

November 14, 1845
Died November 7th, Marguarett Vogh, of Warren County, aged 31 years, of puerperal convulsions.

VICKSBURG DAILY WHIG (Vicksburg, Miss.)
W. H. McCardle, Editor

April 20, 1839
We have just learned that a murder was committed on Choctaw Bayou, parish of Concordia, Louisiana, on Saturday last. A man named J. A. Johnson (the murderer) and a Mr. Jones (the victim) lived on adjoining lands. The parish ran a road through Johnson's land. Johnson complained and declared intentions of violence against any one who might use the road. On Sat. last Jones had occasion to travel the road and Johnson's rifle laid Jones weltering in his blood. The murderer fled.

May 10, 1839
Married at New Orleans, on the 17th ult., at the residence of Louis Burgier, Esq., Surveyor General of the state of Louisiana, by the Rev. Mr. Clapp, Maj. Gen. E. P. Gaines, of the U. S. Army, to Mrs. Myra Clark Whitney, only dau. of the late Daniel Clark, Esq., of this city.

May 13, 1839
Mrs. Eliza Vanzile, of Vicksburg, died of puerperal fever, aged 21 years and 3 months.

September 26, 1839
Died at his plantation in Washington County, on the 20th, John E. Frost, Esq., Attorney at Law of this city, in the 38th year of his age.

Departed this life on the 19th, at his plantation on Big Black, William Bacon, in the 56th year of his age.

September 28, 1839
Sextons report for week ending Sept. 21, 1839:
John Potticary, aged 34 years, of dysentery.
Peter Crowell, aged 35 years, of fever, a resident of Tennessee.

January 8, 1840
Married on the 2d, at the residence of the Honl. John I. Guion, by the Rev. C. K. Marshall, Mr. Samuel Hinman to Miss Adeline Carlile, both of this city.

January 17, 1840
Departed this life on the 21st Dec., Mrs. S. Mariah Dudley, consort of Pulaski Dudley, of Bridgeport, Miss., in the 35th year of her age.

January 29, 1840
Married in this city, on the 24th, by Rev. C. K. Marshall, Mr. James Ferguson, of Warren, to Miss Mary Thompson, of Milliken's Bend.

Married at Augusta, Ky., on the 15th, by the Rev. Burr H. McCown, Mr. John C. Bull, of this city, to Miss Eliza S., daughter of Gen. John Payne, of the former place.

February 5, 1840
Sextons report for week ending February 1, 1840:
Isabella M. Develyn, aged 27 years, of hydrops crariae.
Jacob M'Mullen, aged 23 years, resident of Indiana.

February 13, 1840
Sextons report for week ending February 8, 1840:
Jos. Stephenson, aged 45 years, of typhus pneumonia.
John Conn, aged 59 years.

February 14, 1840
Died on the 13th, in this city, Mrs. Mary Jane, consort of Patk. W. Tompkins, Esq., in the 29th year of her age. Two infant children lose their mother's guardianship.

February 20, 1840
Married in this city yesterday evening, by the Rev. Dr. Weller, John M. Chilton, Esq., to Miss Sarah Norton, both of this city.

March 2, 1840
Departed this life on the 25th, Miss Julia Anna Stith, only daughter of Capt. Stith, of this city, aged 14 years and 2 months.

March 7, 1840
Died, Jeremiah Dennis, aged 45 years, of Ireland.

Married on the 5th, at the residence of Dr. Gwin, by Rev. Chas. K. Marshall, Dr. Wm. T. King to Mrs. Frances A. Clark, of this city.

Married on the 5th, at the residence of H. Hendren, Esq., by Rev. C. K. Marshall, Mr. John H. Lawson to Mrs. Ann H. P. Noble, both of La.

March 10, 1840
Sexton's report for week ending March 7, 1840:
Cornelues Coakly, aged 28 years, erysipelas, resident of Ireland.
Edward Brennan, aged 32 years.

March 18, 1840
Married on the 12th, by Rev. C. K. Marshall, David E. Martin, Esq., to Miss Emily Selser, both of Warren county.

March 20, 1840
Died, Joseph Dent, 42 yrs, of delirium tremens, resident of Vicksburg.

March 21, 1840
Married on Thursday, by Rev. Mr. Hutchinson, Mr. A. D. Mattingly to Miss Mary, daughter of Capt. John Bobb.

April 14, 1840
Sexton's report ending week of April 11, 1840:
Wm. Howard, 21 years, drowned.

Michael Cane, 35 years, resident of Ireland.
Chas. Schevanke, 37 years, drowned, resident of Prussia.

April 24, 1840
Sexton's report ending week of April 18, 1840:
Wm. Knapp, 25 years, consumption, resident of New York.
Mary Hutchcraft, 47 years, gastritis.
Sam J. Dawson, 37 years, general anemia.

May 2, 1840
Married on Thursday evening last, by the Rev. Mr. Hutchison, Mr. Henry N. Dawson to Miss Adeline K., daughter of James Folkes, all of this place.

Married on Thursday evening last, by the Rev. C. K. Marshall, at the residence of the Hon. D. Springer, Mr. William W. Stovall, of Hinds county, to Miss Mary Jewell, of this city.

May 7, 1840
Married on Thursday evening last, at the residence of Mr. O. B. Cobb, Milliken's Bend, Louisiana, by the Rev. Mr. Houghton, Mr. Martin L. Ranney, of this city, to Miss Ruth Cobb.

Died, Hannah Flowers, aged 30 years, of ulceration of the bowels, a resident of Vicksburg.

May 21, 1840
Died at Vicksburg, Xawerie Herzog, aged 30 years, of diarrhea, a resident of Switzerland.

May 23, 1840
Married on the 20th, at the residence of Dr. W. Rossman, Hinds county, by John McGuffie, Esq., Dr. James C. Newman to Miss Laura C. Newman, both of Warren county.

June 6, 1840
Departed this life on the 3d, in the 23d year of her age, Mrs. Mildred Ann Grines, consort of Maj. James P. Bryan.

June 9, 1840
Married on the 29th May last, by the Rev. Mr. McLean, F. Tyler, Esq., formerly of this city, to Miss Virginia A. Townes, daughter of A. T. Townes, Esq., of Yalobusha county, Miss.

Married at Princeton, Miss., on the 28th of May, by the Rev. Mr. Sanders, A. F. Smith, Esq., formerly of this city, to Miss Myra Cox, of that place.

Died at the residence of her husband, in this city, on Saturday last, Mrs. Mary, consort of Isaac Webster, Esq., aged 21 years. She left a husband and child.

Sexton's report ending week of June 6, 1840:
J. S. McPhilips, 28 years, of Ireland.
Mrs. Mildred Bryan, 23 years, of convulsions.
John Dacy, 35 years, of Ireland.

June 16, 1840
Died, Rosanna Reading, aged 23 years, of chronic diarrhea.

June 23, 1840
Died in this county, on the 15th, Mrs. Louisa Croch, consort of James Croch, and daughter of the late Thomas Garret, of Williamson county, Tenn., in the 22d year of her age.

July 2, 1840
Died on the 27th of June, John Harvey McFarland, aged 19 years, son of Mrs. Lucy McFarland, of this county.

Died at Donaldsonville, La., on the 13th, Charles Root, of this Place.

July 9, 1840
Married at Natchez, on the 6th, by the Rev. Mr. Winchester, Mr. James Cocke, of Washington county, Miss., to Mrs. Susan H. Harmanson, of the parish of West Feliciana, La.

Sexton's report ending week of July 4, 1840:
John McFarland, 19 years, phthesis pulmonalia.
Anderson J. Pealer, 32 years, bilious remittent fever.
Timothy Murphy, 45 years, fever, from Ireland.

July 23, 1840
Sexton's report ending week of July 18, 1840:
William O'Brien, 27 years.
Daniel Perry, 24 years, congestion of the brain.
Wm. Turnbull, 45 years, typhoid fever.
Henry Gleichstein, 26 years, bilious remittent fever.

July 28, 1840
Died in Vicksburg, Mrs. M. W. Pike, aged 76 years, of diarrhea.

August 1, 1840
Departed this life in Hinds county, on the 26th, John Wood Tappan, aged 13 years, son of Gen. Tappan, of this city.

August 15, 1840
Married on the 9th day of August, 1840, by the Hon. B. Springer, Mr. John A. Ellison to Mrs. Mary McCauley, all of the county of Warren.

Married on the 13th, by the Hon. B. Springer, Mr. Samuel Spohn to Miss Maria Stuart, all of this city.

Died in Columbia, Arkansas, on the 8th, Augustus O. Arthur, in the 20th year of his age. His remains were brought to this city on the steamer Rodolph, and deposited in the burial ground of the Volunteers, Mr. A. having been a member of the corps of Volunteers.

Sexton's report ending week of August 8, 1840:
James H. Foagey, 22 years, congestive fever, of Tenn.
John Jost, 25 years, congestive fever, of Germany.

September 1, 1840
Died on the 28th of August, at the residence of J. B. Stevens, Esq., Warren co., the Rev. R. M. Prentice, a minister of the Baptist Church, aged 27 years. Mr. Prentice came to this state the 1st of last Jan.

Sexton's report ending week of August 29, 1840:
John Kirney, 35 years.
Jeremiah Herington, 32 years.

September 8, 1840
Sexton's report ending week of September 5, 1840:
Francis Morton, 30 years, bilious fever.
John Collins, 68 years, general debility, of Ireland.

September 19, 1840
Married on the 15th, by the Rev. Carter Jones, John B. Hall, Esq., of Yazoo county, to Miss Levina Steel, of this county.

Died on the 6th, of congestive fever, Mrs. Aurelia Adams, daughter of Asel Fitch, of Rochester, New York, and consort of Mr. R. H. Adams, of this city, aged 27 years.

Died in Bucks Bend, parish of Carroll, La., on the 26th of Aug., 1840, Mr. James Beard, in the 55th year of his age.

Died on the 26th, at his residence in Washington county, Miss., Johon Turnbull, in the 33d year of his age.

October 1, 1840
Died at his residence in Washington county, on the 21st of September, of congestive fever, Mr. James S. Hardy, aged 24 years. He has left both in this country and Virginia many friends and relations.

October 2, 1840
Mr. W. R. T. Chaplain, of Mississippi, was yesterday morning married to Miss Murdock, of Philadelphia, and they were staying at Barnum's Hotel. Just after dinner he retired to his room, where he fell down in a fit, and in a short time expired.

Died on 17th, at residence of Thomas R. Patten, Esq., in Lake Providence, Parish of Carroll, La., Dr. Wm. H. Bower, native of Fauquier co., Va., and for the last 6 years resident and physician of this parish.

October 6, 1840
Died at Vicksburg, on the 2d, Eliz. Jane, dau. of Roland M. Whitman, Esq., of Washington Co., Miss., aged 3 yrs., 10 mos. & 5 days.

October 17, 1840
Married in this city, on the 16th, by the Rev. John R. Hutchison, Mr. Armsted Burwell to Miss Priscilla W. Manlove.

October 22, 1840
Sexton's report ending week of October 3, 1840:
John Kane, 27 years, of Ireland.
Patrick McGuire, 25 years, of Ireland.

Sexton's report ending week of October 17, 1840:
John Hall, 26 years, bilious fever.
John Murphy, 26 years, of Ireland.
W. D. Skates, 25 years, malignant typhus.

October 29, 1840
Died in Vicksburg, Patrick Quinlan, a resident of Ireland.

October 31, 1840
Married on the 22d, at Hickory Level, by the Rev. I. Lane, Dr. James Sterling Peebles, of Attakapas, La., to Miss Mary F. Smith, of Hinds County, Miss.

Married by the Rev. A. H. Halcomb, on the 22d, C. Taylor, of Satartia, to Miss Sarah D. Cassedy, of Warren County.

Died at Satartia, on the 17th, Nathaniel N. Hurst, Esq. Mr. Hurst was a native of western Pa., where he was educated and studied the profession of the law. He came to this state in 1834 or 5, and in 1837 engaged in mercantile business at Satartia.

November 11, 1840
Sexton's report ending week of November 7, 1840:
Isaac E. P. Burns, 21 years.
Wm. H. Crofford, 21 years, from Indiana.

November 24, 1840
Died on the 22d, Joseph W., son of Gen. Benjamin S. and Margaret B. Tappan, aged 15 months.

December 23, 1840
Married on the 17th, by Rev. C. K. Marshall, at residence of Oliear C. Brooks, Esq., Ignatia Flowers to Sarahphina Brooks, all of this co.

December 25, 1840
Sexton's report ending week of December 19, 1840:
Aaron Geofrey, 35 years, shot for an attempt to rob.

January 9, 1841
Sexton's report ending week of January 2, 1841:
Gilbert Gould, 25 years, Catarrhas suffocation.
William Walden, 48 years.
Andrew M'Cuddy, 35 years, intemperance.
Sophia Chandler, 70 years.

January 27, 1841
Married in this city, on the 25th, by the Rev. Mr. Weller, Mr. Thomas Hunt to Miss Martha J. Eason.

January 29, 1841
Sexton's report ending week of January 23, 1841:
Thomas McCrary, 23 years, inflammation of stomach and bowels.
Awry M. Melvin, 15 years, pulmonary apoplexy.

February 18, 1841
Died on the 24th ult., at the plantation of John Cameron, Esq., John Brown, M. D., aged about 30 years.

March 4, 1841
Married on the 3d, by the Rev. Jno. R. Hutchinson, Mr. Samuel Burns, of Natchez, to Miss Delia Clapp, of this city.

March 6, 1841
Married on the 4th, at the residence of John Rundell, by William L. Allen, Esq., the Rev. James F. Adams to Miss Phoebe E. Rundell, all of this county.

Married in Decatur, alabama, on the 18th ult., Dr G. P. Jones, of this city, to Miss Martha Peebles, of Attakapas, La.

March 19, 1841
Died on the 11th, Thomas, son of Thomas and Charlotte Banister, aged 5 years.

March 23, 1841
Sexton's report ending week of March 20, 1841:
John Lewis, 32 years.
J. B. White, 35 years, intemperance.

March 24, 1841
Married yesterday eve., at residence of Thos. J. Randolph, by Rev. John Lane, James Hazelet to Miss Caroline L. Grou, both of this city.

Died suddenly, on the 23d, Angelica Martense, daughter of Richard Wells, Esq.

April 1, 1841
Died in Vicksburg, Wm. Manning, 22 years, resident of Vicksburg.

April 7, 1841
C. B. Porter, aged 34 years, died of inflammation of the stomach and liver. He was from Tenn.

April 14, 1841
Sexton's report ending week of April 10, 1841:
Edward Brouson.
Edwd. Bindy, 39 years.
Wm. Duncan, 45 years, inflammation of stomach.
James York, ?? years, acute gastretis.

April 20, 1841
Dennis McCarty, aged 29 years, died of jaundice, from Ireland.

May 17, 1841
Departed this life, on the 12th, Mrs. Julia Hebron, consort of Col. John Hebron, of this county, in the 33d year of her age. She has left a husband and five small children.

May 18, 1841
Died, Mrs. Evey Geris, aged 60 years, a resident of Vicksburg.

May 29, 1841
Died May 27, Harvey, infant son of Harvey N. and Virginia P. Jenkins, aged 8 months and 15 days.

June 10, 1841
Sexton's report ending week of June 5, 1841:
Martin Feate, 40 years, of Ireland.
William Gill, 21 years, of Illinois.

June 19, 1841
Married Tues. evening last, by the Rev. Mr. Cooper, Mr. Wm. P. Scott, of Vicksburg, to Miss Eliza Jane Alexander, of Lexington, Ky.

Married on the 16th, by John F. Pierson, Esq., Mr. Barney Orrick to Miss Elizabeth Potticary, both of this city.

June 26, 1841
Married on the 21st, by the Rev. John Lane, Alfred W. Brien, Esq., to Miss Amanda M., daughter of Mr. John Cowan, of this county.

July 1, 1841
Married on the 17th ult., at Covington, Ky., by the Rev. J. S, Wilson, Mr. Geo. W. Ball, of Vicksburg, Miss., to Miss Mary Jane, eldest daughter of Jno. K. M'Nickle, Esq.

Died at Louisville, Kentucky, on the morning of the 17th ult., Dr. S. D. McCray, of this county.

July 6, 1841

Died on the 16th ultimo, at Jeffersonville, La., at the residence of Wm. Leviston, Esq., Henry, infant son of Wm. H. Hurst, Esq., of Vicksburg, Miss.

July 15, 1841

Married on the 13th, by the Rev. Dr. Weller, Loyd Ruffin Coleman, Esq., to Miss Harriet L. Moore, daughter of William Moore, both of this city.

Died sometime last month, in Fairfax county, Va., William Swartwout, Esq., a merchant of this city.

Died at his residence in this county, on Sunday last, Silas Hilson.

Died at his residence near Mont Albon, a few days since, John F. Tribble.

July 20, 1841

Married on the 15th, by the Rev. C. K. Marshall, Mr. Jeremiah S. Horra to Miss Martha Triford, both of this city.

Died on the 16th, Margareth, daughter of Henry and Margareth Ahrens, aged 1 year.

July 22, 1841

Died on the 20th of June, at the residence of her father, in Columbia, Ark., Miss Margaret E., daughter of W. W. Gaines, formerly of Warren County, Miss.

July 27, 1841

Sexton's report ending week of July 24, 1841:
W. H. Luben, 35 years, apoplexy.
Rebecca Butler, 41 years, dropsy.

August 5, 1841

Died at his residence near this city, on Tuesday morning, the Rev. James Gwin, in the 72d year of his age. Mr. Gwin was a minister of the Gospel with the Methodist Church.

Died near Yazoo City, on Monday morning last, Stephen Howard, formerly Sheriff of Warren county.

August 10, 1841

Died in this city, on the 9th day of July, William A. Cook, formerly of Virginia. Mr. Cook has resided in Vicksburg about 2 years. His trade was that of a jeweler.

August 17, 1841

Died on the 11th, at her residence in Warren county, of pulmonary consumption, Mrs. Anna Chambers, in the 63d year of her age.

August 19, 1841

James Wilson & Fountain Mosby, sons of David Mosby, deceased, died at the residence of James C. Mosby, Esq., of Warren county, Miss.; James W. on the 11th, aged 10 years & 22 days, and Fountain on the 14th, aged 8 years, 6 months & 7 days.

August 24, 1841

Died last evening, of congestive fever, Mr. R. A. Moffatt, late partner of the firm of Ward Moffatt & Co., New Orleans.

Died on the 16th, near Vicksburg, Charles H. Beal, a native of Massachusetts.

September 4, 1841

Married on the 31st ult., at the residence of Mr. Wm. Brigman, in Warren county, by Wm. L. Allen, Esq., Mr. Jonathan Forbes to Miss Amanda Ferrill, all of this county.

September 9, 1841

Died at the city of Vicksburg, Mrs. Elizabeth Ellison, in the 55th year of her age. She was a member of the Methodist Episcopal Church.

September 14, 1841

Sexton's report ending week of September 11, 1841:
John D. Collins, 24 years, malignant fever.
Mr. Daniel, 24 years, consumption.
Jno. Small, Senr., 62 years, fever.

September 16, 1841

Died at Charleston, Tallahatchie county, on the 4th, of congestive fever, the Rev. Guy R. Pinching, a minister of the Episcopal Church, aged about 28 years, and son-in-law of Thomas F. Walker, of this county. He was a native of Ireland, and a graduate of Trinity College, Dublin. He came to this country in early life.

September 18, 1841

Died in this city, on Wed. night last, John Martin, Esq., a member of the Vicksburg Bar. Mr. M. was a native of Kentucky, for many years a citizen of Tennessee, and for six years a resident of this city.

September 21, 1841

Died in this city yesterday morning, Mr. William P. Little, formerly of Maysville, Kentucky.

Died on the 18th, Wm. Scarbrough, Jr., infant child of Edward and Nancy Scarbrough, aged 2 years.

Sexton's report ending week of September 18, 1841:
Wilson Holcomb, 34 years.
James M'Cleland, 35 years.

S. S. Fox, 35 years, shot by negro.
Lewis Hurbert, 25 years, fever.
James Winn, 21 years, fever.
W. P. King, 40 years, yellow fever.
J. H. Martin, 50 years, malignant remittent fever.
Mrs. Vantine, 41 years, phthisic.
Edw. Begley, 30 years.
Robt. Ritchie, 40 years, delirium tremor.
J. Morton, 35 years, dysentery.
---- Sherrick, 38 years, bilious fever.
Jno. Morris, 52 years, fever.

September 23, 1841
Married at the residence of Mr. J. T. S. Collins, in Springfield, on the 21st, by the Rev. John R. Hutchinson, Mr. Franklin Talbott, of this city, to Miss Caroline G. W. Dakin, of New Orleans.

September 25, 1841
Died in this city, on the 23d, of the prevailing epidemic, Miss Ellen G. Reading, at the residence of her brother, A. B. Reading.

Died on Monday, the 20th, at the residence of her father, in this city, Miss Caroline E., eldest daughter of the late John Martin, Esq., in the 16th year of her age.

September 28, 1841
Died in this city yesterday morning, of the prevailing epidemic, William B. Martin, Esq. (of the firm Martin & McLean), in the 26th year of his age.

September 30, 1841
Married Sept. 9th, at Stonington, Conn., by the Rev. J. Erskine Edwards, Wm. R. Babcock, of Vicksburg, Miss., to Miss Parthenia P., daughter of the late Benj. F. Babcock, of the former place.

Married Sept. 9th, at Stonington, Conn., by the same, C. P. Dixon, of Vicksburg, Miss., to Miss H. Elizabeth, daughter of Ephm. Williams, Esq., of the former place.

Died in this city, on the 22d, commencing his 24th year, of the prevailing epidemic, Mr. George W. Parsons, for nearly 2 years past a citizen of New Orleans, and for the 4 previous, a citizen of Vicksburg.

Died at Clinton, Miss., yesterday morning, of the prevailing epidemic, Richard H. Vail, Esq., in the 25th year of his age.

Died at the Poorhouse of Warren county, Miss., on the 21st ultimo, of yellow fever, Daniel Vanslike, of Cincinnati, Ohio.

October 2, 1841
Sexton's report: Sept. 29 - Oct. 1

Robt. Madox, aged 28 years, bilious fever.
Joseph Muladore, aged 30 years, yellow fever.
Wm. Burke, aged 24 years,
J. Brown, aged 30 years, yellow fever, of Germany.
James D. Foster, aged 21 years, yellow fever.
James Bond, aged 30 years, yellow fever, of Ireland.
Lewis Richards, aged 26 years, yellow fever, of Greenville, Ind.

October 7, 1841
Sexton's report: Oct. 4th - 6th
Thomas Fabel, yellow fever, of Illinois.
James Bond, 38 years, yellow fever.
William Moray, 40 years, yellow fever, of Ireland.
George Evans, 39 years, yellow fever.
---- Booker, 28 years, yellow fever.

Died in this city, of the prevailing epidemic, on 25th of Sept., 1841, Mrs. Sophia Hegeman, widow of the late Dr. Hegeman, of this place.

Died at the residence of Doctor J. B. Morgan, near Clinton, on Sept. 29th, B. G. Davenport, Esq., of this city.

October 9, 1841
Died in this city, on Thursday evening last, of yellow fever, Mr. H. B. Erwin, of Cincinnati.

Sexton's report: Oct. 6th - 8th
George Rogers, aged 40.
R. H. Warren, aged 38, yellow fever.
Mr. Mangley, aged 26.
Mr. Longley, aged 25.
Wm. Jones, aged 38.
F. Scobes, aged 25, fever, of Shawnetown, Ill.

Married at Perch Place, in Hinds county, on the 7th, by the Rev. Geo. Miller, Francis Ilsley, Jr., Esq., of Vicksburg, to Miss Mary B. Dotson, of Hinds.

October 14, 1841
Died in this city of the prevailing epidemic, on the night of the 8th, L. W. Brittingham.

Sexton's report: Oct. 8th - 13th
Jeremiah Shehan, 40 years, yellow fever.
Samuel Runyan, 20 years, bilious fever, Risingsun, Pa.
Stephen Marmon, 4 years.
L. W. Brittingham, 22 years, yellow fever.
Wm. Grockford, 25 years, yellow fever, Jersey City, N. J.
Margaret Vogh, 55 years.
Mr. Cox, 38 years, yellow fever.
Jacob A. Mosback, 31 years, yellow fever.

M. T. Ashley, 28 years, yellow fever.
Infant of Mr. Orrick, 1 month.
Wm. McHenry, 22 years, Ohio.
Henry Houghman, 25 years, yellow fever, Germany.
Israel Sanders, 25 years, yellow fever, Massachusetts.

October 16, 1841
Died at the residence of Major A. G. Creath, on the 4th, R. F. Smith, Esq., late of Columbia, Tenn., of yellow fever.

Departed this life on the 2d, of yellow fever, Mr. Philip Cohen, 26 yrs., a native of Poland, and merchant in this city for the last 18 mos.

October 19, 1841
Sexton's report: Oct. 14th - 19th
Jacob Baker, aged 28, disease-John Barleycorn, of Germany.
John Propst, aged 35, yellow fever, of Germany.
Mrs. Myrer, yellow fever, of Germany.
Hugh Keen, aged 30.
Julia E. Brien, aged 10.
Rodney H. Adams, aged 38, delerium tremens.
John Londergale, aged 34, of St. Louis, Mo.
S. S. Spence, aged 25. delerium tremens.
Michael Reardon, aged 35, delerium tremens.
John Donly, aged 28, yellow fever, of Ireland.
Miss. T. Baker, aged 30.
Edward M. Blies, aged 23, yellow fever, of Cincinnati.

October 21, 1841
Died on the 8th, at Grand Lake, Arkansas, Mr. Caleb Impson, a merchant in this city.

Died in this city, on the 19th, of yellow fever, Col. Alfred Cox, of the firm of Cox, Pinckard & Co. He was formerly a Senator in the Mississippi Legislature from Washington County.

Died on 19th, of yellow fever, Mr. Philip Arrison, citizen of this city.

Died on the 20th, of yellow fever, Mr. Henry Nieman, for the last 2 years a citizen of this city.

Died on the 20th, of yellow fever, Mr. Richard Bosley, a native of England, and for the last few years a resident of this city.

Died of the prevailing epidemic, on the 20th, George Hudson, a native of Massachusetts, and for the last five years a resident of this city.

Died at the residence of his father, in the city of Vicksburg, on the 18th day of September, 1841, in the 8th year of his age, Richard Jay, son of the Hon. James and Martha W. Bland.

October 23, 1841
Died on yesterday evening, John B. Small and Mrs. Harriet Arrison, consort of Wm. Arrison.

October 26, 1841
Died of dropsy, on the 24th of Oct., 1841, in Madison parish, La., Mrs. Mary C., wife of Dr. Julius Culbertson, in the 24th year of her age.

October 28, 1841
Died on the 26th, of yellow fever, Doctor Albert G. Chewning, of this city, in the 27th year of his age. Doctor Chewning was a native of Orange county, Va. and has resided in this city for the last six years.

Died on the 22d, of yellow fever, Mr. James Vose, aged 31 years. Mr. Vose was a native of Bilford, N. H. and had resided in Mississippi 9 years, the last 18 months in Vicksburg.

Died in this city, on Tuesday morning, of the prevailing epidemic, Miss Eliza L. Taylor.

October 30, 1841
Died in this city, on Tuesday evening, of the prevailing epidemic, Mr. Theodore E. Gould.

Died in this city, on yesterday morning, of the prevailing epidemic, Mr. Samuel Folkes, in the 34th year of his age.

Sexton's report: Oct. 28th & 29th
Dennis Tracy, aged 55, intemperance.
W. B. Broadwell, aged 35, hemorrhage of the lungs.
T. E. Gold, aged 30, yellow fever.
Mrs. McGarrey.

November 1, 1841
Mr. Samuel Folkes departed this life this morning, of the prevailing epidemic, in the 34th year of his age. He was of the old firm of S. & M. C. Folkes, of this city. Mr. Folkes was a member of the Methodist Church.

November 2, 1841
Died in this city, Nov. 1st, of yellow fever, Mr. Edward Hart, of New York, aged about 24 years.

Died October 31st, of yellow fever, Wm. P. Scott, for many years of this city.

November 3, 1841
Died at the residence of her father, in this city, on the 21st, in the 15th year of her age, Mrs. Comelia Sophia Winans, wife of Mr. John Winans and daughter of Mr. C. W. Myrer.

November 4, 1841
Sextons report: Oct. 30th - Nov. 3d
Orris Ellmore, aged 33, yellow fever.
John Crider, aged 30, yellow fever.
Daniel Cronan, aged 28, yellow fever.
Wm. Crawford, aged 46, yellow fever.
Wm. P. Scott, aged 50, yellow fever.
Ann Crowder, aged 3, yellow fever.
H. M. Jenkins, aged 34, yellow fever.
Lorenzo D. Swords, aged 26, yellow fever.
Thos. Glancy, aged 30, yellow fever.

November 5, 1841
Died of yellow fever, on the 1st, at the residence of J. T. S. Collins, Esq., Springfield, Mr. Edward Hart, in the 24th year of his age.

November 6, 1841
Departed this life on the 22d, of yellow fever, Mrs. Harriet Sophia Arrison, in the 22d year of her age, consort of Mr. Wm. Arrison, of this city.

November 8, 1841
Died on the 9th, at the residence of his father-in-law, Dr. Edward Johnston, Clark county, Mo., Egbert O. Martin, late of Natchez, Miss., aged 31 years.

Died on the 11th, at his residence in Clark county, Mo., Dr. Edward Johnston, late of Natchez, Miss., aged 61 years.

November 9, 1841
Died on the 7th, of the prevailing epidemic, Mr. James C. Zimmer, in the 26th year of his age, a native of Virginia.

November 13, 1841
Sexton's report: Nov. 4th - 12th
Armand Fargues, aged 40, of France.
Richard Pasco, aged 38, yellow fever.
J. C. Zimmer, aged 26, yellow fever.
A. H. Mitchell, aged 26, liver complaint.
John Miller, aged 28, yellow fever.

Died in this city, Miss Ann B. Dortch, of the prevailing fever on the 4th, aged 48 years. Miss Dortch was a native of East Feliciana, La., but has resided many years in this city, in the family of her brother-in-law, the late Wm. T. Day.

Dr. Weller died at this place, on the 8th, of yellow fever. He was buried at the graveyard adjoining this town. Scarcely were his remains entombed when his son, George Wells, also died. (*Raymond Times*)

November 18, 1841
Married on the 10th, by the Rev. J. R. Hutchison, A. N. Warren, Esq., to Miss Mary E. Thomas, both of Warren county.

November 20, 1841
Died at the residence of his father, B. Whitfield, Esq., in Hinds county, Nov. 13th, Benjamin H. Whitfield, aged 19 years.

Died on the 18th, Aristipus White, infant son of Thomas J. and Laura Ann Hanna.

Sexton's report: Nov. 12th - 19th
John E. Richardson, 31 years, congestion of the brain.
Geo. B. Wright, 30 years, of Lagrange, Mo.

November 30, 1841
Married in this city, on the 28th, by Henry Green, Esq., Mr. Charles Starr to Mrs. Caroline Hamilton.

December 4, 1841
Sexton's report: Nov. 13th - Dec. 8th
Christopher Schmit, 34 years, mania potu.
Thomas Welch, 28 years, horse kicked.
Thomas O'Nell, 27 years, mania potu.

December 11, 1841
Married on the 16th ult., near Livingston, Miss., by the Rev. Dr. J. P. Thomas, Mr. Girard Stites, of this city, to Miss Mary L., daughter of the late John Hodge, Esq., of Madison county.

December 22, 1841
Sexton's report: Dec. 4th - 20th
John Reynolds, 26 years.
Jas. Leiver, 50 Years.
John B. Primer, 65 years, mania potu.
A. D. Adkins, 22 years, inflammation of lungs.
Miss Mary Moore, 23 years.

December 23, 1841
Married Dec. the 16th, by Henry Green, Esq., Mr. William Trowbridge to Miss Catherine Kleimann, of this city.

December 29, 1841
Sexton's report ending week of 25th December:
George Sherod, 25 years, suicide, of Philadelphia.
Julia G. Evans, 21 years.

Married on the 27th, by the Rev. John H. Hutchison, Mr. William Fenimore, of Warren county, to Miss Eliza Wright, of Louisiana.

January 1, 1842
Married 29th, by the Rev. George Moore, Mr. L. S. Houghton to Miss Jane C. Billings, all of this city.

January 4, 1842
Died on Friday morning last, Maria Lucylle, youngest daughter of Wm. J. and Sarah A. Estes, aged 3 years.

January 5, 1842
Valentine Feverbah, aged 40, died of an accident.

January 31, 1842
Died on Friday last, Alexander Peal. His death was caused by an accidental discharge of his gun while hunting, the whole load passing through the wrist, which resulted in lock-jaw.

February 1, 1842
John Blair, aged 26 years, died of inflammation of the brain. He was a resident of Posey City, Iowa.

February 2, 1842
Married in this city, on the 1st, by the Rev. D. C. Page, Mr. Gordon Robinson to Miss Martha P. Taylor, all of Vicksburg.

February 4, 1842
Died at his residence on the 1st February, 1842, in the 31st year of his age, Thomas C. Randolph, a native of Brunswick county, Virginia, and for the last 12 years a merchant of this town. He has left a wife and daughter 5 years old.

February 8, 1842
Sexton's report ending week of February 5th:
James McCarty, 26 years.
Thomas McCoy, 24 years.

February 15, 1842
Died on the 7th, Mrs. Emily Jane Sexton, consort of John M. Sexton, and eldest daughter of the late Benjamin Harris, of this city, in the 21st year of her age.

February 22, 1842
Sexton's report 2 weeks ending February 19th:
Miss Catharine Roberts, 15 years, typhus fever.
James Franks, 28 years.
Lewis Mitchell, 40 years, consumption.

March 17, 1842
Married in this city, on the 15th, by Richards Barnett, Esq., Justice of the Peace, Mr. John Fox to Miss Eve Shriner, all of Vicksburg.

March 18, 1842

Married in this city, on the 17th, by Richard Harnett, Esq., Justice of the Peace, Mr. Henry C. Daniels to Mrs. Nancy Wright.

Died, Bill Byers, 36 years of age, of intemperance, a resident of Vicksburg.

March 31, 1842

Died at residence of Capt. John Tucker, on 21st March, Miss Camilla Runnells, aged 14 years and 5 months, a neice of Ex. Gov. Runnells.

April 7, 1842

Died last eve., of typhus fever, William Moore, a resident of this city.

Sexton's report for two weeks ending April 2:
Michae Nagle, 30 years, fever.
Mary Welch, 29 years, diarrhea.
Edward Bradley, 21 years, swamp fever.
John Davis, 30 years, inflammation of bowels.
John Sharp, 40 years, inflammation of brain.

April 20, 1842

Sexton's report ending week of April 16th:
Mark H. Mayfield, 28 years, consumption.
Mrs. Olivia Littlejohn, 22 years, phthisis pulmonalis.

April 28, 1842

Died of consumption, in the city of Vicksburg, on the 15th, Mrs. Olivia F. Littlejohn, consort of Joseph Littlejohn, and eldest daughter of Jas. Bland, Esq., of this place. She was born in Alexandria, D. C. on the 2d of November, 1819. In 1836 she was married and became a member of the M. E. Church in May 1841.

May 24, 1842

Married at Mount Rose, near this city, on the 22d, by the Rev. P. W. Boyd, James Allen, Esq., of this city, to Mrs. Frances M. Rapaide.

Died on the 20th, Julia, infant daughter of Wm. R. and Harriet J. Norcom, aged 5 months.

May 31, 1842

Married in this city, the 29th, by Rev. Frederick W. Boyd, Rector of Christ Church, Vicksburg, Robert S. French, Esq., to Mary Jane Reid.

June 2, 1842

Married in this city, on the 28th ultimo, by Richards Barnett, Esq., Justice of the Peace, Mr. Moses Blackstock to Miss Martha Winslow, both of the parish of Madison, state of Louisiana.

June 9, 1842

Died, Charles Harbaugh, 22 years, by drowning, resident of Cincinnati.

June 21, 1842
Died on the 15th, at his residence on Old River, in Warren County, Miss., of malignant fever, Mr. Joseph T. Hicks, aged 33 years, a native of Granberry Co., North Carolina, leaving a wife and infant son.

June 23, 1842
Sexton's report ending week of June 18th:
Joem Hall, 40 years, congestive fever.

June 28, 1842
Married in this city, on the 23d, by Rev. Mr. Hutchinson, Mr. Isaac R. Newman to Miss Sevella Vogh.

July 2, 1842
Died in Washington county, Miss., on the 27th ult., Mrs. Mary Emeline, consort of Col. Richard Christmas, Mrs. C. was a native of Williamson county, Tenn.

July 7, 1842
Died 30 June, Isaac Hamilton, an old & respected citizen of this co.

July 9, 1842
Married on the 7th, by the Rev. Carter Jones, Mr. Edward H. Bryan to Mrs. Lucilla Folkes, all of this county.

Sexton's report:
Isaac Hamilton, age 66 years.

July 16, 1842
Died of croup, on the 12th, Andrew, infant son of John A. and Mary A. Ruff, of New Orleans, aged 22 days.

July 19, 1842
Sexton's report week ending July 16th:
Tony Retting, 36 years, bilious fever.
Nancy Walden, and infant.
Isaac Wilson, 25 years, bilious fever.

July 28, 1842
Died at the residence of his uncle, John A. Lane, in Washington county, Miss., on the 23d, of congestive fever, in his 19th year, William R. Fortson, second son of Mrs. Eliza Dortch, of this place.

August 2, 1842
Died on the 26th, at her residence in Hinds Co., near Clinton, Mrs. Elizabeth Kearney, in the 29th year of her age, consort of Mr. Thomas Kearney, and daughter of the late Col. Raymond Robinson, of this co.

August 4, 1842
Married in the town of Monroe, La., on the 21st ultimo, by the Hon.

Lewis F. Lamay, Mr. A. J. Grayson, of Columbia, to Miss Frances J. Timmons, of Monroe.

Sexton's report week ending August 4th:
Edward King, 25 years, drowned.
Wm. Bentsinger, 22 years, bilious fever.

August 16, 1842
Died at Grand Lake, Arkansas, of bilious fever, on the 6th, Mrs. Jane Gillespy, consort of A. M. Sterett, formerly of this city, aged 17 years.

August 23, 1842
Died at the residence of Mrs. Lucy Carroll, on Walnut Bayou, La., on the 17th, Sarah B. Hogan, daughter of Samuel G. Hogan, formerly of Kentucky, aged 6 years and 9 months.

August 25, 1842
Died of congestive fever, at the residence of their father, in the county of Yazoo, on the 12th, Gabriel William, aged 12 years & 6 months, and on the 17th, George Henry, aged 15 years, the eldest and second sons of Peter C. and Elizabeth Goosey.

John Maloy, aged 38 years, died of bilious fever.

August 27, 1842
Died the 24th, in this city, of bilious fever, Charles L. Boyer, formerly a deputy in the Probate Court Clerk's Office, of this county.

August 30, 1842
Died, Chas. L. Bowyer, 25 years, of effusion of the brain.

September 13, 1842
Died at Satartia, on the 3d, Ellen Green, daughter of Peter C. and Elizabeth Goosey, in her 4th year.

James Colt, aged 24 years, died of bilious fever and rupture of a blood vessel of the brain.

September 15, 1842
Died at the residence of Col. G. Kearney, in Madison county, on the 8th, William Foster Cook, son of E. G. and Henrietta V. Cook, aged 2 years, 11 months and 12 days.

September 17, 1842
Married on the 13th, by Wm. L. Allen, Esq., Mr. Asa Chambers and Martha Ann Dyer, both of Warren county.

October 1, 1842
Departed this life in the 32d year of his age, in Warren county, Miss., on the 26th day of September, 1842, William W. Stovall, son of Ralph and Martha Stovall. He has left a wife and little daughter.

October 4, 1842
Died October 1st, of congestive fever, Maj. Peter Mintzer, in the 48th year of his age.

Died, F. L. Barnes, 22 years of age, of inflammation of the brain.

October 6, 1842
Sexton's report, October 1 - 5:
Margaret Welch, 26 years, yellow fever.
John McLane, 28 years, bilious fever.
Mathew Flinn, 20 years, bilious fever.
Sarah E. Swett, yellow fever.

October 8, 1842
Departed this life on the 5th, Miss Sarah Elizabeth Swett, eldest daughter of Daniel and Sarah Swett, of this city, aged 16 yrs., 10 mos.

October 11, 1842
Died on the 1st, Martha Jane, daughter of Richard E. and Mary Hendricks, aged 2 years, 11 months and 22 days.

October 13, 1842
Died on the 18th September, 1842, on Bayou Mason, Madison parish, La., Mary Francis, youngest child and only daughter of Joseph W. and Adaline Williams, formerly of this city.

October 18, 1842
Died in Princeton, Washington county, on the 5th October, of congestive fever, Cyronius C. Denio, second son of C. B. and Emeline Denio, aged 4 years.

October 25, 1842
Sexton's report ending week of October 22:
Mrs. Alice Foley, 28 years, intemperance.
John Martin, 24 years, congestive fever, of Connecticutt.
---- Wonrider, 37 years, bilious fever.

November 1, 1842
Sexton's report ending week of October 29:
---- Donovan, 38 years, mania potu.
John Quinnan, 25 years, mania potu.
Wm. D. Montgomery, 20 years, fever.
Alex. Diamond, 40 years, intermittent fever.
Henrietta Martin, dropsy.
George Hart, 27 years, introsusception.
John Hagerty, 35 years, fever.
Michael Kearney, 33 years, typhus fever.
Edward Devlin, 33 years, typhoid fever.

Married in this city, on the 25th, by the Rev. J. R. Hutchinson, Mr. Jos. P. Hawks to Miss Catharine Neville Barnett.

November 8, 1842
Sexton's report ending week of November 5:
Francis Galagher, 22 years.
Peter Riley, 25 years, intermittent fever.
Jackson Powell, 26 years.
Patrick O'Donald, 30 years, gastritis.
Mrs. Jenkins, 45 years.

November 15, 1842
Sexton's report ending week of November 12:
Jerry Calahan, 35 years, gastritis.
Wm. O'Brian, 38 years, intemperance.
Conrod Fisher, 34 years, gastritis.
Isiah Dameron, 20 years, consumption.
John Collins, 20 years, bilious fever.
Jas. T. Brown, 38 years, convulsions.

November 16, 1842
Died in this city, on the 15th, Nathan Lufbrough Vinson, a native of Georgetown, D. C., in the 23d year of his age.

November 17, 1842
Married in this city, at the residence of E. E. Bruner, on the 10th, by the Rev. Mr. Cooper, Mr. S. R. Bolls to Miss Ann E. Chesley, all of this county.

November 22, 1842
Died at his residence in this city, on Saturday evening last, James Bland, Esq., about 20 years, a resident of this county.

Died at his residence, near Benton, Copiah county, Mr. Ezekial Miller, in the 25th year of his age.

Died, Thos. Molvany, aged 35 years, of general constitutional derangement.

Died, John Carney, aged 40 years, a resident of Vicksburg.

November 29, 1842
Sexton's report ending week of November 26:
Wm. J. Clark, 51 years, consumption.
John Riley, 25 years, inflammation of stomach.
Thos. Kinnan, 44 years, consumption.
Martha Murry, 22 years, dropsy.

December 6, 1842
Sexton's report ending week of December 3:
James Fritz, 41 years, total constitutional.

Patrick Cullin, 28 years, dropsy.
Sarah Chewning, 22 years, of Bolivar county.

Married at the Glidewell House, on the 30th of November, by R. Barnett, Justice of the Peace, Mr. James Richie to Miss Matilda Jeffries.

December 10, 1842
Married on the 8th, at the residence of Mrs. McKay, by Richards Barnett, Esq., Mr. Christopher F. Lawton to Mrs. Sarah Jane Rairdon, both of this county.

December 17, 1842
Married in this city, on the 15th, Mr. J. W. R. Tilden to Mrs, Levina E. Small, both of this city.

December 20, 1842
Married on yesterday morning, at "Live Oak". the residence of Dr. George Smith, by R. Barnett, Esq., Mr. Richard Spann to Miss Martha W. Moseby, all of Warren County.

December 21, 1842
Sexton's report ending week of December 17:
Edward Galagher, 35 years, shot.
Wm. Henry Till, 15, typhus fever.

December 22, 1842
Married on the 20th, by the Rev. C. K. Marshall, Mr. Walter Mudd to Mrs. Lasthina Wools, all of this city.

December 28, 1842
Married on the 27th, at the Glidewell House, in this city, by Richards Barnett, Esq., Mr. Francis W. Delesdenier to Miss Charlotte Foster, both of New Orleans.

December 29, 1842
Married at Hurricane, on the 27th, by the Rev. F. W. Boyd, Rector of Christs Church at Vicksburg, Mr. Thomas E. Robins to Miss Caroline, third daughter of Joseph E. Davis, Esq., all of this county.

Died on the 24th September last, at the residence of Dr. H. G. Boyle, on Bayou Goula, La., D. D. Monroe, formerly of this city.

December 31, 1842
Married on the 29th, at residence of J. T. S. Collins, Esq., by the Rev. F. W. Boyd, Rector of Christs Church, Vicksburg, T. A. Bartlette, Esq., of New Orleans, to Miss Jannette R. De St. Talbot, of this city.

January 3, 1843
Mrs. Mary Campbell, aged 65 years, a resident of Vicksburg, died Dec. 1842.

January 11, 1843
Died on Wednesday evening last, of palpitation of the heart, Thadeus Stith, eldest son of Captain Stith. Mr. Stith was about 22 years of age.

Andrew Fisher, aged 33 years, died of consumption.

January 17, 1843
Sexton's report ending week of January 14:
R. S. Hammond, 38 years, intersusption.
Infant of T. J. Randolph, of Humphrey Co., Tn.
S. B. Gilbert, 38 years.
Infant of F. T. Bell, croup.
John Lewis, 30 years, Delr. Tremens.

January 20, 1843
Died on the 16th, in the 32d year of her age, Mrs. Elizabeth Chapman Hendren, consort of Hadry Hendren, a native of Norfilk, Va., and for the last six years a resident of this city.

Married on the 17th, at the Catholic Church, by the Rev. Mr. O'Reily, Mr. James Kilpatrick to Miss Mary Ellen Green, both of this city.

January 21, 1843
Married on the 19th, at the residence of N. W. Hatch, Esq., by the Rev. John M. Taylor, Mr. Richard Griffith to Miss Sarah B. Hatch, both of this city.

January 26, 1843
Sexton's report ending week of January 21:
Elizabeth P. Hendren, aged 32 years, inflammatory fever.
Thomas W. Radford, aged 36 years, inflammation of bowels.
John Crookey, aged 25 years, inflammation of lungs.
John Weck, aged 35 years, killed by a tree.

January 30, 1843
Married on the 18th, by the Rev. J. Lane, Mr. Robert Wilkins to Caroline V. Spann, both of Warren county.

February 8, 1843
Died at Donaldsonville, La., on the 1st, Francis Ilsley, Sen'r., 63 yrs.

Married on Sun. a.m. last, at New School Pres. Church, by Rev. Mr. Newton, Silas H. Bowman to Mrs. Eliza Jane Scott, both of this city.

February 14, 1843
Married on 2 Feb., by W. N. Peers, Esq., Mr. M. Reed to Miss L. J. Hooter, dau. of M. Hooter, Esq., the great bear hunter of Yazoo Co.

February 24, 1843
Died in this place, on the 16th, Dr. Samuel L. Taliaferro, a native of Virginia, in the 41st year of his age. (*Richmond, La., Compiler*)

February 25, 1843
Married on the 23d, at Lake Washington, Mr. James Irwin, of Lexington, Ky., to Miss Margaret, eldest daughter of Capt. Henry Johnson.

March 7, 1843
Sexton's report ending week of March 4:
Edward Patterson, aged 22 years, pleurisy.

March 16, 1843
Died on the 12th, in his 44th year, Capt. Benjamin H. Stith, of this county, a native of Brunswick County, Virginia.

March 27, 1843
Married on the 16th, at the mouth of Big Sunflower river, by the Rev. Jesse Lea, Daniel A. McKay to Miss Mary Stevenson, late of this co.

March 28, 1843
Married the 23d, at the residence of James McRaven, Esq., near Clinton, by the Rev. Daniel Comfort, Wm. H. Nichol, merchant of Clinton, to Miss Sarah C. Cameron, of Franklin County, in this state.

Sexton's report ending week of March 25:
Infant of A. Auter, 3 years, consumption.
Mr. King, 60 years, of Vicksburg.
Mrs. Rubican, 30 years, of Vicksburg.

March 29, 1843
Married on the 27th, by the Rev. Mr. Russell, Mr. Wm. R. Jones to Miss Eliza Bullinger, both of this city.

April 5, 1843
Died at the residence of her husband, near Brownsville, in Hinds county, on Sunday last, Mrs. Rebecca Bush, wife of Capt. James Bush. Mrs. Bush was a native of North Carolina, but for the last 15 years a resident of this state. She has left a husband and 3 children.

Sexton's report ending week of april 1:
Joseph Chapman, 34 years, mania a potu.
Dr. J. R. Putnam, 30 years, of New Orleans.
Catharine H. Bodley, 3 years, quinsey.

April 14, 1843
Married on the 12th, by the Rev. Mr. Wood, Mr. Andrew Gamble to Miss Patience Potticary, both of this city.

April 18, 1843
Died, Mrs. Myra Pearce, 26 yrs., of consumption, from Louisville, Ky.

April 24, 1843
Died on the 20th ult., Eugenia Jamesella, youngest daughter of Mrs. S. P. Vose, aged 13 months.

Died at Jackson, Miss., on the 11th, Mrs. Martha Bryant, in her 28th year, consort of Nathan Bryant.

Died in Jasper county, April 2, James Brogan, aged 8 years.

Died on the 9th, April, Mrs. Mary Ann Hutchins, consort of Telemachew Hutchins, of Claiborne county, in the 30th year of her age.

Died at Warrenton, Warren county, on the 15th, Dr. James Magee.

Married on the 10th, Judge S. J. Cook to Miss Caroline Baldridge, all of Jefferson county.

Married on the 16th March last, Mr. Martin McNair to Miss Mary Ann Catharine Smith, only daughter of Malcolm Smith, Esq., all of Covington county.

Married on the 6th of April, John A. Adams, Esq., to Miss Sarah A. Blalack, all of Newton county.

Married on 12 April, in Adams Co., J. H. Veazie to Mary Jane Smith.

Married on the 5th April, Mr. Robert M. Lea, of Amite, to Miss Letitia Edwards, of Wilkinson County.

April 25, 1843
Died suddenly at the Vicksburg Female Institute, on the 23d, Miss Lucy Ann Briscoe, only child of John Briscoe, Esq., of Walnut Bayou, La., aged 10 years.

Married on the 23d, by the Rev. John Lane, Mr. Alfred H. Rowlett, to Mrs. Virginia P. Jenkins, all of this city.

May 4, 1843
Died in this city, on the 28th ult., of consumption, Dr. N. B. L. Kinsolving, a native of Albemarle county, Virginia.

May 7, 1843
Died in Yazoo county, on the 25th ult., Mr. John S. Young, a native of South Carolina, but for the last 16 years a resident of this state.

Died at Commerce, Miss., Mrs. Josephine Mitchell, wife of Geo. H. Mitchell, Esq., recently of DeSoto county.

Died at Society Ridge, Hinds county, Miss., on the 27th April, Mrs. Sarah Battle, aged 56, consort of O. P. Battle.

May 9, 1843
Married in Brunswick, Va., on the 22d of March, Mr. Robert P. Harris,

of Warren county, Miss., to Miss Mary A. E. Rice, daughter of the late Col. John B. Rice, of Lawrenceville, Va.

May 10, 1843
Sexton's report ending week of May 6:
Basil Aldwell, 30 years, consumption.
Michael Schaeffer, 37 years, dropsy.

May 16, 1843
Sexton's report ending week of May 13:
Isaac H. Yarnell, 40 years, consumption, Maryland.
Richard Johnson, 35 years.

May 25, 1843
Married on the 21st in Copiah county, Miss., by the Rev. Mr. Mickson, Dr. H. M. Grant, formerly of this city, to Mrs. Sarah Ann Dorsey.

May 27, 1843
Sexton's report ending week of May 27;
Fideli Pedreli, 24 years, delerium tremens.
Catarine Schramm, 37 years.

We record the death of William H. Ward, of Georgetown, Ky. He died on the 20th, of inflammation of the lungs, at the residence of his cousin, H. M. Johnson, Esq., in Yazoo county, in this state.

June 8, 1843
Married on Wednesday evening last, at the residence of Thos. Moore, Esq., Mr. Zachariah Wardlow, late of Alabama, to Mrs. Talba L. Wilkins, of this county.

William Smithy, aged 27 years, of Missouri, died of consumption.

June 15, 1843
Sexton's report ending week of June 10:
Henry Williams, 35 years, killed on railroad, resident of Pennsylvania.
Dr. James Hagan, 38 years, shot with Pistol.

June 20, 1843
Died at his residence in this city, on the 14th, Dudley W. Babcock, a native of Rhode Island, aged 41 years.

Married on Sunday evening, at the residence of William L. Allen, Esq., by the Rev. William H. Taylor, Mr. C. Dickey, of this county, to Miss Adaline Sterdevant, of Yazoo county.

Married on the 15th, by the Rev. Mr. Chapman, Mr. Felix A. Davis, of this city, to Miss Elinor Arrison, formerly of New Port, Ky.

June 22, 1843
Sexton's report ending week of June 17th:
R. B. Herring, 56 years, of intemperance.

June 24, 1843
Married on the 8th, Mr. F. A. Whitney to Miss Elizabeth G. Beazley, of Jackson, Miss.

Married on 31st May, John M. Currier, M. D. Miss Francis Matilda Stewart, both of Wilkinson county.

Married on the 30th, Mr. Jacob J. Chambers to Miss Martha Hope, both of Wilkinson county.

June 27, 1843
George Stramp, aged 45 years, died of bilious fever.

July 1, 1843
Married on the 24th ult., Mr. Z. Kelley, to Miss Anna M. Morris, both of Natchez.

Married on the 22d ult., Mr. Cullen Barrow to Miss Charlotte Vaughn, all of Lowndes county.

Married on the 21st of June, Mr. James Crow o Miss Nancy Irby, all of Claiborne county.

July 4, 1843
Married June 28th, at residence of Col. Wm. Gartley, by Rev. N. N. Wood, R. M. Martin, Esq., of Clinton, to Emily Balfour, of Vernon.

July 8, 1843
Married on the 6th, by the Rev. J. H. Gray, Mr. Ezekiel H. Wright to Mrs. Ann Mariah Beutel, all of this city.

July 11, 1843
Died in this city, on the 8th, Martha Ann Ilsley, infant daughter of Francis and Mary Belinda Ilsley, aged 3 months and 11 days.

Died at the residence of Thos. J. Harper, in this city, on the 7th, Col. Pitt Thomas, for many years a resident of this city.

Died at the residence of Mr. N. W. Hatch, on the 6th, Mrs. Sarah B. Griffith.

Sexton's report ending week of July 8th:
Mary Malady, 28 years, cholera morbus.
Pitt Thomas, 34 years, congestion of the lungs.

July 13, 1843
Died suddenly, at the residence of Dr. Thos. J. Harper, in Vicksburg,

on the 6th, Major Pitt Thomas, in the 35th year of his age.   Maj. Thomas was a native of Southampton county, Va.

July 15, 1843

Died suddenly, on 14th, Emma H., infant daughter of Edwd. R. and Emma Warren, aged 2 years and 7 months.

Died on the 12th, at the residence of James Allen, Esq., near Vicksburg, Mary Allen Rapelje, aged 5 years and 8 months.

Died on the 27th day of June last, at China Grove, her late residence in Hinds County, Mrs. Mary O. Smith, a native of North Carolina. She died of hemorrhage of the lungs. Mrs. Smith was for many years a member of the Presbyterian Church.

Died on the 13th July, 1843, Peter Henry Ahrens, only son of Henry and Margaret Ahrens, aged 2 months and 10 days.

July 20, 1843

Married on the 13th, by Warren Jennings, Esq., Mr. Charles Gee, of Warren County, to Miss Mary Ann Johnston, of Hinds County.

July 25, 1843

Departed this life on the 17th July, 1843, in this city, Mrs. Ann, wife of Mr. John Stinson.

Died in this city, on the 21st, Dr. Willis M. Green.

Died on the 21st, in this city, John Scannell, a native of Ireland, but for several years past a resident of this city.

July 27, 1843

Departed this life on the 21st, Basil G. Wood, in the 26th year of his age. The deceased was a native of Clermont county, Ohio, but had resided the last two years in this city, engaged in trading upon the river.

Sexton's report ending week of July 22:
Mrs. Ann Stinson, 46 years, congestive fever.
John Kroff, 34 years, congestion of brain.
Infant of J. Hazelett, 2 days.
Isaac King, 36 years, influenza.
James Wilson, 38 years, inflammation of bowels.
T. Clark, 34 years, congestive fever.
Samuel Morris, 35 years.
Dr. Willis M. Green, 45 years, influenza.
B. G. Wood, 25 years, fever.
John Scannell, 25 years, effusion of the brain.

August 1, 1843

Sexton's report ending week of July 29:

John Raferty, 38 years, intemperance.
John Tuohy, 35 years.
Michael Koontz, 29 years, fever.
Jacob Gullock, 30 years, bilious fever.
Patrick Fogerty, 23 years.
Mrs. Briggs, inflammation of the bowels.

August 12, 1843
Died near Amsterdam, in Hinds county, on the 7th, of fever, Henry B. Birdsong, a native of Virginia.

August 15, 1843
Died July 28th, in Hinds Co., Miss., William W. R., infant son of Wm. Stovall, deceased, and Mary Stovall, aged 5 months & 12 days.

Died on the 2d, at the residence of her father, R. S. Wheatly, Esq., in this city, Mrs. Catharine B. Chapman, wife of Dr. John L. Chapman, of Washington county, Miss. (*Lou. Journal*)

August 17, 1843
We announce the death of Thomas Hughes Green, youngest son of Col. Thomas J. Green, of this county, aged 2 years and 45 days.

August 22, 1843
Matthew Scannel, aged 24 years, of Vicksburg, died of mania potu.

August 26, 1843
Died in this city, on the 13th, at the residence of Col. T. Thorn, E. G. Hopkins, Esq., late Clerk of the Supreme Court of Mississippi. (*Little Rock Gazette*).

August 29, 1843
Died at Grand Gulf, on the 20th, Albert Tunstall, a native of Louisville, Ky., but for many years past a resident of Mississippi.

August 31, 1843
Henry Jennings, aged 30 years, of Louisiana, died of bilious fever.

September 5, 1843
Married in Raymond, on the 28th ult., at the residence of Jon. L. Stubblefield, Esq., by Hon. H. G. Johnston, Mr. Marsden Hogers to Miss Charlotte R. Barnett.

September 7, 1843
Died on the 29th August, Allice Colley, daughter of Thornton P. and Elizabeth M. Hickey, aged 10 months.

September 16, 1843
Married August 31, by the Rev. Thornton A. Mills, Prof. C. C. Forshey, of Concordia, La., to Miss Martha Williams, daughter of the late Jacob Williams, of Cincinnati, Ohio.

September 19, 1843
Sexton's report ending week of September 16:
Thomas Evans, 29 years, consumption.
John Fea, 30 years.
Infant of Eli Williams, 1 year.
Mathew Barnes, 29 years, typhus fever.

September 28, 1843
Married the 26th, by Richards Barnett, Esq., Mr. Henry McFarland, printer, to Miss Julina Mary, both of this place.

October 3, 1843
Sexton's report ending week of Sept. 30:
John Robinson, 47 years, mania Potu.

October 10, 1843
Sexton's report ending week of Oct. 7:
John Simpson, 29 years, yellow fever.
Patrick Dillon, yellow fever.
E. D. Conklin, 30 years, yellow fever.
Nicholas Duniger, 18 years, yellow fever.
Malinda Freeborn, 18 years, yellow fever.
James Laffy, 40 years, yellow fever.
Elenor Godfrey, 23 years, yellow fever.
Christian Hagan, 23 years, yellow fever.
Hugh Murphy, 40 years, yellow fever.
Thomas C. Johnson, 38 years, congestive fever.
Mary Ann Rose, 27 years, yellow fever.
Virginia Rowlett, 23 years, yellow fever.

October 12, 1843
Married on the 10th, by the Rev. S. Montgomery, Samuel Templeton, Esq., of Warren county, to Miss Martha E., daughter of General James W. Wyley, of Madison county, Miss.

Died at Woodland, the residence of J. Philip Stuart, Warren county, on the 5th October, Elizabeth Yates Stuart, eldest child of John Philip and Mary Eleanor Stuart, aged 10 years, 1 month and 22 days.

October 24, 1843
Died at Lake Bolivar, Miss., on the 18th, William H. Clarke, a native of Virginia, aged about 23 or 25 years.

Sexton's report ending week of Oct. 21:
Lucy Fox, 78 years, cancer.
Samuel Stites, 22 years, yellow fever.
J. B. Price, 22 years, yellow fever.
Neal McCurry, 31 years, yellow fever.
Elizabeth Goodin, 15 years, yellow fever.
Hugh Watt, 29 years, yellow fever.

Dr. King, 31 years, yellow fever.
David Shockney, 58 years, yellow fever.
T. O'Hara, 40 years, yellow fever.
Samuel Spohn, 33 years, yellow fever.
Barney Caradine, 45 years, swamp fever, of La.
Conrad H. Fry, 35 years, yellow fever.
Thomas McDermont, 40 years, yellow fever.

October 27, 1843
Married on 26th, by the Rev. Mr. Boyd, Mr. A. Genella to Miss Louisa Harris, both of this city.

October 30, 1843
Married at Milliken's Bend, parish of Madison, La., on the 10th, Dr. Thomas M. Jackson to Miss Ann E., eldest daughter of Mr. H. P. Moraney, both of the above named place.

October 31, 1843
Sexton's report ending week of Oct. 28:
John V. Craser, 35 years.
William Gray, 38 years, yellow fever.
Elizabeth Cravett, 8 days.
L. W. Whitington, 3 years, yellow fever.
Lucinda Brown, 14 years, yellow fever.
Wm. Pollack, 25 years, yellow fever.
Wm. N. Wood, 38 years, bilious remittent fever.

November 7, 1843
Sexton's report ending week of Nov. 4:
Daniel Lynch, 40 years, yellow fever.
Patrick Corader, 32 years, yellow fever.
William Stevett, 40 years, yellow fever.
William Stlening, 24 years, phthisic.
William Baker, 26 years, yellow fever.
Margaret Daffe, 19 years, of Ireland.
J. W. Robinson, 25 years, yellow fever.
Infant of E. Godfrey, 6 months.
George Penn, 35 years, yellow fever.
Thomas Levy, 38 years.
Frederick Folman, of steamboat *Scott*.
Susan Till, 63 years.
Nancy Blunt, 28 years.

November 9, 1843
Died at his residence in this county, on the 28th, Admiral N. Warren, a native of the state of New York, aged 35 years. He left a widow and an infant son.

Died at his residence in this county, E. D. Walcott, aged 50 years. He left a wife and family of children.

Married on the 5th, by the Rev. F. W. Boyd, Rector of Christ Church, at the residence of Mr. James Allen, Charles B. Babcock, of this city, to Anna Frances Allen, of Newark, N. J.

November 10, 1843

Died at Mechanicsburg, Yazoo County, Miss., of typhus fever, on the 30th October, Craven Dickey, a native of North Carolina.

November 11, 1843

Married at Raymond, Miss., on the 9th, by the Rev. Thomas Ford, Mr. C. G. Kercheval, merchant of this city, to Miss Catharine, daughter of Col. W. C. Demoss, of Raymond.

November 13, 1843

Died at the residence of Richard Edwards, in Warren county, Miss., on the 22d Oct. last, of an affection of the heart, Richard Nesbit. He formerly lived in Philadelphia, but had been a resident of Mississippi for the last 10 or 12 years.

Died at his residence in Warren county, on the 8th, Mr. Thos. Thornley, formerly of Maysville, Ky., aged 40 years.

November 14, 1843

Sexton's report ending week of Nov. 11:
John Weeks, 25 years, of New Orleans, yellow fever.
John Dennis, 29 years.
Thos. Condur, 35 years.
Francis Maguir, 37 years.
John Welsh, 38 years, drowned.
Wm. Whittington, 18 years, gastis entertis.

November 21, 1843

Sexton's report ending week of Nov. 18:
Thos. Plumb, 28 years, intemperance.
Infant of N. Duffy, 18 months.
Thos. Gillum, 23 years, pleurisy, from Arkansas.

December 9, 1843

Married on Thursday evening last, by the Rev. Chapman, Mr. Stephen R. Melvin, of this city, to Miss Mary James, of Pittsburg, Pa.

We announce the death of Mr. James McCutchen, who died at his residence in Washington Co., Miss., on the 27th November. Mr. McCutchen was a native of Ky. He was in the 44th year of his age.

December 11, 1843

Married in Warren county, on the 9th, by the Rev. Mr. Grey, William Biggs, Esq., of the firm of Watts and Biggs, of New Orleans, to Miss Susan A. Flowers.

Departed this life at her residence in Madison Parish, La., on 16th ult., of congestive fever, Mrs. S. Wilkinson, aged 71 years. Mrs. W. had been a resident of our parish for some 50 years. (*Richmond, La. Compiler*).

December 16, 1843
Sexton's report ending week of December 9:
Ephraim Hathaway, 22 years, of Ohio, bilious fever.
Elizabeth B. Sparke, 29 years.

December 18, 1843
Died at St. Helena, 24th Sept., on his homeward passage, Mr. William McMurtrie.

December 20, 1843
Married on the 16th Nov., by the Rev. H. Caldwell, F. H. Robertson, of Clinton, Miss., to Miss Mary Leonora Sadler, of York District, South Carolina, daughter of Ethelwin Sadler, Esq., late of the former place.

January 8, 1843
Married at Oakland, near Natchez, Jan. 4th, by the Rev. Dr. Page, the Rev. Frederick W. Boyd, Rector of Christ Church, Vicksburg, to Miss Mary Eliza Railey, daughter of James Railey, Esq., of Oaklama.

January 22, 1843
Died at Ashland, Washington, Miss., on the 11th day of December last, Benjamin F. Wood, in the 26th year of his age.

January 29, 1844
Married on the 17th, in this city, Mr. Samuel Kaufman, of Madison parish, La., to Miss Fanny Lorch, of Vicksburg.

February 5, 1844
Died in the city of Vicksburg, on Wednesday last, at the age of seven, the third son (namesake) of Sumner Lincoln Fairfield, the Poet.

February 12, 1844
Died in this city, on the 3d, Mrs. Henrietta Barnes, consort of Francis Barnes, of New Orleans, aged 53 years.

Married on the 8th, at Mount Holly, Warren County, by the Rev. James A. Fox, Dr. R. B. Scott to Miss L. I. Walcott, all of this co.

Married on the 1st, by the Rev. James E. Matthews, Mr. Micajah Picket, of Yazoo county, to Jane Eliza Clark, daughter of Gen. Wm. Clark, of Jackson.

Married in Genevis, Vermont, Mr. J. M. Bee to Miss Martha Ann Flower.

February 19, 1844
Died at Rodney, Miss., Feb. 7th, 1844, Mr. Jeremiah Dutch, a stranger

from a steamboat. He seemed to be about 50 years of age, and said he was the son of a minister, formerly settled in New Bedford, Mass., and that he had a brother in Indiana named Ebenezer.

February 26, 1844
Married on the 22d, by the Rev. Mr. Payne, Mr. Henry Geisker to Miss Delia L. Newman, all of this city.

March 11, 1844
Died on the 4th, at the residence of Andrew Knox, Esq., on Lake Washington, Miss., James Kelly, of diarrhea. Mr. Kelly, we believe, was a native of Cincinnati, but had resided in the south several years.

April 1, 1844
Married in Hinds county, on the 17th March, the Rev. Thos. Hassel to Mrs. Liebe, aged 86 and 76 years.

April 15, 1844
Married the 3d by the Rev. N. N. Wood, Mr. James Carter Chappell, to Miss Amanda E. Taylor, both of this city.

Departed this life on the 1st, Miss Josephine, daughter of Mrs. Rachael Alexander, in the 11th year of her age.

April 22, 1844
Married the 21st, by the Rev. George W. Powell, Mr. Wm. Hogan, of this county, to Miss Isabella Baird, of Hinds County.

Died on the 17th, at the house of the Hon. M. C. Folkes, Dr. Thomas M. Seay. Mr. S. was born and raised at Stony Point, in Cumberland county, Va., in the vicinity of which his parents, brothers and sisters still reside. He has fallen a victim to consumption.

Sexton's report ending week of April 20:
S. W. Vannatta, 45 years, pneumonia.
John Ward, 30 years, fever.
Thos. M. Seay, 27 years, consumption.

April 29, 1844
Sexton's report ending week of April 27:
C. B. Breedlove, 22 years, consumption.
John Perkins, 28 years, inflammation of liver and spleen.
Jno. Bockley, 38 years, inflammation of bowels.

May 6, 1844
Sexton's report ending week of May 4:
Joel Paul, 50 years, consumption.
George Thompson, 27 years, deleriun tremens.
James Kenedy, 37 years, bilious pneumonia.

May 13, 1844

Married the 9th, by the Rev. W. C. Payne, Mr. Alexander Legrand to Miss Margaret Ann Batts, both of this city.

Married May 5th, by John Townsend, Esq., Mr. Thomas Kidd to Mrs. Sarah Bolls, all of Warren county.

Sexton's report ending week of May 11:
Dr. J. F. Macklin, 36 years, pistol shot wound.
Nicholas Howlett, 25 years, typhus fever.

Married on the 14th, by the Rev. W. H. Taylor, Mr. Benjamin W. Powell to Miss Olivia Whatley, all of Warren county.

Departed this life on the 4th, at Vicksburg, Mrs. Eliza Hall, consort of Capt. James A. Hall, natives of Virginia, but for the last 14 years citizens of this county, aged 51 years, 9 months and 13 days.

May 27, 1844

Died on the 17th, near Clinton, Miss., of disease of the heart, General Cowles Mead. He was born in Bedford county, Virginia the 18th of October, 1776. In 1806 he came to Mississippi as Secretary of the Territory, under the appointment of Mr. Jefferson.

Sexton's report for 2 weeks ending May 25th:
Margaret Fleming, 51 years, hepititus.
David Hinkston, 47 years, bilious fever.
Barney McMannus, 42 years, consumption.
Infant of J. R. Creasy, 12 months.
Infant of Patrick Kelly, 5 weeks.
Alexander Fronaghu, 26 years, caxalgia.
Robert McMullen, 35 years, mania potu.

June 2, 1844

Married at the residence of H. J. Shackelford, Esq., in this city, on the 25th, by Rev. N. N. Wood, Charles B. Buck, Esq., of Hopkinsville, Ky., to Mrs. Mary E. Davenport, of this city.

June 10, 1844

Married in this city, on the 4th, by the Rev. N. N. Wood, Mr. R. B. Robb to Miss Louisa H. Moss.

Died in this city, on the 28th May, 1844, at the residence of her brother, F. H. Rowe, Mrs. Mary Ann Eaton, wife of the late C. H. Eaton.

Died yesterday morning, J. W. Hitch. Mr. Hitch was formerly of Maryland, but for several years past has been a merchant in this city. He left a wife and one child.

June 17, 1844

Sexton's report for 2 weeks ending June 15:

William Street, 27 years, typhus fever.
Morris Aherns, 32 years.
J. W. Hitch, 45 years, congestion of bowels.
Patrick Donahoe, 30 years, congestion.
Michael McCrath, 40 years, congestive fever.
Elizabeth Blackwell, 52 years.
James Green, 49 years, congestion.

June 24, 1844
Sexton's report ending week of June 22:
Jane Exley, 25 years, inflammation.
Hannah McIntire, 52 years, chronic gastrointentis.

Died very suddenly at his residence in this co., of congestive fever, on the 17th, Mr. John Cowan, in the 53d year of his age. Mr. Cowan was a native of Sevier County, Tenn., and emigrated to this state.

July 1, 1844
Married on the 27th, by the Rev. N. W. Boyd, at the residence of Capt. Lawrence Washington Stith, near Vicksburg, Mr. Philip Finn, merchant, of Alabama, to Miss Harriet Eugenia Thompson, only daughter of Mr. Jacint Laval, of Charleston, South Carolina.

Died, Mr. Michael McDonald, aged 30, of Vicksburg.

July 8, 1844
Died on the 4th, Selia C., youngest daughter of Dr. E. S. and Lavinia Billings, aged 1 year and 2 months.

July 15, 1844
Married at the residence of Col. Wells, on Deer Creek, Washington Co., on the 10th, by Rev. N. N. Wood, of this city, William Myers to Henrietta F. A. Wells, daughter of Col. Wells, both of Deer Creek.

Sexton's report ending week of July 13:
John Croney, aged 30 years, residence Vicksburg.
Wm. Jay, aged 25, bilious fever.
Leila C. Billings, aged 14 months, dropsy of the brain.
Walter Whelaghan, aged 35 years, residence Hinds co., Miss.
Mrs. O'Conner, aged 28 years.
Wm. Johnson, aged 29 years, convulsions.
David Lehman, aged 34 years.
Charles E. Harrison, aged 40 years, delerium tremens.
Thos. Roberts, aged 28 years, fever.
Chas. W. Shuler, aged 21 months, convulsions.
Mrs. Emily M. Martin, aged 40 years, congestive fever.
Caroline Canepa, aged 2 years, congestive fever.

July 22, 1844
Married on the 18th, by John Townsend, Esq., Mr. Gray W. Tucker to Miss Sarah Hawkins, both of this county.

July 29, 1844
Married at the Prentiss House, in this city, on the 21st, by Rev. N. N. Wood, Elijah W. Nance to Miss Lucy Ann Ruby, both of Yazoo City.

Sexton's report ending week of July 20:
Mr. Warren, 38 years.
Richard C. Smith, 25 years, congestive fever.
John R. Armstrong, 15 years, congestive fever.
Margaret Messrshmint, 40 years, congestive fever.

August 5, 1844
Married the 21st July, by the Rev. Thos. Dunn, Doct. John L. Finley, of Providence, La., to Miss Ann B. Pelham, of Batchelors Bend.

Sexton's report ending week of July 27:
Mrs. Frances Edwards, 48 years, dropsy of the brain.
Mr. Johnson, 38 years, consumption.
John Toget, 40 years, swamp fever.
B. H. Cohen, 34, years, congestive fever.
John Clarke, 31 years, congestion of the brain.
John McAvoy, 26 years, fever.
John Turner, 38 years, killed by stabbing.
William Black, 42 years, general debility.
Thomas McMillin, 35 years, dropsy.
Mr. Lovett, 37 years, affection of the leg.
Thomas Donahoe, 39 years, drinking.

August 12, 1844
Sexton's report ending week of Aug. 3:
Mary Ames, 33 years, Vicksburg.
Margaretta M. Day, 9 years, congestive fever.
William Ellis, 23 years, bilious fever.
Bridget Malady, 21 years, bilious fever.

August 26, 1844
Died at the residence of his father, on the 19th, William Townsend, in the 21st year of his age. He left parents, brothers & sisters.

Died on yesterday eve., Caroline, daughter of F. and M. Steigelman.

September 9, 1844
Sexton's report ending week of August 31:
Child of J. A. Lane, aged 5 years, congestive fever.
Daughter of Mrs. Saun, aged 5 years, fever.
Ann Bisban, aged 23 years.
Thomas Goggins, aged 32 years, congestive fever.

September 16, 1844
Sexton's report for 2 weeks ending September 14:
Benjamin Cockrel, 42 years.

Mrs. Sisson, 41 years.
Isaac Pickering, 45 years, congestive fever.
Mrs. E. P. Mosbey, 32 years, dropsy of chest.
E. T. Wagstaff, 27 years, chronic diarrhea.
Mrs. Beagly, 28 years, suicide.

September 23, 1844
Married on 22d, at Laurel Hill, by the Rev. Newton, Thomas W. Tompkins, Esq., of Warrenton, to Catherine Jane McArthur, daughter of Mrs. Sarah McArthur, of Warren County, Miss.

Died, Mrs. Vogle, resident of Vicksburg, of suicide (2 children infanticide).

Mrs. Ann Lynd, aged 65 years, resident of Warren Co., died of fever.

September 30, 1844
Sexton's report ending week of September 28:
Child of Mr. Sulivan, 3 years old.
John Bailey, 35 years, general debility.
Mrs. I. E. Maclin, of Vicksburg.
Child of S. B. Thrift, 5 years.
Child of J. Horsley, 10 days.
Peter Marsh.

October 7, 1844
Sexton's report ending week of Oct. 5:
Infant of J. Butler, 14 months.
Joseph Campbell, 34 years, congestive fever.
John Ulrick, 61 years, a resident of New York, bilious fever.

October 14, 1844
Sexton's report ending week of Oct. 12:
Mrs. Summers, 30 years.
Margeret Slaughter, 25 years, congestive fever.
Thomas Muldon, 33 years, bilious fever.
John O'Neill, 32 years, general debility.

A few months since we witnessed the death of Doct. James F. Maclin, of this city. It now becomes our painful task to record the death of his wife, Mrs. Imogene E. Maclin. She was a member of the Episcopal Church and died at her residence, Vicksburg, Miss., Sept. 24th, 1844. She has left an orphan boy.

October 21, 1844
Sexton's report ending week of Oct. 19:
Miss Hannah E. Killgore, 17 years, congestion of the brain.
John Linden, 38 years, swamp fever.

November 4, 1844
Died on the 24th ult., at the residence of his father, Major Walker, of

this county, Henry F. Walker, aged 30 years, of consumption.

November 18, 1844
Married on the evening of the 13th, by S. B. Harwood, Esq., Mr. Jacob Sartorius to Miss Magdalena Ross, all of this city.

Died in Wilksboro, Illinois, Mrs. Minerva R., wife of J. C. Bond, aged 28 years and 1 month.

Sexton's report ending week of Nov. 9:
E. R. Warren, 38 years.
William Corder, 30 years, consumption.
Rosina Fitzgerald, 28 years, child bed fever.
Martha R. Goodrum, 21 years, bilious fever.
George Meredeth, 23 years.
G. C. Williams, 30 years, hemorrhage of lungs.
Austin Brown, 21 years, consumption.
William Adams, 47 years, chronic diarrhea.

December 23, 1844
Sexton's report ending week of Dec. 21:
John T. Clark, 40 years, dropsy.
Patrick Guinan, 38 years, general debility.
Infant of Mr. Freckman, 2 years.

December 30, 1844
Married near Murfresboro, Tenn., by the Rev. John Lane, on the 29th of October last, Mr. Edward Yager, of Vicksburg, Miss., to Mrs. Mary Ann Green, of Rutherford county.

Departed this life at Biloxi, Hancock county, Miss., on the 21st of December, 1844, Mrs. Mary B. Creath, wife of Albert G. Creath, Esq., of Warren county, Miss., aged 34 years.

James Brown, aged 30 years, a resident of Vicksburg, died of pleurisy.

January 3, 1845
Died Dec. 28, at her residence in Madison county, Mrs. Lanier, formerly from S. Carolina.

January 4, 1845
On Sat. last our court house was the scene of a most appalling case of bloodshed. Dr. Wm. R. Ball, citizen of Barbour Co., Ala., received into his custody, from Danl. Thomas, Esq., Sherriff of this co., Jeremiah B. Granberry, who was indicted of grand larceny. Ball and Granberry left the sheriff's office and about 6 feet from the front door of the courthouse Granberry presented a pistol and discharged it's contents into Ball's stomach. Ball instantly fell, and in a few minuted was dead. Granberry attempted escape, but a son of Ball pursued him. Granberry was confined to jail. On Sun. morning the remains of Mr. Ball were buried with distinguished honors by our citizens.

January 7, 1845
Sexton's report ending week of Jan. 4:
Milly Dunn, 20 years, consumption.

January 8, 1845
Died at his residence, on Bayou Macon, Madison parish, La., the 16th, Thomas Jefferson Gilbert, Esq., of erysipelas, aged 36 years.

January 13, 1845
Died on the 26th ult., at the residence of his father, Lewis Stowers, Esq., in Claiborne County, Miss., Mr. John Stowers, aged 22 years.

January 14, 1845
Sexton's report ending week of Jan. 11:
Dennis Murphy, 35 years, Germany.
R. M. Mudd, 11 years, accidentally shot.

January 21, 1845
Died of chronic hepetitis, on the 13th, Mr. Jesse S. Bonney, aged 34 years, for the last 13 years a citizen of Yazoo County, Miss.

January 23, 1845
Married January 7, 1845, by Samuel B. Harwood, Esq., Henry Lee to Amanda Thomas, all of this city.

January 24, 1845
Married on the 23d, by Samuel B. Harwood, Esq., Mr. Peter Price to Mrs. Martha Stout, all of Warren county.

January 27, 1845
Sextons report:
Jan. 19 – Mary Naghton, 36 years, ruptured blood vessel.
Jan. 19 – T. N. Powell, 27 years, congestion of brain.
Jan. 21 – Houghton Riley, 30 years, inflammation of bowels.
Jan. 24 – Owen Scannell, 45 years, chronic diarrhea.

Married on the 11th, at Warrenton, by Samuel Edwards, Esq., member Board of Police, Mr. Kemp Hurst to Miss Sarah Ann Henderson, all of that place.

January 31, 1845
Married January 28th, 1845, by S. B. Harwood, Esq., Mr. Anthony Kessenger to Mrs. Elizabeth Hurst, all of this city.

February 4, 1845
Married at Macon, Miss., on the 22d ult., by the Rev. D. McNair, Mr. Edmund W. Ferris to Miss Ann M. Marschalk.

February 10, 1845
Patrick Carroll, 28 years of age, died of pneumonia, on the 6th Feb.

February 13, 1845
Married on Tuesday evening, at the residence of Mr. B. F. Hastings, by the Rev. N. N. Wood, Henry T. Moore, Esq., to Miss Emma J. Baker, all of this city.

February 18, 1845
Died on the 16th, John, son of G. W. and M. J. Summers, aged 2 years and 3 months.

February 19, 1845
Married in Cincinnati, on the 27th January last, by the Rev. Mr. Wilson, Mr. James Crooks, of Vicksburg, to Miss Pauline Drayton, of the former place.

February 20, 1845
Bill of Divorce -- Elizabeth B. Goodman -vs- Thomas J. Goodman.

February 25, 1845
Sexton's report ending week of February 22:
John Wisse, 34 years, mania a potu.
Timothy Devine, 33 years, mania a potu.
Infant of W. Porterfield, congestive fever.
Francis Blise, slave, 5 months, disease of lungs.

February 28, 1845
Married at the residence of Mr. Daniel Hillderbrand, in Warren County, on the 13th Feb., by Samuel Edwards, Esq., Mr. Thomas D. Elliott to Miss Nancy Burnham, all of said county.

March 1, 1845
Married on the 25th, by the Rev. A. W. Chapman, Mr. Eugene Newman to Miss Eliza Mitchell, both of this city.

March 3, 1845
Died Feb. 28th, Elizabeth McCarter, aged 24 years, of entreitis, a resident of Hinds county.

March 5, 1845
Bill of Divorce Phineas Gardner -vs- Eliza Jane Gardner.

Married Feb. 28, by the Rev. N. N. Wood, Mr. Solomon Zimmerman to Miss Hannah J. Biggs.

Married by the same, on Sunday evening, Mr. David M. Fisher, to Mrs. Eliza Jones, all of this city.

March 7, 1845
Departed this life on the 5th, at the residence of Henry W. Vick, Esq., in this city, Hobert, eldest son of H. C. Stanard, Esq., of Richmond, Virginia, in the 7th year of his age.

March 8, 1845
Married at the Catholic Church, in this city, on Tuesday evening last, Mr. John Pries to Mrs. Elizabeth Fend, both of this city.

March 18, 1845
Married in Holmes county, on the 22d ult., by the Rev. Joshua Russell, Rev. Daniel L. Russell to Mrs. Sarah Blunt, both of that county.

Died at Columbus, Miss., on the 24th ult., E. F. Calhoun, in the 35th year of his age.

March 19, 1845
Married on the 12th, by the Rev. John Lane, Mr. William J. Cowan to Miss Susan Spann, all of Warren county.

Married in Port Gibson, on the 27th ult., by the Rev. Z. Butler, Rev. Peter Winn to Miss Margaret M. McComb, all of that place.

March 28, 1845
Died of consumption, on the 30th of January last, at the residence of Dr. R. B. Jones, in Marengo county, Alabama, in the 30th year of his age, Dr. R. W. Harper, late a citizen of this place.

Died near Madisonville, on Saturday last, James Williams.

Died in this place, on the 3d, Russell M. Williamson, Esq., of Mississippi, and formerly a resident of this county, aged about 40. (*Columbia Observer*)

March 29, 1845
Died yesterday, Thomas W. Bancks. The deceased came to this country about 8 or 10 years since from England.

March 31, 1845
Married on the 27th, by Rev. M. D. O'Reilly, Jarret R. Cook, Esq., to Miss Minerva M. L. Hines, daughter of Mr. John Hines, all of this co.

April 1, 1845
Married on the 27th day of March, by Judge Springer, Mr. Geo. W. Kendall to Miss Eliza Jane Abbott, late of this county.

Sexton's report:
March 23 - Felix Carroll, 41 years, dropsy.
March 24 - Jane Ford, Missouri.
March 24 - Hugh Memarian, 25 years, intemperance.
March 28 - T. W. Bancks, 30 years, enlargement of the heart.
March 29 - Infant of A. P. McMillan.

April 3, 1845
Married on 26th ult., by the Rev. S. M. Montgomery, Capt. H. B. Balce

to Mrs. A. B. W. Christian, both of this city.

Married on the 1st, by the Rev. L. Wiley, Rev. E. E. Byron, of New Orleans, to Miss Frances E., daughter of B. M. Hines, Esq., of Bolivar County, Miss.

April 8, 1845

Married on the 13th, Mr. James M. Batchelor to Miss Ann Eliza, daughter of the late Dr. Nutt, all of Jefferson county.

April 19, 1845

Died on the 16th, Ellen Bruner, daughter of Wm. F. and Rosanna Bruner, aged about 7 years.

Died on the 16th, Margaret Virginia, daughter of Wm. H. Paxton.

Died on the 13th, at the plantation of A. G. Creath, on the Yazoo river, A. M. Pinckard.

April 22, 1845

Married on the 10th, by Rev. B. H. Williams, John M. Caleb, of Adams Co., to Indiana, daughter of John Booth, Esq., of Claiborne.

On Saturday last, Dr. Wm. B. Smith, near Milldale, in this county, departed this life.

John Cullingsworth, long a resident of this city, died on Sunday last.

Died on Saturday last, Osman Craddick Hall, eldest son of J. J. and Ann J. Hall, of this city, in the 7th year of his age.

We notice in the *Advertiser*, the deaths of two citizens of Holmes county, Mr. Richard Sproles and Mr. Pollard H. Cotts.

Died near Nashville, on the 7th, Mrs. Minerva C. Stephens, relict of the late Rev. Abednego Stephens, and daughter of W. P. Lawrence, Esq., of that city.

Died on the 31st March, at his residence in Panola county, Miss., in the 30th year of his age, Col. Francis M. Oliver, leaving a wife and two children.

Sexton's report:
Apr. 13 - Susan McElroy, 5 years, congestion of lungs.
Apr. 13 - Mrs. Hammet, congestion of lungs.
Apr. 14 - William Pate, 24 years, congestion of lungs.
Apr. 16 - Margaret V. Paxton, 8 months, scarlet fever.
Apr. 16 - Ellen S. Bruner, 7 years, scarlet fever.
Apr. 18 - Mary A. C. Herring, 8 years, scar)et fever.
Apr. 19 - Osman C. Hall, 7 years.

April 26, 1845
Died at Natchez, on board the steamboat *Concordia*, on the 24th, Mr. John B. Aiken, of the firm of Aiken, Gwinn & Co., of this city.

Departed this life the 19th day of April, at his residence in this county, of malignant erysipelas, in the 36th year of his age, Dr. William H. Smith, a native of Brunswick county, Va., and for the last ten years a resident of this county.

April 29, 1845
Married at residence of Mr. Daniel Hilderbrand, on the 23d, in Warren Co., by Samuel Edwards, Mr. William Fallis to Miss Susan Burham.

Died on the night of the 27th, Mary Gwendeline, only child of John and Mary Angelica Connelly, aged 13 months.

Died in Nashville, on the 15th, Mr. John A. McNairy, in the 35th year of his age.

William Eggleston died at his residence in Holmes Co., on the 17th.

May 2, 1845
Departed this life at Vicksburg, Miss., April 15th, Margaret Virginia, daughter of W. H. Paxton, Esq., aged 9 months & 2 days.

Also at Vicksburg, Miss., April 30th, 1845, Eudora Anderson, daughter of Alexander M. Paxton, Esq., aged 3 years and 7 months.

May 6, 1845
Died in this city on Sunday evening last, of scarlet fever, Bertha, eldest daughter of Dr. Morris and Agatha A. M. Emanuel, aged 6 years, 10 months and 3 days.

Married 5th May, 1845, by the Rev. F. W. Boyd, Professor J. C. Passmore, of St. James College, Maryland, to Miss Susan B. Weller, of this city, eldest daughter of the late Geo. Weller.

May 8, 1845
Sexton's report:
May 2 - Hobert McHeynolds, 35 years, congestion of lungs.
May 3 - J. S. Gibbs, 30 years, chronic diarrhea, Little Rock, Ark.
May 3 - Phoebe A. Stites, 2 months, whooping cough.

May 13, 1845
Died on the 11th, at the residence of her parents, in this city, of scarlet fever, Edith Brown, youngest daughter of Dr. Morris and Mrs. Agatha A. M. Emanuel, aged 1 year, 6 months and 5 days.

May 15, 1845
Died of scarlet fever, on Monday last, Eliza Lee, infant daughter of A. L. and Eliza M. Yeiser.

Married at the residence of W. H. Slaughter, in Madison county, on the 13th, Mr. C. C. Davidson to Mrs. Elizabeth H. Dinkins.

Married in this city, on the 17th, by the Rev. Jos. B. Stratton, Mr. Lawren Palmer, of New Orleans, to Miss Maria Louisa Mintzer, late of Vicksburg, Miss.

May 27, 1845

Died on the 24th, of cholera infantum, Elizabeth, daughter of Richard Edwards, Esq., aged 13 months.

May 29, 1845

Married on the 16th, at Chilicothe, Hon. Wm. Allen to Mrs. Effie Coons, daughter of the late Gov. McArthur.

Died in this city, 2 of May, Mary Catharine, daughter of Joseph and Lucinda Genella, aged 2 years.

June 3, 1845

Married in this city, on the 29th ult., by the Rev. F. W. Boyd, Mr. Robert H. Randolph to Mrs. Harriet F. Scott.

Died near Gallatin, Miss., on the 27th ult., Gen. Wiley P. Harris.

Died in Columbus, Miss., on the 24th ult., James M. Weissenger, in the 29th year of his age.

Sexton's report:
May 27 - Mary C. Genella, 2 years, whooping cough.
May 28 - Martha Hicks, 10 months, scarlet fever.
May 29 - John Caney, 35 years, consumption.
May 30 - Thomas Connell, 30 years, inflammation of bowels.

June 5, 1845

Married in this city, on the 3d, by Rev. C. K. Marshall, at the residence of Mr. S. H. Borman, Mr. James Bain, of Claiborne county, to Mrs. Rachael Alexander, of this city.

Died on the 30th of May, Thomas Waitis, infant son of Dr. Wm. R. and Martha S. Ray, of this city.

Died on yesterday, Virginia Rowlett, infant daughter of William and Indiana H. McRay, of this city.

June 10, 1847

Died on the 20th ult., at the residence of J. G. Bell, on Bayou Tensas, La., Mr. D. B. Cox, a native of Richmond, Indiana, in the 28th year of his age.

Died on the 8th, on his plantation in Madison parish, La., Col. W. C. Demoss, a citizen of Hinds county, Miss.

June 12, 1845

Died in Grenada, June 4th, Mrs. Elizabeth R. McRae, wife of John H. McRae, of N. Orleans (whilst on a visit to friends), of a severe attack of fever.

June 17, 1845

Died in this county, on the 10th, Mr. Archibald Cameron, in the 78th year of his age. Mr. Cameron was a native of this county.

Died in this county, on the 31st ult., Mr. John W. Miller, of consumption. Mr. Miller had long been a citizen of this county.

Died on the 29th ult., at the Jefferson House, in this city, James Calloway, who came a passenger from Natchez, on the steamer *Belle of the West*.

Died on the 30th of May, at the residence of his son-in-law, Dr. J. J. Pennington, Princeton, Indiana, the Rev. Nicholan Snethen, of the Methodist Protestant Church, aged 76 years.

Departed this life at his residence in this county, on the 4th of June, Algernon S. Duvall, a native of Frederick Co., Maryland.

June 19, 1845

Sexton's report:
June 9 - Samuel W. Hannah, 17 months, measles.
June 11 - T. W. Hunter, 40 years, eresypelas.

June 21, 1845

Married on 17th, at Clinton, by the Rev. A. Newton, Mr. J. C. Lanier to Miss Mary J. McRaven, all of Hinds county.

Married on the 18th, at the residence of Dr. Wm. L. Balfour, in Mudlunn County, by the Rev. D. R. Cambell, Dr. H. Goldin Blackman to Miss Mary Jane Balfour.

Died at Warrenton, on the 10th, Dr. Ezra Green, a native of Maine, aged about 34 years.

Died on the 8th, at his residence in Jefferson county, Col. Jas. G. Wood, a native of Maryland, in the 75th year of his age.

June 24, 1845

Married on the 22d, by the Rev. M. D. O'Reilly, Dr. Edward A. Pye, to Miss Matilda C. Legrand, all of Madison parish, La.

Sexton's report ending week of June 21:
Eliza M. Mygatt, 37 years, spasmodic affection.

Theodore M. Russell, 4 years, scarlet fever.
Cora Dameron, 7 years, congestion of the lungs.

July 1, 1845

Died in Cincinnati, on the 23d ult., Alden S. Merrifield, late one of the Propriators of the *New Orleans Tropic*.

July 3, 1845

Died in Franklin, Holmes county, on the 24th ult., Thomas W. Dulaney, Esq., aged about 30 years.

July 17, 1845

Married on the 13th, by Judge Springer, Mr. William Kirk to Mrs. Mary Monroe, all of this county.

Died in Raymond, on the 9th, Mrs. Mary F. Peyton, consort of Maj. John B. Peyton.

Sexton's report:
July 6 - A. Dent, 23 years, congestion of the brain.
July 7 - Joanna Vetter, 35 years, dropsy.
July 9 - G. R. Diamond, 6 months, convulsions.
July 10 - M. Rogers, 4 years, convulsions.

July 29, 1845

Sexton's report:
July 20 - James Goulding, aged 35 years, drowned.
July 23 - Thomas McCormick, 38 years, apoplexy.

August 7, 1845

Died August 6th, Leonora, daughter of Jacob and Margaret Vogh, aged about 2 years.

Died August 6th, Julia Ann, daughter of Thos. J. and Mary A. Randolph, aged about 7 years.

August 12, 1845

Married on the 7th, by the Rev. Carter Jones, Mr. Vincent A. Wilkinson, of Yazoo, to Mrs. Julia Sevier, of Warren county,

August 19, 1845

Died at Raymond, on the 2d, Mr. Thomas Downing, in the 74th year of his age. He had been a resident of Mississippi since 1808.

August 28, 1845

Died August 22d, Dr. Dennis V. Falton, of consumption.

September 4, 1845

Married at Bellegrove, Frederick county, Va., by Bishop Meade, Isaac Hite Hay, Esq., of Vicksburg, to Miss Ann Maury, daughter of Dr. Cornelius Baldwin, of Frederick county.

Sexton's report:
Aug. 25 - Samuel M. Boyler, 34 years, chronic diarrhea, Yazoo Co.
Aug. 27 - J. W. Brown, 25 years, suicide.

September 6, 1845
Married 2d Sept., by the Rev. P. Cooper, Rev. Lysander Wiley, of the Mississippi Conference, to Miss Adeline A. Hammet, of Haymond.

The Macon, Miss., *Independent* says that John F. Reat, step-son of the Rev. Geo. Stovall, committed suicide by shooting himself through the heart, on the 18th ult.

September 9, 1845
Sexton's report:
Sept. 4 - Rebecca Mussentine, Yazoo Co., 90 years, consumption.
Sept. 5 - James Finley, aged 31 years, bilious fever.
Sept. 5 - M. Fisher, aged 17 years, congestive fever.

September 11, 1845
Died on yesterday, Thomas M. Coleman, son of Nicholas D. and Lucy A. Coleman, aged 7 years, 5 months and 21 days.

September 16, 1845
Married in Jefferson county, Miss., on the 2d, by Judge Duncan, Mr. Levi Dromgoole, of Madison county, to Miss Zenobia A. Rowlen.

Sexton's report:
Sept. 8 - Ann Wade, 40 years, chronic diarrhea.
Sept. 9 - Robert Jackson, 36 years, chronic diarrhra.
Sept. 9 - Thomas M. Coleman, abscess of lungs.
Sept. 10 - Thomas Anderson, aged 33 years, consumption.
Sept. 10 - Mary Childress, 7 years, scarlet fever.

September 23, 1845
Married on 18th September, by Samuel Edwards, M. B. P., Mr. James Gardner to Miss Minerva Owen.

Died at the residence of P. Marble, in this county, on the 12th, Mrs. Matilda Townsend, consort of John Townsend, in the 45th year of her age. The deceased has left a husband and four children.

Died, James Huie, a citizen of New Orleans, and formerly of Salisbury, N. C., on the 12th.

Died on the 8th, near Richmond, La., Thomas B. Durham, a native of Virginia, aged about 30 years.

September 27, 1845
Married on the 25th, Mr. B. S. Hines, of Warren Co., Miss., formerly of Hancock Co., Georgia, to Levenia Hylander, of Warren Co., Miss.

Died at Panola Plantation, Washington county, Miss., Shalline, only daughter of J. S. and Mary Yerger, aged 1 year, 9 months and 16 days.

September 30, 1845

Died Sept. 24th, T. Burt, aged 35 years, a resident of Warren county, of consumption.

Died of consumption, at Chesterfield, La., September 25th, 1845, Mrs. Adaline Williams, aged 25 years.

October 2, 1845

Married in Madison county, on the 25th ult., Dr. Benjamin Land, of Grenada, to Miss Margaret E. Gage.

October 6, 1845

Sexton's report:
Oct. 3 – James Buckley, 22 years, black tongue.

October 15, 1845

Married on Satruday evening, by N. G. Bryson, Esq., Mr. John F. Ross to Mrs. Ann Armstrong, both of this city.

Died at his residence in this county, of pleurisy, on the 13th, Richard Edwards, Esq., for several years a citizen of this county, leaving a large family.

October 17, 1845

Married on 16th, by Samuel B. Harwood, Esq., Mr. James Bradshaw to Miss Nancy Mason, all of this county.

October 21, 1845

Married on the 16th, by S. B. Harwood, Esq., Mr. J. R. Smith to Mrs. Louisa Alexander, all of this place.

October 24, 1845

Married on the 7th, at the residence of Dr. Wm. Craig in Boyle county, Ky., Mr. John Wesley Vick, of Vicksburg, to Miss Catharine Ann Barbour, daughter of the late Maj. James Barbour, of Danville.

October 27, 1845

Died on the 24th of October, in the 24th year of her age, at the residence of her brother, Richards Barnett, Esq., Mrs. Catharine N. Hawks, consort of Joseph P. Hawks, Esq.

Died October 29, Wm. Chesnut, a resident of New York, aged 22 years, of inflammation of the stomach and bowels.

November 18, 1845

Married on the 13th, Mr. Wm. M. Been to Miss Eleanor A. Crawford, both of Warrenton, Miss.

Married the 17th, by Sam'l. B. Harwood, Esq., Mr. Saml. Goodwyn to Miss Lavinia Pigeon, both of this city.

Died Nov. 13th, Angus C. Chisholm, of La., of disease of the heart.

November 28, 1845

Married on the 25th, at the residence of H. I. Morancy, in Milliken's Bend, La., by the Rev. Mr. O'Reilly, Mr. James B. Kinkead, of Vicksburg, to Mrs. Martha A. Morancy, of the former place.

December 1, 1845

Married November 25, 1845, by Sam. B. Harwood, Esq., Mr. Pollard W. McCarty to Mrs. Matinda Watts, both of this city.

December 2, 1845

Sexton's report:
Nov. 23 - Harrison Rock, of Burlington, Iowa, accidental fall.
Nov. 24 - Mary G. White, puerpural-fever.

December 5, 1845

Married on 27th ult., at the residence of Aaron Wickliffe, Esq., of Washington county, by the Rev. John Lane, John W. King, Esq., of Coahoma county, to Miss Mary E. Wickliffe.

Married in Jackson, on the 25th ult., by the Rev. L. J. Halsey, Alexander Yerger, Esq., to Miss Elizabeth B., daughter of the Hon. Jas. Rucks.

December 9, 1845

Sexton's report:
Dec. 1 - Capt. Wm. Shrodes, of Louisville, Ky., killed by the explosion of a steamboat boiler.

December 17, 1845

Sexton's report:
Dec. 7 - T. E. Fox, 53 years, pneumonia.

December 19, 1845

Died at his residence in Warren county, on the 12th, Uriah Flowers, at the advanced age of 84 years.

December 20, 1845

Married on the 14th, by the Rev. S. M. Montgomery, George B. Clarke, Esq., of Louisiana, to Miss Frances A. Powers, of this city.

December 23, 1847

Married on the 18th, at Brownsville, Hinds county, by the Rev. N. R. Granberry, C. S. Spann, Esq., to Miss Henrietta W. Lanier.

December 24, 1845

Died on yesterday morning, at the residence of Mr. Thomas Shepard, Mrs. Honora Stewart, consort of Mr. J. E. Stewart, of this city.

Died on the morning of the 22d, Isabella Annette, infant daughter of William and Margaret Hay, of this city, aged 2 years.

December 25, 1845

Married Dec. 23d, 1845 by Samuel B. Harwood, Esq., Mr. B. Liverman to Miss Theresa Marks, formerly of Poland, but now of this city.

December 27, 1845

Married at Easton, Md., on the 10th, by Rev. H. M. Mason, D. D., Nathan G. Bryson, of this city, to Emma L., daughter of Jas. Parrott, Esq., of the former place.

Married in Natchez, at the Mansion House, on the 21st, by the Hon. J. S. B. Thatcher, Judge of the Supreme Court, Alfred F. Washburn, Esq., to Miss E. W. Maxwell, teacher in the Natchez Academy.

Died on the 26th, Amanda Vick, aged 4 years and 8 months, and Charles Newet, aged 2 years and 1 month, children of the Rev. C. K. and Amanda Marshall.

Died at the Grand Caillon, La., on the 26th Nov., 1845, Albert J. Quitman, brother of Gen. Quitman, of Adams county, Miss.

December 30, 1845

Sexton's report:
Dec. 22 - Isabella A. Hay, 20 months, scarlet fever.
Dec. 23 - Lehonora Stewart, 22 years, chronic inflammation of the stomach.
Dec. 25 - Owen O'Brien, 35 years, pneumonia.
Dec. 26 - E. R. Strickland, 28 years, consumption.

December 31, 1845

Married the 24th, by the Rev. J. M. Taylor, Mr. John S. Dickerson to Miss Mary Burroughs, both of this city.

January 6, 1846

Sexton's report:
Dec. 29 - Laura W. Hall, 9 years, scarlet fever.
Jan. 2 - Mary Melvin, 40 years, scarlet fever.
Jan. 2 - William Vincent, 32 years, consumption.
Jan. 3 - Elizabeth Mahoney, 30 years.

January 7, 1846

Married January 5, 1846, by Samuel B. Harwood, Esq., Mr. Hardin Nichols to Miss Nancy Stewart, all of this Place.

January 9, 1846
Married in Hinds county, on Thursday morning, by the Rev. N. N. Wood, Mr. O. O. Woodman, of this city, to Miss Caroline Thomas, daughter of Andrew Thomas, Esq., of Hinds county.

January 10, 1846
Died on the 2d, at Milliken's Bend, Caroline M., daughter of Mr. O. B. and Mrs. M. C. Cobb, aged 3 years, 11 months and 16 days.

January 17, 1846
Married on the 15th, by Samuel B. Harwood, Esq., Mr. Jacob Heirsch to Miss Elizabeth Werner, both of this city.

January 20, 1846
Sexton's report:
Jan. 11 - B. Coltrain, 36 years, chronic diarrhea.

January 21, 1846
Departed this life, January 17th, 1846, James W., only child of Samuel and Martha E. Templeton, at their residence in Warren county, Miss., aged 16 months.

Died Monday morning of pleurisy, at the house of Mr. W. J. Estes, of our city, Mr. William Davis, a planter in the lower part of Hinds county, Miss.

Died at their residence, on the 17th, Susan Halsey, only child of John B. and Sarah Ann Hughes, aged 2 years.

January 22, 1846
Married near Yeiser's Store, Hinds county, Miss., January 15, 1846, by the Hon. Amos R. Johnston, Mr. Oscar D. Johnston, of Hinds county, Miss., and late of Monroe county, Kentucky, to Miss Louisa U. W. Peyton, of Hinds county, and late of Maury county, Tennessee

January 27, 1846
Sexton's report:
Jan. 18 - John King, aged 31 years, bleeding at nose, Pennnylvania.
Jan. 20 - Thomas Harrington, aged 35 years, quinsy.
Jan. 21 - Joseph Carson, aged 30 years, convulsions, Alabama.

January 29, 1846
Married January 26th, near Clinton, Miss., by the Rev. Thomas Ford, Mr. Philip P. Werlein, of this city, to Miss Margaret Halsey, of Westhampton, L. I., New York.

January 30, 1846
Married the 27th, by Rev. S. M. Montgomery, Mr. John C. Harwood to Miss Mary E. Day, both of this city.

February 7, 1846
Died on the 5th, Robert, eldest son of James R. McDowell, Esq., of this city.

February 10, 1846
Married at the residence of Mrs. Elizabeth Roberts, on the 4th, by Rev. Mr. Caldwell, Dr. G. W. C. Trezvant to Miss Mary M. Briscoe, all of Warren county.

Died in this city, on Sunday evening last, Edward C. Mielke, formerly of Philadelphia. He was interred in the family burial ground of Mrs. Yerby, the mother of Mrs. Mielke, of Wilkinson county.

February 11, 1846
Died, Robert McDowell, on February 5th, aged 9 years, 8 months and 3 days old.

February 14, 1846
Married February 12, 1846, by S. B. Harwood, Esq., Mr. Thomas B. Mason to Miss Elizabeth Collins, all of this county.

February 17, 1846
Sexton's report:
Feb. 11 – Henry Devine, 40 years, dropsy.
Feb. 14 – Ann Jane Hall, 29 years, consumption.

February 18, 1846
Departed this life February 5th, 1846, at his residence in the county of Yalobusha, Allen Townes, born on the 20th of June, 1772, in the county of New Kent, Virginia, thence he removed to the county of Amelia, Virginia, where he resided upwards of 50 years. He was forty years a member of the Baptist Church.

February 19, 1846
Married on Saturday evening last, by N. G. Bryson, Esq., Mr. Louis Perano to Miss Fronica Buscha, both of this city.

Died on the 14th, in the 30th year of her age, Mrs. Ann Jane Hall, wife of Joshua J. Hall, and only child of Joseph N. Craddick, of this place.

February 24, 1846
Sexton's report:
Feb. 15 – Noah Blackwell, consumption, of Yazoo County.
Feb. 16 – Curley Barnes, scalded on steamboat *Congress*.
Feb. 16 – James Grillo, 35 years, gastrelus.
Feb. 17 – David Hall, 40 years, scalded on steamboat *Congress*, of St. Louis.
Feb. 20 – M. L. McIntire, fall from horse, of Neshoba county.
Feb. 21 – Infant of Dr. W. R. Puckett, convulsions.
Feb. 21 – Richard Johnson, 65 years.

Died in New Orleans, on the 20th, Emma Elizabeth Reading, of scarlet fever, aged 1 year, 6 months and 12 days, the daughter of A. B. and Sophia Reading, formerly of this city.

February 25, 1846

Married February 23d, 1846, by Samuel B. Harwood, Esq., Mr. John Doan to Miss Jane King, both of this county.

February 26, 1846

Died in this city, Mr. Wm. J. Estes, long a resident of this city.

Married on 25th, at the Episcopal Church, by the Rev. S. Patterson, Mr. Albert N. August, of Clinton, Miss., formerly of Richmond, Va., to Miss Virginia E. Wood, of this city.

March 3, 1846

Sexton's report:
Feb. 23 - Emma Elizabeth Reading, scarlet fever.
Feb. 25 - W. J. Estes, 35 years, inflammation of the bowels.
Feb. 28 - James Keenan, of steamboat *Cincinnati*.

March 6, 1846

Died on the 5th, at the residence of her husband, near Vicksburg, Mrn. Helen D. Peck, consort of Dr. Peck.

March 10, 1846

Sexton's report:
Mar. 6 - Turner Houseman, 37 years, scalded.
Mar. 6 - Laura Cecelia Hammett, 2 years, fell in cistern.

Died on the 6th, Laura Cecelia, dau. of Robert & A. Teresa Hammett.

March 17, 1846

Married on the 14th, by S. B. Harwood, Esq., Mr. John M. Jewell to Miss Martha Jane Powers, all of this city.

Died March 13th, William H. Arrison, of Vicksburg, 26 years of age, of pneumonia.

March 27, 1846

Married on the 12th, by the Rev. Mr. Patterson, of Vicksburg, at the residence of T. J. Catchings, Esq., near Bolton's Depot, Hinds county, A. J. Polk, Esq., of Columbia, Tenn., to Miss Mary E. Clendinen.

Married at the residence of Col. Bird Saffold, by the Rev. John N. Waddel, Mr. Willis Herring, of Carroll, to Miss Sarah Saffold, of Newton county.

Married March 25th, 1846, by Samuel B. Harwood, Esq., Mr. Charles W. Read, to Mrs. Sarah Carlisle, both of Hinds county, Miss.

April 4, 1846

Married in Vicksburg, on the 2d, at the residence of Thos. A. Marshall, Esq., by the Rev. A. Davidson, Edward Hoberts, Esq., of the city of Baltimore, to Miss Anne M. Hoblitzell, late of Baltimore, daughter of Saml. Hoblitzell, Cumberland, Md., and neice of H. Stidger, of Vicksburg.

Married at Washington, parish of St. Landry, La., on the 15th, by the Rev. Robert H. Read, Mr. H. S. McFarland, formerly of Vicksburg, to Miss Mary M. Allis, neice of Hon. Judge Dutton, both of Plaquemine.

April 7, 1846

Married on the 2d, in Madison parish, La., by Rev. John Lane, Mr. Jacob Peale, of this city, to Miss Ellen Carbiel, of the former place.

Died March 30th, of consumption, at the residence of the Rt. Rev. Dr. Blanc, Catholic Bishop of this Diocese, the Rev. Michael D. O'Rielly, aged 55 years, lately Cure of the Parish of Vicksburg, Miss.

Sexton's report:
Apr. 1 - Marla A. S. Barnett, 20 yrs, affection of heart, of Yazoo City.
Apr. 2 - David Singleton, 25 years, consumption.

April 9, 1846

Died at Warrenton, Miss., on the 7th, Mrs. Mary Olivia Cambron, consort of Mr. Wm. L. Cambron.

Died in Madison county, on the 24th ult., of Pulmonary consumption, Mrs. Emily, wife of R. M. Martin, and daughter of the late Dr. William Balfour, at the age of 19.

April 14, 1846

Married on the 8th, by Samuel Edwards, Esq., member of the Board of Police, Mr. A. E. Hankinson to Rebecca J. Higdon, all of Warren Co.

Sexton's report:
April 7 - Mary Olivia Cameron, 21 years.
April 8 - Joseph Randolph, 27 years.

April 15, 1846

Married on Monday morning last, by the Rev. Mr. Montgomery, Pastor of the Catholic Church, in this city, Mr. John O'Connor to Miss Esther E. King, both of Warren county.

April 17, 1846

Died in this city on the 16th, of consumption, Mr. P. T. Hubbell, late senior partner of the firm of Hubbell & Wheeler.

Married at Wickland, Nelson Co., Ky., on the 7th, by Rev. J. Farris Smith, Hon. David L. Yulee, of Florida, to Miss Nannie C., daughter of Hon. Charles Wickliffe.

April 21, 1846
Sexton's report:
April 15 – William Gray, 35 years, pleuriny, Caldwell county, Ky.
April 15 – John Moore, 35 years.
April 16 – P. T. Hubbell, 35 years, consumption.

Married the 19th, by the Rev. C. K. Marshall, Mr. William D. Wilson to Miss Mary E. Tidings, both of this city.

Married the 16th, by the Rev. Mr. Cooper, Mr. Tillman Whatley to Miss Sarah McFerren, both of Warren county.

Married at Natchez, on 31st ult., by the Rev. Mr. Stratton, Josiah Winchester, Esq., to Miss Margaret G., eldest daughter of the late Col. Sturges Sprague, all of that city.

April 24, 1846
Married on the 22d, by Rev. Mr. Cooper, Mr. William D. Griffin to Miss Rebecca C., daughter of Geo. Selser, Esq., all of Warren county.

April 30, 1846
Married on the 23d, at the residence of Col. H. W. Vick, in this city, by the Rev. Mr. Patterson, Henry Clay Pindell, Esq., of Lexington, Ky., to Miss James Ann, youngest daughter of the late Capt. James A. Pearce, of Louisville.

May 5, 1846
Married April 30th, 1846, by Sam. B. Harwood, Esq., Mr. Thomas McConnell to Miss Amanda Harvey, both of this city.

Died April 27th, John Adair, aged 34 years, of pneumonia.

May 13, 1846
Married on the 10th, by Saml. B. Harwood, Esq., Mr. John Grondonna to Mrs. Ellen Williams, all of this place.

May 23, 1846
Married in this city, at the residence of Mr. Walter Mudd, on the 21st, by Rev. Mr. Davidson, Mr. Jesse H. Jones, of Higinsport, Ohio, to Miss Abby Cunningham, of Newton, Middlesex county, Massachusetts.

May 28, 1846
Married on the 14th, by the Rev. Mr. Caldwell, Mr. Gabriel Fowler, of Adams county, to Miss Martha Ann, only daughter of Jonathan Melcy, Esq., of Warren county.

June 2, 1846
Died May 29th, Isabella Scott, aged 27 years, of consumption.

June 6, 1846
Married on Wed. morning last, at the residence of E. S. Crawford, by the Rev. S. Montgomery, Col. Josiah Newman, of Carroll county, Miss., to Mrs. Virginia L. Cocke, formerly of Christian county, Ky.

June 13, 1846
Died at St. Joseph, parish of Tensas, La., on the 2d day of June, Mrs. Phebe J. Pierce, daughter of Mr. Joseph Caldwell, of Wheeling, Va., and consort of Thomas N. Pierce, Esq., aged 27 years.

June 16, 1846
Died June 10th, 1846, Mrs. Elizabeth Potticary, aged 43 years, relict of John Potticary. Mrs. Potticary was a native of England, but for many years has resided in Vicksburg.

Sexton's report:
June 11 – Elizabeth Potticary, inflammation of bowels & stomach.
June 11 – Richard Abbott, 40 years, consumption.

June 20, 1846
Married on 17th, at the residence of Capt. John F. Walker, by Rev. Montgomery, Henry L. Bennett, Esq., to Mrs. E. A. Williamson, both of Madison Parish, La.

June 23, 1846
Married on 17th, at the residence of A. A. McWillie, Esq., in Madison county, by the Rev. Mr. Campbell, Petee Anderson, Esq., of New Orleans, to Mrs. Louisa Foster.

June 27, 1846
Married on Thursday evening last, Mr. Hardy Hendren to Mrs. Vose, both of this city.

July 2, 1846
Sexton's report:
June 23 – Eliza Hendray, 33 years.
June 24 – A. B. McFarland, 22 years, Pneumonia, Lafayette county.

July 7, 1846
Sexton's report:
June 28 – Margaret Ann McGarvis, 24 years, by violence, of New Orleans.
July 1 – Wm. Barrickeman, 40 years, consumption, of Indiana.
July 2 – John L. Henderson, 41 years, of Marshall county.

July 9, 1846
Married on the 2d, by the Rev. S. Caldwell, Mr. G. F. Rard to Mrs. Mary A. Gee, of Warren county.

July 11, 1846
Died on the 28th May last, at the residence of her uncle, J. P. Willis–

ton, Esq., of Northampton, Mass., Mrs. Julia Wood, formerly of Vicksburg, aged 32 years.

July 14, 1846
Married at Cincinnati, Ohio, on July 1st, by Rev. N. L. Rice, Luther Nichols, Jr., of this city, to Miss Anna, daughter of J. Whitaker, Esq., of Cincinnati.

July 16, 1846
Married on the 11th, by S. B. Harwood, Esq., Mr. John King to Miss Nancy Stout, both of this county.

Sexton's report:
July 5 - Hugh Dicert, 25 years, congestive fever.
July 11 - Bridget McGrain, 36 years.

July 18, 1846
Married on the 15th, by the Rev. Samuel Patterson, Mr. James W. Melvin to Miss Irma Louise Josephine, daughter of the late Joseph L. DeNorris, all of this city.

Died at Louisville, Kentucky, on the 26th of June last, Mr. Winfield S. Valentine, in the 28th year of his age.

July 21, 1846
Married July 18th, 1846, by S. B. Harwood, Esq., Mr. John Betz to Miss Eve Hoth, of this city.

Died on the 18th, Samuel A. Bedford, aged 25 years, of congestion of the lungs, a resident of Yazoo county.

July 25, 1846
Died on Thursday morning last, in this city, of whooping cough, Alexander Brooks, infant son of William and Indiana McRae.

July 28, 1846
Married in Franklin, Tenn., on the 4th ult.. Mr. James P. Sessions, of Miss., to Miss Anna G., daughter of the late Col. Thomas Hardeman.

Died at Warrenton, Warren county, Miss., on the 19th, Olivia, daughter of O. C. and Misella A. Henry, aged 2 years and 8 days.

August 4, 1846
Died July 31st, James Baine, aged 48 years, of consumption, a resident of Claiborne county.

August 15, 1846
Died on the 10th of July, Benjamin Baldwin, only son of George B. and Balsora Williams, aged 7 years, 9 months and 3 days, of inflammation of the bowels and brain.

August 20, 1846

Married the 12th, at the residence of Mr. Richards, by the Rev. John Lane, John G. Parham, Jun., to Miss Mary E. Blunt, both of this co.

Married 30th July, at the residence of Mrs. McCutchen, by the Rev. Mr. Gridley, Mr. Newman J. Nelson, of Washington county, to Miss Mary Ward, of Louisville.

Died on the 19th, Virginius, infant son of B. S. and M. B. Tappan.

Sexton's report:
August 13 - John Atwood, 19 years, congestive fever, of Yazoo county.
August 15 - Robert Rogers, 34 years, congestive fever, of Hinds county.

August 22, 1846

Died in this city, on the 21st, John F. Ross, long a citizen of this city.

August 25, 1846

Died yesterday evening, Emma, daughter of Martin L. and Ruth Ranney, aged 5 years.

Sexton's report:
Aug. 18 - Augustus Lambert, 45 years, chronic diarrhea.
Aug. 21 - John F. Ross, 47 years, gout.

September 1, 1846

Married at Baton Rouge, on the 25th ult., by the Rev. J. Woodbridle, Benjamin F. Tisdale, Esq., of New Orleans, to Maria M., youngest daughter of the late James M. Pike, of Lexington, Ky.

Died August 27th, Andrew White, aged 40 years, of convulsions.

September 3, 1846

Married in this city, 1st, at Thatcher's Hotel, by N. G. Brynon, Esq., Mr. William Regan, of Yazoo City, to Mrs. Mary Ann Butler, of Port Gibson, Miss.

September 8, 1846

Married on the 2d, by the Rev. B. R. Truly, Mr. William S. Lum, of Vicksburg, to Miss Mary A., daughter of the Rev. Thomas Griffin, of Madison county.

September 15, 1846

Died, September 9th, John Glasscock, aged 31 years, of typhus fever, Parish of Avoyelles, La.

September 17, 1846

Died in this city, on the 15th, Mr. Peter Hossley, for many years a citizen of this place.

Married on the 14th, at the residence of Mr. Charles H. Vinton, by N. G. Bryson, Esq., Mr. James M. Blackshear to Miss Eliza Jane Hollingshead, all of this city.

Married on the 31st ult., by the Rev. E. Schon, Mr. Charles W. Miller, of this city, to Miss Livina Ann Conover, of Cincinnati.

September 19, 1846

Married on the 17th, by the Rev. A. W. Chapman, Mr. David G. Hardaway to Miss Adaline W. Neely, both of this county.

September 26, 1846

Married in Cincinnati, on the 13th, Mr. Hiram Harrison, of Yazoo City, to Miss Annie Baker, of that city.

Also, on the eve of their departure as missionaries to India, the Rev. John Chandler to Miss Charlotte Hopkins, all of that city.

September 29, 1846

Married in Henry county, Tenn., on the 7th, Mr. George W. Wilson, of Vicksburg, to Miss Caroline E. Johnson, of said county.

Died yesterday, Mr. Benjamin W. Bancks, in the 29th year of his age.

Died Sept. 21, John Remus, 27 years of age, from a fall from a horse.

October 8, 1846

Sexton's report:
Sept. 28 - B. W. Bancks, 29 years, congestion.
Sept. 29 - Thomas Donahoe, killed by stabbing, of Hinds county.
Oct. 1 - Frances Bambush, 3 months, inflammation of bowels.

October 13, 1846

Married on the 8th, by Rev. Henderson, Mr. Samuel Richardson to Miss Henderson, all of Warrenton.

October 17, 1846

Married on the 15th, at the Episcopal Church, by Rev. Mr. Patterson, Basil G. Kiger, Esq., to Miss Caroline Isabella Gwin, all of this city.

Died on Wednesday morning last, Mr. Charles G. Kercheval, of Raymond, Miss.

October 24, 1846

Married on 21st, at the residence of Mrs. Pinching, by Rev. S. Patterson, Robert W. Birney, Esq., of Youngs Point, La., to Mary Fredonia Williamson, daughter of the late R. M. Williamson, of this city.

October 27, 1846

Married 22d, in the county of Hinds, at the residence of Mrs. F.

Whitaker, by Rev. S. M. Montgomery, Captain J. Burckett, of this city, to Miss Charlotte L. Whitaker.

October 29, 1846

Died at the residence of her father in this county, on the 25th, of congestive fever, Florence C., daughter of E. W. and Minerva Morris, aged 15 years.

Died 25th, of consumption, Mr. Thomas G. Williamson, an old citizen of this city.

Sexton's report:
Oct. 19 - Edward Dunn, 40 years, consumption.
Oct. 24 - Thomas Monnahan, 30 years, stabbing, of Jackson, Miss.

October 31, 1846

Died in the parish of Carroll, Louisiana, on the 3d day of October, 1846, John P. Taylor, aged about 50 years. Mr. Taylor was born and raised in Claibourne county, Miss., and had only resided in Louisiana for the last six years.

November 3, 1846

Sexton's report:
Oct. 25 - Thomas Williamson, 30 years, dropsy.
Oct. 26 - Mary Ann Hackett, 3 years.
Oct. 30 - J. M. Vetter, 40 years, suicide.

November 4, 1846

Married in Nashville, at the residence of Joseoh Woods, Esq., by Rt. Rev. Bishop Miles, D. D., Raymond Augustin Rourk, of Vicksburg, to Miaa Jane M. West, of the former place.

November 5, 1846

Departed this life at her late residence in this county, Mrs. Artimisia Blount in the 45th year of her age, of pulmonary consumption.

November 10, 1846

Died Nov. 3, Jolin Thinkler, aged 42 years, of fever.

November 12, 1846

Died of bronchitis, on the 27th, at the residence of Rev. Robert Caldwell, of this place, Clinton Dameron, aged 6 months and 6 days, infant son of Dr. Matthew and Mrs. Margaret Ann Deavenport, of Lawrenceburg, Tenn., latterly of Pulaski, and formerly of Hinds county, Miss.

November 19, 1846

Married on the 17th, by Rev. Mr. Montgomery, Mr. Jacob Vogh to Mrs. Priscilla G. Strong, both of this city.

Died 23d, at the residence of Mrs. Fretwell, in this city, Wm. F. Ames, for many years a citizen of this place.

December 2, 1846
Sexton's report:
Nov. 23 - William F. Ames, 33 years, neuralgea.
Nov. 25 - James H. Oldcraft, 28 years, consumption.

December 15, 1846
Sexton's report:
Dec. 8 - Charles Prickles, 23 years, diarrhea.
Dec. 12 - Adam Conner, 30 years, intemperance.

December 16, 1846
Married in Kentucky, on the 1st, by the Rev. Jacob Creath, Mr. Cowles G. Meade, of Miss., to Miss Sallie Woolfolk, daughter of Col. Joseph Woolfolk, of Woodford county.

December 19, 1846
List of deaths in hospital at Malamoros, since Nov. 15, 1846:
   Murphy James, 2d artillery, comp. K
   McCill W., 2d dragoons, comp. B
   Swink, J., Kentucky cavalry
   Freeman J., 1st artillery, comp. H
   Wick Walter, 1st reg't. Indiana Vol.
   Philips James, 1st reg't Indiana Vol.
   Archer James, 2nd artillery, comp. I
   Atchison J., 3d reg't. Illinois Vol.
   Martin S., Tennessee cavalry
   Lawrence A., 1st reg't. Indiana Vol.
   Winslow, quar. master's department
   Hearly E., 3d reg't. Indiana Vol.
   Berry W., 3d reg't, Illinois Vol.

December 24, 1846
Died on the 23d, Mary, infant daughter of J. G. and Victoria Berry, aged 4 months.

Died December 14th, John J. Lowe, aged 42 years, of dropsy.

January 1, 1847
Married in this city, on the 31st December, by N. G. Bryson, Esq., William H. Thum to Eliza E. Gilliland, both of Lauderdale Co., Tenn.

Departed this life on the 15th December, 1847, in Hinds county, Miss., Mrs. Martha Ann Turner, consort of John C. Turner, and eldest daughter of Col. John and Mary Gibson, in the 33d year of her age. Mrs. T. was a member of the Methodist Episcopal Church.

January 5, 1847
Married in Isequena county, on the 21st December, by Rev. Dr. Dunn, Dr. I. W. Pettiway to Miss Julia J. Nelson, daughter of Major Samuel Nelson, of that county.

Married at the residence of John T. Fortson, Esq., in Isequena county, 3d January, 1847, by Rev. Dr. Dunn, Edmund R. Travis, Esq., of Lake Porvidence, La., to Miss Elizabeth A. Lortson, of Isaquena.

Died December 28th, George Miller, aged 40 years, of consumption.

January 7, 1847

Departed this life the 31st ult., Sarah Silviah, infant daughter of Dr. I. H. and Mary E. Cook, aged 1 year and 4 days.

January 8, 1847

Married yesterday evening, in this city, by Saml. B. Harwood, Esq., Mr. John G. Wilson (of Marshall Relief Guards), to Miss Margaret A. Dent, of this city.

January 12, 1847

Sexton's report:
Jan. 3 - Isaac Lynch, 25 years, accidental fall, Copiah Co.
Jan. 5 - James Cargrow, 25 years, intemperance.
Jan. 9 - Emeline Myers, 18 months, Rankin county.

January 13, 1847

Married Jan. 7th, Mr. James E. Whitiker to Miss Sarah Rabb, both of this county.

Died on the 2d of January, Mrs. Sarah Ann Walcott, long a resident of Warren county.

January 16, 1847

Died January 8th, Stephen M. Jackson, of Bachelor's bend, Miss., and formerly of Petersburg, Va., in the 47th year of his age.

January 19, 1847

Married on the 14th, by Rev. C. K. Marshall, Randal Gibson, Esq., to Mrs. Louisiana McCaleb, both of Warren county.

Married on the 6th, by the same, Mr. Edmund J. Drake to Miss Mary Swords, both of this city.

January 21, 1847

Married in Christ's Church, Vicksburg, on Tuesday evening, by the Rt. Rev. Bishop Otey, Mr. Joseph H. Todd to Miss Catharine Weller, daughter of the late Rev. George Weller, all of this city.

January 26, 1847

Married on the 21st January, 1847, by Rev. Mr. Patterson, Mr. John M. Selser to Mrs. Mary E. Warren, both of Warren county.

Died on yesterday morning, Jane, consort of Wm. Laughlin, of this city. (Picayune, 20th).

Sexton's report:
Jan. 17 - W. H. Langley, 19 years, Marshall Co., pneumonia.
Jan. 19 - Chasley Ray, 25 years, Marshall Co., typhus pneumonia.
Jan. 20 - J. R. Rerwood, 18 years, Alabama, cold.
Jan. 20 - A. A. Carter, 50 years, Clinton, Miss., consumption.
Jan. 20 - J. H. Godwin, 30 years, chronic diarrhea.
Jan. 21 - John Ellis, 45 years, Fort Tobias, chronic inflammation
Jan. 21 - Rice Bayley, 45 years, pneumonia.

January 27, 1847
Married on the 25th, by Rev. Dr. Leavel, at the Methodist Church, Mr. Thomas J. Scott to Miss Elizabeth V. Fretwell, all of this city.

January 29, 1847
Died on Wednesday evening, Mrs. Mary L. Stites, consort of Mr. Girard Stites, merchant of this city.

Died at the residence of his father, William Henderson, eldest son of Wm. and Margaret Hay, aged 11 years and 2 months.

February 2, 1847
Sexton's report:
Jan. 25 - Mr. Wier, Pneumonia.
Jan. 26 - H. H. Finney, 28 years, shot.
Jan. 27 - Charles Hazleton, pneumonia.
Jan. 28 - Mary L. Stites, 23 years, 6 months, consumption.
Jan. 29 - S. C. Malone, 45 years, pneumonia, Evansville, La.
Jan. 30 - Wm. Councell, 30 years, malignant typhus fever.

February 3, 1847
Died at his residence in this city, on the 30th ult., William Councell, Esq., of the firm of Jack & Councell, aged 30 years. The deceased was born in Denton, on the eastern shore of Maryland, and for the last 10 years resided in this place.

February 9, 1847
Died February 1st, Wm. Mulvahill, aged 45 years, of dropsy.

February 11, 1847
Married in this county, near Warrenton, 4th Feb., by Rev. Stephen Patterson, of Christ Church, Benjamin Crump to Miss Delia Green.

February 16, 1847
Sexton's report:
Feb. 9 - Samuel C. Price, 35 years, dropsy of brain.

February 17, 1847
Died at his residence near Warrenton, in this county, February 11th, of pneumonia, Mr. Samuel M. Hanna, aged about 38 years.

Died in this city, on the 14th, in the 28th year of her age, Mrs. Mary E., consort of the Rev. S. M. Montgomery, Pastor of the Vicksburg Presbytarian Church.

February 18, 1847

Died of scarlet fever, on the 26th ult., William H. H., aged 6 years and 11 months, and on the 1st, Richard, aged 8 years and 6 months, and on the 9th, Arra Ann, aged 9 years and 9 months, children of George and Eliza Hawkins.

February 23, 1847

Sexton's report:
Feb. 14 - Mary Eliza Montgomery, 28 years, consumption.
Feb. 16 - Adam Knapp, 22 years, effusion of the brain.
Feb. 20 - Conrad Steigelman, 38 years, convulsions.

February 24, 1847

Died on the 15th, at his residence near Satartia, Yazoo county, Mr. James Stewart, in the 35th year of his age.

February 27, 1847

Married by the Rev. Mr. Leavel, on Thursday evening, Mr. G. Washington Hanna, formerly of Baltimore, to Miss Caledoria Wilkinson, formerly of Louisiana, all of the city of Vicksburg.

March 2, 1847

Married in Yazoo City, on the 25th February, by the Rev. H. McInnis, Mr. S. H. Wilson to Miss Mary F. Whitman.

Died February 24th, Ephraim Dickey, aged 18 years, of scarlet fever.

March 3, 1847

Married on the 1st, by Rev. S. H. Montgomery, Mr. Franklin W. Lanter to Miss Margaret M. J. Bruner, all of Vicksburg, Miss.

March 5, 1847

Died on board the steamboat *Gondolier*, a few miles below Warrenton, on the 3d, Mr. L. J. Robinson, of Pittsburgh, Pa.

March 9, 1847

Died March 2d, William Irwin, aged 35 years, of consumption.

March 12, 1847

Married in Hinds Co., on the 25th ult., by Rev. Tho. Ford, Dr. Alfred Patton to Mrs. Priscilla Ingram, daughter of Daniel Thomas, Esq.

March 13, 1847

Died yesterday, William Moore Coleman, son of Lloyd R. Coleman.

March 17, 1847

Died March 12th, Helen Woodburn, aged 42 years, of cancer.

March 23, 1847
Sexton's report:
Mar. 16 - John F. White, 37 years, accidental fall.
Mar. 19 - John Webb, 50 years.
Mar. 20 - Lydia Jewell, 75 years, chronic diarrhea.

March 30, 1847
Died March 18th, I. N. Glidewell, 38 years of age, of disease of the lungs, from New Orleans.

April 3, 1847
Died in this city yesterday morning, of consumption, Nathan S. Drake, leaving a wife and 3 children.

Married on 31st of March, 1847, by Saml. Edwards, M. B. P., Maj. David T. Briggs to Miss Mahetabel Melvin, both of Warren county.

Married at the Catholic Church in this city, on the 4th, by the Rev. S. H. Montgomery, Mr. H. H. Simmons to Miss Tar--- Slydon, both of Vicksburg.

April 8, 1847
Died at his residence, Greenville, Bachelor's Bend, Washington county, Miss., Dr. Edward Bentley Church.

April 10, 1847
Died at the residence of her son, the Hon. Benjamin Springer, on the 20th of March, 1847, Mrs. Lydia Jewell, in the 75th year of her age. Mrs. Jewell was born in Marshfield, Massachusetts, from which place she removed to Litchfield.

April 13, 1847
Sexton's report:
April 3 - Edward B. Church, 40 years, congestion of lungs, Batchelor's Bend.
April 5 - Hiram Duncan, 32 years, malignant typhus fever.

Married 8th, by the Rev. Mr. Pearce, of Port Gibson, Mr. Andrew G. Hyland, of this county, to Miss Martha Jane Briscoe, of Claiborne Co.

April 15, 1847
Died on yesterday, of scarlet fever, Eugenia, aged 8 years and 10 months, daughter of Dr. T. J. and Mrs. Harper.

April 16, 1847
Died on Monday last, of scarlet fever, Arthur H., infant son of W. L. F. and Madaline Slaughter, in the 4th year of his age.

April 20, 1847
Sexton's report:

April 14 - Joseph S. Canfield, 45 years, dropsy.
April 16 - John Brunel, 50 years, drowned.

April 22, 1847

Died at the residence of Capt. Fountain Wood, of this city, on the 18th of March last, Ann Elizabeth Birdsong, who was born in Sussex county, Virginia, on the 28th of April, 1833, and was brought to this state by her parents, William W. and Eliza Frances Birdsong, in the spring of 1834, to Hinds county.

April 24, 1847

Married on Monday evening, by S. B. Harwood, Esq., Mr. Edward Tickell to Mrs. Elizabeth Price, of this city.

Married on Thursday evening last, by the same, Mr. George W. Brown, of this city, to Miss Penelope A. Winn, of Arkansas.

April 27, 1847

Died in this city, on the 24th, Mary Elizabeth, daughter of Andrew and Patience Gamble, aged 4 years.

April 28, 1847

Sexton's report:
April 21 - J. Huley, 60 years, pneumonia, Yazoo City.
April 23 - John Corregain, 21 years, fever.
April 24 - Mary E. Gamble, 3 years & 3 months, scarlet fever.

May 1, 1847

Married on the 29th, at the residence of F. F. Bowen, Esq., by the Rev. Stephen Patterson, Jno. Shelton, Esq., of Raymond, to Miss Catherine V. Brown, of this place.

Died on yesterday, of scarlet fever, Andrew Jackson, son of Mr. & Mrs. Gamble, aged 1 year and 9 months.

May 4, 1847

Sexton's report:
April 26 - William E. Adams, 43 years, malignant typhoid fever.
April 27 - Catharine Frail, 26 years, Germany.

May 11, 1847

Martha Brothers, aged 37 years, a resident of Vicksburg, died of inflammation of the stomach and bowels, on May 6th.

May 19, 1847

Married in this city, at the residence of Dr. Raley, on the 10th, by Rev. Mr. Montgomery, Robert B. Harris to Miss Charlotte Hollinshead.

Died in this city, on the 14th, of scarlet fever, Marion Davidge, son of Charles and Lucy Buck, aged 7 years.

Sexton's report:
May 12 - John Lamaze, 28 years, malignant scarlet fever.

May 20, 1847
Married 18th, by Rev. Dr. H. Leavel, Gen. G. D. Mitchell, of this city, to Miss Caroline P., eldest daughter of Mr. Wesley W. Neely, of Warren County.

May 25, 1847
Sexton's report:
May 16 - Joshua Lonsberry, 30 years, consumption.

May 27, 1847
Died on the 25th, Dr. Daniel McGill, a native of North Carolina, but for the last 12 or 13 years a resident of this city.

June 8, 1847
Sexton's report:
May 31 - Lt. R. L. Moore, aged 35 years, killed at Battle of Buena Vista.
May 31 - Wm. H. McMahon, aged 35 years, fits.
June 5 - Gottleib Burke, 34 years, dropsy.

June 22, 1847
Died June 15th, of accidental discharge of cannon, Antonio Pau, aged 35 years.

June 29, 1847
Sexton's report:
June 21 - Thomas White, 26 years, killed at Battle of Buena Vista.
June 21 - John Dawson, 23 years, bilious fever.
June 24 - Cornelius Martin, 23 years, chronic diarrhea, 1st Indiana Regt.

Died in this city, on the 14th June, John G., only son of Rev. A. W. and Mary A. Chapman.

July 8, 1847
Died at his residence in Warren county, on 17th June, Dr. James H. Gregory, aged 43 years. He left a widow and five children.

Died July 1st, Bridget O'Brien, aged 45 years, of Vicksburg.

July 13, 1847
Died July 9th, Jane Canavon, aged 25 years, of typhus fever, a resident of Vicksburg.

July 14, 1847
Died on the 8th, of congestive fever, Mr. William L. Thomas, in the 22d year of his age.

Departed this life on the 28th day of June, at the residence of her brother, John T. Branch, Esq., of Northampton county, North Carolina, Mrs. Mary A., wife of N. T. Williams, of Vicksburg, and daughter of Thomas Branch, Esq., in the 33d year of her age.

July 17, 1847

Married on the 6th, by the Rev. John Lane, Mr. J. P. Porter to Miss Catharine J. Barefield, all of this county.

July 20, 1847

Married on the 12th, by Rev. Mr. Stratton, Mr. James A. Coulson, of Vicksburg, to Miss Harriet Amanda Barfield, of Natchez.

July 21, 1847

Died July 14th, of congestive fever, Henry Ahrens, aged 34 years.

July 27, 1847

Sexton's report:
July 19 - Asa Leathers, 30 years.
July 22 - Timothy Lane, 30 years.

July 28, 1847

Died at the residence of Thos. L. Dobyns, Esq., in Jefferson county, Miss., on the 7th, his second son, Richard Dobyns, aged 3 years and 10 months.

Married on the 13th, by the Rev. Dr. Leavel, Dr. Edward W. Lane to Miss Laura, daughter of Wm. Lum, Esq., all of this county.

Married on the 18th, in Warren county, on Hurricane Island, at the residence of Col. Flowers, by Sam B. Harwood, Esq., Mr. Thomas J. Coe, of the First Mississippi Rifles, to Miss Sarah Ann Young, both of this county.

Married in Madisonville, on the 14th, by Rev. J. T. Russell, Hon. James R. Burrus, of Yazoo, to Miss Laurentina Ophelia, eldest daughter of W. F. Walker.

Married in Benton, on the 30th June, by the Hon. J. R. Burrus, Geo. B. Wilkinson, Esq., to Miss Cordelia, eldest daughter of the Hon. R. S. G. Perkins.

July 31, 1847

Married on Thursday morning last, in this city, Col. John McClellan, of Nashville, to Miss Eliza S. Punchard, of this city.

VICKSBURG REGISTER (Vicksburg, Miss.)
William Mills, Editor

January 22, 1834

Died on the 21st, of scarlet fever, John, son of W. W. Gaines, Esq., of this place.

Departed this life on the 19th, of bilious fever, Mr. David Heiser, in the 23d year of his age, a native of Paris, Bourbon County, Ky.

Married on Wednesday evening last, by the Rev. Mr. McRoberts, James J. Chewning, Esq., to Miss Sarah M. Sims, all of this place.

Married on the 14th, J. P. Harrison, Esq., of this place, to Miss Sydney Ann Norton, of Adams County.

Married on the 16th, Russel Smith, Esq., to Mrs. Mary Mason, both of Warren County.

February 26, 1834

Died 24th ultimo, David L. Shackleford, of this city.

Married 25th, by the Rev. S. S. M'Roberts, Mr. William R. Campbell, Esq., to Miss Margaret P. H. Tiedeman, of Vicksburg.

March 5, 1834

Departed this life on the 27th February last, Mr. Smith Fawcett, about the 34th year of his age.

March 12, 1834

Departed this life on the 2d, Frances Julia Ann, infant daughter of R. D. and Clarisa Ann Muir, of this city, aged 16 months.

Died suddenly at his residence in Holmes County, on the 4th, Major William L. Arick.

March 26, 1834

Married on the 13th, Dr. Thos. Anderson to Mrs. Ann E. Nolan.

Married on the 22d, by S. W. Cowan, Esq., Mr. Benjamin Rutherford, of Tennessee, to Miss Ruth Sophia Newningham, of this city.

Died on the 13th, David Parkison, (of the firm Rappleye, Davis & Co.), of this place, formerly of Florence, Ala.

April 24, 1834

Died on the 15th last, at the age of 23, Mrs. Eveline Glass, consort of Mr. James Glass. She has left three infant children.

Married on Tuesday evening last, by the Rev. John Lane, Mr. John Elliott to Miss Henrietta Barker, all of this county.

May 1, 1834
Married on the 27th, by the Rev. J. J. Roberts, Mr. James Page, late of Amite County, Miss., and now of Hinds, to Miss Susan Hudson, late of Covington County, Miss.

May 22, 1834
Departed this life at the residence of her mother, Mrs. M. Deloach, in Holmes Co., on the 16th day of May, Mrs. Obedience W. Harmer, consort of Rev. Dr. William R. Harmer, aged 36 yrs., 3 mos. and 5 days.

Died at Natchez, on the 13th, T. T. Grayson, Esq., attorney at law.

May 29, 1834
Married in New Orleans, on the 8th, by the Rev. R. D. Smith, Mr. Jas. R. McDowell to Miss Jane M. Mills, both of Vicksburg, Miss.

Married at the residence of Mr. Mark Anderson, by R. J. McGinty, Esq., on the 26th, Mr. David Lyons to Mrs. Lovice Friar.

June 5, 1834
Died on the 16th, at the residence of Mrs. E. A. Yeiser, Mr. F. Wm. Yeiser, late of Baltimore, Md.

June 12, 1834
Married the 10th, at the residence of Major Thomas T. Merryman, by Samuel W. Cowan, Esq., Mr. John Harmon to Miss Margaret M'Lane, all of this county.

June 19, 1834
Married the 15th, by the Rev. J. M. Baker, Dr. Walter R. Pucket to Miss Ann Matilda Cochran, both of this county.

June 26, 1834
Died of cholera, at Providence, La., on the 17th, Mr. Edward Mitchell, formerly a resident of this place.

July 3, 1834
Died at Jackson, Arkansas Territory, on the 8th of May last, R. C. Fitzgerald, of dropsy of the lower abdomen, Mr. Fitzgerald was about 28 or 29 years old, and formerly lived with Oliver C. Brooks, of Warren County.

July 24, 1834
Died in Vernon, Madison County, Miss., on the 8th, William B. Mennefee, in the 24th year of his age. Some two years since Mr. Mennefee removed from Culpepper County, Va.

Married on the 17th June, by the Honorable Wm. Mills, Mr. Henry F. Buesley to Miss Mary Ann Walls, all of this city.

Married on the same day, by Samuel W. Cowen, Esq., Mr. John Goodrum to Miss Elizabeth Bond, all of this county.

July 31, 1834
Married on the 17th, by the Rev. Dr. Wm. R. Harmer, Col. Wm. Johnson, merchant of Tchula, Holmes County, to Mrs. Caroline C. McBee, of the same county.

Married in this city, on Thursday evening last, by James Cornell, Esq., Mr. Wm. R. Spears to Mrs. Charlotte Stuart.

Died on the 24th day of July, at Milliken's Bend, La., in the 22d year of her age, Mary, the wife of Mr. Oliver B. Cobb, of that place.

Departed this life at the residence of his mother, of congestive fever, Mr. William C. Deloach, in the 27th year of his age.

August 7, 1834
Departed this life on the 23d, at the residence of his father, in the parish of Carroll, state of Louisiana, Mr. John Stanford Hood, third son of Harbird and Nancy Hood, in the 27th year of his age.

August 14, 1834
Died at Lake Bolivar, Washington County, Miss., on the 15th ultimo, Mrs. Sarah C. Smith, consort of Mr. Reddick Smith, and sister of Bennet M. Hines, Esq., in the 40th year of her age.

Married in this city, on Tuesday evening last, by James Cornell, Esq., Mr. James Wilkerson to Miss Armissa Salan.

August 28, 1834
Died the 23d, William Lee Green, eldest son of Thomas M. Green, in the 10th year of his age.

September 18, 1834
Died in this co., on 30th August last, at the residence of Jno. Cowan, Samuel W. Cowan. He was a vigilant and faithful public officer.

Died at Benton, Miss., on the 3d Sept., from an unfortunate recounter, Dr. John M. M'Morrough, formerly of Virginia, but for several years a resident of this state, leaving a wife and children.

Died on the 6th, at his residence near this place, in the 44th year of his age, Dr. Hartwell Harris, a native of Brunswick County, Virginia, and for the last ten years a citizen of Warren County.

October 2, 1834
Married the 30th September, by the Rev. Mr. McRoberts, Mr. Joseph A. H. Anderson, of Vicksburg, to Miss Tunstella E. A. Kinkead, of Clinton.

Married the 23d September, by the Rev. John Lane, Mr. William M. Gibson to Miss Elby Gibson, all of this county.

October 9, 1834
Married in this city, on the 6th, by James Cornell, Esq., Mr. John Barefield to Miss Margaret Bolls, all of this county.

Died on the 9th, of congestive fever, Patrick R., son of Allen Sharkey, aged 3 years and 6 months, living in Coila, Carroll County, Miss.

Died in this county, on the 20th ult., Mr. Edward Currie, an esteemed citizen and farmer, in the 48th year of his age.

November 6, 1834
Departed this life in Holmes County, Miss., on the 10th, of cyanche tonsillaris, Mr. Jordan Wiltshire, son of Charles Wiltshire, Esq., in the 25th year of his age.

Drowned from on board the steam boat *Choctaw*, nearly opposite the Little Sunflower river, a passenger by the name of J. Derby, reported to be from Salem, Massachusetts.

November 20, 1834
Died at Amsterdam, Miss., on the 3d October last, Mr. Donald Matheson, aged 32, a native of Scotland.

December 11, 1834
Married on the 25th of November, by the Rev. S. S. McRoberts, John Templeton, Esq., to Miss A. M. Dawson, both of this place.

Married on the 27th day of November, in Viffeennes, Ind., Simson L. George, Esq., of Vicksburg, Miss., to Miss Mary Ann Bruner, of the former place.

Married on the 8th Dec., R. J. Lyons, Esq., merchant of Vicksburg, to Miss Eliza Ann Harrison, of Wilkinson County, Miss.

December 18, 1834
Married the 16th, by William Everett, Esq., Mr. John M. Hawkins, to Miss Evelina Jane Colbert, both of Warren County.

Died at the residence of his father, on the 14th, Joseph, only son of Robert and Virginia E. Riddle, aged 18 months.

Died in this place this morning, of pleurisy, Robert Crittenden, Esq., of Little Rock, Arkansas Territory.

Died in this city, on Monday morning last, the Hon. Fountain Winston, late Lt. Governor of Mississippi, and Senator at the time of his death, in the State Legislature, from Adams County.

January 22, 1835
Departed this life on the 30th day of December, 1834, at his residence in the parish of Carroll, Louisiana, Mr. Harbord Hood, aged about 56 years, one of the oldest settlers of Lake Providence.

Departed this life on the 31st ult., Mrs. Elizabeth Russell, wife of Wm. C. Russell, Esq. Mrs. Russell, whose maiden name was Thompson, emigrated from Chapel Hill, North Carolina, in company with her husband, to the state of Tennessee in 1828, where she remained until the spring of 1834, when she removed to Warren County, Miss.

Died on the 6th, Mrs. Mary Estes, wife of William Estes, Esq., aged 43 years.

Married on the 4th, by the Rev. Dr. Wm. B. Harmer, Mr. Dufphey Burroughs to Miss Elizabeth Boyd, all of Yazoo County.

Married Jan. 14, by the Rev. S. S. McRoberts, Mr. Samuel S. Fox to Miss Elizabeth Brown, both of this city.

February 19, 1835

Died on the 18th, at his residence in this place, John D. Carriel, Esq., of consumption, formerly of Florence, Ala., but for the last 3 years a resident of this place.

Died on February 6, 1835, in Warren Co., near Vicksburg, Mr. John Linsey, of Giles Co., Tennessee. He has left a wife and six children.

March 19, 1835

Died on the 11th, at the residence of Samuel Terrell, Esq., of Hinds County, his wife, Diana Terrell, in the 41st year of her age.

April 23, 1835

Died at his residence in this city, on the 21st April, Richard Fretwell.

Married on the 22d, by the Rev. John Lane, Wm. Mills, Esq., to Mrs. Minerva G. Elliott, both of Warren County.

Married on the 9th, at the residence of her father, by Wm. Everett, Esq., Mr. George Hawkins to Miss Eliza Ann Wilson, daughter of Joseph E. Wilson, all of this county.

April 30, 1835

Died on the 23d, at the residence of C. Steele, Esq., of this town, his wife, Eliza, aged about 28 years.

Died on the 19th, Mr. William Bullitt, of the firm of Bullitt, Ship & Co., of this city. (*N. O. Bulletin*)

May 14, 1835

Married on the 5th, by Hon. Felix Bosworth, Bartlett Browder, Esq., of the parish of Carroll, La., to Narcissa Jane Hughlett, of Tennessee.

May 21, 1835

Married on the 20th, by the Rev. John Lane, Mr. John FeBrodnax to Miss Mary E. Vick, both of this city.

May 28, 1835

Died on the 23d, at his residence near Montalbon, Mr. Andrew Bolls, in his 58th year. Mr. Bolls was a native of Mississippi.

Died in Vicksburg, Miss., on the 26th, Mr. W. C. Godwin, late of Nansemond County, Virginia.

Married 24th, by the Rev. S. S. McRoberts, A. N. Warren, Esq., to Miss Emily E. Ferguson, both of this city.

Married at Fort Adams, on 21st, by the Rev. Mr. Brown, Mr. Charles Ridgley Lewis, of Hinds County, second son of Major S. W. Lewis to Miss Laura Lavinia Sewell, of Maryland.

Married 26th, by the Rev. S. S. McRoberts, Mr. A. B. Reading to Miss Sophia Anderson, both of this city.

June 11, 1835

Married in Yazoo County, on the 2d, Mr. James Vose to Miss Sophronia H. Punchard.

Married the 7th, by the Rev. Benjamin Haughton, Mr. John M. Stuky, late of Lancaster, Ohio, to Miss Mary M. Leggett, of this place.

Departed this life on the 1st, in the 23d year of her age, at the residence of her mother, Mrs. Asa Brahston, near Washington, Miss., Mrs. Anne Marin, wife of Mr. John Vick, of this county.

June 18, 1835

Married at Pucchenubbee, Carroll County, on the 3d, by the Rev. James R. West, Colonel Wm. G. Kendall, of Carrollton, to Miss Mary Philomelia, daughter of Col. John L. Irwin, formerly of Jefferson Co.

Died on the 17th, Isaac J. Ross, of bilious fever.

Died on the 3d, at Lake Providence, parish of Carroll, La., of the measles, Louisa Ann, daughter of Horace and Minerva Prentice, aged 2 years and 5 months.

June 25, 1835

Married on the 18th, by David Hendrick, Esq., Mr. Stanford H. Harding, late of Harding County, Tennessee, to Miss Jane M. Watson, of Queen's Hill, Miss.

July 2, 1835

Married on the 11th, by Jas. Bland, Esq., Mr. Simon T. Lane to Miss Caroline Marshall, all of this county.

Died at Bayou Mason,, in the parish of Carroll, state of Louisiana, on the 4th day of June, 1835. Samuel Hawley, aged about 80 years, a native of Massachusetts, and once a soldier of the Revolutionary army.

Died at Bayou Mason, parish of Carroll, Louisiana, the 30th March, 1835, John Dempsey, Sen., aged about 70 years, among the first settlers on Lake Providence.

July 9, 1835

Died at Mississippi Springs, on the 2d, Mary Rhodes, daughter of James E. Sharkey, aged 2 years.

Died on the 6th, Dr. Hugh S. Bodley, of this city, formerly of Lexington, Ky.

Married on the 24th June, by R. J. McGinty, Esq., Mr. Wm. Two, of this city, to Mrs. L. M. Thomas, formerly of Cincinnati.

Married on the 7th, by the Rev. Benjamin A. Haughton, Mr. Henry H. Ellison to Mrs. Sarah Ann Bolls, both of Hinds County.

July 16, 1835

A few days anterior to the 4th of July, various circumstances excited suspicion of a few citizens of Madison County, in the neighborhood of Beattie's Bluff, of an insurrection among the slaves about to occur. It was soon ascertained that two individuals, by name Cotton and Saunders, both of them steam doctors by profession, were concerned and both were immediately apprehended. A committee of investigation was immediately organized, composed of 13 respectable citizens. They discovered that the evidence of a conspiracy was conclusive, and that the guilt of Cotton and Saunders was beyond doubt, ordered them to a public execution, by hanging, which took place in the town of Livingston, on the 4th day of July. Before Cotton was hung, he made repeated confessions of his guilt, and furnished a detail of the plan and a list of prominent conspirators. It seems from Cotton's confession he was an accomplice of the celebrated Murrel. We are told that five white men altogether have been hung in Livingston. Ruel Blake, one of the prime movers of the conspiracy, fled but was apprehended in Vicksburg, carried back to Livingston, tried and executed yesterday. We were just informed that Hunter, one of the chiefs of the conspiracy, has been apprehended near Benton, Yazoo County. (Note: The above were Joshua Cotton, William Saunders, and John A. Murrell.)

Married on the 15th, Col. Edwin G. Cook to Miss Henrietta Harris, both of this county.

Died of congestive fever, on the 10th, Mary Ross, aged 9 years, eldest daughter of Isaac J. and Silviah C. Ross, of this county.

Died on the 20th, at the residence of Dr. J. Smith, of this county, of congestive fever, Augustine Maclin, aged about 20 years. Mr. Maclin was a native of Virginia.

Died on the 19th, John W, Jones, a resident of Clinton, Miss., but formerly of this place.

Died suddenly, on the 20th, at his residence in this county, Eugene Magee, Esq., a practioner of law, and at his death a member of the Senate of the State of Mississippi.

July 30, 1835

Married 27th, by Wm. Everett, Esq., Mr. William Godfrey, to Miss Frances Ann Richardson, both formerly of Norfolk, Va.

Died on the 22d, at the hospital of Warren County, Miss., Robert Miller, of Meadville, Penn.

Died on the 29th, at the same place, Solomon Bradbury, of Tennessee.

Died on 22d, William Henry, youngest child of H. G. and Elizabeth E. Foster, aged 15 months and 10 days.

August 27, 1835

Died at the residence of Richard Harrison, in Jefferson County, Henrietta Matilda, daughter of Francis and Louisiana McCaleb, of congestive fever, aged 4 years, 4 months and 25 days.

Died on the 19th, at Thompson's Well, in Yazoo County, Miss., Charles Higley, Esq., of the late firm of Messrs. Higley, Walker and Co., a native of Connecticut.

September 3, 1835

Died on the 29th ult., Minerva A. Ross, youngest and only daughter of Isaac J. and Silviah C. Ross, of bilious fever, aged 6 years, 11 months and 5 days.

September 17, 1835

Married on the 1st, by the Rev. Benjamin Houghton, Mr. James Crichlow to Miss Sarah Ross, both of Vicksburg.

Died the 16th of August, at the residence of Mr. John Turnbull, in Washington County, Mrs. Catherine Olivia Gervais, consort of Col. St. Clair Gervais.

Died on the 15th of September, at the residence of Mrs. Catherine Hanes, in this place, Mrs. Caroline Petty, consort of P. H. Petty.

October 1, 1835

Died 26th Sept., W. H. Robinson, a native of Penn., aged 27 years. He left a wife. He was a member of the Rifle Company at Vicksburg.

October 22, 1835

Recently departed this life, the infant son of Thomas J. Green, aged 4 years.

Died in Sartartia, on Sunday evening last, in his 21st year, Mr. Frederick W. Hodge, formerly of New Hampshire.

November 12, 1835
Died at her residence, Sylvan Vale, in this county, on the 2d, Mrs. Mary E. Smith, consort of Russell Smith, Esq.

December 3, 1835
Married the 12th of November, by Wm. Everett, Esq., Mr. William Turner to Miss Jane Gasford, all of this city.

Married 15th November, by Wm. Everett, Esq., Doct. John T. Dorsey to Miss Mary F. Bass, both of Louisiana.

Married on the 19th November, by the same, Mr. J. W. Miller to Mrs. Ann Thompson, all of this county.

December 24, 1835
Married on the 20th of Dec., 1835, Mr. Albert G. Robertson, of Hopkins County, Ky., to Miss Elizabeth A. F. Cowan, of Warren County, Miss.

Married in East Hartford, Conn., Mr. Walter Pitkin, of this place, of the firm of Seeger & Pitkin, to Miss Catharine B. Stanley.

February 4, 1836
Married the 26th ultimo, by the Rev. John Lane, Mr. T. C. Randolph, of this place, to Miss Mary J. R. Scott, of Warren County.

Departed this life on the 31st ult., in Hinds County, of hydrothorax, Mr. N. B. Gibbs, in the 18th year of his age. Mr. Gibbs was a native of South Carolina, but for the last 2 years a resident of this state.

February 11, 1836
Died at Mont Albon, on the 10th, Mr. Alex. McLeod, aged about 23 years. The deceased was for many years a resident of Warren Co.

Duncan S. Walker died on the 31st of December last, off of St. Jago, Cuba, whither he had gone for his health.

February 18, 1836
Died on the 8th, Mr. James S. Boyd, of the firm of Bruegard and Boyd, lately of Cincinnati.

Died a few days since in Havana, Island of Cuba, J. P. McGilly Cuddy, of the firm of G. B. Tate & Co., Vicksburg.

February 25, 1836
Died at the residence of her mother, on the 18th, Miss Martha J. Cochran, aged 15 years.

March 3, 1836
Married 1st of March, 1836, at the residence of James L. Dunn, by Wm. Everett, Esq., Mr. Martin Anding, of this city, to Mrs. Celeste Dunn, of Yazoo County.

March 17, 1836
Married last evening, at the residence of A. G. McNutt, by Rev. S. S. McRoberts, Ferdinand Sims, Esq., Attorney at Law of this place, to Miss Sarah A. McNutt, late of Rockbridge County, Va.

Died at Palmyra, Mississippi, on the 4th of March, Shelton Clark, aged about 30 years, formerly of Cincinnati, Ohio.

April 13, 1836
Died on the 2d ult., Mrs. Eliza R. Greenleaf, consort of Daniel Greenleaf, Esq., at their residence 6 miles from Vicksburg, aged 22 years. Her disease was consumption.

April 23, 1836
Married on the 20th ult., by the Rev. Benj. A. Haughton, Mr. Joseph Littlejohn to Miss Olivia E., daughter of James Bland, Esq., all of this city.

Married in Hinds County, on Wednesday evening last, by the Rev. Dr. Hammet, of this city, Mr. James Hall, formerly of Prince George County, Va., to Mrs. Eliza Smith, formerly of Sussex County, Va.

May 5, 1836
Married the 29th ult., by the Rev. Benj. A. Haughton, Dr. Benjamin J. Hicks, of Vicksburg, to Miss Martha M., daughter of John Cowan, Esq., at his residence in Warren County.

Married on Tuesday evening last, by the Rev. Dr. Hammet, Hugh R. Austin, Esq., of Hinds County, to Eliza A., daughter of Jesse B. Ragan, Esq., of this county.

May 12, 1836
Married on Thursday evening last, by the Rev. Dr. Hammet, Stephen S. Booth, Esq., formerly of Surry County, Virginia, to Miss Ann E., daughter of the late Roswell Valentine, of this county.

June 23, 1836
Married on the 16th, by the Rev. T. C. Brown, Washington Rossman, M. D., of Mont Albon, to Miss Letitia A., daughter of Isaac N. Selser, of Hinds County.

Married on the 11th, Mr. R. J. Blatchford to Miss Amelia Mary Anne Bengough, both of Natchez.

Died at Vicksburg, the 20th of June, Mrs. Martha Emanuel, late of Northumberland Cty., Virginia, the consort of Mr. Samuel Emanuel.

June 30, 1836
Married in this city, on the 15th, by the Rev. Dr. Hammet, John H. Bransford, Esq., formerly of Cumberland County, Virginia, to Miss

Mary Virginia, daughter of the late Lawson Pucket, Esq., of Chesterfield County, Virginia.

We record the death of Mrs. Susan Latham, consort of Mr. Harvey Latham, of Madison, who expired on the 23d.

July 14, 1836

Died at Providence, Louisiana, on the 1st day of July, Mrs. Caroline Chambliss, aged 18 years, 4 months and 17 days, daughter of Mrs. Harriet Davison, and grand-daughter of Genl. Joseph Kerr, consort of Thomas J. Chambliss, merchant. She had on the 29th ultimo given birth to a male infant (dead born).

Married on the 3d, by E. M. Maxey, Esq., Mr. Benedict Riney to Mrs. Nancy Bryant.

Married on the 3d, by R. J. McGinty, Esq., at the residence of Noel Rushing, Esq., Mr. Alexander Ludley to Miss Louisa Cain.

A duel was fought last evening, near this place, between two midshipmen, Mr. Key (son of F. Key of this city), and Mr. Shearman, formerly of Boston, which resulted in the death of Mr. Key, the ball passing through his breast the second fire.

July 28, 1836

Died in Yazoo County, on the 16th, Mrs. Mary Francis, wife of Mr. Samuel Punchard, and daughter of James W. Haseltine, Esq., of Francestown, N. H., in the 22d year of her age.

August 11, 1836

Departed this life at the Parsonage, on the 5th, in the 16th year of his age, Francis John, second son of Rev. James A. Fox, of Warren Co.

August 25, 1836

Departed this life, on the 14th day of August, 1836, at Lake Providence, Louisiana, Cynthia Holland Macquillen, consort of Capt. Joseph Macquillen, in the 37th year of her age, the fifth daughter of the late Robert Prince, Esq., of Jefferson County, Miss., and in early days, of the state of Tennessee. She leaves a husband and six children.

September 1, 1836

Departed this life on the 26th, at the residence of Wm. C. Doss, Martha Virginia, dau. of Hartwell Vick, aged 5 yrs., 1 month and 26 days.

Married on the 18th, at the Mississippi Springs, by S. Pratt, Esq., Mr. Amos R. Johnston, Editor of the *Clinton Gazette*, to Miss Harriet A., daughter of the Rev. E. Battle, of Clinton.

Married on the 31st July, by the Rev. Doct. French, Mr. William A. Tufts, merchant of Vicksburg, Miss., to Miss Martha Tabb, eldest daughter of Henry Tabb, deceased, of this Borough. (*Norfolk Beacon*)

September 15, 1836

Died on the 13th, T. Victor, Esq., aged about 25. Mr. Victor was a native of Lynchburg, in the state of Virginia, and only came to this country 8 months since. He was buried with military honors by the volunteers, a corps of which he was a member.

Died on the same day, E. Varley, Esq., aged about 40.

Departed this life on the 5th Sept., 1836, at the residence of Mr. R. J. Chambliss, near the town of Providence, La., John Abner Everett, infant son of Mrs. Lucinda S. Chambliss and the late Abner Everett, deceased. He was nearly four years old, and left one elder brother.

Died of congestive fever, on the 1st, at his residence in Yazoo County, Dr. Duncan Turnbull, aged 41 years, a native of Glassglow, Scotland, and late of Baltimore, Md. The deceased had recently emigrated to this state.

Married on the 6th, by J. N. Bittner, Esq., Mr. G. Duty to Mrs. Lavina Cathers, all of this county.

September 29, 1836

Died on the 30th day of August, James D. Wade, for some time a resident of this city. Mr. Wade was a member of an association of carpenters and housejoiners.

Died on the 22d, at the residence of her father, Mary Fulton, second daughter of Thomas F. Walker, of this place, aged 22 years.

October 6, 1836

Married on the 22d September, 1836, by the Rev. John Lane, Mr. John J. Gresham to Miss Penelope Newsom, both of this city.

Died on the 20th of September, 1836, at the residence of his father near Warrenton, Miss., John Ellison Ray, son of Valentine C. Ray, born November, 1834, aged 2 years, 10 months and 14 days.

Died at Providence, La., on the 20th day of September, 1836, William B. Leech, Esq., Attorney & Counsellor at Law.

October 13, 1836

Married the 21st ult., by the Rev. A. G. Burton, Mr. William J. Estes, formerly of this city, to Miss Sarah Ann, daughter of William Redditt, Esq., of Carroll County, Miss.

Departed this life on the 5th, Miss Esther M. Gibbs, aged 21 years and 10 months.

Died of typhus fever, on the 28th ult., at the plantation of Joseph Robertson, on Deer Creek, Washington County, Joseph L., son of Wm. T. Robertson, of Brandon, Miss., in the 14th year of his age.

October 27, 1836
Died at Belle Monte, Louisa County, Virginia, on the 12th, of puerperal convulsions, Mrs. Isabella A. Mills, consort of Dr. Wm. Mills, Jr., of Yazoo County, Miss.

Died on the 22d, Mr. Edmund Gregorie, aged 21 years.

November 10, 1836
Died in Vicksburg, on the 26th of October, Mrs. Mary Glass. She was left a widow in 1824 or 1825, with a family of small children. She has been a member of the M. E. Church some 10 or 12 years.

We announce the death of Dr. Samuel Shane, who departed this life this morning in about the 35th year of his age. Dr. Shane emigrated from Baltimore about 12 months ago.

November 24, 1836
Departed this life on the 10th, at the residence of her brother, Mr. Wm. Vick, Mrs. Mary T. Henderson, a native of Virginia, daughter of Newet and Elizabeth Vick.

December 8, 1836
Married on the 24th of Nov., by Rev. Mr. Cox, of the Protestant Episcopal Church, of this city, Edward L. Shannon, merchant of this city, to Miss Ann C., daughter of John Kealofer, Esq., of Hagerstown, Md.

Died at Woodland, Yazoo County, at the residence of Mr. John B. Pease, Mrs. Lydia Pease, the wife of Henry H. Pease, of Manchester, Miss., and daughter of Doctor Stephen Harris, of Warwich, R. I.

Died the 4th, Martha Prissilla, dau. of Valentine C. Ray, aged 12 mos.

The funeral sermon of the Rev. Randal Gibson, Sen., deceased, will be delivered in the Methodist Church near Samuel Lum's Camp Ground, on the 11th, by the Rev. W. Winans.

December 29, 1836
Married on the 22d, by E. H. Maxey, Esq., Mr. Daniel Hilderbrand to Miss Eliza Fitzhugh, all of Warren County.

January 5, 1837
Married on Thursday last, Mr. G. B. Williams to Miss Balzorah Mackey, by William Everett, Esq., all of this county.

January 12, 1837
Died at his residence in this city, on the 19th, of a pulmonary disease, Dr. James E. Pettway, aged 30 years, formerly of Sussex County, Virginia. Doctor Pettway emigrated to this county 8 years since.

February 1, 1837
Died at Un. Point, Concordia Parish, La., on the 21st Dec. last, Mrs. Zilpha Stanbrough, consort of David Stanbrough, aged 33 years.

Died very suddenly, in Vicksburg, on the night of the 18th, John Turnbull, Esq., in the 64th year of his age.

Died January 24th, Ambrose D. Downs, a native of this county.

February 22, 1837

Married on the 7th, by the Rev. Mr. Cox, George J. Rapalje to Miss Frances M. Glass, all of this county.

Died on the 15th, Elizabeth McNeill, daughter and only child of Robert and Virginia A. Riddle, aged 24 months.

Bill for Divorce -- Henry Morris -vs- Lucinda Morris.

March 15, 1837

Married the 7th, by the Rev. J. R. McCall, Mr. B. Davis, merchant, to Miss Catharine McKay, both of this city.

March 29, 1837

Married on 23d, by the Hon. James Bland, Mr. George Richards to Miss Hester Ann Selser.

Died on Sun. last, Mrs. Martha C. Ward, consort of Mr. P. W. Ward.

April 12, 1837

Bill for Divorce -- Emanuel Millsap -vs- Catharine Millsap.

April 19, 1837

Died in Vicksburg, on the 17th, Caroline, daughter of Daniel and Sarah Sweet, aged 6 years, formerly of Georgetown, D. C.

Died in Manchester, Miss., on the 4th April, 1837, Lewis S. Pease, aged 30 years, of inflammation of the lungs.

May 17, 1837

Died on the 14th, in this city, Theodore Webster, aged 6 years, son of Geo. W. Webster, of this city.

May 24, 1837

Died in Vicksburg, on the 16th, Horatio G. Johnson, aged 23 years, of inflammation of the lungs.

May 31, 1837

Married on the 18th, Mr. Richard H. Jenkins, merchant, to Miss Lovicia M. Patterson, both of this city.

Died a few weeks since, on Deer Creek, Catahoula Parish, La., Chas. M'Kenzie, native of Scotland, formerly soldier of British army.

June 7, 1837

Sexton's report:

May 31 - James Abbot, 62 years, residence vicksburg.
June 1 - J. W. Swiney, aged 17 years, congestive fever.

June 14, 1837
Married last evening, by the Rev. Joseph Travis, Mr. Thomas Henry Goodall, of this city, merchant, to Miss Catherine, second daughter of Elias Phenny, Esq., of Lexington, Mass.

July 19, 1837
Sexton's report:
July 10 - Rowland Hendrich, 25 years, residence Kentucky.
July 10 - Sarah M. Chewning, 24 years, peritomites.
July 11 - John Cole, residence Indiana, congestive fever.
July 13 - A. Law.

Died at her residence in this city, on the 10th, Mrs. Sarah Chewning, in the 22d year of her age, wife of Mr. James J. Chewning.

Died at Bridgeport, Hinds County, Miss., of congestive fever, on 27th June, Mr. Thomas H. Mortimer, aged about 25 years.

July 26, 1837
Departed this life the 13th day of July, 1837, at Lake Providence, La., Mrs. Martha Chambliss, consort of Mr. Nathaniel Chambliss, and daughter of Mr. James Beard, in the 24th year of her age. Mrs. Chambliss had been a member of the Methodist Episcopal Church.

Married on the 19th, by the Rev. J. R. McCall, Mr. William N. Wood, of this city, to Miss Amanda M. McCall, late of Lancaster, Kentucky.

Sexton's report:
July 16 - James Chathroe, 22 years.
July 21 - A. Montandon, 38 years, residence Vicksburg.
July 22 - John Wilkins, 39 years, residence Vicksburg.
July 22 - Frederick Laiker, 29 years, bilious fever.
July 23 - Harvey Campbell, 35 years.

August 2, 1837
Died at Oakham, Warren County, Miss., on the 25th day of July, Chiron Brooks, only son of Oliver C. Brooks, Esq., aged 6 years.

August 9, 1837
Departed this life on the 24th ult., Loftus Henry Gray, aged 11 months, youngest son of N. Gray, Esq., of this city.

Died at Bridgeport, Hinds County, Miss., on 6th August, Dr. Daniel S. Carmichael, aged about 22 years. He was from Marion District, South Carolina.

Sexton's report:
July 24 - E. Rogers, 35 years, yellow jaundice.
July 27 - Paul Sackman.

July 27 - Frederick Cruso, 32 years.
July 27 - Charles Miller, 23 years, congestive fever.
July 28 - Sarah Whitney, 25 years.
July 29 - Andrew M. Chapin, 28 years.
July 29 - James Drinkwater.
July 30 - Jacob Sleight, 29 years, congestive fever.
July 31 - Jacob Lagell, 32 years.
Aug. 2 - Thos. Nagley, 32 years.
Aug. 2 - Sarah Briggs, 40 years.
Aug. 2 - George Joiner, 40 years.
Aug. 2 - Mrs. Horn, 30 years.

August 23, 1837

Married in Benton, on the 3d, by the Rev. J. B. Crawford, Mr. Samuel W. Punchard, of Yazoo Co., to Miss Mary C. Munger, formerly of S.C.

Died at Prarie Makage, La., Sarah Cynthia and Susan Mary, daughters of Dr. Baker, the former on the 11th, and the latter on the 15th of July.

Sexton's report:
Aug. 8 - Mrs. Kirby, 27 years, bilious fever.
Aug. 9 - John King, bilious fever.
Aug. 10 - William King (a negro), 22 years, bilious fever.
Aug. 11 - Henry Wharton, congestive fever.
Aug. 16 - Charles Sharkey - 32 years, bilious fever.
Aug. 16 - Mrs. Butcher.
Aug. 17 - John Crosby, 30 years, congestive fever.
Aug. 19 - Enoch Batterton, congestive fever.
Aug. 20 - Richd. Cockrill, 24 yrs., Nashville, Tenn., congestive fever.
Aug. 20 - John W. Smith, 28 years, Rockford, Ind., congestive fever.

August 30, 1837

Died on the 22d, of congestive fever, at Vicksburg, Miss Celeste Day, eldest daughter of Wm. T. Day, Esq.

Died on the 23d, Mrs. Eliza Foster, wife of Joseph Foster, bookbinder, late of N. Orleans, and formerly of the city of New York. Mrs. Foster was the daughter of Mrs. Sarah Garson, of New York.

Died in Vicksburg, on the 22d, of congestive fever, in the 22d year of his age, Ira Scull, son of John H. and Elizabeth Scull, of Claremont County, Ohio.

Sextons report:
Aug. 21 - Felix Banderel, 28 years, congestive fever.
Aug. 22 - Wm. D. Short, 30 years, inflammation of lungs.
Aug. 22 - Herman Schmid, 26 years.
Aug. 22 - Andrew Eberer, 32 years, Germany, congestive fever.
Aug. 23 - Mrs. Eliza Foster, 37 years, congestive fever.
Aug. 24 - Michael O. Conner, congestive fever.
Aug. 24 - Thomas H. Bean, 31 years, consumption.

Aug. 26 - Mary Ann Triford, 53 yrs., Baltimore, inflammation of bowels.

September 6, 1837

Died on Saturday last, at his residence in this town, Hon. Thomas Emerson, in the 64th year of his age. Judge E. has filled several offices in Tennessee.

Died on the 23d, William D. Short, aged about 30 years. His remains were deposited in the earth by the Masonic Fraternity.

Died in Vicksburg, 30th Aug., of ulcerated sore throat, Mary Catharine, aged 18 months, daughter of Dr. Morris Emanuel.

Sexton's report:
Aug. 29 - Samuel Baker, 30 years.
Aug. 30 - Peter Riley, 30 years.
Aug. 28 - Washington Hendren, 4 years, congestive fever.
Sept. 1 - Sarah Pourell, 28 years, congestive fever.

September 13, 1837

Married the 7th, by Rev. T. C. Brown, Mr. Percival Marble, of this city, to Miss Elizabeth, daughter of John Townsend, Esq., of Mont Albon.

Departed this life in Bridge Port, Miss., on the 23d, William E. Whipple, aged 20 years. Mr. Whipple was formerly from Pawtucket, R. I., where his relatives now reside.

Died in Milliken's Bend, La., of consumption, on September 2d, Daniel O'Heytour, a native of Alabama.

Sexton's report:
Sept. 1 - James Keiran, 35 years, congestive fever.
Sept. 5 - Joseph Haverstraw, 25 years, congestive fever.

September 20, 1837

Married on Sunday evening last, by E. H. Maxey, Esq., Harvey M. Jenkins, Esq., to Miss Virginia Rozell.

Sexton's report:
Sept. 11 - John Frederick, 35 years, fever.
Sept. 12 - James Rooney, 28 years, N. Orleans.
Sept. 13 - Hamilton Hosack, 34 years, Cincinnati, yellow fever.
Sept. 14 - C. Cattinazzi, 34 years, fever.
Sept. 15 - Mrs. Morssie.

September 27, 1837

Married in Shelbyville, Ky., on the 24th August, by the Rev. R. Dearing, Mr. Alexander F. Newman, of the firm of Harwood, Newman & Co., of Vicksburg, to Miss Margaret Isabella, daughter of Mr. Jno. McGaugherty, of the former place.

Died in this city, last evening, Mr. J. M. Ross, Esq.

Sexton's report:
Sept. 19 - Wm. Henry, 24 years, Tenn.
Sept. 19 - John Watcher, 22 years.
Sept. 21 - Hannah Burroughs, 51 years, bilious fever.
Sept. 21 - Paul Powel, 22 years.
Sept. 22 - Charles Meade, 25 years.
Sept. 22 - Jeremiah Donovan, 25 years, Co. of Cork, Ireland, inflammation of stomach.
Sept. 22 - Dennis C. Henadin, 44 years, Ireland.
Sept. 22 - Francis M'Hattan, 22 years.

October 4, 1837

Died at his plantation on the Sunflower, on the 12th ultimo, Cyrus Griffin, Esq., formerly of Boston, Massachusetts. Mr. Griffin came to this state in 1826, and entered the practice of law at Natchez. He subsequently edited the Southern Galaxy printed at that place.

October 11, 1837

Departed this life on the 28th, at his late residence in this place, Charles C. Mayson, Esq., Treasurer of the State. Mr. Mayson was a native of South Carolina.

Sexton's report:
Sept. 24 - James Teer, 30 years, Downs Co., Ireland.
Sept. 26 - Jacob Burley, 28 years.
Sept. 26 - Andrew Hough, 32 years.
Sept. 27 - A. Cuthen, 42 years.
Sept. 29 - Timothy Delung, 30 years.
Oct. 3 - Jacob Yost, 28 years.
Oct. 4 - James Hughes, 32 years.
Oct. 4 - John Impson, 12 years.
Oct. 7 - John Wells, 16 years, Ohio.
Oct. 7 - Joseph Wilson, 35 years.

October 18, 1837

Married on 16th, by the Rev. Mr. Hutchinson, Miles C. Folkes, Esq., to Miss Rebecca A. Manlove, both of this city.

Died on the 11th, at his residence in this county, Hugh M. Mackey.

Dr. Thomas Davis fell a victim to the prevailing epidemic, on the 4th.

October 25, 1837

Sexton's report:
Oct. 18 - John Cunningham, 32 years.
Oct. 19 - J. L. Guion's boy.
Oct. 20 - John Hamilton, 23 years, Warm Springs, Bath Co., Va.
Oct. 20 - James O'Neil, 29 years, Boston.

November 1, 1837

Sexton's report:
Oct. 23 – John Reed, 29 years, residence Pittsburg.
Oct. 28 – Ambrose Seiders, 35 years, Maine, fever.
Oct. 28 – Henry Bonneman, Cincinnati.

November 8, 1837

Died in Natchez, 29th of October, Mr. George B. Hubbard, in the 24th year of his age, a native of Norfolk, Va., whence he emigrated two years since.

Died November 4th, Mrs. Louisa Paxton, the consort of W. H. Paxton, Esq., and daughter of Mr. Lawrence W. Smith, of Fayette Co., Tenn.

November 29, 1837

Sexton's report:
Nov. 1 – Anthony Flasbly, 25 years, Baltimore.
Nov. 4 – Thos. Fanen, 45 years.
Nov. 4 – Rebecca Louisa Paxton, 21 years.
Nov. 6 – Jacob Redney, 34 years.
Nov. 6 – A. A. Richardson, 35 years, drowned.
Nov. 18 – John Gray, 37 years.
Nov. 18 – John Vantone, 33 years.
Nov. 18 – Charles Trarll, 50 years.
Nov. 18 – John Gray, 38 years, Tenn., bowel complaint.

January 4, 1838

Married Dec. 25, 1837, by the Rev. William Allen, the Rev. Robert G. Green to Mrs. Elizabeth Boren, of Warren County.

January 9, 1838

Died on the 6th, William Henry, infant of F. Sims, Esq., of this city, aged 13 months.

January 10, 1838

Died Jan. 10th, J. S. Blackburn, Esq., late of Virginia, a member of the Vicksburg Bar.

January 12, 1838

Died in Lake Providence, parish of Carroll, La., at Holly Place, the residence of his parents, William Lester, eldest son of ---- and Elizabeth Lester Bosworth.

January 17, 1838

Married on Monday evening last, by the Rev. Mr. Chaney, Thos. J. Hanna, Esq., of Baltimore, to Miss Laura White, of this place.

January 27, 1838

We record the death of Chester Ringgold, Esq., a member of the Jefferson Bar, and lately chosen Attorney of the District. He expired in Fayette, on Friday evening last.

February 1, 1838
Mrs. Elizabeth Winn, consort of Bushrod Winn, of this city, departed this life on the 31st. She has left an infant daughter and a husband.

February 8, 1838
Died yesterday morning, Mr. D. W. Sutton, of the late firm of Sutton & Brown, of this city. Mr. S. was a native of New York.

Thos. G. Ellis, Esq., departed this life at the plantation of Mr. John Routh, on Lake St. Joseph, La.

February 9, 1838
Married in Warren County, on the 8th ult., by the Rev. John Lane, Mr. P. W. Defrance to Miss Emily J. Sessions, both of this county.

VICKSBURG SENTINEL (Vicksburg, Miss.)
John Jenkins, Editor & Proprietor

March 5, 1845
Married in this city, on the 27th ult., by the Rev. N. N. Wood, Mr. Solomon Zimmerman to Miss Hannah J. Briggs.

Married on the 2d, in this city, by the Rev. N. N. Wood, Mr. Davis M. Fisher to Mrs. Eliza Jones.

March 13, 1845
The *Liberty Advocate*, Amite Co., Miss., has the following: During the evening of the 26th ult., an affray took place at the house of Ezekiel Boatner, in this county, which resulted in the death of John Robinson, from a blow inflicted on the head with a chair, by Boatner. He died early on the morning of the 27th. Mr. Boatner was not to be found.

March 17, 1845
Sexton's report:
March 8 - John Duffy, 40 years, dropsy.
March 15 - T. F. Gibbons, 25 years, chronic diarrhea.

March 18, 1845
Married in Natchez, on the 26th February, by the Rev. Mr. Page, Jefferson Davis, Esq., of Warren, to Miss Varia B., daughter of Wm. B. Howell, Esq. of Adams County.

March 29, 1845
Married on the 27th, by the Rev. M. D. O'Reily, Jarret R. Cook, Esq., to Miss Minerva Mary Louisa Hines, second daughter of Mr. John Hines, of this county.

April 11, 1845
Married the 9th, by the Rev. Mr. Montgomery, Mrs. Martha Ballard, of this city, to Mr. James J. Chewning, of Sunflower County, Miss.

Married on the 8th, at Milliken's Bend, parish of Madison, La., by the Rev. M. D. O'Reily, Doctor James R. Riggs to Miss Mary C., daughter of Mr. Fitzwilliam, all of the same parish.

May 14, 1845

Sexton's report:
May 10 - R. D. Smith, 42 years, malignant erysipelas.

June 13, 1845

Married at the house of William Trowbridge, in this city, on the 12th, by the Rev. Samuel M. Montgomery, Mr. James O'Neill to Mrs. Sarah Gill, both of Warren County.

Sexton's report:
June 2 - McLeim, 25 years, chronic diarrhea.

July 16, 1845

Sexton's report:
July 6 - A. Deat, 23 years, congestion of the brain.
July 7 - Joanna Miller, 35 years, dropsy.

September 10, 1845

Sexton's report:
Sept. 4 - Rebecca Mussentine, 30 years, consumption, Yazoo Co.

September 17, 1845

Sexton's report:
Sept. 8 - Ann Wade, 40 years, chronic diarrhea.
Sept. 9 - Robert Johnson, 30 years, chronic diarrhea.
Sept. 10 - Thomas Anderson, 33 years, consumption, Hinds Co.

October 1, 1845

Died September 24, T. Bart, of Warren Co., aged 35 years, of consumption.

October 6, 1845

Sexton's report:
Sept. 28 - Adalind Williams, 25 years, consumption, of Louisiana.

October 15, 1845

An unfortunate affray occurred in our village on Sun. last, between Mr. Samuel Swisher, keeper of the Eagle Hotel, and Col. F. A. Bailey, a planter of this county, which resulted in the death of the latter.

October 22, 1845

Sexton's report:
Oct. 12 - H. H. Stites, 31 years, swamp fever, Yazoo County.
Oct. 13 - Henry Garnett, Yazoo County.

VICKSBURG WEEKLY SENTINEL (Vicksburg, Miss.)
By John Jenkins and F. C. Jones

January 26, 1848
Married on the 18th, by the Right Rev. Jos. H. Otey, Fulton Anderson, Esq., to Miss Mary Ann, elder daughter of Geo. S. Yerger, Esq., all of this city.

February 9, 1848
Died in Vicksburg, on the 2d, George Limerick, aged 25 years, of congestive fever.

February 16, 1848
Married on the evening of the 10th, at her residence, by the Rev. Dr. Crawford, Mr. Joseph S. Acuff to Mrs. Nancy J. Higdon, all of this co.

Married on Sunday evening last, by the Rev. Mr. Patterson, Col. Joshua J. Hall, of Texas, to Mrs. Virginia A. Meikle, of this city.

Died at the residence of Mr. Parham, on Walnut Bayou, parish of Madison, La., on the 22d ult., John Shannon, Esq., of that parish, aged about 34 years.

Died in Hinds County, at the residence of her husband, Thomas Bolton, Mrs. Mary Bolton, aged 54 years.

Died on the 10th, Edward Griffin, aged 37 years, of mania potu.

March 15, 1848
Died on the 11th, Martin L. Ranny, aged 33 years, of consumption, a resident of Vicksburg.

Married on the 9th, by the Rev. A. W. Chapman, at the residence of Col. A. C. Downs, Mr. Albert M. Newman to Miss Minerva I. Baldwin, both of this county.

April 12, 1848
Died at the residence of his father, on Cherry Street, April 4th, Harold Travis Nutt, aged 5 years, 2 months and 18 days.

Died on the 7th, Frederick Davis, aged 23 years, of consumption.

Died on the 6th, John Casian, aged 30 years, of old age.

April 19, 1848
Died on the 14th, John Cornell, aged 21 years, of enlargement of the spleen, a resident of Lake Bolivar, Miss.

April 26, 1848
Died on April 16th, Sarah Blake, aged 62 years, of dropsy.

Married on the 20th, at the residence of Mr. Wm. Bobb, near this city, by Rev. W. Carey Crane, James E. Carnes, Esq. (Editor of the *Vicksburg Whig*), to Miss Emily F. Thompson, of Hopkinsville, Ky.

May 10, 1848
Died on the 5th, Samuel H. Simpson, aged 9 months and 20 days, only son of Adam and Margaret Simpson.

Died on the 3d, Geo. Sanford, aged 30 years, suicide.

May 17, 1848
Died at the residence of Dr. J. G. Parham, near this city, on the 9th, Henry Mason, youngest child of Dr. Geo. and Mrs. Mary J. Smith, formerly of Greenville Co., Virginia, aged 2 years, 8 months and 7 days.

Died the 10th, Lucy, infant dau. of N. G. Bryson, Esq., Mayor of city.

Died on the 10th, Matilda Hutchinson, aged 26 years.

May 24, 1848
Died on the 19th, J. Townsend, aged 23 years, of Arkansas.

May 31, 1848
Died in this city, on the 2nd, Mr. Margarett Phillips, wife of Mr. Benjamin Phillips, in the 28th year of her age, a native of London, England, and for the last nine years a resident of Vicksburg.

Died May 21st, John Gimp, aged 30 years, of suicide.

Died on the 26th, Ellen Nowlan, aged 35 years, of typhus fever.

June 21, 1848
Died on the 15th, aged 1 year and 2 days, William, infant son of A. M. and Mary Ann Boyd, of this county.

July 5, 1848
Married on the 18th, at the residence of Dr. J. P. Woolfolk, of Isaquena County, Mr. James R. Harvey to Miss Eleanor W. Benton.

Died on the 29th June, Sophia Onis, 27 years, of congestive fever.

July 26, 1848
Married the 18th, at Diamond Place, Miss., by Rev. Patterson, E. C. Laughlin, of New Orleans, to Mrs. Florida McCaleb, of former place.

Married in New Orleans, on the 13th, by Rev. Dr. Scott, Alex. T. Steele, Esq., to Miss Maria L. Taylor.

August 2, 1848
Died recently, at her residence in Newton, Mrs. Saffold, consort of Col. Bird Saffold, of that county.

Sexton's report:
July 23 - Wm. Bell, 60, general debility, of Warren Co.
July 24 - John Sully, 27, mania a potu.
July 24 - Geo. W. Steigleman, 5, drowned.

July 27 – Patrick Ellwood, 26, diarrhea and intemperance.
July 28 – M. P. Deloach, 42, consumption, of Isaquena.
July 29 – Peter Connell, 25.

August 9, 1848

Married the 3d, by Rev. A. Newton, Rev. Thos. Magruder, of Madison Co., to Caroline E., dau. of the late Duncan McArthur, of Warren Co.

August 30, 1848

Died in this city, on the 21st, Mr. D. M. Wallace, of consumption.

Sexton's report:
Aug. 21 – Danl. Driscall, 37, chronic diarrhea.
Aug. 25 – Daniel Dunlap, congestive fever.
Aug. 25 – Wm. B. Alverson, 25, chronic diarrhea.
Aug. 26 – Moses Sanderson, 35, disease of the lungs.

September 30, 1848

Sexton's report:
Sept. 3 – David Miller, 35. bilious typhoid fever.
Sept. 6 – Thos. Broderick, 21, disease of the head, resident of Ireland.
Sept. 8 – Charles Gillies, 25 years, yellow fever.
Sept. 8 – W. Scott Weaver, 22, shot.
Sept. 9 – James Beulan, 35, general bad health.

Married in Carrollton, Miss., on the 30th ult., by Rev. John D. Neal, Mr. William H. Clements, of the Mississippi Democrat office, to Miss Margaret, eldest daughter of Col. Richard Nelson.

October 4, 1848

Sexton's report:
Sept. 24 – Amos Robinson, 25, yellow fever.
Sept. 24 – William Wright, 20, yellow fever.
Sept. 25 – Henry Giesker, 36, malignant fever.
Sept. 26 – Jesse May, 30, fever.
Sept. 26 – Ellen McCarty, 40, inflammation of lungs.
Sept. 28 – Thos. Donague, 32, consumption.
Sept. 29 – Patrick Leahy, 35, bilious fever.
Sept. 29 – Wm. Wilkinson, 23, congestion of lungs.
Sept. 29 – Elizabeth Adams, 42, chronic diarrhea.

October 25, 1848

Married on the 21st ult., by the Rev. W. Carey Crane, Mr. Patrick O'Connor to Miss Susan Ellis, all of Warren County.

December 6, 1848

Died November 29th, Timothy Davis, aged 28 years.

January 3, 1849

Married on the 13th ult., Major Richard Griffith, Treasurer of the State of Mississippi, to Miss Sarah A. E., daughter of Benjamin Whitfield, Esq., all of Hinds County.

Married Dec. 26, 1848, by Rev. S. W. Sexton, Mr. William M. Jenkins to Miss Sarah Ann, daughter of John Slater, Esq., all of this co.

Died on the 23d of December last, of asiatic cholera, at the city of Vicksburg, Vincent M. Lewis, in the 50th year of his age. Mr. L. was a native of Virginia and a graduate of Princeton College.

Sexton's report:
Dec. 26 - John Salley, 30, asiatic cholera.
Dec. 27 - John M. Johnson, 31, asiatic cholera.
Dec. 27 - Jesse Hopkins, 29, asiatic cholera.
Dec. 27 - John Price, 58, asiatic cholera.
Dec. 27 - Patrick Donnelly, 35, asiatic cholera.
Dec. 28 - Mr. Coakley, 22, consumption.
Dec. 28 - Danl. Peer Gear, 29, chronic diarrhea.
Dec. 30 - Alexander Halford, 88, asiatic cholera.
Dec. 30 - Patrick Doyle, 40, chronic diarrhea.
Dec. 30 - Peter Daley, 40, asiatic cholera.
Dec. 30 - Timothy Welsh, 35, asiatic cholera.
Dec. 30 - Matthew Gill, 30, asiatic cholera.
Dec. 30 - Thomas Kane, 52, asiatic cholera.

January 17, 1849

Departed this life on the 7th, of asiatic cholera, Valentine Vogh, in the 27th year of his age. The deceased was born in Germany, but for many years a resident of this country.

Died of cholera, on the 8th, Mr. Isaac R. Newman, in the 32d year of his age. He was a native of Mississippi. He married at the age of 25 and leaves a widow and two children.

Sexton's report:
Jan. 7 - Henry Hill, 36 years, dropsy.
Jan. 12 - Agnes M. Brown, 47 years, disease of the heart.

February 14, 1849

Sexton's report:
Feb. 5 - David Lewis, of intemperance.
Feb. 6 - Eber Rowe, 33, consumption.
Feb. 7 - Charles Yancy, 31, cholera, of Providence, La.
Feb. 7 - Patrick Ragan, 21, jaundice and intermittent fever.
Feb. 7 - Anthony McRoberts, 40, fits.
Feb. 7 - I. F. Rousseau, 38, consumption.

March 28, 1849

Married in New Orleans, 15th, by Rev. Dr. Twichell, W. A. Haines to Miss Mary Thompson, all of this place.

Married on the 22d, by the Rev. S. W. Sexton, Dr. M. H. Wall, of Cadiz, Ky., to Miss Catharine S. Harris, of Warren County, Miss.

Died in Holmes County, at the residence of her father, Robert J. Davis, 11th, Mary Ellen, consort of Geo. W. Mabry, aged 19 years, 5 months and 17 days.

Died, James Anderson, aged 30 years, of pleurisy, on the 23d.

Died on the 20th, Catherine Straub, aged 40 years, on a steamboat.

WASHINGTON REPUBLICAN (Washington, Miss.)
Published by Andrew Marschalk

April 27, 1813
Married in Jefferson County, on the 11th, by Samuel Dunbar, Esq., Mr. Hiram Baldwin to Mrs. Ann Heard, both of said county.

May 18, 1813
Died in Philadelphia, on the 19th ultimo, Doctor Benjamin Rush, full of years and honors.

June 16, 1813
Died at Bayou St. John, in the 58th year of his age, Col. John Girault, for many years a resident of Natchez. He left widow and large family.

July 21, 1813
On the 22d, Mrs. Ann Wilkinson, of Homochito, Adams County, departed this life, in the 57th year of her age, and was interred in the family grave yeard of Montfort Calvit, Esq., near Washington. She was a native of Charles County, Maryland.

August 11, 1813
Died on the 14th ult., Ensign Richard Cocke, of the 3d Regt. U. S. Infantry, of a severe fever. Ensign Cocke was a native of North Carolina.

Married on the 9th ultimo, at Fredericksburg, Virginia, the Hon. Josiah Simpson, one of the Superior Judges of this Territory, to Miss Ann Stanard, daughter of the late William Stanard, Esq., of that place.

August 25, 1813
Died at Selcertown, on the 16th, Col. Abraham Morhouse, a citizen of Louisiana. Col. Morhouse was a native of the state of New York.

September 29, 1813
Died at Dauphin Island, on the 4th, Capt. James B. Wilkinson, of the 3d U. S. Regiment of Infantry, eldest son of Major Gen. Wilkinson.

October 13, 1813
Died in the county of Adams, on the 17th September, in the 79th year of his age, Mr. Robert Lowry, Sr., formerly of Sumpter District, South Carolina.

Died on Sunday night last, in Jefferson County, the Rev. Wilson Bolls, aged 43 years, 40 of which he resided in this territory.

October 27, 1813
Married on Sunday evening last, Capt. David Greenleaf, of this county, to Mrs. Gore, of this place.

November 3, 1813
Died in the city of Natchez, on Sunday night last, Capt. N. Nichols.

January 12, 1814
Married on Thursday evening last, in this place, Mr. J. H. M'Comas, merchant of Natchez, to Miss Anne Wyllis.

January 26, 1814
Married on the 12th, in Amite County, Mr. Wm. Holmes to Miss Dorcas Nelson, eldest daughter of Col. David Nelson, of that county.

Married the 16th, in Warren Co., Col. Benj. Hicks to Eunice Brown.

February 23, 1814
Adam Tooley, Esquire, of this co., departed this life on the 18th, aged 72 years, for 25 years a member of the Methodist Episcopal Church.

March 9, 1814
Died at his residence in Selcertown, Adams Co., on the 3d, Reuben Morhouse, aged 47 years, 4 days. He was a native of New York.

March 16, 1814
Died on the 15th of February last, First Lieut. Joseph M. Wilcox, of the 3rd Regiment of U. S. Inf., about 21 years of age, a native of Connecticutt, but lately a resident of the state of Ohio.

March 30, 1814
Departed this life on Monday night last, Mrs. Mary Defrance, wife of Mr. Abram Defrance.

April 20, 1814
Departed this life on Thursday last, Miss Mary Henderson, second daughter of John Henderson, Esq., merchant of Natchez.

May 18, 1814
Died on the 6th, Mrs. Jane Smith, consort of Mr. Israel Smith. She left a husband and nine children.

Died on the 10th of March last, between Fort Findley and Fort M'Arthur, on his return home from the army, Captain Joseph Carpenter, senior editor of the *Western Spy*.

June 1, 1814
Departed this life, on the 23d ult., in Amite County, Mr. Jonathan Hicks.

June 8, 1814
Died on Sunday morning last, in the 42d year of her age, Mrs. Susanna Marschalk, the consort of the editor of this paper.

July 27, 1814
Died on the 25th, Mrs. Elizabeth Williams, wife of the late Governor Williams of this Territory, at his residence near the town of Washington.

August 31, 1814
Died yesterday afternoon, at the house of Henry Dangerfield, in this town, Col. Nehemiah Tilton, Register of the land office, aged 67 yrs.

Died the 20th, at his residence near this place, Capt. Francis Gildart.

October 5, 1814
Major Andrew Hunter Holmes, the youngest brother of his Excellency David Holmes, Governor of the Mississippi Territory, fell in the field of battle, at Fort Mackinaw, on the 4th day of August, 1814, in the 22d year of his age. He was a native of Virginia.

October 12, 1814
Died at St. Louis, on the 18th ult., Brig. Gen. Benjamin Howard, of the U. S. Army.

November 9, 1814
Died on the 2d, Capt. Jonh Bisland, junior, in the 27th year of his age.

November 23, 1814
Died on the 12th, Mrs. Esther King, wife of Maj. R. King, aged 47 yrs.

January 4, 1815
Died at his plantation on Homochitto, on Thursday last, William Conner, Esq.

February 22, 1815
Died on Sunday evening last, Henry Dangerfield, Esq., Secretary of this Territory and Register of the Land Office west of Pearl River.

April 5, 1815
Died the 25th ult., at his plantation on Pine Ridge, Maj. Richard King, born Morris Co., New Jersey, on the 14th of Sept., 1760, from whence he emigrated and arrived in this territory on the 1st day of Jan., 1774.

July 15, 1815
Departed this life at his plantation in this territory, Col. Richard Sparks, late of the 2d United States Infantry, aged about 52 years.

October 28, 1815
Died yesterday morning, Mr. James McCurdy, Editor of *The Natchez Intelligencer.*

WASHINGTON REPUBLICAN & NATCHEZ INTELLIGENCER
(Washington, Miss.)
Published by Andrew Marschalk

December 13, 1815

Died in this city, on Thursday last, in the 32d year of his age, Mr. Oliver W. Foller, a native of Providence, Rhode Island.

Died in the county of Amite, on the 27th November, in the 42d year of her age, Mrs. Penelope Gayden, consort of Mr. Agrippa Gayden.

January 10, 1816

Died on the 4th, at Woodville, Wilkinson County, in the 24th year of his age, Mr. Ezekiel Foreman, merchant of that place.

January 31, 1816

Died in Jefferson County, on the 19th, Mrs. Patsey Harrison, in the 53d year of her age.

February 7, 1816

Died in the county of St. Tammany, near Madisonville, La., about the 22d ult., Mrs. Eliza B. Morgan, consort of General David B. Morgan, aged 26 years and 5 months.

May 8, 1816

Died in this city, on the 3d, Mr. William Forget, a native of Pennsylvania, in the 31st year of his age.

May 15, 1816

Died in the neighborhood of Greenville, Jefferson County, on the 7th, Mrs. Mary Balch, in the 24th year of her age.

May 29, 1816

Departed this life yesterday afternoon, of an inflammation of the lungs, in the 8th year of his age, Thomas Jefferson, son of Puckshunnubbee, a principal chief of the Choctaw nation of Indians.

June 19, 1816

On Wednesday, the 12th, departed this life, in the 26th year of her age, at the seat of the late Gen. Claiborne, near this city, Mrs. Isabella Charlotte H. Claiborne, consort of Doctor Thomas Augustine Claiborne, late of the Navy of the United State.

The bodies of Henry Irvine and Patty Nall were yesterday found near this place, murdered in a most shocking manner, apparently with an ax, as the head of both were nearly separated from their bodies and their skulls much fractured. They had been missing from the 6th to the 11th, when they were discovered. Suspicion is on a Sargent Fox and a woman by the name of Fanny Newman, who had quarreled with the deceased and been heard to utter threats against them. (Natchitoches, La.)

July 17, 1816

Died on the 14th, in Jefferson County, near Union Town, Mr. Derick P. January, a native of Philadelphia, but long a resident of Kentucky, and this territory. He has left a wife and two small boys.

Married on Sunday evening last, by Theodore Stark, Esq., Mr. Joseph Leonard to Miss Eunice Greenleaf, daughter of D. Greenleaf, Esq., all of this county.

August 7, 1816

Died on the 31st of July, of typhus fever, Mrs. Jane Ross, consort of John Ross, Esq., of Jefferson County, aged 21 years and 11 days.

August 21, 1816

Married on Wednesday evening last, by S. Brooks, Esq., Dr. G. H. Hunter, of New Orleans to Miss Ann M. Girault, of this city.

Married on the same evening, by S. Brooks, Esq., Mr. E. G. Head, merchant of this city, to Miss Maria Throckmorton.

Married the same evening, Mr. Robert Dunbar to Miss Sarah Shotard.

October 9, 1816

Died on the 27th of September, in Franklin County, Mr. Reuben Gibson, formerly of South Carolina, but for many years an inhabitant of this territory.

October 16, 1816

Died at Elysian Fields, on the 22d ultimo, in the 24th year of his age, Mr. Robert Pleasants Davis, son of Micajah Davis.

October 30, 1816

Married on the 20th, Mr. Charles Davis, merchant of Liberty, Amite County, to Mrs. Parthena Leith, of the same county.

November 13, 1816

Married on the 5th, by Wm. Lemon, Esq., Capt. Samuel Sousby, of Jefferson County, to Miss Elizabeth Foster, daughter of Mr. Thomas Foster, of this county.

Departed this life, on the 1st Nov., Miss Mahala Caroline Ross, eldest daughter of Mr. Samuel Ross, of Adams County, aged 17 years, 3 months and 21 days.

November 20, 1816

Married at Beach Grove, Jefferson County, on the 14th, Joseph MacQuillen, Esq., merchant of Port Gibson, to Miss Cynthia Holland Prince, daughter of Robert Prince, Esq., of the former place.

Married on the same day, James Irwin, Esq., of Claiborne County, to Miss Maria Newman, daughter of Benjamin Newman, Esq., of Jefferson County.

December 18, 1816

Died on the 15th, at his residence in the town of Washington, Doctor John C. Cox.

January 22, 1816

Died at his plantation near Natchez, on the 20th, Mr. Nathaniel Ivey, aged 54 years, a native of Virginia, but many years a resident of this territory.

January 29, 1817

Married in Jefferson County, by the Rev. Joseph Bullen, Dr. Benjamin M. Bullen to Miss Elizabeth Dixon.

February 12, 1817

Died on Thursday last, at Selser Town, Mr. Charles V. Larimere, a native of France, and late a teacher of dancing.

February 19, 1817

Married in Pike County, on the 2d, by Barnabas Allen, Esq., Mr. William Dickson, of Georgia, to Miss Harriet Catchings, of that place.

February 26, 1817

Died at his late residence (Liberty, Amite Co., M. T.), on the 10th, Mr. Joseph King, about 28 years of age, a native of South Carolina.

March 5, 1817

Died on Monday last, Christian Harmon, aged 59, a native of Germany.

Died at Covington, Ken., 4th ult., Andrew Burt, formerly of this city.

April 9, 1817

Died in New York, on the 3d ultimo, Mrs. Elizabeth Servoss, wife of Mr. Thomas L. Servoss, formerly of this city.

Married at Alexandria, on Thursday evening last, Mr. Hugh Chain, one of the editors of the *Louisiana Rambler*, to Miss Matilda Anderson, both of that place.

May 14, 1817

Died on the 10th, Alexander Fowler, aged 25 years, only son of Mr. James Fowler, of this city.

Married Thurs. eve. last, Robt. Feagan to Emelia Ratliff, both of here.

May 21, 1817

Married on Sunday evening last, by William Lemon, Esq., Mr. Bennet M. Hynes to Miss Ruth Newman, daughter of Mr. Ezekiel Newman, all of this county.

June 14, 1817
Died at his county seat near Natchez, on the 5th, James M'Intosh, Esq., in the 50th year of his age.

July 5, 1817
Died on the 26th ult., in the parish of Concordia, by a fall from a horse, William Rives, aged 29 years, 5 months.

Died on the 22d ult., Mrs. Anne Guice, in the 55th year of her age, wife of Jonathan Guice, Sen., of Franklin County.

July 26, 1817
Departed this life on the 23d, near this city, Mr. Andrew Haslet, son of the late Doctor Andrew Haslet, of the city of Baltimore, aged 28 years. He emigrated with his relation, Dr. Smith, to this territory, and on the 2d of Feb. last was married to Miss Ann A. Conrad.

August 2, 1817
Mr. Hugh Davis, son of the late Colonel Hugh Davis of Wilkinson County, in this territory, was drowned on the 12th July, in the Homochitto River.

One of the most horrid murders ever perpetrated at Fort Adams in this territory was on or about the 24th ultimo. Mr. John S. Horn, of Kentucky, had lately descended the river with a boat load of produce and halting at this place one of his hands left him; in consequence of which he employed a certain Israel Kemp. Elisha M'Conathy and the above named Kemp left here on the 23d and the next day arrived at Fort Adams. Kemp, in the dead of night (as is supposed) killed Horn with an axe and shot M'Conathy. Both bodies were thrown overboard. Kemp has been conveyed to Wilkinson jail to stand trial in November next.

Another murder was committed at Liberty, Amite County, by a man named Tucker, on the person of ---- Cotton. Tucker has fled.

August 9, 1817
Departed this life on the 3d, Miss Ann Eliza Virginia Claiborne, the daughter and eldest child of the late General Ferdinand L. Claiborne.

Died in this city, on the 5th, Major Overton M. Cosby, of Warren Co.

August 16, 1817
Died on the 7th, near this city, Mr. James Brown, the only child of Capt. James Brown, late of New York.

Departed this life on the 14th, Capt. Daniel Hull, aged 30 years, brother of Com. Isaac Hull. From the age of 15 to 29 he followed the profession of a sailor. He came to this city in December last and established a plantation.

Died a few days since, at his residence in Pike County, Mr. Richard Conn, a native of Ireland. He has left a wife and eight children.

September 18, 1817
Died at the Walnut Hills, on the 31st ult., Mrs. Elizabeth McAlister, aged 43 years, consort of Capt. John McAlister, a resident of that settlement. She left a husband and four children.

Married on Wednesday evening last, by the Rev. Daniel Smith, F. A. Browder, Esq., of Bayou Sara, to Miss Isabella A. Henderson, daughter of John Henderson, Esq., of this city.

Married on the 7th, Mr. Amos Alexander to Miss Lavina Ford, youngest daughter of Mr. Robin Ford, all of this county.

October 4, 1817
Died on the 27th ult., at Baton Rouge, with the prevailing fever, Major George C. Allen, formerly of the old 7th Regiment. He was interred on the 28th at Baton Rouge.

December 6, 1817
Married at Concordia, La., on the 23d ult., by the Hon. Judge Dunlap, William F. Smith, Esq., to Miss Ann E. Reagan, daughter of Capt. Geo. Reagan, of said place.

December 20, 1817
Died at Franklin, on the 16th, James Keith, Esq., attorney at law.

Married on the 16th, by the Rev. Mr. Manafee, Mr. Augustin Freeland, of Claiborne County, to Miss Eliza Magruder, of Adams County.

December 27, 1817
Died at his residence near Port Gibson, on the 19th, Samuel Gibson, aged 69, and for 45 years a resident of this state.

THE WEEKLY CHRONICLE (Natchez, Miss.)
Printed by John W. Winn & CO.

December 7, 1808
Died at Fort Concordia, on the evening of the 5th, James Ferrall, Esq., 39. a native of Ireland.

March 1, 1809
Died on Friday, the 24th ultimo, at his plantation near Sandy Creek, Abraham Merlin, Esq., a respectable inhabitant of this territory.

April 29, 1809
Died on the 28th, Jona. Davis, Esq., Collector of this District.

May 6, 1809
Died on Monday morning, 1st April, Mrs. Celeste Bowmar, consort of Capt. Joseph Bowmar.

Married on Sunday, the 30th ult., by Hon. Thomas Rodney, Mr. George Newman to Miss Charlotte Dunbar, daughter of Mr. Robert Dunbar.

Married on Thursday, 4th, Mr. Mitchell to Miss Betsy Burney, daughter of Mr. David Burney.

May 27, 1809

Married in Adams County, on Saturday evening, the 20th, by the Hon. Samuel Brooks, Mr. Daniel D. Elliott, merchant of this city, to Miss Catherine Surget, daughter of Mrs. C. Surget.

June 3, 1809

Married in the county of Rapide, Orleans Territory, on Monday, the 22d ult., by Hon. Judge Claiborne, Mr. Archibald Terrell, merchant of this city, to Miss Anne Martin, daughter of the late Major Abraham Martin.

Married in this county, Mr. Philip Hill, of this city, to Miss Torry, of Morgan's Fork.

Died on the night of the 16th, of a wound he received on Monday, of a duel, Lieut. Bowie, of the U. S. Light Dragoons.

Departed this life on the 11th ult., Mrs. Sarah Cassels, wife of Henry Cassels, Jun., Esq., of Amite County, Mississippi Territory.

September 9, 1809

Died this a.m., Mr. William Davis, late of Meadville, Pennsylvania.

December 9, 1809

Departed this life on the 5th, Mrs. Elen Davis, consort of Col. Hugh Davis, of Wilkinson County.

Died in this city, on Sunday evening last, Col. Joseph Pannell.

Died on the 9th October last, in Mifflin Co., Pennsylvania, the Rev. David Snodgrass, for several years past an inhabitant of this territory.

May 28, 1810

Died yesterday morning, the 27th, Mrs. Sarah Hubbs, widow of the late Thomas Hubbs, of the Territory of Orleans.

Married on Sunday the 20th, by the Hon. Samuel Brooks, Mr. William Wright, merchant, to Miss Mary N. Hoggatt, all of this county.

Married on Thursday the 24th, by the same, Mr. John Mary Joseph Ducayet, to Miss Flora Catharine Ritter, all of this town.

Married yesterday, the 27th, by the same, Mr. James Campbell Wilkins, merchant of this place, to Miss Charlotte Bingaman, daughter of Mr. Adam Bingaman, of Adams County.

WEEKLY SENTINEL (Vicksburg, Miss.)
Printed & Published by John Shannon & Co.

September 29, 1846

Sexton's report:
Sept. 15 - Peter Hossley, 29 years, congestion.
Sept. 18 - D. D. Sullivan, 38, falling off bank.
Sept. 18 - John Donovan, 40, Ireland.

November 3, 1846

Died 25 Oct., 1846, at Vicksburg, Thomas Williamson, formerly of Hagerstown, Md. He had been a resident of this place ten years.

November 10, 1846

Charles S. Williams contracted disease on the Rio Grande, in the enemy's country, and after obtaining an honorable discharge from the army (Raymond Fencibles), on the 19th his spirit took flight.

Married in Christ Church, on Thurs. eve., by Rev. Stephen Patterson, Mr. Joseph P. Hawks to Mrs. M. J. Rebecca Randolph, all of this city.

Married in Nashville, the 27th of October, at the residence of Joseph Woods, Esq., by the Rt. Rev. Bishop Miles, D. D., Raymond A. Bourk, Esq., of this city, to Miss Jane M. West, of the former place.

Married at Canaan, on the 4th, at the residence of Maj. J. B. Williamson, by the Rev. Mr. Patterson, Mr. Sidney G. Miller, of New York, to Miss Frances Williamson, of Vicksburg.

Died Nov. 3d, John Thinkler, aged 42 years, of fever.

December 2, 1846

Sexton's report:
Nov. 23 - M. F. Ames, 23 years, neuralgia.
Nov. 25 - James A. Oldcroft, 28 years, consumption.

Married on the 12th, by the Rev. Mr. Caldwell, Mr. Wm. A. Bovard to Miss Ellen E. Glasscock, all of Warren County.

December 16, 1846

Sexton's report:
Dec. 8 - Charles Puckles, 23 years, diarrhea.
Dec. 12 - Adam Conner, 30 years, intemperance.

December 30, 1846

Sexton's report:
Dec. 23 - Daniel Wallace, 28 years, inflammation of the brain.
Dec. 25 - Margaret Porterfield, 22 years, pueperel fever.

January 6, 1847

Married at Lexington, on the 26th ult., by the Rev. John Skinner, of the Presbytarian Church, James G. Paxton, Esq., Attorney at Law, to Ann

M. White, daughter of Matthew White, Esq., merchant, all of Lexington.

Died Dec. 14th, John J. Lowe, aged 42 years, of dropsy.

January 13, 1847

Sexton's report:
Jan. 3 - Isaac Lynch, 25 years, Copiah Co., accidental fall.
Jan. 5 - James Cargrow, 25 years, intemperance.

We are informed that on last Sabbath evening, John Reeves, a citizen of Lexington, killed a man by the name of Herrn, formerly a citizen of this county. Herrn was intoxicated and on coming to Mr. Reeve's grocery he swore he would ride into the house and made an attempt to do so, but Reeves met him at the door and struck him with a stick. He died in about 12 hours.

January 20, 1847

Sexton's report:
Jan. 13 - M. S. Tucker, 23 years, cold plague, of Marshall County.
Jan. 14 - E. M. Turner, 40 years, of Texas.
Jan. 16 - C. C. Briggs, 38 years, congestive chill.

February 3, 1847

Sexton's report:
Jan. 29 - G. C. Malone, 25 years, of Evansville, Ind., pneumonia.

February 10, 1847

Died on the 9th, James L., only son of Mr. & Mrs. Wm. Thomas, of this place. The deceased was in his tenth year.

February 24, 1847

Sexton's report:
Feb. 14 - Mary Eliza Montgomery, 28 years, consumption.
Feb. 16 - Adam Knapp, 22 years, effusion of the brain.
Feb. 20 - Conrad Steigelman, 38 years, convulsions.

March 10, 1847

Married in Yazoo City, on the 25th ult., by the Rev. R. McInnis, Mr. S. H. Wilson to Miss Mary F. Whitman.

Sexton's report:
March 3 - L. J. Robinson, of Pittsburgh, Pa.
March 6 - Wm. H. Easom, 17 years, malignant typhus fever.

April 7, 1847

Sexton's report:
March 28 - Lesley Evans, 25 years, consumption.
March 28 - L. Mulegan, 40 years.
March 29 - Allen Dickerman, 30 years, pneumonia, of St. Louis.
April 2 - N. S. Drake, 38 years, consumption.

April 28, 1847
Sexton's report:
April 21 - J. Hurley, 60 years, of Yazoo Co., pneumonia.
April 22 - John Carngain, 21 years, fever.

May 19, 1847
Died the 12th, William Gordon Robinson, aged 4 years and 6 months, eldest son of Gordon and Martha P. Robinson, of this city.

May 26, 1847
Married 18th, by Rev. Dr. H. Leavel, Col. G. D. Mitchell, of this city, to Miss Caroline P., eldest daughter of Mr. Wesley W. Neely, of Warren County.

June 2, 1847
Died in this city, on the 25th, Dr. Daniel McGill, in the 43d year of his age, of a violent attack of neuralgia. Dr. McGill was a native of North Carolina, but had been a resident of this city for the last ten years.

Sexton's report:
May 24 - Noland Myers, 52 years.
May 26 - J. G. Camp, 30 years, erysipelas.

June 9, 1847
Died on the 7th, aged about 29 years, Jacob Shuler.

Sexton's report:
June 5 - Gottleib Wahl, 34 years, dropsy.

June 16, 1847
Married in Morehouse Parish, La., on the 9th, Mr. Thomas B. Pierce, of this city, formerly of Cincinnati, Ohio, to Miss Mary Ann Woodburn, recently of this city.

July 28, 1847
Major W. R. Thompson, formerly of Lauderdale County, Tenn., lately went to Chicot County, Arkansas, where he died at the residence of Col. W. C. Russell, on the 18th, of congestive fever. He was in the 24th year of his age.

August 4, 1847
Died July 29th, Patrick Coleman, 35 years, of convulsions.

August 11, 1847
Bill for Divorce -- Catherine Wilmurth -vs- Ralph P. Wilmurth.

Sexton's report:
Aug. 1 - A. R. Sears, 20 years, chronic diarrhea.
Aug. 3 - Mary Laughlin, 30 years, chronic diarrhea, of Ireland.

August 18, 1847

Died on the 1st, at the residence of Mr. J. D. Peebles, near Bolton's Depot, Hinds Co., Albert R. Sears, of Sharon, Conn., aged 20 years, brother of John Sears, Jr., of Mercien & Sears, of this city.

Died on the 10th, of inflammation of the bowels, at his residence in Warren County, Miss., Mr. Lawrence G. Heath, a native of Granville County, Va., aged 48 years.

Married the 12th, at residence of Jos. E. Davis, Esq., by Rev. S. M. Montgomery, Robert M. Martin to Miss Mary M. Davis, all of this co.

Married on the 12th, at the residence of M. C. Folkes, Esq., by the Rev. S. M. Montgomery, Mr. Charles W. Dwight to Mrs. E. B. Goodman, all of this city.

Sexton's report:
Aug. 13 – James Bumsich, 21 years, chronic diarrhea.
Aug. 13 – Joseph Sungenati, 37 years, ascites.
Aug. 13 – Catharine Curtin, 50 years, consumption.
Aug. 14 – Thomas McManus, 33 years, fit.

August 25, 1847

Married on the 18th, at the residence of Dr. H. Hill, in this county, by the Rev. S. M. Montgomery, Mr. Robert H. Smith, of Hinds County, to Miss Frances M. Elliot, of Warren.

September 8, 1847

Married on the 2d, at the residence of Washington E. Green, Esq., by Rev. S. H. Montgomery, Mr. Daniel Morgan, of Vicksburg, to Miss Mary Ellen Cookley, of Zanesville, Ohio.

Married on the 2d, at the residence of Mr. Martin Hackler, in Hinds Co., by J. I. Lewis, Esq., Mr. Isaac S. Johnson, of Warren Co., to Miss Margaret Hackler, of Hinds County.

September 29, 1847

Sexton's report:
Sept. 23 – Henry Blake, 21 years, bilious remittent fever.
Sept. 24 – Daniel Montgomery, 34 years, yellow fever.

October 6, 1847

Died the 25th September, of congestion of the lungs, at the residence of her father, on Joe's Bayou, Madison parish, La., Mrs. Ann Eliza Fretwell, wife of Dr. John R. Fretwell, and only daughter of Col. Bennett H. and Elizabeth Bell, formerly of Halifax Co., North Carolina.

Sexton's report:
Sept. 28 – Nancy Lilly, 36 years, bilious remittent fever.
Sept. 30 – Augustus Gray, 27 years, delirium tremen.

October 27, 1847

Sexton's report:

Oct. 20 – Henry Hopkins, 50 years, yellow fever.
Oct. 22 – James McManus, 32 years, yellow fever.

November 3, 1847
Sexton's report:
Oct. 11 – Charles Smith, 35 years, yellow fever.
Oct. 12 – Andrew Wise, 45 years, bilious cholic.
Oct. 13 – John Daws, 30 years, delirium tremens.
Oct. 13 – Edward Leonard, 30 years.

November 10, 1847
Sexton's report:
Nov. 2 – Thomas Ramage, 34 years, consumption.
Nov. 3 – David Fitzpatrick, 36 years, fever.

November 17, 1847
Sexton's report:
Nov. 7 – Peter Bell, 40 years, mania a potu.

November 24, 1847
Sexton's report:
Nov. 18 – E. H. Crimm, 25 years, consumption.
Nov. 20 – D. Weisse, 22 years.

December 1, 1847
Married on the 25th, by the Rev. Mr. Montgomery, Mr. Ambrose B. Niles to Miss Elizabeth Nichols, all of this city.

Sexton's report:
Nov. 21 – F. W. Rouse, 30 years, congestion of the brain.
Nov. 24 – John H. Rice, 26 years, quinsey, of Kentucky.

December 15, 1847
Died December 7th, John Cox, aged 48 years, of chronic diarrhea.

Died in the city of Mexico, on the 18th of September last, of a wound received in the battle of Churubusco, Marcellus L. Wright, 9th Regiment U. S. Infantry, aged 17 years, 7 months and 1 day. The deceased was a native of Vermont and a brother of J. Gilbert Wright, Esq., of Hinds County, Miss., formerly a resident of this city..

Dr. Jonathan Lafayette Owings, came to an untimely end, by drowning, on the 7th, in the Mississippi River. He had been for the past two years a resident of Holly Springs, Marshall Co., Miss., engaged in the practice of dentistry.

December 22, 1847
Sexton's report:
December 12 – J. Stransbury, 35 years, consumption, of Louisiana.
December 17 – Timothy Roferty, 28 years, chronic diarrhea.

Married on the 14th, by the Rev. Mr. Montgomery, David Coopland Gay to Mrs. Sally N. Nicholson.

December 29, 1847

Married on the 22d, at the residence of Charles Baker, Esq., of Warren County, by the Rev. Mr. Chapman, of this city, Mr. Adam J. Snyder, of the steamer Exit, to Miss Elizabeth J. Heath.

Married on the 8th, by the Rev. Thomas Ford, Mr. Hiram R. Lott to Miss M. A. E. Williams, all of Hinds County.

Married on the 14th, by the Rev. Thomas Ford, Mr. Wm. H. Hampton to Miss Martha L. Thomas, daughter of Daniel Thomas, Esq., all of Hinds County.

Married on the 16th, by the Rev. A. W. Chapman, Mr. John D. Cato to Miss Martha Whatley, both of this county.

Married on the 16th, by the same, Capt. C. C. Williams, of the steamer Exit, to Mrs. Charlotte Hair, of this county.

January 5, 1848

Died December 30th, Thomas F. Wry, aged 44 years, of chronic diarrhea, a resident of Pontotoc County, Miss.

January 12, 1848

Sexton's report:
Jan. 2 - Garret Linchen, 30 years, of Louisiana.
Jan. 2 - Michael Foley, 37, consumption.

January 19, 1848

Sexton's report:
Jan. 9 - James Buntin, 23 years, pneumonia.
Jan. 9 - James Montgomery, 48 years, consumption.
Jan. 10 - Alexander R. Depew, 65 years, fungus hometodes.
Jan. 10 - E. C. Danley, 53 years, apoplexy.
Jan. 11 - John Fox, 30 years.
Jan. 12 - James Purley, 23 years, pneumonia.
Jan. 15 - Frederick Huntman, 27 years, consumption.

THE WOODVILLE REPUBLICAN (Woodville, Miss.)
Published by William A. A. Chisholm

December 18, 1823

Died in this town, on Friday last, William F. Noland.

It becomes our painful task to record the death of Doctor James A. Maxwell, in the 45th year of his age. He expired yesterday afternoon. (Washington City, Nov. 22)

Died in this city, on Wednesday morning, Capt. William Barrow, aged about 60 years, an inhabitant of the Parish of Feliciana, in the State of

Louisiana. He has left Mrs. Benoist, a widow, his daughter, in Philadelphia, and a younger daughter in that city. He had placed his son and nephew at the Columbian College, near this city, and was on his way from Philadelphia to Wheeling, to his residence, when he was taken ill of typhus fever.

January 1, 1824

A most deliberate murder was committed yesterday morning, at the White Horse tavern, about a mile from this city, on the body of Dr. Drahan, lately from Baton Rouge, by a man named Carlisle. He made his escape immediately, but was apprehended last evening by Mr. Gridley, an officer of the peace.

Married on Monday evening last, by the Rev. Mr. Fox, Maj. A. M. Feltus, merchant of this place, to Miss Eliza Ann Ventress, daughter of the late Mr. Lovick Ventress, of this county.

Married on the evening of the 24th, by the Rev. Mark Moore, Dr. Jesse Saunders, of Alabama, to Miss Maria Davis, of this city.

Married on the same evening, by the Rev. Mark Moore, Samuel Davis, Esq., to Miss Mary Williams, both of this county.

Died on the 29th ultimo, Wm. A. Richardson, Esq., of Wilkinson County, Miss.

January 6, 1824

A most daring and atrocious murder was committed on Wednesday night, on the person of Mr. John Miller, of this town. Mr. Miller was entering the door of Mr. Hawkins billiard room, when some villain discharged a musket or pistol at his back, loaded with buck shot, several of which entered his head and shoulder. He lived only a few minutes.

January 15, 1824

Married at Port Gibson, on Friday, the 9th, by James Cornell, Esq., Mr. John Brent, formerly a citizen of this town, to Mrs. Harriet Shaw.

February 10, 1824

Died at his residence, near Pinckneyville, on the 2d, in his 56th year, Thomas Dawson, Esq., one of the first settlers in that neighborhood.

Died at the residence of his mother, in this neighborhood, on the 5th, Mr. Jared C. Beasley.

February 17, 1824

Died in this town, Tues. eve., the 10th, Thomas Aspinal, merchant.

We regret to announce the death of Mrs. Eleanor W. Gildart, wife of Francis Gildart, Esq., in the 23d year of her age.

March 2, 1824

Died here this morning, Mrs. Mary E. Davis, consort of Robert Davis.

Died at Woodville, on Sunday morning, the 22d ultimo, of a paralytic affection, Hezekiah B. Hull, Esq., Counsellor at Law, in the 36th year of his age.

March 9, 1824

Married on Tuesday, the 2d, by Thomas Dawson, Esq., Mr. Henry T. Thom to Miss M. Dawson, all of this county.

Died here, on the 6th, Catherine Gill, infant dau. of H. M. Gill, Esq.

April 27, 1824

Married on the 11th, by Jeremiah Downs, Esquire, Mr. Richard Kidd, to A. E. Chaney, both of Pinckneyville.

May 11, 1824

Died on the 8th, at the residence of Genl. Joor, Mrs. Sarah H. Shaw, consort of John F. Shaw.

June 1, 1824

Married in Illinois, Mr. Robert K. Fleming, late editor of the *Republican Advocate*, to Miss Lucinda Leland.

June 8, 1824

Died on the 2d, Capt. John Hughes, a citizen of this town.

Died the 5th, at the residence of Hugh Connell, Miss Lucretia Smith.

June 15, 1824

Died at his residence near here, on Sun. last, Dr. Micajah Frazier.

Died here yesterday, Matilda, infant dau. of the late Dr. Wm. Langley.

Died at Elmsley, this morning, Mrs. Bethia Liddell, consort of Moses Liddell, Esq.

Died in this parish of Feliciana, on the 11th, Capt. Jedediah Smith, a planter of that parish.

July 24, 1824

Married at Natchez, on Mon. eve. last, by Rev. Mr. Pilmore, the Hon. Gerard C. Brandon, of this county, to Miss Betsy Stanton, of that city.

August 3, 1824

Died in this town, on the 30th ult., Lucy Ann, infant daughter of George B. Collier, Esq.

August 18, 1824

Died in this town, on the 18th, William Doss, son of Geo. W. Doss.

August 27, 1824

Died in this town, on the 23d, Penelope, infant dau. of H. Cage, Esq.

September 14, 1824
Died in Pinckneyville, on Sunday the 12th, Mr. George F. Randolph, Jnr., aged 23 years.

Since the above was written, Mrs. Rachel Randolph, consort of George F. Randolph, Jnr., departed this life, on Monday last.

September 28, 1824
Died at the residence of Mr. M. F. DeGraffenreid, near this place, on the 25th, Major Chapman White.

October 5, 1824
Died at the house of Mr. Thomas S. Chew, in the parish of Feliciana, on the morning of the 2d, the Reverend Mark Moore.

October 19, 1824
Married on 7th September, by the Rev. Robert Patterson, Iveson G. Lea, Esq., to Miss Mary Ann Harriet Batchelor, daughter of Thomas Batchelor, Esq., both of Liberty, Miss.

Died at the residence of Thomas Batchelor, Esq., in Liberty, Miss., on 29th September, of bilious fever, Iveson G. Lea, Esq., Attorney at Law, aged 22 years.

November 23, 1824
Married on Wednesday, the 17th, by Howell Moreland, Esquire, Mr. Levi Prewett, of this place, to Miss Millberry Hamilton, of the parish of Feliciana.

Date Missing
Yesterday's mail brought the melancholy tidings of the death of Francis Baker, Esq., of this city. His body was found about 5 miles from Maysville, Ky., on the 8th ult., with his throat cut and his head bruised in a most shocking manner. (Natchez, Nov. 27)

December 11, 1824
Departed this life, the 27th ultimo, at his residence near Pinckneyville, Colonel William Yerby, in the 47th year of his age.

March 29, 1825
Died on the 26th, at the residence of her mother, Mrs. Mary Collier, consort of G. B. Collier, Esq., of this town.

April 5, 1825
Died on the 24th March, at the residence of A. M. Feltos, Esq., near Woodville, Mrs. Elizabeth Ventress, relict of the late Lovick Ventress, Esq., in the 55th year of her age.

April 19, 1825
Married on Thursday evening last, by Benjamin Eccles, Esq., Mr. Henry Richardson to Miss Louisa Keller, all of Jackson, La.

April 27, 1825
Married at Fort Adams, on the 19th, Mr. William Richardson to Mrs. Elizabeth Curts.

May 14, 1825
Married on Thursday evening last, Mr. George Nimon to Mrs. Martha B. May, both of this place.

June 18, 1825
Married at Sligo, on the 16th, by the Rev. James A. Fox, Mr. Tignal Jones Stewart to Miss Sally Ann Randolph, eldest daughter of Judge Randolph.

Married at Ashley Place, on Wednesday evening 15th, by the Rev. J. A. Fox, Mr. Lemuel Pitcher to Mrs. Mary Stark.

Married at Cherryfield, on the 16th, by the Rev. William Winans, Mr. Samuel Tuell to Mrs. Hughes.

Died on the 13th, Martha, youngest daughter of Mr. Hugh Connell.

June 25, 1825
Died in this town, on the 21st, Louisa, infant daughter of Mr. Reuben L. Bonner.

July 2, 1825
Died here, on the 27th ultimo, Enoch, infant son of Mr. Elisha Gower.

August 13, 1825
Died on the 10th, William R. Bruce, infant son of Mr. John L. Bruce.

August 20, 1825
Died in this place, at the house of his daughter, Mrs. Post, on the 18th, Mr. L. Fourniquet.

September 10, 1825
Departed this life, at Ashwood Place, on Wednesday morning last, Thomas Poindexter, Esqr., formerly of Fredricksburg, Virginia.

September 24, 1825
Died at Washington, Miss., on the 20th, Dr. William P. Foster, Editor of the Ariel, published in the city of Natchez.

October 8, 1825
Married in Port Gibson, on the 2d, by the Rev. Randal Gibson, Mr. Abram Green to Mrs. Ann Maxwell, relict of the late Dr. James A. Maxwell.

October 22, 1825

Sexton's report:
Oct. 8 - Mrs. Paulina Biggs, bilious fever.

Oct. 10 - ---- Adams, aged 57 years, remittent fever.
Oct. 10 - Henry Stephens, age 25 years, malignant fever.
Oct. 12 - Theo. M. Rogers, aged 28 years, intemperance.

October 29, 1825

Departed this life at the city of Natchez, in the 25th year of his age, of the prevailing epidemic, Mr. William Loring Callender, formerly of this place. Mr. Callender was a native of Wilmington, North Carolina, and emigrated to this state about 2 years since.

November 26, 1825

Departed this life at Cabin Hall, the residence of the late Col. William Yerby, Mrs. Francis Yerby, nearly 97 years of age.

Governor Walter Leake, a Revolutionary Patriot, died on the 17th, at Mount Salus, his residence in Hinds County. He was a native of Virginia and emigrated to Mississippi while a territory.

December 3, 1825

Married on Thursday evening last, by Benj. Eccles, Esqr., George B. Collier, Esqr., to Miss Sarah Clarkson, both of this county.

On Sunday last, a Coroner's Inquest was held on the body of Mr. Thomas Jackson, found dead about 3 miles from this town. The jury formed an opinion that the deceased came by his death from a blow received on his head, and by being shot near the right ear, by some unknown person.

December 20, 1825

Married on Thursday evening last, by the Rev. J. A. Fox, Francis Gildart, Esq., to Miss Judith Bailey, all of this county.

January 10, 1826

Died at the residence of Wm. Buckner, in this county, on the 7th ult., by the Rev. Benjamin Davis, Minister of the Baptist Church, in the 44th year of his age.

February 21, 1826

Married on Thursday evening last, by the Rev. James A. Ranaldson, Dr. Edward T. Farish to Miss Eliza A. Smith, all of this county.

March 7, 1826

Married on Wednesday evening last, by the Rev. George A. Irion, William W. Yerby, Attorney at Law of Amite County, to Miss Thirsa Ann Hadley, of this county.

March 18, 1826

Married on Sunday evening last, by Benjamin Eccles, Esq., Mr. John Iler to Miss Mary Rutledge, daughter of Mr. Dudley Rutledge, all of this county.

Married on the same evening, by F. E. Stephens, Esq., Mr. James Saunders to Miss Lucretia Swaize, all of this county.

May 27, 1826

Departed this life at her residence near Woodville, on Friday morning, the 19th, at a very advanced age, Mrs. Janette C. Stewart, consort of the late Capt. John Stewart.

June 10, 1826

Married on Thursday evening, the 1st, by John Brice, Esqr., Mr. James Fanner, to Miss Mary Ann Roach, all of this county.

Married on Wednesday evening last, by Benjamin Eccles, Esq., Mr. Wm. L. Cason, to Miss Jane Cook, all of this county.

July 8, 1826

Another Revolutionary hero gone -- departed this life at his residence at Sligo, in the county, on the 3d, Col. Henry Hampton, in the 84th year of his age.

July 15, 1826

Died on the 7th June, at his residence in Buckingham, Edward Patterson, aged seventy. During the Revolutionary War he was a faithful soldier.

July 22, 1826

Married on Thursday evening, the 13th, by Lemuel Miles, Esq., Mr. Zachariah Canfield to Miss Julia P. Jones, both of this county.

Died in this place, on Sunday morning last, the 16th, Mrs. Mary Hammett, consort of Mr. William Hammett.

July 29, 1826

Married in this county, on the 29th ult., by Judge Williams, Mr. Edmond Ginn to Mrs. Eliza Ann Harrison.

September 2, 1826

Married at Judge Hampton's, in this county, on the 31st ult., by Benjamin Eccles, Esq., Mr. Thomas S. Herbert to Miss Susan F. Hughes, daughter of the late Capt. John Hughes.

September 9, 1826

Married Tues. last, by the Hon. Thomas H. Prosser, Frederick A. Browder, Esq., of Feliciana Parish, to Mrs. Harriet Hook, of this co.

Died at Elysian Fields, Amite County, Mrs. Mary Davis, in the 81st year of her age.

February 27, 1830

Married on Thursday night, 25th, by Wm. T. Lewis, Esq., Mr. Michael Woods to Miss Susan H. M'Alpine, daughter of John M'Alpine, Esq., all of Wilkinson.

May 15, 1830
Died on Wednesday, 12th, at the residence of his father, William, youngest child of the Hon. E. M'Gehee, of this vicinage.

June 12, 1830
Married on Tuesday, 1st, by Rev. J. C. Burrus, Mr. Daniel Peck to Mrs. Louisa H. Ligon, of Wilkinson.

June 26, 1830
Died in Woodville, on the 19th of this month, Mrs. Mary, wife of George H. Gordon.

July 3, 1830
We heard this morning, of the decease of Robert H. Adams, Esq., late Senator from this state to Congress.

July 10, 1830
Died on the 7th, at the house of John Frazier, near Ft. Adams, Capt. Thomas B. Dougherty, in the 58th year of his age. He was a native of Pittsburgh.

Died on Wednesday, 30th ultimo, in this town, Mr. William L. Ellesberry, in the 22d year of his age.

July 17, 1830
Married at Natchez, on Tuesday, 6th July, by the Rev. Geo. Potts, Fielding Davis, Esqr., Sheriff of this county, to Miss Lucinda Newman, of that city.

Married last evening, July 16th, at the Hotel of Messrs. Buckner & Canfield, by Daniel Bass, Esqr., Mr. George Poindexter, Jr., to Miss Henrietta Baillie, all of this county.

It is with painful emotions we record the demise of our friend, Asa Colver, who died on the evening of the 9th, at his residence near Fort Adams, of bilious remittent fever.

July 24, 1830
Departed this life on the 22d, at the residence of H. Connell, Esqr., of this county, Mr. Robert C. Mitchell, Jr., lately of Alabama.

July 31, 1830
Married on Tuesday evening last, by Wm. Terrell Lewis, Esqr., Mr. Lazarus Drake to Mrs. Martha Spears, all of this county.

Died at her residence, on the 16th, Mrs. Harriet Browder, consort of Frederick A. Browder, Esq., of this county.

August 21, 1830
Died in the parish of Concordia, La., on the 13th, Mr. John A. Shields, formerly of this county.

Departed this life on Sunday night, the 8th, at the residence of the late Gerard Brandon, Colonel James Smith, a native of South Carolina, but for many years a citizen of this county.

August 28, 1830

Married on Tuesday evening last, Mr. Wiley W. Richardson to Miss Margaret Reid, both of this county.

Died in this county, on the 23d, Cornelia, daughter of Mr. Thos. S. Herbert.

September 11, 1830

Married on Wednesday last, by Daniel Bass, Esqr., Rev. Andrew Adams to Mrs. Bailley.

Died at his residence in this county, near Fort Adams, on the 27th ult., Mr. Edmond Ginn, a highly respectable planter.

Died lately at Natchez, Julius C. M'Connell, Esqr., formerly of this place.

September 18, 1830

Died at the residence of Calvin Smith, Esquire, Second Creek, on Saturday, August 28, aged 17 years, Martha A. Smith, wife of Mr. C. S. Smith, and daughter of the late Mr. Kary, of La.

Died at his residence in this county, on the 13th, Mr. Moses Gordon.

We record the demise of our friend, Wm. Cross. He died on the morning of the 9th, of congestive fever.

Died on the 15th, in the 5th year of her age, Caroline, daughter of the late N. H. Bryant.

Died the 15th, in 3d year of her age, Jane, daughter of Robert Norwood.

Died on the 15th, Polly Curry, consort of Thos. Curry, of this county.

Died at Princeton, on the morning of the 29th, Mr. Philip A. Gilbert, Representative elect to the State Legislature, from Washington County.

Died lately, in Washington City, Geo. Graham, Commissioner of the General Land Office.

Died near Woodville, on the 16th, Mr. Asa Kimball.

Married on Thursday evening, the 16th, by John Mayes, Esqr., Mr. Ransom Graham to Mrs. Biddy Pickens, daughter of Littleberry Thomson, near Fort Adams.

Married on the same evening, by John Mayes, Esqr., Mr. Edward Duff to Miss Delila Thomson, daughter of Littleberry Thomson.

September 25, 1830

Married on the 16th, by Daniel Bass, Esqr., Mr. Christopher Bartlett to Mrs. Margaret Parker.

October 2, 1830

Departed this life on Tuesday, the 21st, near Whitestown, Thomas Scott, in the 63d year of his age.

Died in this county, on the 25th ult., Mr. Easias Kaigler, a respectable planter.

Died on Sunday, the 12th, at the residence of Jas. H. Murray, Esqr., in this town, Dabney Carr Cosby, Esqr., Counselor at Law. (*Port Gibson Correspondent*)

We announce the death of our late fellow townsman, the Honorable Robert Stark, Secretary of State. He died at his summer residence on Mill Creek, on Saturday evening last, in the 66th year of his age, and was buried at the family burying ground in the town of Columbia. (The father of the subject of this notice, Col. Robert Stark was put in handcuffs and confined for 12 months, while his son Robert, then the eldest of the family, was thus engaged in the service of his country. The present Mrs. Sophia Gildart, was about 11 years of age, and left in charge of her younger brothers and sisters, when the Tories plundered them of everything, and left this little family destitute).

October 16, 1830

Died on the 30th of September, at the Hotel of William P. Gadberry, Esq., John H. Fernandis, Esq., A. M. L. D., in the 32d year of his age.

October 23, 1830

Died on Thursday night last, the 21st, at the residence of Maj. J. L. Trask, in this county, of bilious fever, the Rev. John C. Porter, Rector of Trinity Church, Natchez, in the 24th year of his age. He was a native of Albany, New York.

Died at the residence of her father, near Manchester, S. C., on the 14th Sept., Mrs. Mary Rebecca McDuffie, consort of the Hon. George McDuffie, and daughter of Richard Singleton, Esq.

Died in New Orleans, on the 15th, Thos. Lee, merchant of that place.

Died in Vicksburg, on the 12th, Mr. Henry Simonton, aged about 30 years.

Died at his plantation, in Jefferson County, on the 10th, Robt. McCray, aged 65 years.

Died in Claiborne County, on the 10th, Dr. David D. Downing, an eminent physician.

October 30, 1830

Died on Wednesday night, the 27th, at Ashly, her residence in Wilkinson County, Miss., Mrs. Sophia Gildart, relict of the late Capt. Francis Gildart, in the 64th year of her age. Mrs. Gildart was the 3d daughter of Col. Robert Stark, Sr., of South Carolina, where near the town of Columbia she was born, emigrated to Frederick County, Va., living there many years with her husband, the family moved to Carthage, Tennessee, having emigrated from thence to Washington, in this state.

November 6, 1830

Married in Claiborne County, on the 20th ult., Mr. Andrew Ellis to Miss Jane Scott.

November 13, 1830

Died in Claiborne County, on the 1st, Miss Margaret Briscoe, daughter of Wm. Briscoe, aged 19 years.

Died at Port Gibson, on the 1st, Dr. P. B. Wilcox, a native of Ky., aged 28 years.

Died in Claiborne County, on the 1st, Mr. Abram Barnes, aged 46 years, on the 30th ult., Mrs. Hansey Marble, consort of Eerra Marble. On the 4th, Mr. Reuben White, aged 21 years.

Died at his residence in this county, on the 15th, Mr. Wm. Lindsay.

Died in Monticello, Miss., on the 27th ult., Mr. James Coursey.

Married at the Hurricane (Adams County), on the 21st ult., Mr. David McAleb, Jun., to Miss Florida A. Davis, eldest daughter of Joseph E. Davis, Esq.

Married on the 11th, Mr. John P. Runnells to Miss Sarah Coleman, all of Claiborne County.

Married in West Feliciana, La., on the 4th, Mr. Peter Southerland to Mrs. Mary Ann Roberts, both of this county.

November 20, 1830

Died at the residence of Wm. Eccles, on the 20th, Judge Carraway, in the 68th year of his age.

We announce the death of Jacob Hyland, Esq., one of the proprietors of this paper. He departed this life at his residence in this county, on Tuesday, the 9th.

Married on the 12th, by C. Vanhouten, Esq., Gen. D. Davis to Miss Julia Burr, all of Amite County.

November 27, 1830
Married on Thursday last, by the Rev. J. C. Burrus, Mr. George Joor to Miss Laura Singleton, daughter of Hiram Singleton, all of this county.

Married on the 16th, by Judge Guion, Mr. John Tarbe, merchant of Natchez, to Miss Ann Bouis, of the parish of Concordia, La., niece of Mr. John P. Arnaud.

Died in West Feliciana, on the 20th, Mr. Anthony H. McDermott.

December 4, 1830
Died on the morning of the 19th, at his late residence near Natchez, Doct. Seaborn Jones Noble, a native of Georgia.

December 11, 1830
Married on Wednesday, 1st Dec., by John Robertson, Esq., Zachariah Cox to Miss Eliza Randell, daughter of the Rev. Joel Randell, all of this county.

Married on Thursday evening, the 26th November, by George B. Crutcher, Esq., Mr. William A. Hardwick, of Clinton, to Mrs. Amelia Walker, of Hinds County.

December 18, 1830
Married on Thursday evening last, by the Hon. Thomas H. Prosser, Bennett H. Barrow, Esq., of West Feliciana, to Miss Emily Joor, daughter of Maj. Genl. John Joor, of this county.

December 31, 1830
Married on Sunday, 26th December, by Rev. Thos. C. Brown, Mr. John F. Ailes, of Monroe, La., to Miss Elizabeth H. Smith, daughter of Mr. Thomas Smith, of this county.

Married on Thursday last, by Joseph Patterson, Esqr., Mr. Duncan C. Henderson to Miss Mary Ann Ogden, daughter of Mr. John Ogden, all of this county.

Died on Thursday morning, the 30th December, Mr. Joseph P. Henley, a native of the state of Virginia.

Died on Sunday night, the 1st, January, 1831, Eleanor Eugenia, youngest daughter of Wm. W. Yerby, Esqr.

January 3, 1833
Married on Sunday last, by Joseph Green, Esq., Mr. Wm. Dodd to Miss Ann Cotter, all of this town.

January 12, 1833
Married on Thursday evening last, by the Rev. Mr. Bertron, Doctor Samuel Lessley to Miss Mary Kaigler, daughter of Mr. William Kaigler, all of this county.

Married on Thursday, 27th December, by Bishop Wm. F. Mathews, Mr. John A. Beckem to Miss Jane B. Coleman, all of this county.

January 19, 1833

Married in this town, January 2d, by the Rev. Mr. Weller, Mr. Lewis Charles Levin, of Mississippi, to Miss Ann Hays, daughter of Andrew Hays, Esq. (*Nashville Banner*)

Died at the residence of her uncle, Judge Johnson, on the 16th, of scarlet fever, Rachael Neal, daughter of William Dillahunty, in the 9th year of her age.

January 26, 1833

Married at the residence of J. P. Gilbert, Esqr., in Raymond, on the 17th of January, by the Rev. Mr. Comfort, of Clinton, Meredith S. Breckenridge, Esqr., formerly of Staunton, Va., one of the firm of Wallace & Breckenridge, merchants of the former place, to Miss Eliza Ann Dawson, daughter of the late Judge Dawson, of Wilkinson County.

February 9, 1833

Died at Holmesville, Pike County, Miss., on the 17th, Mr. James L. Reed, a citizen of that place.

February 16, 1833

Married in this town, on the 15th, by C. C. West, Esq., Edward Morton, member of the American Theatre, New Orleans, to Miss Catherine Jane Casseals, of the same city.

Died in this town, on Saturday last, Mr. Edward Feltus, Clerk of the Probate Court of Wilkinson County.

February 23, 1833

Died on the 12th, Thomas, infant son of Mr. G. L. Lovelace, 22 mos.

March 2, 1833

James Reid departed this life on the evening of the 26th ult.

Married on the 20th February last, by William Stewart, Esqr., Doct. Solomon Weathersby to Miss Julia Ann Bennet, all of Amite County.

March 23, 1833

Died in this town, on the 21st, Mrs. Anne Toole.

March 30, 1833

Married on the 24th, by the Rev'd. J. C. Burruss, at the residence of Governor A. M. Scott, near Woodville, Preston W. Farrar, Esq., to Miss Eliza J. Scott, only daughter of Governor Scott.

Married at Natchez, on the 25th, by the Rev. Geo. Potts, Doct. Charles H. Stone, of Woodville, to Miss Mary G. Newman, of the city of Natchez.

Married on the 28th, by Bythall Haynes, Esq., Mr. David Boland to Miss Drusilla McGraw, daughter of Darling McGraw, all of this county.

April 6, 1833

Died at Whitestown, on the 4th, Mr. Henry Ferguson, aged 30 years.

Died in this city, on Monday night last, of pulmonary disease, Mr. Nelson Wooster, in the 23d year of his age.

April 27, 1833

Married on Thursday, the 18th, by the Hon. John B. Dawson, General William L. Brandon, of this county, to Miss Ann Eliza Ratliff, of West Feliciana.

Married on Thursday, 18th, by Bythell Haynes, Esq., Mr. William C. Irwin, of Yazoo County, to Miss Margaret A., daughter of Mr. Daniel Anderson, of Wilkinson.

May 4, 1833

Married on 23d April last, by Joseph Patterson, Esqr., Mr. Noland M. Luckett, of Jefferson County, Kentucky, to Miss Ann C. Tigner, daughter of Capt. Wm. Tigner, of this county.

Died near Whitesville, in this co., on Sat. last, Mr. Thomas W. West.

May 11, 1833

Died at his residence in this county, one mile west of Woodville, on the 5th, Mr. David Calliham, in the 67th year of his age. Mr. Calliham has resided in this county for many years.

May 18, 1833

Married on Tuesday evening, 7th, by Rev. James A. Ranaldson, Mr. Thomas E. Shannon, of this county, to Miss Pamela Woods, daughter of Mr. Isham Woods, of the parish of West Feliciana, La.

May 25, 1833

Married at the residence of John A. Grimball, Secretary of State, by the Rev. Mr. Bryant, Mr. David McRae, of Green City, to Miss Eliza A. Grimball, of Hinds.

June 1, 1833

Married by the Hon. Joseph Ford, Major S. M. Catching, of Pike, to Miss Eady S. Drake, of Marion County, Mississippi.

June 8, 1833

Married on Thursday evening last, by the Hon. A. S. Randolph, Mr. Lewis Davis to Miss Martha Octavia West, daughter of the late Thomas W. West, all of this county.

June 15, 1833

Married on Tues. eve. last, by Daniel Bass, Esq., Mr. Richard T. Christmas, to Mary M. Sims, dau. of Capt. John Sims, all of this co.

Married on the 9th of June, by the Rev. T. C. Brown, Mr. Hugh McCrane to Mrs. Elizabeth Coon, all of this county.

June 29, 1833

Died at Cherry-Field, in this county, on Saturday, 15th, Mrs. Susan Hampton, aged 72 years, consort of the late Col. Henry Hampton.

July 6, 1833

Died at his residence on Buffaloe, in this county, on Saturday morning last, in the 68th year of his age, Mr. John Brown. Mr. B. has been a resident of this county for the last 28 years.

July 13, 1833

Mrs. Mary H. Webb, wife of Dr. Noah Webb, died in Pinckneyville, on the third day of the present month, in the 20th year of her age.

Died at his residence near Woodville, Colonel Charles Stewart, in the 24th year of his age. He died on the 8th day of July. Col. Stewart was born in the state of Mississippi. Col. Charles Stewart was the only unmarried child of Mr. Charles Stewart.

July 20, 1833

Married on 11th July, by John Dunckley, Esqr., Mr. William A. Brown to Miss Margaret B. Turbeville, 3d daughter of Mr. Samuel Turbeville, all of this county.

Died on the 15th, at Arrundale, the residence of Francis A. Evans, Mary R., youngest daughter of Mrs. M. P. Foley, aged 8 years.

Departed this life on the 3d day of July, Commodore Brooks, aged 5 years, 11 months and 27 days.

July 27, 1833

Died at her residence, near this place, on Wednesday morning last, Mrs. Mary Cattiham, consort of the late David Cattiham.

John Butler, of Amite County, in this state, who on the 15th September last, at a shooting match, killed his nephew-in-law, John Knox, and fled to Texas, has been taken, and on Monday last was lodged in the jail of this county.

August 17, 1833

Departed this life, on the 13th, in the 50th year of her age, Mrs. Nancy Lewis, wife of Col. John S. Lewis, of this town. Mrs. L. had been, for many years, a member of the Methodist Church.

Died on the 16th, at Fort Adams, Christopher E. Hall Miller, aged 7 months, only son of William Miller.

Died lately, at Port Gibson, Dr. James S. Carraway, formerly of this town.

August 31, 1833

Died on the 26th, William G. Ogden, son of George Ogden, of this county, in the 27th year of his age. He left a wife and one infant son.

Departed this life, Duncan Stewart, Esq., in the 28th year of his age.

September 7, 1833

Departed this life on the 3d, of malignant fever, in the 27th year of his age, Samuel Brown, a native of Newburyport, Massachusetts, and for some time past a resident of this village.

Departed this life, at her residence in this place, on the 2d, Mrs. Lenora Gordon, consort of Col. George H. Gordon, in the 18th year of her age.

Departed this life at his residence on Fool's Creek, on the 1st September, John Dunckley, Esq., in the 55th year of his age. He died of congestive fever.

September 14, 1833

Died on the 6th, in the 5th year of her age, Sarah Eleanor, eldest daughter of Walthall Burton, of this county.

Departed this life, at Fort Adams, on the 30th ult., Thomas D., infant son of Mr. John McNulty.

Departed this life at Liberty, Amite County, on the 18th ult., Juliet T., and on the 2d, William, only children of Mr. John Walker, of that co.

Departed this life in New Orleans, on the 1st of September, Solon Hill, Esq., formerly a citizen of this county.

September 21, 1833

Departed this life, Charles Henry, on the 19th, and Susannah Virginia, on the day following, children of James and Harriet B. White, of this town.

Died near Clinton, Louisiana, on the 11th, of the prevailing fever, Lawrence B. Davis, of Baltimore, Maryland.

Died on the 11th, of the prevailing fever, William, youngest son of John and Eliza Dillahunty, aged 18 months and 20 days.

Died on the 11th, near Fort Adams, James Mayes, in the 19th year of his age, a native of this state.

September 28, 1833

Died on the 15th, in this town, John Joor, eldest son of William T. and Emily Mayes, in the 5th year of his age.

Died on the 15th, Mrs. Susan T., consort of John W. Gildart, Esq.

Died, Mr. James Mayes, formerly of this county.

October 19, 1833
Died in this town, on Thursday evening, Doct. A. L. Keagy.

Doctor Edward T. Farish died in the Choctaw Nation, on the 7th.

Married in Woodville, on the 17th Oct., Doct. Young Burke to Miss Sarah Matilda Smith, daughter of the late P---wood Smith.

Alonzo Phelps, who was charged by the verdict of a Coroner's jury with the murder of Owen Rhodes, was on last Saturday lodged in the jail of this county.

October 26, 1833
Died on the 21st, Mrs. Patsey Connell, consort of Hugh Connell, Esq.

Died on the 24th, Mr. Wm. Newell.

Died on the 16th, Mr. Daniel Murphrey, in the 23d year of his age.

Died at his residence in East Feliciana, on the 19th, Capt. W. J. Boatner, in the 44th year of his age.

Died on Monday, the 7th, at the house of R. M. Williamson, Esq., in Madison County, N. G. Howard, Esq., late a representative from Rankin County in the State Legislature.

Died in Yazoo County, last week, Dr. Floyd, a physician, and formerly a representative in the State Legislature from that county.

Died on the 10th, at Clinton, Miss., Major Thomas W. Gwin, of Washington County, Miss., late of Sumner County, Tennessee.

November 9, 1833
Died on the 31st ult., William Netterville, in the 69th year of his age.

Died on the 30th ult., Mr. William B. Conner.

Died on Thursday, 31st ult., Mr. George W. Carter.

Died lately, in this county, Mr. Robert E. Love.

November 16, 1833
Married on Sunday evening last, by the Rev. Mr. Burtron, Doct. J. C. Patrick to Mrs. Eliza Connell, all of this county.

November 30, 1833
Married on the 21st, by James Jenkins, Esqr., Mr. William Haynes, of Wilkinson, to Miss Elizabeth, daughter of Peter Faust, of Amite.

John T. Semple was born the 4th November, 1804, and departed this life on the 24th of the same month, 1833, aged 29 years and 20 days.

December 7, 1833
Mrs. Martha Patrick, a respectable lady of this district, hung herself on Monday morning last, aged about 22 years.

January 4, 1834
Died at his residence in this county, on the 25th December last, Mr. Jesse Brown.

January 18, 1834
Died at his residence in this parish, on the 26th ult., Luther L. Smith, Esq., leaving a wife and several children. (*St. Francisville Phoenix*)

January 25, 1834
Died at his father's residence in Donegal, on the 7th, Kinchen Holliman, son of Mr. Z. Walker, aged 9 years.

Died in Woodville, on Wednesday night last, at the house of Mr. Stephen Johnson, Mr. Hatlett Potter, a native of the state of New York, and for several years a citizen of this county.

Married on Thursday last, 23d, by Daniel Bass, Esqr., Mr. Adam I. Chambers to Miss Sarah N. Sims.

Married on the 16th, by the Rev. Mr. Bertron, Mr. Robert Turner to Mrs. Frances Ann Shepherd.

Married on the 12th, by Bythell Haynes, Esqr., Mr. Stephen Poyner, of Franklin, Tennessee, to Miss Ann Ratcliff.

February 1, 1834
Died on 24th January, at the house of his son, at Bayou Sara, of a sudden attack of pleurisy, Mr. Jesse Deloach, in the 55th year of his age, and for the last 23 years a planter of this state.

February 8, 1834
Married 7th February, at the Woodville Hotel, by Danl. Bass, Esqr., Mr. Charles J. B. F. Castell to Miss Louisa Henrietta Micoud, both of New Orleans.

February 15, 1834
Died on the 26th ult., Mrs. Rebecca Lewis, of Woodville, aged 46.

February 22, 1834
Married on the 13th, by the Rev. T. C. Brown, Mr. Samuel Davis to Miss Emma M., daughter of Charles Edwards, all of this county.

Died on Monday evening last, Mr. John R. Holliday Lewis, eldest son of Maj. S. W. Lewis, of Fort Adams.

March 1, 1834
Married on 27th ult., by N. Scudder, Esq., Mr. John Jenks to Miss Ariann Jackson, all of this county.

March 15, 1834
Died on the 2d, Mrs. Isabella Knight, consort of the late Henry Knight, aged about 50.

March 22, 1834
Died yesterday, in this city, William Wirt, Esq., aged about 62 years.

April 12, 1834
Married on the 8th, by N. Scudder, Esq., Mr. William McNeely to Miss Mary A., daughter of John W. Seymour, Esq., all of this county.

Married on the 10th, by the same, Mr. Moses Pool to Miss Mary, daughter of Joseph Henderson, all of this county.

May 17, 1834
Died on the 7th, at the house of Mr. Philip Noland, in this county, in the 24th year of her age, Mrs. Levice Norwood, consort of Mr. Robert Norwood. The deceased left an infant child and husband.

June 7, 1834
Married on the 5th, by the Hon. A. S. Randolph, William S. Griffin, Esqr., to Miss Ann C., daughter of the Hon. Moses Liddell, all of Wilkinson County.

Married on the 20th ult., by N. Scudder, Esq., Mr. Levi D. Doughty to Miss Matilda Sape, all of this county.

Bill of Divorce -- Western Muse -vs- Cassander Muse.

July 5, 1834
Died at his residence near Woodville, on the 4th, Mr. Benj. H. Lewis.

Died at his father's residence in this county, on the 3d, of gastric fever, William Arthur, eldest son of Col. F. R. Richardson.

Died on the 2d July, Duncan Noland, son of John J. and Mary Collins, aged 3 years and 4 months.

Died at the house of Maj. F. Mayes, in this county, on the 23rd ultimo, Mr. J. J. Mayes, aged 19 years.

Died the 29th June, at Arundale, the residence of Francis Evans, Esq., Ellen Keary, consort of Rev. J. C. Burrus, aged 19 yrs. and 10 mos.

July 12, 1834
Died at the residence of Mrs. Mary S. Ogden, near Woodville, on the 9th of July, Mary Elizabeth, only child of Henry and Anna Vose, aged 1 year and 8 months.

July 26, 1834
Died on the 22d, Mr. Samuel Glass, formerly of Pittsburgh, Penn.

Died at his residence in East Feliciana, on the 24th, Col. Green B. Davis, of congestive fever.

August 2, 1834
Married on 27th July, by Nathaniel Scudder, Esqr., Mr. Asa Anderson to Mrs. Margaret Coates, all of this county.

We record the death of Mrs. Eveline R. Mayes, consort of Benjamin M. Mayes, of this county. She departed this life on the 26th ult., of phthisis pulmonahs, aged 30 years and 7 days.

August 30, 1834
Married on the 28th, by N. Scudder, Esq., Mr. William Payne to Miss Susan Hubbard, all of this county.

Married in Woodville, 27th, by Daniel Bass, Esqr., Captain John Philbrick to Mrs. Susan Scott, all of this county.

Died the 16th August, at Liberty, Amite County, Mrs. Penelope Whitney, aged 32 years, consort of Minor M. Whitney.

September 13, 1834
Died in this place, on Wednesday evening last, of congestive fever, Mr. Joseph A. Foster, in the 32d year of his age.

September 20, 1834
Died in this town, on the 19th, Julia Ann Clingan, in the 7th year of her age.

November 1, 1834
Died this morning, Mr. John C. Hicks, a citizen of this county.

November 8, 1834
Married 23d October, by Joseph Patterson, Esqr., Mr. Peter Leatherman to Mrs. Charity Smith, all of this county.

November 22, 1834
Married on the 12th, by Rev. Silas H. Hazard, Elijah M. Davis, Esqr., to Sarah Ann W., second daughter of the Hon. William Lattimore.

Died on the 18th, at her residence in Woodville, Mrs. Mary M. Conrad, consort of Mr. Peter Conrad. The deceased was a native of Germany, who together with her husband and family emigrated to this country many years since.

January 3, 1835
Died on the 26th December, Mrs. Ann Tuell, a member of the Methodist Episcopal Church for many years.

Married on the 30th ultimo, by Rev. T. C. Brown, Mr. David A. Palmer, of La., to Miss Martha A., daughter of Mr. Charles Hester, of this county.

Married by N. Scudder, on the 12th ult., Mr. William Penny to Mrs. Elizabeth Brown, all of this county.

Married on the 30th ult., by N. Scudder, Esqr., Mr. Moses Stewart, of Adams County, to Miss Elizabeth White, of this county.

Married on the 1st, by N. Scudder, Esqr., Mr. Benjamin Walker to Miss Emeline Deloach, all of this county.

February 7, 1835

Married on Thursday evening last, by Daniel Bass, Esq., Chauncey S. Kellogg, Esq., to Miss Rebecca B. C. Waller, daughter of Mrs. Rebecca F. Coleman, all of this county.

Married on the 5th, by the Rev. T. C. Brown, Mr. Wm. Alexander to Miss Eliza, daughter of Jonathan Combs, all of this county.

Died at Fort Adams, on 30 Jan. last, John McNulty, aged 34 years.

February 28, 1835

Died the 22d, Mrs. Maria Ashly, wife of John Ashly, Esqr. of this co.

Died in New Orleans, on the 20th, Maj. Jeremiah Noland, a citizen of this county.

Died in Amite County, on the 16th, Mrs. Elizabeth Dunn, wife of Maj. Sylvester Dunn.

March 7, 1835

Died at her residence in this county, on Sunday last, Mrs. Jamesy Hicks, consort of the late John C. Hicks.

March 21, 1835

Married on the 19th, by the Rev. T. C. Brown, Mr. Joseph B. S. Wyatt, of Tennessee, to Miss Josephine Netterville, daughter of Mr. Thos. Netterville, of this county.

April 11, 1835

Married on 5th, by John Mays, Esqr., Mr. John Iler to Miss Amanda Turner, all of this county.

May 9, 1835

Married on the 8th by the Rev. T. C. Brown, Mr. Wright B. Orr to Miss Martha N., daughter of Mr. James B. Richardson, all of this county.

May 30, 1835

Married on the 28th, by the Rev. Wm. Winans, the Hon. James Walker to Miss Mary B. Newell, all of this county.

Died on Friday, the 22d, Mr. Abram Iler.

June 20, 1835
Married on Sunday morning at the Methodist Church, by the Rev. Thos. C. Brown, Mr. M. A. Jenkins, of Benton, Miss., to Miss Roselie P. Carter, of this county.

Died on Friday morning, the 18th, Charles West, infant son of Thos. J. Hamilton.

July 11, 1835
Died this morning, in the 6th year of her age, Martha Jane, eldest daughter of Wm. A. A. Chisholm, of this county.

July 18, 1835
Died on the 13th, in the 17th year of her age, Eleanor C. Carter, daughter of G. W. & M. B. Carter.

July 25, 1835
Married on 23d, by Rev. T. C. Brown, John Conway, formerly of Amite County, to Rebecca M., dau. of Mr. Josiah Gayle, of Amite County.

Married on the 23d, by the Rev. T. C. Brown, Mr. John B. Therrel to Miss Jane A. Dunlap, all of this county.

August 1, 1835
Died near Woodville, on Sunday, 26th July, Eliza Ann, daughter of Mr. Samuel Tillotson, of Liberty, Miss., aged 9 years, 3 months.

August 8, 1835
Died July 30th, 1835, at her residence on Buffaloe, in this county, in the 49th year of her age, Mrs. Sarah Smith, consort of the late Prestwood Smith.

Died at the residence of her mother, near Woodville, on the 13th ult., Eleanor C. Carter, aged 16 years, dau. of the late Geo. W. Carter.

August 15, 1835
Died in Woodville, on the 9th, Mrs. Elizabeth A. Henley, consort of the late Joseph P. Henley.

August 22, 1835
Married on 11th August, by John Ashley, Esq., Mr. Thomas Ford to Miss Mary Cole, all of this county.

August 29, 1835
Died on the 20th day of August, 1835, Robert C. Blount, in the 4th year of his age, son of Mr. Traverse Blount.

September 12, 1835
Married on the 6th, by the Rev. T. C. Brown, Mr. John F. Scott to Miss Eliza, daughter of Mr. Samuel Goodrich, all of this county.

Died on the 8th, at the residence of the Hon. Moses Liddell, William S. Griffin, Esq.

Died on the 15th August last, at the residence of Mr. George Brown, Mr. William Brown, in the 69th year of his age.

September 19, 1835

Died on the 10th, Henry C. Connell, eldest son of the late John Connell, aged about 7 years.

Died in Woodville, on the 13th, of congestive fever, Mr. J. A. Wells, aged about 27 years, a native of New York City. The deceased was formerly a member of Brown's Circus.

Died on the 13th, Mr. H. P. Lipscomb.

Died the 15th Sept., at his residence near Woodville, William Stewart.

Died the 7th, Mrs. Eliza Ann Dillahunty, dau. of the late Mark and Ann Kirkby, of New York, and wife of John N. Dillahunty, Esq., of this co.

September 26, 1835

Married on the 10th, by Nathan E. Raymond, Esqr., Mr. Thomas I. Lanier, of North Carolina, to Mrs. Ellen Old, of this county.

October 3, 1835

Married on the 27th of September, by the Rev. T. C. Brown, Mr. George Jonte to Miss Minerva Oglesby.

Married on the 1st, by the Rev. John C. Burruss, Capt. Robert Semple to Leonora, second daughter of Hugh Connell, Esq., all of this co.

Married on the 1st, by the Rev. Samuel Dawson, Mr. Alexander S. Iler to Miss Malissa Turner, all of this county.

Died in this county, on the 31st August last, Mr. Joshua L. Pearce.

October 10, 1835

Married on Sept. 17, by John Mayes, Esq., Mr. A. P. Reid to Miss Mary E. Presbury, of Maryland.

October 17, 1835

Married on the 15th, by Joseph H. Street, Esq., Mr. Miles E. Lilley to Miss Virginia Waters, all of this county.

Married on the 11th, by John McCrea, Esq., Mr. Elijah R. Brown to Miss Martha M. Gaulden.

November 14, 1835

Married at Natchez, 5th Nov., by Rev. Geo. Potts, Albert G. Foster, of this town, to Miss Sara Jane, daughter of Mr. Joseph Newman.

Married on the 12th November, 1835, by H. Street, Esq., Mr. Thomas M. Iler to Miss Mahala, youngest daughter of Mr. Mabry Morris, of this county.

December 12, 1835

Departed this life, at his residence in Amite County, on the 15th, Mr. Elias Boatner, about eighty years of age.

December 19, 1835

Married on the 10th, by Jos. H. Street, Esqr., Mr. William Cizzee to Mrs. Jane Anderson, all of Wilkinson County.

Died on the 25th of Nov., at the residence of his late brother, Maj. J. L. Trask, Col. I. E. Trask, of Springfield, Mass.

Died on the 25th Nov., at his residence near Pinckneyville, Mr. Ruffin Deloach, aged about 75 years.

January 16, 1836

Married in the parish of East Feliciana, on the 5th, Mr. David Hester, of Wilkinson, to Miss Anne R. Scott, of Louisiana.

January 23, 1836

Married at the residence of his mother, in the county of Wilkinson, on the 23d Dec., 1835. by Jos. H. Street, Esq., Mr. Wm. D. White to Miss Rebecca Ann Ross; all of said county.

Married at the residence of Mr. Geo. E. Frazier, in Wilkinson County, on the 31st Dec'r., 1835, by Jos. H. Street, Esqr., Mr. Samuel Estis to Miss Frances Eliza Frazier, all of said county.

Married at Woodville, in the State of Mississippi, on the 21st of November, 1835, by Joseph H. Street, Esqr., Mr. Joseph Jewell, of Point Coupee, La., to Miss Jane Eliza Lewis, of New Orleans.

February 6, 1836

Departed this life on the 30th of January, Mr. Elisha Hodges, of this county, leaving a wife and three children.

Married at the residence of Mr. William Glover, in this county, on the 5th, by the Rev. Samuel Dawson, Mr. Daniel Miller to Mrs. Martha S. Huff, all of this county.

February 13, 1836

Married on the 31st of January, by J. H. Street, Esq., Mr. David Carter to Miss Ann Netterville, all of this county.

February 20, 1836

Died on the 13th February, Mrs. Frances Dunckley, in the 60th year of her age.

Married on the 11th February, 1836, by the Rev. William Winans, Horace D. Kellogg, Esq., to Mrs. Mary Ann Stewart, all of this place.

Married in February, 1836, by the Hon. A. S. Randolph, Mr. William Reid to Miss Jane Riddle.

Married on the 17th February, 1836, by the Rev. Benj'n. Shaw, Mr. Levi Blount to Miss Lavinia Calder.

Married on the 24th January, 1836, by John Ashly, Esq., Mr. Joseph J. Moss to Miss Martha Coats.

Married on the 19th January, 1836, by V. N. Harris, Esq., Mr. Thomas Wisner to Miss Emily Rawlins.

March 12, 1836

Died at his residence near Woodville, on the 5th, Mr. James Leech.

Died in Woodville, on the 8th, Mr. Joel Landrum.

April 2, 1836

Married by the Rev. J. Wooldridge, near Jackson, La., on the 23d March, Col. John S. Lewis, of Woodville, Miss. to Miss Eunice W. Higgins, of Ellsworth, Me.

Married on the 31st March, Mr. Matthias Overman to Miss Ellen Roache, both of this county.

April 30, 1836

Married on the 26th, by V. N. Harris, Esq., Mr. John A. Warren to Miss Mary Ann Cole, both of this county.

May 14, 1836

Married on the 11th, by the Rev. B. Shaw, Mr. John P. Harris, merchant of Woodville, to Miss Eliza S. Cosby.

May 21, 1836

Married on the 12th May, by the Hon. A. S. Randolph, Mr. Mason E. Saunders to Mrs. Jane Noland, all of this county.

Married on the 12th May, by the Hon. C. P. Smith, Mr. Robert Norwood to Miss E. E. C. Lewis, all of this county.

Married on the 16th May, by the Rev'd. Samuel Dawson, Mr. William B. Woods to Miss Sophronia Courtney, all of this county.

Died on the 19th, James Bailey, infant son of Doct. J. Saunders, of this place.

June 25, 1836

Married in Cincinnati, Ohio, Col. Geo. H. Gordon, of this place, to Miss Ellen White, of the former place.

Married on the 16th, by V. N. Harris, Esq., Mr. Jackson Carroll Whetstone to Miss Eleanor C. Rawlins, of this county.

Married on the 20th, by the same, Mr. Jos. N. Walker to Miss Lavina Dodd, of La.

July 23, 1836

Married on Thursday, the 14th, by Bythell Haynes, Esq., Mr. William Tillery, of Amite County, to Miss Martha L. King, of this county.

Married on the 17th, by V. N. Harris, Esq., Mr. William E. L. Baum to Miss Sarah Dancer, all of this county.

August 6, 1836

Married on the 28th, by the Rev. James Smylie, Henry G. Street, Esq., of Meadville, to Mrs. Victorie Caroline Buckholts, of this county. (*Liberty Advocate*)

August 20, 1836

Married on the 7th, at the Episcopal Church, by the Rev. Spencer Wall, Mr. Truman Powell to Mrs. Sarah W. Feltus, all of this county.

Married on the 11th, by Rev. Wm. Winans, Mr. Hiram Frayard to Mrs. Adaline Newell, all of this county.

Died at Fort Adams, in July, Mr. Dudley Rutledge, an old and respectable citizen of this county.

August 27, 1836

Departed this life, on the 13th, at the residence of his uncle, Maj. J. L. Trask, Mr. I. T. Browning. The deceased has left an aged father and mother in the State of Massachusetts.

September 3, 1836

Married the 31st of August last, by J. B. Jones, Esq., Mr. James Craig Bell to Miss Mary Tool, all of this county.

Married on the 1st of Sept., by the Rev. Samuel Dawson, Mr. George Helmer, to Miss Mary Ann Silvey, all of this county.

September 10, 1836

Died the 19th of August, Mr. Hugh M'Craine, with congestive fever. He has left a wife and five children.

September 24, 1836

Died near Fort Adams, in this county, on the 21st, Mr. Philip Noland.

October 1, 1836

Died on the 18th ult., Moses Miles, son of R. L. Bonner, in the 3d year of his age.

October 15, 1836
Married on the 13th, by V. N. Harris, Esq., Mr. Henry Dixon Holland to Miss Rachael Hope, all of this county.

October 29, 1836
Married on the 27th October, by the Hon. N. Scudder, Mr. John Knighten, of Yazoo County, to Miss Julina Meek, of Wilkinson.

Married on the 20th, by J. B. Jones, Esq., Mr. Johnsa Dorsey to Miss Sarah Glass.

Married on the 27th, by J. B. Jones, Esq., Mr. Michael Hootsell to Miss Eliza Ann Mayes.

November 19, 1836
Died on the 10th, Mr. Southard Aitsbury, of this county, in the 38th year of his age.

Married in Woodville, on 17th Nov., by the Rev. B. Shaw, Mr. Alfred Swingle to Miss Laura E. Toole.

December 10, 1836
Married on the 1st, by the Hon. N. Scudder, Mr. Elbert Mock, of Franklin County, to Miss Mary Ann Meek, of this county.

Married on the 4th, by the same, Mr. Abram Decker to Mrs. Susan Webb, of this county.

December 17, 1836
Died at the residence of Clement B. Penrose, Esq., Mrs. Eliza Rosana McMurdo, aged 24 years.

December 24, 1836
Died on Nov. the 16th, Miss Susanna Langford, a member of the Methodist Church.

January 7, 1837
Married on the 1st Jan'y., 1837, by the Rev. S. Dawson, Mr. Jesse Enlow to Miss Eveline Lusk, all of this county.

Married on the 5th, by V. N. Harris, Esq., Mr. Jas. S. Moon to Miss Mary Ann Fenner, all of this county.

January 14, 1837
Married on the 8th January, 1837, by V. N. Harris, Esq., Mr. George Shropshire to Miss Mary Jane Anderson.

January 21, 1837
Married on 15th January, 1837, by the Hon. N. Scudder, Mr. John Stembridge to Miss Matilda Anderson, all of this county.

Married on the same evening, by V. N. Harris, Esq., Mr. James Smith to Miss Elizabeth Cole, all of this county.

Married on the 19th January, 1837, by V. N. Harris, Esq., Mr. Tho. E. Cory, of Franklin County, to Miss Esther McGraw, of Wilkinson.

January 28, 1837

Married on 25th January, 1837, by the Hon. N. Scudder, Francis A. Fair to Eliza Hall, both of West Feliciana, La.

Died on the 21st, Mr. John Wiley, a citizen of this county.

February 18, 1837

Died at the residence of Maj. S. F. Mayes, John Foster, on the 26th ult., in the 80th year of his age. He came to this state from South Carolina. In the year 1825 he moved to Texas and procured a large quantity of land. At the commencement of the late war, the deceased being very old, came to Mississippi, leaving four sons in Texas.

Died in this town, on the 13th, Abram Scott, infant son of the Hon. Preston W. Farrar.

Married on the 12th Feb., 1837, by -- B. Jones, Esq., Mr. John Glass to Miss Elizabeth Woodard, all of this county.

February 25, 1837

Married on the 21st, by the Hon. N. Scudder, Mr. Henry L. Cason to Miss Marinda Varnell, all of this county.

Died the 16th of February, 1837, Mrs. Ann Currie, consort of Mr. Jacob C. Currie, in the 29th year of her age, leaving a husband and five small children.

March 4, 1837

Died 9th of February, Mr. John O. Williams. He has left a wife and two small children.

March 11, 1837

Died in West Feliciana, on the 6th, Mrs. Ann B. M. Whitaker, consort of Mr. J. B. Whitaker, in the 20th year of her age.

Died near Woodville, on the 7th, William Haile, Esq., formerly member of Congress from Mississippi.

Died in Rankin County, Franklin E. Plummer, Esq., drowned in crossing a small but very much swollen stream. He was a member of the State Legislature for several years.

March 18, 1837

Died on the 12th in this town, Chas. L. Hyatt.

Died lately at Rodney, in Jefferson County, Thomas J. Hamilton, a citizen of this town.

March 25, 1837
Died on the 18th, in this town, Mrs. Emily Wisner, consort of Mr. Tho. Wisner.

April 22, 1837
Died here, on the 21st, Dr. Saml. Leslie, of pulmonary consumption.

May 13, 1837
Married by the Hon. N. Scudder, 4th, Mr. Wilkinson M. Doles, to Miss Lydia Noland, all of this county.

May 20, 1837
Married 9th, by the Hon. N. Scudder, Mr. Jeremiah D. Noland to Miss Ellen Ann Downs, all of this county.

Died on the 15th, Mr. John McCready, a citizen of this county.

May 27, 1837
Married 25th May, by Rev. Mr. Marshall, Mr. Charles Pascoe to Miss Ann R. Thomas, all of Woodville.

Married on the 23d May, by John McCren, Esq., Mr. David Yarbrough to Miss Sarah Walton, both of East Feliciana, La.

June 10, 1837
Died on 23d May, at the residence of Mr. Sterling, on the Onachitta, Mrs. Mary Cook, wife of Mr. D. P. A. Cook, formerly of this county.

June 24, 1837
Died on the 19th, Mr. Jehu Quine, of this county.

Died on the 20th, Mr. Mordecai Quine, of this county.

Died on the 20th, Mrs. Sarah E., consort of Mr. W. P. Burton.

Married on the 21st, by the Rev. A. D. Wooldridge, Mr. J. C. Dougherty, of Jackson, La., to Miss Mary Louisa, daughter of Dr. S. Robinson, of Pinckneyville, Miss.

July 8, 1837
Married in this town, on the 28th June, by the Rev. John F. Fish, Mr. Robt. B. McAlpine to Miss Jennette Ann Eccles.

Died in this town the 26th, Margaret Ann, only child of Henry J. and Margaret Bass, aged 15 months and 18 days.

July 15, 1837
Married on the 11th, by the Rev. Mr. Fish, Mr. Robert A. Wilkinson, of La., to Mrs. Mary F. Gildart, of this place.

Died on the 13th, C. S. Kellogg, Esq.

August 26, 1837

Departed this life August 19th, Capt. Peter Smith, in the 71st year of his age. Capt. Smith was a native of North Carolina, emigrating to Mississippi as early as 1782, when the country was a wilderness.

Departed this life on Fri. last, Charles Ridgely Lewis, aged 22 years, the youngest son of Major S. W. Lewis. (Fort Adams, Aug. 19, 1837)

September 2, 1837

Maj. B. W. Edwards died at his plantation in Holmes County on the 18th ult.

James Meek, Esq., died at his residence in this county, on the 24th ult., in the 48th year of his age.

Mr. H. M. Burt, died at the plantation of Col. John S. Lewis, near Woodville, on the 25th ult.

Frances Ann Virginia, youngest child of Thos. F. Gravis, died in Woodville on the 25th ult.

September 16, 1837

Departed this life, on the 12th, James M. Bradford, Esq., the senior editor of the Louisiana Journal, a distinguished member of the Bar in the Third Judicial District, and for upwards of thirty years a resident of the Territory, and subsequently the State of Louisiana. He died of a wound in the abdomen, given in an affray by one of our citizens, Mr. John McDermott. (*Louisiana Journal*)

September 23, 1837

Died at Fort Adams, on the 5th Sept., 1837, John Ogden, Esq., an old citizen of Wilkinson County and many years a member of the Baptist Church. He has left a wife and ten children.

Married on the 21st, by the Rev. Mr. Marshall, Mr. Augustus W. Forsythe to Miss Mary R. Shields, both of this city.

October 7, 1837

Died on the 17th ult., at Jerico (his residence) in Amite County, Mr. Jacob Boatner, long a citizen of this state and South Carolina.

October 14, 1837

Departed this life, the 26th ultimo, of phrenetis, Dr. Wm. Butler Hooke, in the 24th year of his age.

Married on the 12th, by the Rev. Benjamin Shaw, Mr. Henry E. Sale, merchant of Woodville, to Miss Maria E., daughter of the Hon. John B. Posey, of Wilkinson County.

October 21, 1837
Married on the 17th, by the Hon. N. Scudder, Mr. E. A. Knowlton to Mrs. Ann Ratliff, all of this place.

Died on the 5th of October, Eliza Jane Williams, aged 4 years and 8 months, daughter of Ebenezer Williams.

Died at his residence near Pinckneyville, this morning, Oct. 21st, Dr. John F. Carmichael.

October 28, 1837
Died at his late residence in this town, the 24th, Dr. Dick H. Eggleston, in the 41st year of his age. Dr. Eggleston was a native of Amelia County, Virginia, receiving his medical degree in 1819, at the University of Pennsylvania, and came to this state in 1820.

November 4, 1837
Doct. John F. Carmichael departed this life at his Cold Springs plantation, on the 21st ultimo, in the 74th year of his age. He was one of the oldest settlers of the state of Mississippi. After graduating at Philadelphia he entered the army in 1789, a Surgeon-mate.

November 25, 1837
Married on the 22d, by the Hon. N. Scudder, Mr. W. W. Munson, to Miss Matilda Adeline Howell, both of West Feliciana, Louisiana.

December 2, 1837
Married on the 30th ult, by John McCron, Esq., Mr. Lewis A. Yarbrough to Miss Elizabeth Humphreys, of Wilkinson County.

Departed this life November the 23d, Dr. Alexander M. Kennan, a native of Kentucky, in the 31st year of his age.

Died on the 27th ult, in this town, at the residence of Mr. J. A. Scott, Mr. A. J. Gray.

December 9, 1837
Married at Natchez, Miss., on the 1st, by the Rev. Mr. Page, William Howard West, of this place, to Miss Sara Olivia Dunbar, of Adams County.

Died the 2nd of Dec'r., Dr. C. B. Magoun, a native of New Hampshire, but for several years past a resident of this county, and successful practitioner of medicine.

December 16, 1837
Died at his late residence in this place, on the 3d, Doctor Calvin B. Magoun, in the 39th year of his age.

Died on the 11th December, 1837, Augustus D. Hester, of Wilkinson County, Miss., aged 26 years and 29 days.

January 6, 1838
Married on the 25th ult., by the Rev. Samuel Dawson, Mr. Thomas McDonald to Miss D. Leatherman.

Married on the 28th ult., by Judge Scudder, Mr. Jas. M. Iler to Miss Caroline Ginn, all of this county.

Married on the 4th, by the Rev. Mr. Winans, Charles C. Cage, Esq., to Miss Catharine J. Stewart.

January 13, 1838
Married the 28th ult., by the Rev. Samuel Dawson, Mr. Syvester C. Estess to Miss Emeline Murphy, all of this county.

Married the 11th January, by the Hon. M. Scudder, John Slade, Esq., to Mrs. Louisa Hayes, all of this county.

January 27, 1838
Died at his plantation in this county, on the 16th, in the 35th year of his age, Mr. Wm. W. Kaigler, leaving a wife and child.

February 3, 1838
Died on the 19th October, of congestive fever, Clement Biddle Penrose, Esq., aged 35 years.

March 10, 1838
Married on the 3d, by the Rev. S. Dawson, Mr. John Wisner to Miss Tebitha Ellsberry, all of this county.

March 17, 1838
Died on the 11th, at the residence of Wm. F. Paquinett, William G. Poindexter, eldest child of John G. Poindexter, in the 6th year of his age.

Daniel Bartlet was found dead on the 8th, near the residence of Mr. Thos. White, on Buffaloe. It is supposed he died in a fit.

March 31, 1838
Died the 17th, in this town, Mrs. Elizabeth Herbert.

April 7, 1838
Married on the 1st April, by the Rev. S. Dawson, Mr. Leath Miller to Miss Lackey T. Parmer, all of this county.

April 14, 1838
Married April 12th, by the Rev. Mr. Collins, Mr. Edward Stevens to Miss Elizabeth Hubbard, all of this place.

April 28, 1838
Married on the 19th, by the Hon. N. Scudder, Mr. B. W. Wright to Miss Rebecca J. Watkins, all of this county.

May 5, 1838

Married on the 26th April, at the residence of Mr. James N. Brown, by the Rev. A. T. Simmons, Mr. George R. Draughan to Miss Mary L. D. Winningham, all of West Feliciana Parish, La.

Married on the 3d, by the Hon. N. Scudder, Mr. James Oneal to Miss Priscilla Fogleman, of La.

May 12, 1838

Married on the 3d, by the Rev. S. Dawson, Mr. Daniel Commer to Miss Nancy A. Lanehart, all of this county.

May 19, 1838

Married on the 14th, by the Rev. Samuel Dawson, Mr. John Forbes to Miss Lucinda C. Brown, all of this county.

May 26, 1838

Married in Kingston, N. H., April 30th, Doct. C. S. Magoun, of this place, to Miss Sarah B. Sanborn, daughter of J. H. Sanborn, Esq., of the former place.

Married on the 24th, Mr. H. M. Button to Miss Adaline Cain, all of this county.

June 9, 1838

Married on the 7th, by C. C. West, Esq., Mr. Samuel Dearmond to Miss Sarah Fairchild.

June 23, 1838

Married 21st June, 1838, by the Rev. Mr. Collins, Mr. William Halsey to Miss M. S. Chapman, all of this place.

Married on the 26th ult., at Tuscumbia, Alabama, by the Rev. C. Richardson, Rev. John G. Burrus, of Mississippi, to Miss Emily L. Nutting, of Massachusetts.

June 30, 1838

Died in this county, on his Old River plantation, on the 27th, Mr. Wm. Kaigler.

Died in this town, on the 17th, Col. John W. Gildart, about 45 years.

July 7, 1838

Married the 3d July, 1838, by the Hon. N. Scudder, Mr. Victor N. H. Netterville to Miss Caroline Dunckley, all of this county.

July 21, 1838

Died near Woodville, Miss., on the 14th, of congestive fever, Mr. Pliney Tower, of Springfield, Vermont, aged 25 years.

Died at Fort Adams, on the 12th, Master James Miller, aged 13 years.

August 4, 1838

Samuel Gwin, Esq., Cashier of the Union Bank of Mississippi, died in New Orleans on Saturday last. His death was occasioned by drinking ice water.

Married on the 29th July, by Rev. Samuel Dawson, Mr. Wm. Woods to Miss Mary A. Mosley.

Married on the 26th July, by Rev. Samuel Dawson, Mr. Benjamin F. Sibley to Miss Eliza H. Hornsby, all of this county.

Married on the 2d, by the Rev. Wm. Winans, Mr. Wm. D. Postlewaite to Miss Sophia T. Carter, all of this county.

August 18, 1838

Died on the 13th, Ann Wilson, daughter of Mr. Thomas Ellis, aged 5 years, 7 months and 13 days.

September 15, 1838

Died on the 11th, at Laurel Hill, Louisiana, in the 5th year of his age, Christopher Ashley, only son of C. W. Bancks, Civil Engineer.

Died on the 14th, Charles C., youngest son of Maj. Thos. G. West.

Died on the 9th September, of congestive fever, Isaac Smith, son of D. Bass, Esq., aged 11 years.

September 22, 1838

Died 19th Sept., Harriet Ann Allen, dau. of W. D. Allen, aged 10 yrs.

October 13, 1838

Died in this place, on the 10th, in the 22d year of his age, Mr. J. M. Kercheval.

Married in Woodville, on Wednesday evening last, by John B. Jones, Esq., Mr. Peter Kelley to Miss Lessley, both of this town and county.

Married on the 2d, by the Rev. Wm. Winans, Mr. James J. Graves, late editor of the *Liberty Advocate*, to Miss Mary A. A. Anderson, daughter of Capt. John B. Anderson, both of Amite.

November 3, 1838

Married on 21st October, 1838, by the Hon. N. Scudder, Mr. Samuel Bell to Miss Esther Ann Fenner, all of this county.

December 1, 1838

Departed this life on 28th, Mrs. Leonora Semple, consort of Col. Robert Semple, in the 20th year of her age.

December 22, 1838

Married on the 13th, by the Hon. N. Scudder, Mr. J. J. Stockett to Miss Mary Olivia McKenzie, all of this county.

December 29, 1838
Married on the 27th, by the Rev. Samuel Dawson, Mr. James M. Holmes to Miss Mary Carsa, both of this county.

January 5, 1839
Married on the 3d, by the Hon. N. Scudder, A. M. Star, of this place, to Miss Elizabeth Parker, of Cincinnati, Ohio.

January 19, 1839
Married on the 17th, by N. Scudder, Esq., Mr. Benjamin C. Stuart to Miss Martha C., daughter of Maj. F. S. Mays, all of this county.

Died on the 8th, Mrs. Rebecca Ogden.

Died in the 17th, Mrs. Lanehart, consort of Mr. Abraham Lanehart.

February 9, 1839
Died Feb. 5th, at his late residence in Woodville, Mr. James C. Weekley, in the 59th year of his age.

February 16, 1839
Married on the 15th, by the Rev. R. A. Stewart, Mr. George Martin, merchant of this place, to Miss Margaret Dickson, of this county.

Married on the 2d, by John McRea, Esq., Mr. F. Brindley to Miss Harriet Butler, both of East Feliciana Parish, Louisiana.

Died near Woodville, 12th, Charles Radcliffe, infant son of Jas. C. and Mary P. Bell.

Died the 25th, Maria Louise Fraser, wife of Wm. T. Fraser, merchant of this place, aged 20 yrs, 8 mos. She has left two small children.

March 2, 1839
Died in this place, on the 23d of February last, Mr. Frederick O. Jenkins, late of Baltimore, Md., aged about 24 years.

March 9, 1839
Died at the house of Wm. D. Allen, in this county, on the 4th, of consumption, James Jackson Landrum, in the 25th year of his age.

March 16, 1839
Married on 7th March, by Rev. S. Dawson, Mr. John Lyons to Miss Julia Ann Sapp, all of this county.

Married on the 14th, by Truman Powell, Esq., Mr. Robert T. Ogden to Miss Amanda Caroline Tigner, both of this county.

March 23, 1839
Died in this place on the 22d, Mrs. Sarah B. Magoun, wife of Dr. C. S. Magoun, and daughter of Jacob H. Sanborn, Esq., of Kingston, N. H.

April 20, 1839

Died at her residence near this place, Mrs. Mary Stewart, on the 14th.

Died at his residence in this county, on the 19th, Dr. Jas. Lyne.

Married on the 9th, by the Hon. N. Scudder, Monsieur Palemond Broussard to Mademoiselle Elesina Broussard, of Attakapas, La.

Married on the 18th, by the same, Mr. Wm. W. Shillings to Mrs. Lavina Swigart, all of this county.

May 4, 1839

Married on the 2d, by T. Powell, Esq., Mr. John D. Kaigler to Mrs. Catharine F. Kaigler, both of this county.

Departed this life, on the 3d, Mrs. Caroline Netterville, consort of Mr. Victor N. H. Netterville.

May 11, 1839

Married on the 9th, by the Rev. J. F. Fish, Mr. Francis D. Richardson, of Attakapas, Louisiana, to Miss Bethia F. Liddell, daughter of Moses Liddell, of this county.

Married on the 2d, Mr. Caleb Swayze to Miss Nancy Jeter, both of Wilkinson County.

Died in this place, of scarlet fever, on the 6th, Lemuel, only son of Mrs. Celia Ann Prewett, aged 5 years and 6 months.

Married in Amite County, on the 16th, by the Rev. Charles Felder, Mr. William T. Jones, of Wilkinson, to Miss Mary Magdalene, daughter of Col. Holloway Huff, of the latter county.

Died at Louisville, Kentucky, on the 27th April last, Mr. James C. Dodge, for many years a citizen of this county.

May 25, 1839

Married on the 21st, by the Rev. Wm. Winans, Mr. John Whittaker to Mrs. Robina Rogers.

Married on the 23d, by the Rev. Elijah Steele, Mr. William P. Dickson to Miss Margaret L. C. Winans.

Married on the 23d, by the Rev. John Fish, Mr. Charles A. Thornton to Miss Cornelia V. Randolph.

June 1, 1839

Married at Washington, Miss., on the 21st ult., by the Rev. J. F. Fish, Charles Lancaster, of Woodville (formerly of Philadelphia), to Miss Rosena E., daughter of Isaac Dunbar, Esq.

June 8, 1839
Married on the 4th, by the Rev'd. B. Shaw, Col. William T. Lewis to Miss Harriet Eliza Davis, youngest daughter of Mrs. Susan Davis.

Departed this life at her residence, on the 30th ultimo, Mrs. Elizabeth Yerby, relict of the late Col. William Yerby, of this county.

June 29, 1839
Died recently in Columbus, Miss., B. W. Benson, Secretary of the State of Mississippi.

Died here, on the 20th, Emma Jane, only child of Mr. Charles Pascoe.

July 6, 1839
Died in this place, on the 29th ult., Thomas Leigh, Esq., from a wound received in a recounter with Fielding Davis, Esq. Mr. L. was the son of the Hon. B. W. Leigh, the late distinguished U. S. Senator.

Died at the residence of her son, Mr. Joshua Presler, of this county, on the 9th ult., Mrs. Jael Presler, relict of Mr. Peter Presler, dec'd., in the 106th year of her age. She emigrated to this country with her husband in the year 1789.

July 20, 1839
Died in this county, on the 25th of June, Frances Matilda, aged 8 months and 5 days, daughter of Dr. P. E. H. Lovelace, of Wilkinson.

July 27, 1839
Married on the 25th, by the Hon. N. Scudder, Mr. Elisha F. Moreland to Miss Catharine F. Chambers, all of this county.

August 17, 1839
Married on the 11th, by the Hon. N. Scudder, Mr. Jesse Ogden to Miss Caroline E. Poole, all of this county.

August 24, 1839
Married on the 22d, by N. Scudder, Mr. James F. Brown to Miss Susannah, daughter of Charles Netterville, Sr., of this county.

Died in the town of Fort Adams, on the 3d, Mr. Charles S. Venport, in the 36th year of his age, a native of the State of Virginia.

Died on the 4th, in Pike County, this state, Rebecca C. Kaigler, wife of Mr. John Kaigler, in the 59th year of her age.

August 31, 1839
Died in this town, on Wednesday last, Mrs. Priscilla Moise, consort of Dr. E. W. Moise, late of Charleston, South Carolina.

September 14, 1839
Died in this county, on the 4th, Mrs. Mary L. Moore, consort of A. T. Moore, Esq.

Died on the 11th, Mrs. Early, consort of H. G. Early.

Died on the 12th, Mr. P. W. Ogden.

September 28, 1839

Married on Thursday evening last, by C. C. West, Esq., Mr. Thomas Allen to Mrs. Lavina Pearce, La.

Died in this town, on the 27th, Mr. Walter N. Barrel, of Bayou Sara.

October 26, 1839

Died on the morning of the 21st, at the residence of her father, Mrs. Lydia F. King, wife of Captain Samuel King, of Adams County, in the 31st year of her age.

Died at his residence in this co., on the 23d, Judge Thos. H. Prosser.

November 2, 1839

Died on the 15th of October, of yellow fever, in Barker's Settlement, Louisiana, Mr. John A. Fell, formerly of Fort Adams, and of the firm of Fell and Sanders, of this county, and a native of Hartford County, N. C., in the 42d year of his age.

Died at the Cold Springs, Wilkinson County, Miss., on the 24th Oct., of bilious fever, Luther Pardee, aged near 22 years. Mr. P. was formerly from Livona, Livingston County, N. Y.

Died in Woodville, on the 31st October, Mr. Alexander Mitchell.

November 9, 1839

Married last evening, Rev. J. F. Fish, of Watertown, Jefferson Co., to Miss Julia Antionette, daugher of John I. Mumford, of this city.

Married in Woodville, on Tuesday last, by Cato. C. West., Esq., Pierce N. Durano, of the parish of Avoyles, Louisiana, to Miss Elizabeth Boman, of New Orleans.

November 16, 1839

Departed this life on the 24th of October, at the residence of her husband, Mrs. Sophia Bancks, consort of C. W. Bancks, Engineer on the West Feliciana Rail Road. The deceased was a native of England and emigrated to this country some four or five years since.

November 23, 1839

Married on the 17th, by Truman Powell, Esq., Merrill Smith to Miss Mary Ann Humphries, both of this county.

Married on the 14th, by the Rev. J. Dawson, on the sand bar opposite Concordia, below Fort Adams, Mr. Christopher Bougho to Miss Sarah Wilson, both of Louisiana.

January 4, 1840
Married on the 1st, by the Rev. B. Shaw, Dr. C. S. Magoun to Mrs. Celia Ann Prewett, all of this town.

Married at Bayou Tunica, on the 29th ult., by Thomas Dawson, Esq., Mr. John A. Key, of this county, to Mrs. Sarah Kent, daughter of Mrs. Sarah Rawlins, of West Feliciana, La.

January 11, 1840
Married on the 9th, by the Rev. Elijah Steele, Mr. Wilson P. Burton to Miss Margaret Quine, both of this county.

Married on the 5th, by the Rev. Elijah Steele, Mr. J. G. Woodard, late of New York, to Miss Mary Ann Shaffer, of this place.

January 18, 1840
Married on the 16th, by the Rev'd. B. Shaw, Benj. F. Herbert, Esqr., to Miss Elizabeth C. Hamilton, both of this county.

January 25, 1840
Died in East Kingston, N. H., on the 30th December, 1839, Mrs. B. Magoun, consort of Simon Magoun, Esq.

February 1, 1840
Married on Thursday evening last, by the Rev. B. Shaw, Mr. Charles Sims to Miss Philadelphia Gordon, all of this county.

February 8, 1840
Married on Thursday evening last, by the Rev. William Winans, Mr. George E. Frazier to Miss Ann Eliza Cage, all of this county.

February 15, 1840
Married on the 11th, by the Rev. E. Steel, Mr. Jefferson M. Morris to Miss Mary A. Martin, all of this county.

February 22, 1840
Married on the 20th, by Truman Powell, Esqr., Mr. William A. King to Eliza E. Netterville, both of this county.

February 29, 1840
Died at his residence in Avoyelles Parish, La., Thomas Landrum, formerly of this county, in the 39th year of his age, leaving a wife and two small children.

March 7, 1840
Died in New Orleans, on 20th February last, Mrs. Eleanor Eliza, wife of Mr. Francis Haley, Jr., aged 32 years.

March 14, 1840
Died at Liberty, Miss., on the 1st, Mr. Isaac O. Benthall, formerly of this county.

March 21, 1840
Died at his residence in this county, on the 15th, Jacob Elsberry, in the 80th year of his age.

Died in this town, on Sunday morning last, Drury Spurlock.

Died Mon. a.m. last, of whooping cough and dentition, McAfee, youngest son of Col. F. R. and S. M. Richardson, aged 6 mos.

March 28, 1840
Married on the 22d, by the Rev. Mr. Winans, Mr. Thomas H. Bacon, of Trigg County, Kentucky, to Mrs. Frances Jones, of this county.

Died on the 18th, Mrs. Robina E. Whitaker, of this county.

April 4, 1840
Married on the 19th ult., by Felix Embree, Esq., Mr. Samuel Dearmond to Miss Susan Richardson, both of East Feliciana Parish, La.

April 25, 1840
Married on the 23d, by Rev. B. Shaw, Mr. James Lovie to Miss Eliza Kaigler, all of this place.

May 16, 1840
Married on the 7th, at Bellview, by John G. Poindexter, Esq., Mr. George Row, of Louisiana, to Miss Margaret Bell, of Wilkinson County.

Married on the 14th, Mr. William Magee to Miss Rebecca Wisner, all of this county.

June 6, 1840
Married on the 20th ult., by John G. Poindexter, Esq., Mr. David T. W. Cook to Miss Sarah Godley, all of this county.

Married in the city of New Orleans, on the 25th ult., Mr. Joseph Kann, of this town, to Miss Louise Morese, of the former city.

Married on Thursday evening last, at Cold Springs, Claiborne County, Miss., by the Rev. John Lane, William H. McCardle, Esq., senior editor of the Vicksburg Whig, to Miss Emily Caroline Byrnes, only daughter of the late Robert Ralston Byrnes, Esq.

June 13, 1840
Departed this life on the 17th of May last, in the 24th year of his age, Benjamin M. Hubbard, of Louisiana, formerly of this county.

Married on the 4th, by the Rev. Benjamin Shaw, Mr. Owen Kilbourn, of Jackson, La., to Miss Mary A. E. Tyron, of Wilkinson County, Miss.

Married on the 9th ultimo, in Marion, Perry County, Alabama, by the Rev. Peter Crawford, General Samuel Houston, Ex-President of Texas, to Miss Margaret M. Lea, of Marion.

Died in Woodville, on the 7th, Mrs. Elizabeth H. Kaigler, in the 45th year of her age.

June 27, 1840

Married on the 18th, by Rev. S. Dawson, Mr. Abram Lanehart to Mrs. Sarah J. Fenner, all of this county.

Died on the 18th, Martha, youngest daughter of Mr. George and Mrs. Martha Morris, of this county.

Died in this town, on Sunday morning last, of apoplexy, Henry Deal.

July 4, 1840

Died on the 26th day of June, of consumption, Mrs. Hannah Turberville. She had long been a member of the Methodist Church.

Died on Monday, the 29th ult., at her residence, Mrs. Martha Lyne, consort of the late James Lyne.

July 11, 1840

Died July 5th, Miss Ellen Augusta Kaigler, aged 7 years, 4 months and 2 days.

July 18, 1840

Died on the 9th, at Fort Adams, Mr. Wm. Harrison Williams, in the 20th year of his age. Mr. Williams was a native of Warren Co., Ohio.

July 25, 1840

Died at the residence of Ananias Pate, Wilkinson County, on the 14th, Sarah Jane, infant daughter of James D. and Eleanor E. Pate, aged 9 months and 3 days.

August 1, 1840

Died on the 25th ult., Mary Prudence, infant daughter of Wm. and Mary Halsey, of this place.

August 8, 1840

Died at her late residence in Woodville, Miss., on the 27th of July, in the 84th year of her age, Mrs. Margaret Hampton, relict of Major John Hampton, an officer of the War of the Revolution, and for 30 years a member of the Senate of South Carolina. Mrs. Hampton emigrated to this state with her husband in 1815.

Died in this co., on the 3d, Jeremiah, youngest son of Joseph Collins.

August 15, 1840

Married on the 13th, by T. Powell, Esq., Mr. James P. Murrey to Miss Jane Cupit, all of this county.

August 29, 1840

Died on the 20th August, 1840, at his father's residence six miles east of Woodville, in this county, Joseph Johnson, son of Jesse and Maria L. Saunders, six years of age.

Died in Woodville, on the 26th, in the 11th year of her age, Susanna, daughter of the late John Bryant.

Married on the 20th, by Rev'd. Henry Thom, Mr. William Wilson to Miss Ellen Combs, all of this county.

September 5, 1840

Died on the 30th ult., at his residence on Buffalo, in this county, Mr. Joseph Fenner, in the 85th year of his age.

Died on the 25th of August, Harriet McGehee, daughter of Mrs. Mary B. Carter, in the 12th year of her age.

September 12, 1840

Married 1st Sept., by the Rev. E. Steel, Mr. B. F. Yerby to Miss Catharine Gildart, daughter of the Hon. Francis Gildart, all of this county.

Married on the 31st August, by T. Powell, Esq., Mr. Thomas McCante to Miss Catherine McGinnis, all of this town.

September 19, 1840

Married 17th, by the Rev. Mr. Steel, Mr. Wm. H. Woods to Miss Ann Martha Oswald, daughter of Col. T. H. Oswald, all of this county.

October 3, 1840

Died this morning, at the residence of Judge Wade, of La., Mrs. Wm. L. Brandon, of this county.

October 17, 1840

Married on the 13th, by the Rev. Wm. C. Craine, Dr. Henry N. Martin to Miss Lucy A. Adams, all of this county.

October 24, 1840

Married on the 22d, by the Hon. Francis Gildart, Mr. D. C. Lewis to Mrs. Martha N. Orr, all of this county.

Died in this town, on the 18th, Mr. Daniel Bass.

Died on the same day, at his residence in this county, Mr. Mabry Morris, aged about 80 years.

Died on the 22d ultimo, in Adams County, Miss., Victoria Ann, daughter of Jesse Bell, aged 2 years, 3 months and 19 days.

November 14, 1840
Married on Thursday last, by Judge C. L. Dubuisson, Mr. Gerard Brandon, of Wilkinson County, to Miss Charlotte S., daughter of Nathaniel Hoggatt, Esqr., of this county. (*Natchez Free Trader*)

December 5, 1840
Married in New Orleans, on the 26th ult., by the Rev. Mr. Wheaton, Mr. Jno. F. Winkley to Miss Susan Todd, all of that city.

December 19, 1840
Died at his mother's residence, 12 miles east of Woodville, on December 6th, 1840, of consumption, Daniel Williams Davis, in the 28th year of his age.

Died at her father's residence in Woodville, December 13th, 1840, Rachel Johnson, infant daughter of Jesse and Maria L. Saunders.

January 2, 1841
Married on the 30th Dec. last, by the Rev'd. S. Dawson, Mr. John H. Butt, of La., to Miss Catharine Westberry, of this county.

January 9, 1841
Died at his residence in Ft. Adams, on the 30th Dec., 1840, James Crow, aged 69 years.

January 16, 1841
Married 30th Dec., 1840, by the Hon. F. Gildart, Mr. Henry J. Knight, of this county, to Miss E. Wells, of West Feliciana, La.

February 13, 1841
Died on the 8th, Col. R. L. Throckmorton, of this county, aged 48 years. The subject of this notice was a native of Adams County and for 30 years a resident of Natchez, whence he removed to this county some four years since.

Married on 9th of February, 1841, by the Hon. F. Gildart, Doct. Andrew R. Kilpatrick, of Rapide Parish, La., to Miss Martha Ogden of this county.

March 6, 1841
Died on the 4th of March, 1841, at the late residence of his father, Robt. T. Ogden, in the 25th year of his age.

March 13, 1841
Married on the 11th, at the residence of the late Col. Throckmorton, by the Rev. Wm. C. Crane, Major Patrick F. Keary to Miss Helen Davis, all of Wilkinson County.

March 27, 1841
Married on the 24th, by the Hon. Francis Gildart, Mr. Michael DeMonet to Miss Jane Turbeville, all of this place.

April 3, 1841
Died on the 31st of March, 1841, Mrs. Harriet Woods, late consort of Capt. Isham F. Woods, at their residence in the parish of West Feliciana, Louisiana, aged 55 years. She was born March 7th, 1786, in South Carolina, and emigrated with her late husband to this country, in 1817.

April 10, 1841
Married on the 4th April, by the Rev. Mr. Jones, Mr. William Beach to Miss Esther Netterville, all of this county.

Married on Tuesday 6th, by the Rev. Mr. Stanton, Mr. Chester A. Bulkley to Miss Clara V. Holt, all of this place.

April 24, 1841
Married on the 21st, by the Rev. R. L. Stanton, Mr. Robt. B. Dean to Miss Martha A. Turbeville, all of this county.

We are called upon to chronicle the death of Robert Riddle, Esqr., late cashier of the Planters Bank in this city. (Vicksburg Whig)

May 1, 1841
Married the 22d of April, by the Rev. Samuel Dawson, Mr. Terry Echols to Miss Rutha P. Jones, all of this county.

May 8, 1841
Married on the 6th, by the Rev. Benjamin Jones, Dr. Charles D. Waddill to Miss Matilda C. McGraw, all of this county.

May 15, 1841
Married in the parish of West Feliciana, La., on the 1st May, 1841, by the Rev. Mr. Lewis, Dr. J. L. Donnellan, of Woodville, to Mrs. C. C. Sargeant.

May 22, 1841
Died on the 21st, Gilbert, son of Mr. John G. Woodard, of this town, aged 8 months.

May 29, 1841
Died in Fort Adams, May the 27th, Mr. Samuel Kline, in the 32 year of his age, formerly of Pennsylvania.

Died on the 26th, Mr. Joseph Brown, of this county, in the 48th year of his age.

June 12, 1841
Married on the 18th of May, 1841, by Felix Embree, Esq., Mr. Stephen D. Wilkinson, of Amite, to Miss Eliza Anderson, of Wilkinson Co.

Married on the 27th of May, 1841, by Felix Embree, Esq., Mr. John K. Pickett, of Louisiana, to Mrs. Martha Kilpatrick, of Wilkinson County.

June 19, 1841
Died in Fort Adams, on the 11th of May, William Chenery, a native of Portland, Maine, but for the last 3 years a resident of this county.

June 26, 1841
Married on 16th, by Rev. Saml. Dawson, Jno. Roach to Rachael Brown.

Married on the same night, by Rev. Samuel Dawson, Mr. Robt. Simmons to Miss Eliza Brown, all of this county.

July 3, 1841
Died at Alexandria, La., on the 10th ult., Mrs. Sarah Jane Dawson, consort of Robert Dawson, aged about 30 years.

July 10, 1841
Married on the 8th, by the Rev'd. William Winans, Mr. Isaac B. Draughan to Miss Mary F. Lindsey, all of this county.

July 17, 1841
Died on the 4th, at his residence in Yazoo County, in the 51st year of his age, Wm. Reid, formerly a resident of this county.

August 7, 1841
Married on the 5th, by the Rev. Mr. Stanton, Thuxton Davidson, Esqr., to Mrs. Caroline S. Farish, all of this place.

Died on 23d ult., Mr. Mathew N. Brandon, of Pinckneyville, in this co.

August 14, 1841
Died on Percy's Creek, in this county, on the 12th, Susan, youngest daughter of Geo. B. Collier, Esq., aged about 11 years.

Died in Amite County, on the 5th, Mrs. Susan Arbuthnot, consort of Mr. Wm. Arbuthnot, formerly of this county.

September 18, 1841
Died on the 10th, in the city of New Orleans, at the residence of Mr. James Ross, the Rev. Elijah Steele, Minister of the Poydras Street Methodist Church, in the 26th year of his age.

Married on the 13th, by the Rev. Thos. C. Brown, Mr. Thomas L. Young to Miss Elizabeth McGill, all of this county.

Married on the 14th, by Rev. S. Dawson, Mr. David L. Carter to Miss Ophelia Gibson, all of this county.

Died on the 13th, David Holmes Connell, youngest son of Hugh Connell, Esq., of this town.

September 25, 1841
Married on Thursday evening, by the Hon. Jas. I. Weems, Col. Robert Semple, of Wilkinson Co., Miss., to Miss Francena R. Wade, of La.

October 2, 1841
Departed this life on the 27th ult., Mrs. Laura Smith, consort of Judge C. P. Smith, of this county.

October 9, 1841
Died on the 7th Oct., Mr. Henry Y. Collins, for many years a merchant of this town.

October 16, 1841
Died on the 12th of October, 1841, Mr. Arthur Daniel, for many years past a citizen of this county.

November 27, 1841
Married on the 11th, by the Rev. T. C. Brown, Mr. Nathaniel Still to Mrs. Elizabeth H. Brown, all of this county.

Married on the 22d, by Rev. T. C. Brown, Mr. Absalom Langford to Miss Elizabeth Stewart, all of this county.

Married on the 29th of October, by Felix Embree, Esq., Mr. John Crow to Mrs. Martha Drake, all of this county.

December 4, 1841
Married on the 3d Nov., by the Rev. P. L. Stanton, Mr. Thomas M. Gill to Miss Mary H. T. Bush, daughter of Capt. Wm. S. Bush, all of this county.

Married on Tuesday evening last, by the same, Thomas W. Hays, Esq., to Miss Ellen Ellis, daughter of Mr. Thomas Ellis, of Cold Springs.

Married on Thursday evening last, by the same, Mr. John J. McGraw to Miss Ann O. Palmer, daughter of Mr. Alva Palmer, all of this county.

Married on the 2d, by the Rev. T. C. Brown, Mr. Charles A. Edwards to Miss Narcissa J. James, all of this county.

December 11, 1841
Married on the 7th, by the Rev. T. C. Brown, Mr. Wm. W. Dawson to Miss Penelope Knight, all of this county.

December 18, 1841
Married 15th December, 1841, by the Rev. Wm. E. Mathews, Mr. Robert B. Richardson to Mrs. Mary E. H. Hatfield, all of this county.

December 25, 1841
Married on the 21st, by the Hon. Francis Gildart, Mr. John J. Kearsey to Miss Julia H. Shaffer, all of this town.

Married on the 16th, by the Rev. T. C. Brown, Mr. Daniel L. Flinn to Miss Dinah T. Dawson, all of this county.

Married on Thursday evening last, by the Rev. R. L. Stanton, Salmon Aretus Phelps, Esqr., to Miss Hannah Hoyt Buckley, all of Woodville.

Died at the residence of Dr. Magoun, in this county, Calvin S. Magoun, aged 14 months.

January 1, 1842

Married the 22d December, 1841, by the Rev. Wm. Winans, Mr. Edward J. McGehee to Miss Ann Beverly Carter, all of this county.

Married on the 24th of December, 1841, by M. Overman, Esq., Mr. Jeremiah Palmer to Miss Minerva Blount, both of the parish of East Baton Rouge, Louisiana.

January 15, 1842

Married on the 8th of January, 1842, by M. Overman, Esq., Mr. Hampton Swinney to Miss Sarah Ann Lisleby, both of the parish of East Baton Rouge, La.

Married on the 13th, by the Rev'd. Robert W. Kennon, Mr. Robert A. McCraine to Miss Elizabeth Cupit, all of this county.

February 5, 1842

Married on the 3d, by M. Overman, Esq., Mr. Wm. Emry to Miss Amanda Leake, all of this county.

February 12, 1842

Died at his residence, on Ford's Creek, on the 9th February, 1842, Mr. William B. Dunckley.

April 9, 1842

Married on the 5th, by Rev. Samuel Dawson, Mr. Moses Cavin to Miss Sarah Shropshire, all of this county.

Married on the 6th, at the residence of Mr. James Baird, by Rev. Wm. Winans, Mr. Wm. W. Armistead to Miss Mary White, of Amite Co.

April 16, 1842

Married at the residence of Dr. Holt, in Woodville, on the 10th, by Rev. R. W. Kennan, Mr. Piere Martin Ozanne, of New Orleans, to Mrs. Beatrice Agnes Bruner, of the former place.

April 23, 1842

Married at Fort Adams, on the 20th, by the Rev'd. R. W. Kennon, Mr. Francis M. Richardson, of Fort Adams, to Miss Eliza Ann Dorsey, of Louisville, Ky.

Married at Jackson, Miss., on the 12th, by the Rev. C. K. Marshall, John D. Freeman, Esq., of that city, Attorney General for the State of

Mississippi, to Miss Eliza Ardine, daughter of the Hon. George Adams.

April 30, 1842
Departed this life on the 11th, at his residence in this county, Thomas Batchelor, Esq. The deceased has resided for a long time in Amite County.

Died in Jackson, on Monday last, Dr. Joseph M. Sitler.

May 7, 1842
Died in the parish of Point Coupee, La., on the 24th, Dr. Thomas Lyne, formerly of this place.

May 14, 1842
Departed this life on the 10th, Mrs. Jane C. Cage, consort of Mr. Polaski Cage.

May 21, 1842
Died suddenly, on Wednesday morning last, at his late homestead, Thomas Smith, Esq., in his 80th year.

May 28, 1842
Died the 23d, at his residence in this county, Mr. Charles Edwards.

June 11, 1842
Married on 2d June, by the Rev. Mr. Brogard, Mr. Jno. A. J. Hamilton to Miss Gertrude K. Hall, both of this parish.

June 18, 1842
Married in Amite County, on Tuesday last, by the Rev. R. L. Staunton, Mr. J. J. Bulow Johnson to Miss Emily S. Gayle.

June 25, 1842
Died the 19th, at the residence of Mrs. Frazier, in this county, Stephen Platner, Jr., aged 7 years and 7 months.

July 9, 1842
Married on the 3d, by the Rev. Samuel Dawson, Mr. Turner B. Euell to Miss Annes Comer, all of this county.

July 16, 1842
Died on the 7th of July, Sarah Ellen, infant daughter of M. Overman.

Died in Woodville, on 10th July, 1842, Mrs. Mary Weakly, consort of the late James C. Weakly.

September 3, 1842
Married in this place, on Wednesday last, by the Rev. Sam. Watson, Mr. Thos. M. Oswald, of Wilkinson County, Miss., to Miss M. M. J. G. Barkley, of this city.

Married on the 25th of August ult., by Judge Gildart, Mr. Jas. M. Bailey to Miss Saray Hays, both of Wilkinson County.

Married on the 1st of Sept., by Judge Gildart, Mr. Robt. Thompson to Miss Eliza C. Shaffer, both of this town.

October 15, 1842

Married on the 22d of September, by the Rev. Wm. Winans, Charles S. Dickison, of Tennessee, to Miss Martha W., daughter of the late James B. Baird, of this county.

October 22, 1842

Married at St. Paul's Church, on the 15th, by the Rev. W. C. Crane, Hon. Cotesworth Pinckney Smith to Miss Catharine Jackson.

October 29, 1842

Died at Laurell's plantation, East Baton Rouge, La., William James Collins, formerly of Wilkinson County, Miss., aged 17 years, 1 month and 20 days.

November 19, 1842

Married on the 9th, by the Rev. Mr. Drake, Isaac D. Gildart, Esq., of this place, to Miss Caroline Collins, of Adams County.

Married on the 10th, by the Rev. T. C. Brown, Mr. Samuel W. Foster to Miss Emily J. Brooks, all of this place.

December 24, 1842

Married on the 15th, by the Rev'd. J. Woodbridge, Alfred A. Williams, Esqr., of this town, to Miss Catharine Stewart, eldest daughter of Col. Nolan Stewart, of West Baton Rouge.

Died at his residence in Adams County, on the 26th ultimo, in the 45th year of his age, Mr. Jesse Bell.

January 7, 1843

Married in this county, by the Hon. F. Gildart, Mr. S. S. Bowman to Miss Sarah M. Hamilton, daughter of James Hamilton, Esqr., of West Feliciana, La.

Alexander Hughes was accidently killed by the upsetting of his cart, on the 30th Dec., 1842.

January 21, 1843

Married on the 15th, by F. Cooley, Esq., Mr. Wm. V. Gray to Miss Mary Ann Brown, all of this county.

Died on the 7th, Col. Theodore Starke, of this county.

January 28, 1843

Died at the residence of Mr. Wm. Stamps, in this county, on the 25th, of consumption, Mr. Richard Parker.

February 4, 1843
Married on the 30th Jan., 1843, by the Rev. T. C. Brown, Mr. Robert P. Davis to Miss Margaret M. Bell, all of this county.

February 11, 1843
Married at Whitesville, January 31, by the Rev. W. E. Mathews, Mr. Josiah Ayres, of New York, to Miss Margaret S. A. Graves, of this co.

Married in St. Paul's Church, Woodville, on the 7th, by the Rev. W. C. Crane, Alfred T. Moore, Esq., of Canton, Miss., to Miss Mary E. Lewis, of this county.

February 18, 1843
Married on Thursday evening last, by the Rev. R. L. Stanton, Mr. Benjamin H. Williams, of the firm of Cline and Williams, of Fort Adams, to Miss Martha M. Reily, of this county.

February 25, 1843
Married on the 19th February, 1843, by Francis Cooley, Esqr., Mr. Isaac N. Brown, of West Feliciana, La., to Miss Georgia Virginia Oswald, daughter of Col. T. H. Oswald, of this place.

Died at the residence of Rev. William C. Craine, in this town, on the 18th, Rev. Mr. Payne.

Died at the residence of Col. W. S. Hamilton, in this place, on the 23d, Mrs. Penelope Stewart.

March 11, 1843
Died on the 9th, W. J. Stamps, a student of Bethany College, in the 17th year of his age, a resident of Wilkinson County, Miss.

March 18, 1843
Died in this city, on Sunday evening last, Mrs. Mary Y., consort of Mr. John W. Fuqua, aged about 21 years, youngest daughter of Major S. W. Lewis, of this county.

March 25, 1843
Died on the 15th, of inflammation of the lungs, Mr. Abraham Lanehart, aged 52 years. He was a member of the Methodist Church.

April 1, 1843
Married the 23d ult., by the Rev. T. C. Brown, Mr. Lodwick N. Vaden to Miss Harriet, daughter of Benjamin Ferguson, of this county.

Married on the 30th ult., by the Rev. T. C. Brown, Mr. John G. Lindsey to Miss Martha Leatherman, all of this county.

April 8, 1843
Married on the 2d day of April, 1843, by the Hon. F. Gildart, Mr. Elisha F. Moreland and Miss Orinda E. Hope, all of this county.

Married the 2d, by the Rev. T. C. Brown, Mr. Wm. M. Williams and Mrs. Elizabeth B. Smith, all of this county.

April 15, 1843

Married by Elder W. E. Mathews, on 5th of April, Mr. Robert M. Lea, of Amite, to Miss Letitia Edwards, of Wilkinson County.

May 27, 1843

Married the 23d, by the Hon. F. Gildart, Mr. Victor N. H. Netterville to Miss Clarinda Catharine, daughter of the late A. P. Slocumb, Esq., of this county.

June 3, 1843

Married May 31st, by the Rev. Wm. C. Crane, John M. Currier, M. D., to Mrs. Frances Matilda Stewart, both of Wilkinson County.

Married on the 30th, by the Hon. F. Gildart, Mr. Jacob J. Chambers to Miss Martha Hope, both of this county.

Died on the 28th ult., Eliza Ann, daughter of A. M. Feltus, Esq., of this place, aged 2 years and 2 months.

June 10, 1843

Married the 8th of June, by F. Cooley, Esq., Mr. Thomas Woodsides to Miss Emily Lacy Land, both of this county.

July 22, 1843

Married July 11, by Rev. H. T. Thoms, Mr. David Phipps to Miss Mary E. Stephenson, all of this county.

July 29, 1843

Married on Wednesday morning last, in the Presbyterian Church, in this town, by the Rev. James Purviance, Rev. Robert Livingston Stanton to Mrs. Anna Maria Blackford.

Died in Woodville, July 22d, Henry N., son of George and M. W. Martin, aged 11 months.

Died in Wilkinson County, on the 17th, William F. Woods, son of William H. and Ann M. Woods, aged 2 years and 6 days.

August 19, 1843

Died on the 13th, near Bayou Sara, William Richardson Joor, in the 25th year of his age.

September 9, 1843

Married on the 30th ult., by Francis Cooley, Esq., Mr. Isaac Alexander to Miss Martha Langford.

Married on the 31st ult., by Francis Cooley, Esq., Mr. Jesse M. Netterville to Miss Catharine R. Lanehart.

September 23, 1843

Married on the 16th, by Hon. Francis Gildart, Dr. D. Clay Lea, of Amite County, to Miss N. Elizabeth Edward, of Wilkinson.

Died on the 8th, at his residence in the parish of West Feliciana, La., Captain Isham F. Woods.

Died in this town on the 20th, of congestive fever, William Weed, Jr., in the 17th year of his age.

Died here on the 19th, Thomas Herbert, son of Dr. R. H. McDaniel.

Died at the residence of his parents, in the parish of West Feliciana, La., Francis A. Evans, Jr., just entered his 17th year.

September 30, 1843

Married in this town, on the 23d, by Rev. R. L. Stanton, Mr. Silas Lindley to Miss Rachael Gray.

Died in this place, on the 28th, Mr. Albert G. Foster, of consumption.

October 7, 1843

Died 30th September, in the 13th year of his age, Francis William McGehee, son of Judge Edward McGehee.

October 21, 1843

Died on the 17th, Eliza Jane, daughter of Wm. D. Allen, of Wilkinson county, Miss., aged 7 years, 2 months and 22 days.

Died on the 13th, Mrs. Lucetta A. Phares, late of the parish of East Feliciana, La., aged about 36 years.

October 28, 1843

Died on the 19th, Clara, oldest daughter of Chester A. and Clara V. Buckley, aged 1 year, 9 months and 6 days.

November 4, 1843

Died on the 24th ultimo, of typhoid bilious fever, Mrs. Mary Ann McNeely, wife of Mr. Wm. McNeely, of this county.

December 2, 1843

Married on the 28th ult., in this place, by M. Overman, Esq., Mr. John F. Wills to Miss Eliza C. Glover.

Married on the 27th ult., in this place, by M. Overman, Esq., Geo. W. Eagan to Miss Ann Eliza Brown.

February 6, 1847

Married on Thursday evening last, by Rev. T. C. Brown, Mr. Nolan D. Stewart to Miss Mary Jane Reneau, both of this county.

Died on the 27th ult., Mrs. Rebecca Tabitha, wife of James Hanham, aged 34 years.

February 27, 1847

Died on the 16th, near Whitesville, in this county, M. Wm. M. Smith, aged 40 years.

March 6, 1847

Died in this place, on Wednesday last, Mr. A. C. Lanehart, aged about 28 years. The deceased has left a wife and child.

Died this morning, Mrs. Susan C. Worsham, aged 22 years, late of Franklin County, Tenn.

April 3, 1847

Married on the 23d ult., in Clinton, La., by Rev. David Pipes, Mr. Joseph Newell, of this place, to Miss Cornelia H. M. Brewer, of Wilbraham, Mass.

Married on the 25th ult., by Rev. John A. Smylie, Joseph Redhead, M. D. of Wilkinson, to Miss Mary Gayden, of Amite.

May 1, 1847

Married yesterday morning, by Rev. H. Beach, Sam'l. E. Brown to Rebecca E. Mattingly, both of Jackson, La.

May 29, 1847

Died in this place, on Saturday last, Mr. Berry L. Davis.

Died in this place, on Tuesday morning last, Mr. William Weed, aged about 40 years.

June 5, 1847

Married on the 12th ult., by the Rev. Mr. Speers, of Natchez, Henry Strong, M. D., of this county, to Miss Eliza L. Collins, of Adams Co.

June 26, 1847

Died last night at the residence of B. H. Davis, Esq., James N. Dowty, Esq., of consumption. Mr. D. has filled the office of Deputy Sheriff of this county for the last eight years.

August 21, 1847

Died at the plantation of S. S. Boyd, Esq., near Pinckneyville, on Wednesday last, Mr. S. P. Hudson, aged about 37 years.

August 28, 1847

Married on the 24th, by Rev. Chas. Beach, Mr. Thomas Hill to Miss Adomeline Landry.

Married on the same day, by L. K. Barber, Esq., Mr. Frederick Brindley to Miss Eveline Sophronia Kennedy.

Died at East Pascagoula, on August 17th, Miss Mary Ann, eldest daughter of Mrs. E. P. McNulty, of Rose Hill, Wilkinson Co., Miss.

October 9, 1847

Married August 19th, in New York, by the Rev. Mr. Kingsbury, Dr. Chas. J. Hester, of East Feliciana Parish, Louisiana, to Miss Laura Ann Kellogg, of Adams County, Miss.

October 16, 1847

Married on the 7th, at the residence of Mr. John Wisner, by R. Dawson, Esq., Mr. Jesse Ogden to Miss Sarah Eveline Elsbury.

Married on the same day, at the same place, by the same, Mr. Jesse Lanehart to Miss Rebecca Jane Guffy, all of this county.

January 8, 1848

Married on the 6th, by the Rev. T. C. Brown, Esq., Mr. John H. Leatherman to Miss Mary E. Chisholm.

Married in Natchez, on Thursday morning, by Rev. W. H. Watkins, Mr. Robert Tekle, of this county, to Miss Emeline, daughter of John Robinson, Esq., of Natchez.

January 15, 1848

Departed this life on Saturday night, Jan. 8th, 1848, Maj. Samuel W. Lewis, aged 65 years. Baltimore, Md. was the place of his nativity. He rendered service at the seige of Baltimore during the last war.

January 22, 1848

Married on the 13th, by Sam. Bell, Esq., Walter Morrison to Miss Lovica M. Presler.

Married on the same day, by Rev. Dr. Winans, Duncan S. Cage and Miss Sarah Jane Connell.

Married on the 14th, Thomas Helmer to Miss Evilene Jackson.

Married on the 15th, by Sam. Bell, Esq., Joshua Charrier to Miss Zelia Juno.

Married on the 7th, by C. Farish, Esq., Frederick Theilman and Mrs. Catharine Webb.

Married on the 20th, by same, John G. Henderson and Elizabeth Flint.

February 5, 1848

Died on the 31st ult., at his residence in Fort Adams, Mr. John L. Wall, in the 49th year of his age.

February 26, 1848

Married in Woodville, on the 25th, by Claiborne Farish, Esq., Col. W. J. Hodge to Miss Margaret P. Ellis.

March 11, 1848
Married in Bolivar Co., on the 13th of February, by Rev. Mr. Porter, Col. Calvin H. Nicholson to Miss Caroline C. Smith, of Woodville.

March 18, 1848
Died in this town on the 1st ultimo, Mrs. Elizabeth Posey, the relict of the Hon. John B. Posey, deceased. Mrs. Posey was in the 60th year of her age, and a native of Beaufort District, South Carolina. Mrs. Posey emigrated to Mississippi in 1810.

April 17, 1848
Married on Wednesday evening last, by Rev. Mr. Beach, Mr. Joshua Glass and Miss Cornelia Herbert Leatherman, both of this county.

Died at his residence in this county, on the 7th, Mr. Zachariah Walker, aged 64 years. The deceased settled in this county in the year 1801.

May 1, 1848
Married on Thursday evening last, by Rev. Mr. Lewis of Bayou Sara, Mr. Charles Matthews, of Louisiana, to Miss Penelope Stewart, of this county.

Departed this life on the 22d ult., of consumption, John Timon, aged about 56 years.

May 8, 1848
Married Thurs. evening last, by Rev. B. Jones, Mr. Samuel W. Riley, of Wilkinson, to Miss Mary Charlotte Boatner, of East Feliciana.

Died in this co., on the 7th, Mrs. Lavinia Netterville, of consumption.

May 15, 1848
Died on the 11th, of inflammation of the liver, Mrs. Brandon, the wife of ex-Governor G. C. Brandon.

Died on the 12th, Mrs. Maria Sale, wife of H. E. Sale, Esq., of consumption. She was the daughter of the late Judge Jno. B. Posey.

May 23, 1848
Married on Tansy Island, in this county, Mr. Lorenzo Dow Ives to Miss R. Cleavland.

May 30, 1848
Married 29th, in the Presbyterian Church, by Rev. Mr. Buch, Hon. J. Alexander Ventress to Miss Charlotte Pinchen, both of this county.

June 13, 1848
On Sat. morn., 10th, as several gentlemen were starting for the home of Thos. J. Browns, Esq., of this co., on a hunt, the pack began to fight and Benj. M. Cage, endeavoring to separate the dogs, using the

breach of his gun for that purpose, was shot through the body by the accidental discharge of the piece, and expired Sunday morning. Mr. Gage, a young lawyer, served in B. Co., of the 1st Miss. Rifles in the Mexican War.

July 4, 1848

Married on the 22d, by R. Dawson, Esq., Mr. John Kaiser, of Adams County, to Miss Mary Ann McCraine, of Wilkinson County.

Married on the 21st, by N. E. Raymond, Esq., Mr. James Holden to Miss Mary Phipps, all of this county.

Died on Tuesday night last, Mrs. Martha Morris, consort of Mr. George Morris, Sen., of this county, aged 43 years. She was a member of the Presbytarian Church.

July 11, 1848

Died on the 5th, Mr. M. M. Hester, aged 28 years.

Died on June 30th, at her residence near Whitesville, Miss., Mrs. Amanda J. Smith, consort of John P. Smith.

August 1, 1848

Died at the residence of her aunt, in this county, on Saturday last, Mrs. Sarah Jane Duvall, of the measles.

Died in Lexington, on 10th, Mrs. Sarah Strother, resident of this place.

Died in Isaquena Co., on the 17th ult., Geo. Joors, formerly of this co.

August 22, 1848

Died on the 24th of June, at her residence in Rapides Parish, La., Mrs. E. McIntosh, aged 71 years, formerly of this county. Also, Mrs. Mary Allin, a daughter of Mrs. McIntosh, aged about 40 years.

September 26, 1848

Died at Bridgehampton, Saffolk County, Long Island, New York, Mary Pierson, wife of Franklin Soule, aged 25 years.

October 31, 1848

Married on the 26th, by R. Dawson, Esq., Mr. David Hopkins to Miss Letitia Ann Scott, all of this county.

WOODVILLE REPUBLICAN &
WILKINSON WEEKLY ADVERTISER
(Woodville, Miss.)
Published by Chisholm & King

January 8, 1827

On Friday last, Mr. E. Magee, overseer for Major Montgomery, at Dog River, in this county, was most inhumanly murdered by the slaves belonging to his brick yard.

January 23, 1827

Married in this county on Thursday evening, the 4th, by Benj. Eccles, Esqr., Mr. Jesse Bell to Miss Elizabeth Ann Jones, daughter of Mr. Isaac Jones, all of this county.

Married on the same evening, by Benjamin Eccles, Esqr., Mr. James Varnell to Miss Thirsa Ann McGraw, all of this county.

February 2, 1827

Married in this county, on Thursday evening, the 1st, by Rev. Jacob Creath, Mr. John Dunbar, merchant of this place, to Miss Ann Calliham, all of this county.

Died at his residence in this county, on Wednesday morning last, the Hon. John P. Hampton, Judge of the Third Judicial District of this State.

March 10, 1827

Married on Sunday, the 4th, by the Rev'd. James A. Fox, Mr. William D. Allen to Miss Martha Scott Landrum, all of this county.

Died at his residence in Amite County, on the 21st ult., the Rev. Mathew Bowman, in the 63d year of his age.

March 17, 1827

Died at his residence in this co., on the 16th, Dr. William P. Trask.

Married in this county, on Thursday evening last, by the Rev. William Winans, Doctor Francis A. McWilliams to Miss Jennette S. Nesmith.

April 21, 1827

Married in the parish of West Feliciana, on the 19th, Mr. Jesse Davis to Miss Ann Marley.

April 28, 1827

Married on the 29th ult., by the Rev. Mr. Borrella, Mr. T. DeValcourt, editor of the Attakapas Gazette, to Miss Felionise Guidry, all of St. Martinsville, La.

May 5, 1827

Married on Thursday evening last, by the Rev. James A. Fox, the Hon. William Haile, to Miss Nancy Joor, eldest daughter of Major General John Joor, all of this county.

May 12, 1827

Married on Sunday evening last, by the Rev. George A. Irion, Mr. John King to Miss Jemima G. Harris, all of this county.

Married on the 29th ult., at Burlington, the residence of D. Vertner, Esq., by the Rev. John Wurts Cloud, Colonel Joseph Callender,

Cashier of the Branch Bank at Port Gibson, to Miss Sarah Breazeale, of the same place.

Died at her residence in this county, on the 8th, Mrs. Martha Roach.

Died on the 9th, Mr. David I. Gray.

May 26, 1827

Departed this life on the 20th, Doct. W. C. Smith.

Married on the 22d, by L. Miles, Esq., Mr. Saml. N. Ratcliff to Mrs. Nancy Hayes, all of this county.

June 2, 1827

Died in this county, on the 30th ult., Capt. Stewart Cole.

Died in this town, this morning, Mr. Daniel Hart.

Departed this life on the 1st, Miss Jemima Edwards, and on the 4th, her sister, Mrs. Sarah Davis, leaving more than a thousand dollars to the children of her sister, Elizabeth Dunn.

Married on the 31st ult., by the Rev. Thomas Brown, Mr. Walthall Burton to Miss Terresa Ann Therrell, all of this county.

June 9, 1827

Departed this life on the 8th, Mr. Caleb Wilcox, at his saw mill near Caledonia Springs. He received a mortal wound on his left thigh from one of the dogs that drew up the logs from the water on to the mill, which broke his thigh bone.

June 23, 1827

Married on Thursday evening last, by the Rev. Mr. Pipkin, Mr. Lorenzo D. Brown to Miss Sarah Stocket, all of this county.

June 30, 1827

Married the 28th, by the Rev. B. Pipkin, the Rev. Thos. C. Brown, of this county, to Mrs. Elizabeth Bingaman, of Louisiana.

Married on the same evening, by the Rev. B. Pipkin, Mr. Joseph P. Henley, to Miss Elizabeth A. Wesbrook, all of this place.

August 4, 1827

Married on the 31st ultimo, by Bishop Jacob Creath, Jr., Daniel O. Williams, M. D., to Miss Mary Jane Lacy, both of this county.

Married Thurs. eve. last, by James S. Carraway, Esq., Mr. Thomas P. Curry to Miss Mary Hayes, dau. of Mr. James Hayes, all of this co.

August 18, 1827

Married on Thursday evening, the 16th, by James S. Carraway, Esq., Mr. Joseph Poursh to Miss Sally Armstrong, both of this county.

August 25, 1827
Died on the 23d, Sarah Bela D. and Mary S. Clarkson, daughters of Mr. Charles S. Clarkson, of Greenwood, 12 miles west of Woodville, the one in her ninth and the other in her seventh year.

September 8, 1827
Married on the 6th, by Lemuel Miles, Esq., Mr. Robt. S. Morris to Miss Susan Knight, all of this county.

Died at the residence of his father, near Pinckneyville, on the 1st, Mr. Thomas M. Deloach, about 30 years of age.

Died in Amite County, on the 23d ult., Dodley Jones, son of D. and Mary Jones, 4 years, 4 months and 13 days.

September 15, 1827
Died on Saturday evening last, at the residence of her husband, near this place, Mrs. Sophia Bradford, wife of James M. Bradford, Attorney and Counsellor at Law. (St. Francisville)

September 22, 1827
Married on Thursday evening last, by the Rev. James A. Fox, Mr. William T. Mayes, to Miss Emily Merseilles, all of this county.

Married on same evening, by Rev'd. W. Winans, the Rev'd. Peyton S. Graves, of New Orleans, to Miss Aurelay G. Bruce, of this town.

Departed this life on Monday morning last, Mrs. H. Bush, consort of the late Capt. Isaac Bush.

September 29, 1827
Departed this life on the 24th, James Wilson, eldest son of Mr. James Wilson, merchant of this place, aged 3 years and 2 months.

Married on Sunday evening last, by the Rev. William Winans, Maj. John G. Richardson to Mrs. Mary Winingham, all of this county.

October 6, 1827
Departed this life, 28th September, at Cold Springs, Mrs. R. Raymond, consort of Dr. N. E. Raymond, aged 40 years, of pulmonary consumption. She was a member of the Presbyterian Church.

Married on Thursday evening last, by the Rev'd. George A. Irion, Mr. William Dowty to Miss Malissa M. Smith, daughter of Mr. Z. Smith, all of this county.

October 13, 1827
Died at his residence in this county, on the 8th, John H. Davis, Esq.

Died in West Baton Rouge, on the 4th, Mr. Peter L. Victor, Surgeon Dentist.

October 20, 1827

Died in this town, on Monday morning last, in the 16th year of her age, of bilious fever, Mrs. Mary Dorothy Temons, consort of Mr. John H. Temons, and daughter of Mr. Peter Conrad.

Married in this county, on the 18th, by Howell Moreland, Esqr., Mr. Daniel Slack to Miss Harriet Bush, daughter of the late Capt. Isaac Bush.

Married on the same evening, by John Mcgee, Esq., Mr. William Conner to Miss Martha Leatherman, daughter of Mr. Daniel Leatherman.

November 3, 1827

Died in this county, on the 2d, Mrs. Elizabeth J. Gray, consort of the late David I. Gray.

Died in St. Francisville, on the 24th ultimo, Mrs. Ann O'Donald, consort of Mr. Charles O'Donald.

Information has reached us of the death of the Lady of Judge Edward McGehee. She died at Montgomery, Alabama, on the 20th ult.

November 10, 1827

Departed this life on the 20th of Oct., in the State of Alabama, Mrs. Harriet A. R. McGehee, wife of Edward McGehee, Esq., of this co.

November 17, 1827

Died in this county, on the 14th, Mr. Robert B. Beasley.

December 1, 1827

Married on Tuesday, the 20th, by L. Miles, Esqr., Major J. W. Jeter, of Adamsville, to Mrs. Susan Porter, all of this county.

December 8, 1827

Married on the 29th ult., by Jacob Chambers, Esqr., Mr. Thomas Benthal to Miss Cynthia Jackson, all of this county.

December 15, 1827

Married at the Cottage, on the 13th, by the Rev. George A. Irion, Robert L. Dunn, Esqr., of Amite County, to Mrs. Eliza W. Nicholson.

December 22, 1827

Married on Thursday evening last, by the Rev'd. Dr. Cooper, Edmund H. Wailes, Esqr., to Miss Jane B. Newell, eldest daughter of Mr. Geo. B. Newell, of this county.

INDEX

ABBOTT, Eliza Jane 140 Richard 155 James 182
ABRAMS, M H 24 Susan Nephthali 24
ACOR, John 17
ACUFF, Joseph S 189 Nancy J 189
ADAIR, John 11 154
ADAMS, 212 Andrew 215 Ann M 34 Aurelia 102 Daniel W 34 Elisha B 1 Eliza 13 Eliza Ardine 74 254 Elizabeth 191 George 74 254 James F 104 John A 123 Lucy A 248 Mary Ann 10 Phoebe E 104 R H 102 Rebecca Jane 13 Robert H 13 214 Rodney H 110 Sarah A 123 Stephen 10 Thomas B 56 84 William 137 William E 165
ADKINS, A D 113
AHERN, Hannah 92 John 92
AHERNS, Morris 134 Henry 106 126 167
AHRENS, Margaret 126 Margareth 106 Peter Henry 126
AIKEN, John B 142
AILES, Elizabeth H 218 John F 218
AINSWORTH, James 22 Jane 52
AITSBURY, Southard 233
ALBERTSON, Benjamin 33 71 Eliza Winslow 33 Louisa 33
ALDRIDGE, Clark 14
ALDWELL, Basil 5 124 William 4
ALEXANDER, Amanda 95 Amos 200 Eliza 227 Eliza Jane 105 Elizabeth Ann 79 George 46 Isaac 24 257 Josephine 132 Lanora 56 Lavina 200 Louisa 147 Martha 24 257 Matilda 53

ALEXANDER (continued) Mrs 88 Rachael 132 143 S 79 Wm 53 56 227
ALFORD, Asenith 56 Turney 56
ALLEN, Anna Frances 130 Barnabas 198 Barnabus 55 Daniel 88 Effie 143 Eliza Jane 258 Frances M 115 Gen 71 George C 200 Harriet Ann 240 James 115 126 130 James J 71 Lavina 244 Martha Scott 263 Mary P 49 Narcissa Ann 55 Robert 95 Sarah 40 88 Sarah Ann 24 Thomas 244 Thos B 40 W D 240 William 143 186 William D 241 258 263 William L 104 107 117 124
ALLIN, Mary 262
ALLIS, Mary M 153
ALSWORTH, John N 38 Minerva Jane 38
ALVERSON, Wm B 191
AMBROSE, Mary 17
AMES, M F 202 Mary 135 William F 159 160
ANDERSON, Ann E 168 Asa 226 C A 31 Daniel 220 Eliza 250 Fulton 189 Hester Elizabeth 96 Isaac 25 James 193 Jane 230 John B 240 Joseph A H 170 Joseph G 53 Louisa 155 Margaret 226 Margaret A 220 Mark 169 Martha 27 Martha J 53 Mary A A 240 Mary Ann 189 Mary Jane 233 Matilda 198 233 Petee 155 Sarah 25 Sophia 173 Thomas 146 168 188 Tunstella E A 170 W P 27
ANDING, Celeste 176 Martin 176
ANDREW, Rev Bishop 75
ANDREWS, Martha K 65 Mary 25

ANTOINE, Hiram 26
ARBUTHNOT, Susan 251 Wm 251
ARCHER, James 69 160 Mary Ann 69
ARICK, Gertrude Eliza 41 William L 168
ARMISTEAD, Mary 253 Wm W 253
ARMSTRONG, Andrew 35 Ann 147 John R 6 135 Mrs Charles 6 Sally 264
ARNAUD, John P 218
ARNOLD, Armenia 26 John B 45 Maria B 44 Mary G 48 Medoria 45 Prescilla 38
ARRINGTON, John H 40 Patience A 40
ARRISON, Elinor 124 Harriet 111 Harriet Sophia 112 Philip 110 William H 11 152 Wm 111 112
ARTHUR, Augustus O 102 E A W 1 Joseph H 1
ASHLEY, John 228 231 M T 110
ASKEW, James 62
ATCHISON, J 160
ATKINSON, Elizabeth 46 M 46
ATWOOD, John 157
AUGUST, Albert N 152 Virginia E 152
AUSTIN, Catharine 93 Eliza A 177 Hugh R 177 James 93 Rev Mr 11 Wm J 21
AUTER, A 122
AYRES, Josiah 256 Margaret S A 256
BABCOCK, Anna Frances 130 Benj F 108 Charles B 130 Dudley W 124 Parthenia P 108 Wm R 108
BACON, Elizabeth H 38 Frances 246 Thomas H 246 William 98
BAILEY, F A 188 Jas M 255 John 136 John H 63 Judith 212 Medoria 45 Saray 255
BAILIFF, Mary C 97 Thomas 97
BAILLEY, Mrs 215
BAILLIE, Henrietta 214
BAIN, James 143 Rachael 143
BAINE, James 156
BAIRD, Isabella 31 132 James 253 James B 255 Margaret E 49 Martha W 255

BAKER, Annie 158 Charles 207 Dr 183 Emma J 139 Francis 210 J M 169 Jacob 110 Samuel 184 Sarah Cynthia 183 Susan Mary 183 T 110 William 129
BALCE, A B W 140 141 H B 140
BALCH, H B 8 Mary 196
BALDRIDGE, Caroline 123
BALDWIN, A L 33 Ann 193 Ann Maury 145 Cornelius 145 Hiram 193
BALFOUR, Emily 11 125 153 Mary Jane 9 44 144 William 11 153 Wm L 9 144
BALL, Geo W 105 Mary Jane 105 Wm R 137
BALLANCE, Eliza 13 James 13
BALLARD, Martha 187
BALLDWIN, Minerva I 189
BAMBUSH, Frances 158
BANCKS, Benjamain W 158 C W 240 244 Christopher Ashley 240 Sophia 244 T W 8 140 Thomas W 140
BANCROFT, Aaron 27 Jane P 27
BANDEREL, Felix 183
BANISTER, Charlotte 104 Thomas 104
BANKES, George D 16 17
BANKS, G G 63 Lucy 62
BANKSTON, B G 38 Lucinda 38
BARBER, Eliza 30 31 L K 30 31 259
BARBOUR, Catharine Ann 147 James 147
BARCLAY, Ann Frances 30 John 30 Sarah Eliza 30
BAREFIELD, Catharine J 167 Hugh 11 John 171 Margaret 171 Susanna 11 Theodosia 67
BARFIELD, Eliza 59 Harriet Amanda 167 John 57
BARHAM, Elizabeth 94
BARKER, Henrietta 168
BARKLEY, M M J G 254
BARLOW, John 16 57
BARNARD, Eliza Jane 18 Thomas 18 33
BARNES, Abram 217 Curley 151 F L 118 Frances H 28 Francis 131 G G 62 Gibson 28 Henrietta 131 Lucy 62

BARNES (continued)
  Martha 52 Mathew 128 Rev Mr 32
BARNETT, Catharine 147
  Catharine Neville 119 Charlotte R 127 James W 3 Maria A 11 Marla A S 153 Mary T 3 R 120 Richard 4 Richards 114 115 120 128 147
BARREL, Walter N 244
BARRETT, William 67
BARRICKEMAN, Wm 155
BARRICKENIN, William 12
BARRIS, Nancy E 43 Robert E 43
BARROW, Bennett H 218 Benoist 207 208 Charlotte 125 Cullen 125 Emily 218 Sarah E 84 Seth L 84 William 207
BARROWS, David N 36 Mary E 36
BARRY, Bartley C 22 Catherine D 23 Mr 16
BART, T 188
BARTLET, Daniel 238
BARTLETT, Christopher 216 Margaret 216
BARTLETTE, Jannette R 120 T A 120
BARTLOW, Frederick 15
BASS, D 240 Daniel 214 215 216 220 224 226 227 248 Elijah 67 Henry J 235 Isaac Smith 240 Job 67 Julia 42 Margaret 235 Margaret Ann 235 Mary F 176 Virginia E 46
BATCHELOR, Ann Eliza 141 James M 141 Mary Ann Harriet 210 Thomas 210 254
BATHIS, Mary 17
BATTAILE, M J 29 Wm 29
BATTELLE, Jonathan 21
BATTERTON, Enoch 183
BATTLE, E 178 Harriet A 178 Jethro Orren 47 O P 123 Orren Datus 47 Sarah 123 Sarah F 47
BATTS, Margaret Ann 133
BAUGH, Dr 38
BAUGHN, George Thomas 49
BAUM, Sarah 232 William E L 232
BAYLEY, Rice 162
BAYNTON, Cornelia 14 Jno 14

BAZILLE, F G 39 Polly 39
BEACH, Chas 259 Esther 250 H 259 Rev Mr 261 William 250
BEADLES, Ed P 19
BEAGLY, Mrs 136
BEAL, Charles H 107
BEAN, Eliza 42 Thomas H 183 William 42
BEARD, James 102 182 Martha 182 William G 8
BEASLEY, James F 73 Jared C 208 Lucy Ann Frances 75 Robert B 266 Samuel P 73 75
BEATTY, Mary 43
BEAZLEY, Elizabeth G 76 125 Hannah 84 Lucy A F 85 S P 85 Samuel P 76 78 84 Susannah 85 William S 78
BECK, Susan 13 Thomas W 13
BECKEM, Jane B 219 John A 219
BECKLEY, Mary Jane 40 Wm S 40
BEDFORD, 20 Samuel A 156
BEE, J M 131 Martha Ann 131
BEEN, Eleanor A 147 Wm M 147
BEESLEY, William 57
BEESLY, Sarah A 50
BEGLEY, Edw 108
BELL, Amanda 52 Ann Eliza 205 Bennett H 205 Charles F 40 Charles Radcliffe 241 Elizabeth 205 Elizabeth Ann 263 Esther Ann 240 F T 121 J 27 J G 143 James Craig 232 Jas C 241 Jesse 248 255 263 Jo 88 Margaret 246 Margaret M 256 Mary 232 Mary C 40 Mary P 241 Peter 206 Sam 260 Samuel 240 Victoria Ann 248 Wm 190 Wm M 27
BELSINGER, Fred 16
BELT, Jane M 84 Jas H 84 T J 84
BENGOUGH, Amelia Mary Anne 177
BENNEDICT, E 31 N 31
BENNET, Julia Ann 219
BENNETT, E A 155 Henry L 155
BENSINGER, E 40 Ferdinand 40
BENSON, B W 243 Minerva O 32
BENTHAL, Cynthia 266 Thomas 266

BENTHALL, Isaac O 245
BENTON, Eleanor W 190 John W 32
BENTSINGER, Wm 117
BERKENFENT, Louisa 35
BERNARD, Felix 25
BERRY, Elizabeth 56 J G 160 Mary 160 Mrs E 31 Sarah 68 Susan 47 Thomas 68 Thomas Y 66 Victoria 160 W 160
BERT, T 7
BERTRON, Rev Mr 68 218 224
BET, Mahalet 30
BETZ, Eve 156 John 156
BEULAN, James 191
BEUTEL, Ann Mariah 125
BIBB, Fannie May 81 Fanny May 11 Joseph 11 81
BICKERSTAFF, Henry 21 Robert 21
BIELLER, Ann 45
BIGGS, Hannah J 139 Paulina 211 Susan A 130 William 130
BILLINGS, E S 134 Jane C 114 Lavinia 134 Leila C 134 Selia C 134
BILLINGSLEY, M W 38
BINDY, Edwd 105
BINGAMAN, Adam 18 201 Charlotte 201 E Jane 18 Elizabeth 264
BINGHAM, Eunice Ann 97 Margaret F 96
BIRCH, Anne Remson 13 George 13
BIRDSONG, Ann E 37 Ann Elizabeth 165 Eliza Frances 165 George T 37 Henry B 127 Laura V 37 William W 165
BIRNEY, Mary Fredonia 158 Robert W 158
BISBAN, Ann 135
BISHOP, Emily 55 H W 51 52
BISLAND, Jonh 195 Peter 15
BITTNER, J N 179
BIVENS, Cytheria E 47
BLACK, Frances Merwin 39 James R 7 Mary Jane 50 Peter 14 15 William 135
BLACKBURN, Irving 26 J S 186
BLACKFORD, Anna Maria 257

BLACKMAN, Goldin 144 H Golden 9 H Goldin 44 Mary Jane 9 44 144
BLACKSHEAR, Eliza Jane 158 James M 158
BLACKSTOCK, Martha 4 115 Moses 4 115
BLACKWELL, Elizabeth 134 Noah 151
BLAIR, Anna M 48 John 73 114
BLAKE, Henry 205 Martha Ann 26 37 77 Mary E 75 Nancy 54 Nancy H 52 Ruel 174 Sarah 189 William G 26 75 77 William R 52 54 Wm J 37
BLALACK, Sarah A 123
BLANC, Rt Rev Dr 153
BLAND, James 110 119 177 181 Jas 115 173 Martha W 110 Olivia E 177 Olivia F 115 Richard Jay 110
BLANE, Rt Rev Dr 11
BLATCHFORD, Amelia Mary Anne 177 R J 177
BLEDSOE, Giles 16 James 19 Martha 13 Richmond 13
BLENKINSOP, Rev Mr 87
BLIES, Edward M 110
BLISE, Francis 139
BLOUNT, Artimisia 159 Lavinia 231 Levi 231 Malinda 22 Minerva 253 Robert C 22 228 Sarah 42 Traverse 228
BLOXTON, Mary 12
BLUNDELL, D F 48 James 48
BLUNT, Mary E 157 Nancy 129 Sarah 140
BOATNER, Elias 230 Ezekiel 187 Jacob 236 Mary Charlotte 261 W J 223
BOBB, John 99 Mary 99 Wm 189
BOCKLEY, Jno 132
BODDIE, George W 31 78 Louisa A 31 78
BODLEY, Catharine H 122 Hugh S 174
BOLAND, David 220 Drusilla 220
BOLLS, Andrew 173 Ann E 119 Margaret 171 Martha Jane 69 Mary 38 Mary Jane 67 Matthew 69 S R 119 Sarah 6 133

BOLLS (continued)
   Sarah Ann 174 Wilson 194
BOLTON, Mary 189 Thomas 189
BOMAN, Elizabeth 244
BOND, Elizabeth 169 J C 137
   James 109 Minerva R 137
BONE, David 66 William Henry 66
BONNEMAN, Henry 186
BONNER, Louisa 211 Moses Miles 232 R L 232 Reuben L 211
BONNEY, Jesse S 138
BOOKER, 109
BOOTH, Ann E 177 Indiana 141 John 141 Joseph 97 Stephen S 177
BORDWELL, Ann 76 Charles 76
BOREAM, Anne Remson 13
BOREN, Elizabeth 186
BORLAND, Mary Isabel 44 Solon 44
BORMAN, S H 143
BORRELLA, Rev Mr 263
BOSLEY, Richard 110
BOSWORTH, Elizabeth Lester 186 Felix 172 William Lester 186
BOUCHELLE, E F 40 Maria T 40
BOUGHO, Christopher 244 Sarah 244
BOUIS, Ann 218
BOURDEN, Reuben 15
BOURK, Jane M 202 Raymond A 202
BOVARD, Ellen E 202 Wm A 202
BOWEN, A G 67 E L 53 57 F F 165 Mary 26
BOWER, Wm H 102
BOWIE, Lieut 201
BOWMAN, Eliza Jane 121 Mathew 263 S S 255 Sarah M 255 Silas H 121
BOWMAR, Celeste 200 Joseph 200
BOWYER, Charles L 4 117
BOYD, A M 190 Eliza 27 90 Elizabeth 172 Eveline T 74 F W 78 120 130 142 143 Frederick W 115 131 Gordon D 88 J H 27 74 75 76 77 James H 73 90 James S 176

BOYD (continued)
   Jane Elizabeth 36 Mary Ann 190 Mary Eliza 131 N W 134 P W 115 Rev Mr 129 S S 259 William 190
BOYER, Charles L 117
BOYLAN, Samuel M 47
BOYLE, Charlotte A 36 H G 120 William 36
BOYLEN, Samuel M 9
BOYLER, Samuel M 146
BRACEY, William 22
BRADBURY, Solomon 175
BRADFORD, Edward 67 James M 236 265 Martha J 47 Mary L 81 Nancy A 41 Sophia 265 Virginia 67
BRADLEY, Augustus H 24 Edward 115 Levisa 29 Sarah A E 24
BRADSHAW, James 147 Nancy 147
BRAHSTON, Anne Marin 173 Mrs Asa 173
BRANCH, John T 167 Mary A 167 Thomas 167
BRANDON, Ann Eliza 220 Betsy 209 Charlotte S 249 G C 261 Gerard 215 249 Gerard C 209 Mathew N 251 Mrs 261 Mrs Wm L 248 William L 220
BRANSFORD, John H 177 Mary Virginia 177 178
BRAY, Angelitha 75 Calvin 75
BREAZEALE, Sarah 264
BRECKENRIDGE, Eliza Ann 219 Meredith S 219
BREEDLOVE, C B 132
BREELAND, Polly 39
BRENNAN, Edward 99
BRENT, Harriet 208 John 208 Laura H 31
BREWER, Cornelia H M 259
BRICE, John 213
BRIDGES, Abram 20 Margaret 20 Morgan 95 Peter 56 Wm 95
BRIEN, Alfred W 105 Amanda M 105 J W 74 Julia E 110
BRIGGER, Elizabeth 72
BRIGGS, C C 203 David T 164 Gray 14 Hannah J 187 Harriett 14 Mahetabel 164 Mrs 5 127

BRIGGS (continued)
Robert Williams 35 Sarah 183
Susan A 28 William 28
BRIGMAN, Wm 107
BRINDLEY, Eveline Sophronia 259 F 241 Frederick 259 Harriet 241
BRISBAN, Ann 7
BRISCOE, John 30 123 Lucy Ann 123 Margaret 217 Martha 30 Martha Jane 164 Mary 68 Mary M 151 Wm 68 217
BRITTINGHAM, L W 109
BROADWELL, W B 111
BRODERICK, Thos 191
BRODHEAD, Mary Wyatt 23 Samuel A 23
BROGAN, James 123
BROGARD, Rev Mr 254
BROMGOGLE, Levi 47 Zenobia A 47
BROOKS, Chiron 182 Commodore 221 Emily J 255 James G 65 Mary C 46 Oliear C 103 Oliver C 169 182 S 197 Samuel 201 Sarahphina 103
BROOMFIELD, Ann 53 John 53
BROTHERS, Martha 165
BROUSON, Edward 105
BROUSSARD, Elesina 242 Palemond 242
BROWDER, Bartlett 172 F A 200 Frederick A 213 214 Harriet 213 214 Isabella A 200 Narcissa Jane 172
BROWN, 187 Adeline Louisa 52 Agnes M 192 Albert G 44 59 Alfred 97 Ann Eliza 258 Anne W 72 Austin 137 Cath 40 Catherine V 165 Charles K 52 Edwin R 59 Elijah R 229 Eliza 251 Elizabeth 172 227 264 Elizabeth A 41 Elizabeth H 252 Eunice 194 Frances 54 George 229 George W 165 Georgia Virginia 256 Henry 40 Isaac N 256 J 109 J W 9 146 James 137 199 James F 243 James N 239 Jas T 119 Jesse 224 John 104 221 Joseph 52 250 Lorenzo D 264 Lucinda 6 129 Lucinda C 239

BROWN (continued)
Margaret B 221 Martha M 229 Mary Ann 255 Mary E 84 Mary L 28 Mattha B 97 Nancy C P 52 Penelope A 165 Rachael 251 Rebecca E 259 Rev Mr 173 Robert 72 Sam'l 222 Sam'l E 259 Sarah 59 264 Sarah A E 24 Silas 19 20 23 54 Susannah 243 T C 1 177 184 221 224 227 228 229 252 253 255 256 257 258 260 Thomas 264 Thos C 218 228 251 264 Thos J 261 William 229 William A 221
BROWNING, I T 232
BROWNRIGG, John H 64
BRUCE, Aurelay G 265 John L 211 Mrs 16 William R 211
BRUEGARD, 176
BRUNEL, John 165
BRUNER, 4 Ann 93 Beatrice Agnes 253 E E 93 119 Ellen 141 Ellen S 8 141 Margaret M J 163 Mary Ann 171 Rosanna 141 Wm F 141
BRUNSICH, James 205
BRYAN, Edward H 116 James P 100 Keziah M 50 Lucilla 116 Mildred 101 Nancy R 50
BRYANT, B C 34 Caroline 215 D 34 John 248 Martha 123 N H 215 Nancy 178 Nathan 27 123 Rev Mr 220 Susanna 248
BRYNON, N G 157
BRYSON, Emma L 149 Lucy 190 N G 147 151 158 160 190 Nathan G 149
BUCH, Rev Mr 86 261
BUCHANAN, Henry 35 S A 35
BUCK, Charles 165 Charles B 133 Lucy 165 Marion Davidge 165 Mary E 133
BUCKHOLTS, Victorie C 232
BUCKLEY, Chester A 258 Clara 258 Clara V 258 Hannah Hoyt 253 James 147
BUCKNER, E Rush 39 Enos Rush 82 97 Georgeana 97 Georgeanna 82 Georgiana 39 Mr 214 Wm 212
BUESLEY, Henry F 169 Mary Ann 169

BUFFKIN, Gideon 57
BUIE, G M 38 John Whitfield 33 Minerva Jane 38
BULKLEY, Chester A 250 Clara V 250
BULL, Eliza S 98 John C 98
BULLEN, Benjamin M 198 Elizabeth 198 Joseph 198 Mordecai Dudley 70 Samuel 70 Zenobia A 47
BULLINGER, Eliza 122
BULLINGTON, Margaret 73
BULLITT, William 172
BULLOCK, E J 49 J L W 49
BULLUS, Ann M 34
BUMPASS, J A 62
BUNBAR, James 90
BUNCH, Nancy 78
BUNTIN, James 207
BURCH, J 65 S 25
BURCKETT, Charlotte L 159 J 159
BURFORD, Mary E 27
BURGIER, Louis 98
BURHAM, Susan 142
BURK, Louisa H 88
BURKE, Gottleib 166 Sarah Matilda 223 Wm 109 Young 223
BURKHALTER, Jesse 23 John 29 Ruth 29
BURLEY, Jacob 185
BURNETT, Agness Ann 20 Daniel 20
BURNEY, Betsy 201 David 201 James D 45 Mary 45
BURNHAM, Nancy 139
BURNLEY, Edwin 52 Susan 52
BURNS, ---insley 71 Delia 104 Isaac E P 103 Martha 71 Samuel 104 William 87
BURR, Julia 217
BURRESS, Eliz 14 John C 14
BURRISS, J C 91
BURROUGHS, Dufphey 172 Elizabeth 172 Hannah 184 Mary 149
BURROWS, Rev Mr 17
BURRUS, Ellen Keary 225 Emily L 239 J C 214 218 225 James R 167 John C 18 John G 239 Laurentina Ophelia 167

BURRUSS, J C 219 John C 229
BURT, Andrew 198 H M 236 T 147
BURTON, A G 179 George W 8 Margaret 245 Nancy 53 Sarah E 235 Sarah Eleanor 222 Sarah M 24 Terresa Ann 264 W P 235 Walthall 222 264 Wilson P 245
BURTRON, Rev Mr 223
BURWELL, Armsted 103 Priscilla W 102
BUSCHA, Fronica 151
BUSH, H 265 Harriet 266 Isaac 265 266 James 122 Jas 45 Lucinda M 39 Mary H T 252 Rebecca 122 Richard 41 Sarah Ann 45 Wm S 252
BUTCHER, Mrs 183
BUTLER, B 47 C G 47 Christian 47 Harriet 241 J 136 John 221 John M 95 Martha Jane 95 Mary Ann 157 Rebecca 106 Z 67 140
BUTT, Catharine 249 John H 249
BUTTON, Adaline 239 H M 239
BUTTS, Angelina E 46 David 46
BYERS, Bill 115
BYNUM John 37 Rebecca 37
BYRNES, Emily Caroline 64 246 Robert Ralston 64 246
BYRON, E E 141 Frances E 141
CABALL, Elvia K 60 William S 60
CABANISS, A B 28 Susan 28
CABELL, Elizabeth 76
CABLE, Jacob 65
CAGE, Ann Eliza 245 Benj M 261 262 Catharine J 238 Charles C 238 Duncan S 260 H 209 Jane C 254 Jesse 34 Penelope 209 Polaski 254 Sarah Jane 260
CAIN, Adaline 239 Louisa 178 Michael 100
CALAHAN, Jerry 119
CALDER, Lavinia 231
CALDWELL, H 131 Isabella Jane 25 Joseph 155 Phebe J 155 Rev Mr 151 154 202 Robert 159 S 155
CALEB, Indiana 141 John M 141
CALHOUN, Adam Gordon 25

CALHOUN (continued)
  E F 140 Ewing F 42 Henry W
  25
CALLENDER, Joseph 263 Sarah
  263 264 William Loring 212
CALLIHAM, Ann 263 David 220
CALLOWAY, James 144
CALVERT, Feliciana 48
CALVIT, Tacitus 14
CAMBELL, D R 144
CAMBRON, Mary Olivia 153 Wm
  L 153
CAMERON, Archibald 44 144
  John 104 Mary Olivia 153
  Sarah C 122
CAMP, J G 204 N W 79 Norman
  W 36 41
CAMPBELL, Ancyvilia 24
  Charles 24 D R 9 Duncan A 96
  Elizabeth Ann 55 Harvey 182
  Jn 91 John 12 55 Joseph 136
  Margaret P H 168 Mary 120
  Mary P 45 Peter G 8 Rev Mr
  155 Sarah 68 Virginia 67 William R 168
CANAVON, Jane 166
CANEPA, Caroline 134
CANEY, John 143
CANFIELD, Joseph S 165 Julia P
  213 Mr 214 Zachariah 213
CANLEY, Mrs R 80
CANNON, Amanda H 37 W B 56
CARADINE, Barney 129
CARAWAY, Laban 96
CARBIEL, Ellen 153
CAREY, Harriet J 45 Silas J 45
CARGROW, James 161 203
CARLILE, Adeline 98
CARLISLE, 208 Campbell 19
  Sarah 152
CARMICHAEL, Daniel S 182 John
  F 237
CARNES, Emily F 189 James E
  189
CARNEY, John 119
CARNGAIN, John 204
CAROL, Mr 17
CAROTHERS, Lydia O 71
  Thomas 71
CAROUTH, Joseph 67
CAROUTHERS, Eliza 42
CARP, N W 48

CARPENTER, Ann 38 Horace 39
  69 Joseph 194 Mary Hassan 38
  Orville 38
CARRAWAY, Eliza B 37 James S
  221 264 Jas E 37 Judge 217
CARRIEL, John D 172
CARROLL, 19 Felix 8 140 Lucy
  117 Patrick 7 138
CARSA, Mary 241
CARSON, Catherine 92 James 92
  Jane 213 Jane M 83 Joseph 10
  47 150 Wm L 213
CARTER, A A 162 Abner 96 Ann
  230 Ann Beverly 253 David 230
  David L 251 Eleanor C 228
  Elizabeth 96 Elizabeth M 7
  George W 223 228 Jacob 37 M
  B 228 Mary B 248 Ophelia 251
  Rosalie P 228 Sophia T 240 W
  96
CARTWRIGHT, Fenton 14
CARTY, Ann 76
CARUTHERS, Samuel M 47
CASIAN, John 189
CASON, Henry L 234 Marinda 234
CASSEALS, Catherine Jane 219
CASSEDY, Sarah D 103
CASSELS, Sarah 201
CASSIDY, Jane 59
CASSITY, Eveline 59 Harriett A
  55
CASTELL, Charles J B F 224
  Louisa Henrietta 224
CASWELL, G K 21
CATCHING, B 59 B H 59 Bej
  Franklin 59 Eady 220 Nancy 53
  Phillip Scott 53 S M 220 Silas
  59
CATCHINGS, E J 49 Harriet 198
  Nancy M J 75 T J 152 Thomas
  J 75
CATES, Alfred B 39
CATHERS, Lavina 179
CATLIN, Ann H 46
CATO, John D 207 Martha 207
CATTIHAM, David 221 Mary 221
CATTINAZZI, C 184
CAUSEY, Jonas 25
CAVIN, Moses 253 Sarah 253
CECIL, James 14
CHAIN, Hugh 198 Matilda 198
CHAISE, Rev Mr 14

CHAMBERLAIN, J 67 69 Jere 67 Jeremiah 67 Rev Dr 66
CHAMBERS, Adam I 224 Anna 106 Asa 79 86 117 Catharine F 243 H C 28 Jacob 266 Jacob J 125 257 Lucretia J 28 Margaret M 79 Martha 125 257 Martha Ann 117 Sarah N 224
CHAMBLISS, Caroline 178 Lucinda S 179 Martha 182 Nathaniel 182 R J 179 Thomas J 178
CHAMPION, Martha 23 Willis 23
CHANDLER, Charlotte 158 John 158 Sophia 104
CHANEY, A E 209 Rev Mr 186
CHAPIN, Andrew M 183
CHAPLAIN, W R T 102
CHAPMAN, A W 7 139 158 166 189 207 Ann E 86 B D 86 Catharine B 127 John G 166 John L 127 John R 37 Joseph 122 M S 239 Mary A 166 Nancy K 48 Peyton Cook 34 Rev 130 Rev Mr 124 207 Samantha Jane 34 Sarah 37
CHAPPELL, Amanda E 132 James Carter 132
CHARRIER, Joshua 260 Zelia 260
CHATHROE, James 182
CHEATHAM, Sarah 37
CHENERY, William 251
CHERRY, Jane M 83 Wilie 83
CHESLEY, Ann E 119
CHESNUT, Wm 147
CHEW, Rebecca F 28 Thomas S 210
CHEWNING, Albert G 111 James J 168 182 187 Martha 187 Sarah 120 Sarah M 168 182
CHILDRESS, Caroline M 61 Martha 61 Martha Ann 61 Mary 146
CHILTON, John M 99 Sarah 99
CHISHOLM, 262 Angus C 148 Martha Jane 228 Mary E 260 William A A 207 228
CHRISTIAN, A B W 141 Allen 44
CHRISTIN, Mrs A B W 8
CHRISTMAS, Mary Emeline 116 Mary M 220 Richard 116 Richard T 220
CHRISTY, Joseph 2

CHUNN, Mr 26
CHURCH, Edward B 164 Edward Bentley 164
CIZZEE, Jane 230 William 230
CLAIBORNE, Charlotte H 196 Courtney Ann 91 Eliza Virginia 199 Ferdinand L 91 199 Hon Judge 201 Thomas Augustine 196
CLAPP, Balinda A 66 Delia 104 Rev Mr 98
CLARK, Caroline 35 Daniel 98 Elia Amelia 47 Elizabeth 91 Frances A 99 Giles H 27 Hannah S 38 Harriet 42 James R 27 Jane Eliza 131 John T 137 Joshua G 12 Louisa A 31 78 Louisa P 72 Moses 47 Robert 87 Sarah G 81 Shelton 177 T 126 William 31 35 42 72 78 81 131 Wm J 119
CLARKE, Amelia 26 Frances A 57 148 George B 148 James B 23 John 135 Joshua G 91 Mary Wyatt 23 Moses 26 Theodore Allen 26 William H 128
CLARKSON, Charles S 265 Mary S 265 Sarah 212 Sarah Bela D 265
CLAY, Curtis 53 Ellen L 53
CLAYPOOLE, Abraham G 92
CLAYTON, Ann 67 James 65 Lucinda 67 Martha K 65 Mary Ann 48
CLEAVER, Amos 89
CLEAVLAND, R 261
CLEMENTS, Margaret 191 William H 191
CLENDINEN, Mary E 152
CLEVELAND, Anna E 85 B T 85
CLIFTON, C R 11 81
CLINE, 256
CLINGAN, Julia Ann 226
CLOUD, Dr 69 John Wurts 263 Sarah 69
CLOWER, Mary 45
COAKLEY, Mr 192
COAKLY, Cornelues 99
COATES, Margaret 226
COATS, Martha 231
COBB, Alex 31 Caroline A 31 Caroline M 150 Charles R 14

COBB (continued)
  M C 150 Mary 170 O B 100 150 Oliver B 170 Ruth 100
COCHRAN, Ann Matilda 169 Jane N 69 John 24 Martha J 176 S A 69
COCKE, James 101 Richard 193 Susan H 101 Virginia L 155
COCKREL, Benjamin 135
COCKRILL, Richd 183
COCKS, Drusilla 92
COE, Sarah Ann 167 Thomas J 167
COFFEE, Eugenia 12 81 Mary C 82
COGAN, Martha E 68
COGGIN, Eliza J P 75
COHEA, Elizabeth Courtney 27 Maria Frances 89 Mary 64 Perry 27 64 73 85 B H 135 Philip 110
COIT, Mary Ann 16 Thomas C 16
COLBERT, Evelina Jane 171
COLE, Elizabeth 234 John 182 Mary 228 Mary Ann 231 Rebecca 40 Stewart 264
COLEMAN, Arena 51 Asa 65 Aurelius 43 Harriet L 71 106 Israel 64 Jane B 219 Lloyd R 163 Loyd R 71 Loyd Ruffin 106 Lucy A 146 Lydia O 71 Martha C 43 Martha Caroline 24 Mary 65 Melissa Ann 36 Mrs P 65 Nicholas D 146 Patrick 204 Rebecca F 227 Sarah 217 T J 43 Thomas A 146 Thomas J 24 Thomas M 146 William Moore 163
COLHOUN, E Jane 18 G 18
COLLIER, G B 210 George B 209 212 251 Lucy Ann 209 Mary 210 Sarah 212 Susan 251
COLLINS, Caroline 255 Duncan Noland 225 Eliza 40 Eliza L 259 Elizabeth 10 151 Henry Y 252 J T S 108 112 120 Jeremiah 247 John 102 119 John D 107 John J 225 Joseph 247 Mary 225 Mary A J 87 Rev Mr 238 239 Thomas F 87 William James 255
COLT, James 117
COLTHARP, Martha Jane 95
COLTRAIN, B 150
COLVER, Asa 214
COMBS, Eliza 227 Ellen 248 Jonathan 227
COMER, Annes 254
COMFORD, Daniel 79 Elizabeth Ann 79
COMFORT, D 32 Daniel 60 61 122 Rev Mr 4 219
COMMER, Daniel 239 Nancy A 239
COMPTON, Adeline 67 Stephen 67
CONANT, Mrs 83
CONDIFT, Eliza 39 W G 39
CONDUR, Thos 130
CONGER, Mary 38 Sidney 38
CONKLIN, E D 27 128
CONN, John 99 Richard 200
CONNELL, David Holmes 251 Eliza 223 H 214 Henry C 229 Hugh 209 211 229 251 John 229 Leonora 229 Martha 211 Patsey 223 Peter 191 Sarah Jane 260 Thomas 143
CONNELLY, John 142 Mary Angelica 142 Mary Gwendeline 142
CONNER, Adam 160 202 Martha 266 Michael O 183 William 195 266 William B 223
CONOVER, Livina Ann 158
CONRAD, Ann A 199 Mary M 226 Peter 226
CONWAY, John 228 Rebecca M 228
COOK, Caroline 123 David T W 246 E G 117 Edwin G 174 Euriticity 89 Fanny 43 Henrietta 174 Henrietta V 117 I H 161 Isabella 51 Jane 213 Jarret R 42 140 187 Mary 235 Mary E 161 Minerva L 42 Minerva M L 140 Minerva Mary Louisa 187 P A 235 S J 123 Sarah 246 Sarah Silviah 161 William A 106 William Foster 117 William W 51 Wm F 22
COOKLEY, Mary Ellen 205
COOLEY, F 255 257 Francis 256 257

COON, Christina 42 Elizabeth 221 Wm 42
COONS, Effie 143
COOPER, D 13 Judge 48 P 76 146 Preston 77 Rev Dr 91 266 Rev Mr 105 119 154 Sarah 30
COOPWOOD, Olevia 46
COOR, Harriet 55 J W 55 John 53
COPES, J S 41 81 Janes H 81
COPLEY, G W 45 M A 45
CORADER, Patrick 129
CORDELL, Joseph 36 Mary J 36
CORDER, William 137
CORDTS, Catherine Sophia 35
COREA, Perry 85
CORMICK, B 69
CORNELL, James 170 171 208 John 189 John S 23
CORREGAIN, John 165
CORY, Esther 234 Tho E 234
COSBY, Dabney Carr 216 Eliza S 231 Overton M 199
COTTER, Ann 218
COTTON, 199 A J 97 Agnes 97 Frederick 14 John A 70 Joshua 174
COTTS, Pollard H 141
COUGER, Elizabeth A 29
COULSON, Harriet Amanda 167 James A 167
COUNCELL, William 162
COURSEY, James 217
COURTNEY, Sophronia 231
COVINGTON, B M 13 Louisa C 13 Mary 38 Salatine 38 William 96
COWAN, Amanda M 105 Jno 170 John 105 134 177 Martha M 177 S R 8 S W 168 Samuel W 169 170 Susan 140 W J 8 William J 140
COWDON, James 20
COWEN, Samuel W 169
COX, Alfred 110 Cornelia F 32 D B 143 Eliza 218 James B 32 John 206 John C 198 Mr 109 Myra 100 Rev Mr 180 181 Zachariah 218
CRADDICK, Ann Jane 151 Joseph N 151
CRAIG, Wm 147

CRAINE, William C 256 Wm 248
CRANE, A 28 Jane 28 W C 255 256 W Carey 189 191 Wm C 249 257
CRARY, John 85 John W 86 Louisa Maria 86
CRASER, John V 129
CRAVETT, Elizabeth 129
CRAWFORD, B 49 Coningham 61 E S 155 Eleanor A 147 J B 183 Peter 247 Rev Dr 189 Robert 32 Vantromp 79 Wm 112
CRAWLEY, Elizabeth 48
CREASY, J R 133
CREATH, A G 43 141 Albert G 137 G 110 Jacob 160 263 Jacob Jr 264 Mary B 137
CREECY, Brooke 6 Henrietta B 6 James R 6 Luther S 1
CREIGHTON, H C 85
CRICHLOW, James 175 Sarah 175
CRIDER, John 112
CRIMM, E H 206
CRISSWELL, E 81 Janes H 81
CRITTENDEN, Robert 171
CROCH, James 101 Louisa 101
CROFFORD, Wm H 103
CRONAN, Daniel 112
CRONEY, John 134
CROOK, A E 47 J W 47
CROOKEY, John 121
CROOKS, James 139 Pauline 139
CROPPER, Rev Dr 74 T C 32
CROSBY, John 183
CROSS, Wm 215
CROUCH, Peter 94
CROW, James 125 249 John 252 Martha 252 Nancy 125
CROWDER, Ann 112
CROWEL, Mr 93
CROWELL, Peter 98
CRUMP, Benjamin 162 Delia 162 James M 1 2
CRUMPLER, D D 74 Myra E 74
CRUSER, Elizabeth 6 John V 6
CRUSO, Frederick 183
CRUTCHER, George B 218
CRUTE, Isabella S 46
CUDDY, J P McGilly 176
CULBERSON, Thomas 68

CULBERTSON, Julius 111 Mary C 111
CULLIN, Patrick 120
CULLINGSWORTH, John 141
CUMMENS, James 7
CUNNINGHAM, Abby 154 Jane 86 John 185
CUPIT, Elizabeth 253 Jane 247
CURRIE, Ann 234 Edward 171 Jacob C 234
CURRIER, Frances Matilda 257 Francis Matilda 125 John M 125 257
CURRIN, Robert S 46 Sophronia 46
CURRY, Mary 264 Polly 215 Thomas P 264 Thos 215
CURTIN, Catharine 205
CURTIS, Israel C 70 Thomas 70
CURTS, Elizabeth 211
CUTHEN, A 185
DACY, John 101
DAFFE, Margaret 129
DAKIN, Caroline G W 108
DALEY, Peter 192
DAMERON, Cora 145 Isiah 119
DANCER, Sarah 232
DANDRIDGE, Martha 49
DANGERFIELD, Edmond 17 Henry 195 Mary E 13 Mrs E M 17
DANIEL, A 17 Arthur 252 Henry C 74 Mary 74 Mr 107
DANIELS, Henry C 115 Nancy 115 Smith C 69
DANLEY, E C 207
DART, Julia Ann 3
DAVENPORT, B G 109 Mary E 133
DAVID, D 217
DAVIDSON, A 153 C C 143 Caroline S 251 Elizabeth H 143 Heneretta 31 Rev Mr 154 Thuxton 251
DAVINE, Timothy 7
DAVIS, 168 Ann 263 B 181 B H 259 Benjamin 212 Berry L 259 Caroline 120 Catharine 181 Charles 197 Christopher J 44 Cynthia 39 Daniel Williams 249 Elen 201 Elijah M 226 Elinor 124 Eliza Jane 71

DAVIS (continued) Ellen 26 Emma M 224 Felix A 124 Fielding 214 243 Florida A 217 Frederick 189 Green B 226 Harriet Eliza 243 Helen 249 Hugh 199 201 J L G 38 Jefferson 8 42 187 Jesse 263 Jno R 5 John 115 John H 265 Jona 200 Jos E 205 Joseph E 120 217 Julia 217 Lawrence B 222 Lewis 220 Louisa 4 Lucinda 214 Margaret M 256 Margaretta 5 Margaretta A 5 Margt J 38 Maria 208 Maria Frances 89 Martha Octavia 220 Mary 208 213 Mary E 43 208 Mary Ellen 193 Mary M 205 Micajah 197 N 39 Parthena 197 Robt 208 Robt J 193 Robt P 256 Robt Pleasants 197 Robt V 29 Samuel 208 224 Sarah 264 Sarah A 90 Sarah Ann W 226 Thos 185 Tim 191 Varia B 8 187 Varion B 42 Wm 150 201 Wm L 89
DAVISON, Caroline 178 Harriet 178
DAWE, P W 51
DAWS, John 206
DAWSON, A M 171 Adeline K 100 Amanda 25 Dinah T 253 Eliza Ann 219 Henry N 100 J 244 John 166 John B 220 Judge 219 M 209 Mary Jane 50 Penelope 252 R 260 262 Robert 251 S 233 247 249 Sam J 100 Samuel 229 230 231 232 238 239 240 241 250 251 253 254 Sarah Jane 251 Thomas 208 209 245 Thomas S 50 Wm W 252
DAY, Celeste 183 Elizabeth B 5 Margaretta M 135 Mary E 150 Wm T 112 183
DE WITT, Thos 52
DEAL, Henry 247
DEAN, Martha A 250 Robt B 250
DEARING, R 184 William R 31
DEARMOND, Samuel 239 246 Sarah 239 Susan 246
DEASE, Mary A 30 O C 95
DEAT, A 188
DEAVENPORT, Clinton Dameron 159 Margaret Ann 159

DEAVENPORT (continued) Matthew 159
DECATUR, Francis 42 Julia 42
DECKER, Abram 233 Susan 233
DEFRANCE, Abram 194 Emily J 187 Mary 194 P W 187
DEGEN, Elizabeth 20
DEGRAFFENREID, M F 210
DELANY, 19
DELESDENIER, Charlotte 120 Francis W 120
DELOACH, Emeline 227 Jesse 224 M 169 M P 191 Obedience W 169 Ruffin 230 Thomas M 265 William C 170
DELUNG, Timothy 185
DEMONET, Jane 249 Michael 249
DEMOSS, Catharine 130 W C 130 144
DEMPSEY, John 174
DENIO, C B 118 Cyronius C 118 Emeline 118
DENNIS, Jeremiah 99 John 130
DENORRIS, Irma Louise Josephine 156 Joseph L 156
DENSON, Mrs 36 William 36
DENT, A 145 Joseph 99 Margaret A 161 Martha L 13
DEPEW, Alexander R 207
DEPRIEST, Louisa 36
DERBIGNY, Peter 93
DERBY, J 171
DESAINTTALBOT, Jannette R 120
DEVALCOURT, Felionise 263 T 263
DEVELYN, Isabella M 99
DEVILINE, H 93
DEVINE, Henry 35 151 Timothy 139
DEVLIN, Edward 118
DIAMOND, Alex 118 G R 145
DIBRELL, B T 25
DICERT, Hugh 12 156
DICKERMAN, Allen 203
DICKERSON, George M 27 John S 149 Mary 149
DICKEY, 60 Adaline 124 C 124 Craven 130 Ephraim 163
DICKINSON, George M 39
DICKISON, Charles S 255 Martha W 255

DICKMAN, Julia 72 Mr 72
DICKS, Eliza 40 George J 40
DICKSON, David 20 62 90 David C 54 David H 60 Eliza 24 Harriet 198 Margaret 241 Margaret L C 242 Margaret Reed 62 Martha C 51 Nancey E 54 Sophia Jones 20 William 51 90 198 William P 242
DILCS, Martha 61
DILLAHUNTY, Eliza 222 Eliza Ann 229 Isabella 36 John 222 229 Rachael Neal 219 Rufus M 36 William 219 222
DILLARD, B B 63 Emily 35 Sophia S 37
DILLIARD, Henry M 60
DILLON, Patrick 128
DINKINS, Elizabeth H 143 Lucy 87
DINSMORE, James 14 Martha K 14
DIVINE, Henry 10 Mary 65
DIXON, B 33 C P 108 Elizabeth 198 George D 30 H Elizabeth 108 Henry St John 33 82 John B 28 L V 72 88 Lucy Virginia 88 Mary B 30 Mary L 28 Philip 54 R L 82 Sarah J 88
DOAN, Jane 11 152 John 11 152
DOBSON, 60
DOBYNS, Richard 167 Thos L 167
DODD, Ann 218 Lavina 232 Wm 218
DODGE, James C 242
DOGGETT, D S 2
DOLES, Lydia 235 Wilkinson M 235
DONAGUE, Thos 191
DONAHOE, Patrick 134 Thomas 135 158
DONAN, P 61 62 64 74 75 Peter 74
DONLY, John 110
DONNELLAN, C C 250 J L 250
DONNELLY, Patrick 192
DONOHOO, Ann M 44
DONOVAN, 118 Jeremiah 2 185 John 202 Mary 5 Michael 5
DORSEY, Eliza Ann 253 Elizabeth Anne 6 Franklin H 40 John T 176 Johnsa 233

DORSEY (continued)
  Mary F 176 Richard B 50
  Richard S 6 Sarah 233 Sarah
  Ann 124 Washington 49
DORTCH, Albert Gallatin 26 Ann
  B 112 Eliza 116 Mary 26
DOSS, Geo W 209 William 209
  Wm C 178
DOTSON, Mary B 109
DOUGHATY, Geo W 81
DOUGHERTY, J C 235 Mary
  Louisa 235 Thomas B 214
DOUGHTY, Levi D 225 Matilda
  225
DOUGLASS, Elizabeth A 29 G W
  35 Virginia 35 Walter J 29
DOVE, Nancy J 56
DOWDLE, Rebecca 32
DOWLING, Charlie 38 Nancy 38
  David D 217 Rev Mr 1 Thomas
  145
DOWNS, A C 189 Ambrose D 181
  Ellen Ann 235 Jeremiah 209
DOWTY, James N 259 Malissa M
  265 William 265
DOXEY, John L 47
DOYLE, Patrick 192
DOZIER, John 95 Lavinia 95 W B
  95
DRAHAN, Dr 19 208
DRAKE, B M 78 Benj M 17 Eady
  S 220 Edmund J 161 Lazarus
  214 Martha 214 252 Mary 161
  N S 203 Nathan S 164 Rev Mr
  56 71 89 91 255
DRANE, Matilda 43 Wesley 43
DRAUGHAN, George R 239 Isaac
  B 251 Mary F 251 Mary L D
  239
DRAYTON, Pauline 139
DREYFUS, Levi 25
DRINKWATER, James 183
DRISCALL, Danl 191
DROMGOOLE, Levi 146 Zenobia
  A 146
DRYFUSS, J 39
DUBUISSON, C L 249
DUCAYET, Flora Catharine 201
  John Mary Joseph 201
DUCKER, John 65
DUDLEY, Charles 85 Harriet 85
  Mary Wortland 85

DUDLEY (continued)
  Pulaski 98 S Mariah 98
DUFF, Delila 216 Edward 216
DUFFY, John 187 N 130
DUGGAN, Elizabeth 70 Thomas H
  70
DUGHARTY, Prudence 81
DULANEY, Margaret S 81
  Thomas W 145 William J 81
DUNBAR, Ann 263 Caroline 90
  Charlotte 201 Clarinda 42
  Isaac 242 Jo 82 John 42 263
  Robert 197 201 Robert Sr 23
  Rosena E 242 Samuel 193 Sara
  Olivia 237 Sarah 197 William
  91
DUNCAN, Hiram 164 Hon Judge
  47 Judge 146 Mrs E 25 Samuel
  18 Samuel P 18 Wm 105
DUNCKLEY, Caroline 239
  Frances 230 John 221 222
  William B 253
DUNIGAN, Armenia 26 John 26
DUNIGER, Nicholas 128
DUNKLIN, Joseph J 85 Martha
  Jane 88
DUNLAP, Andrew 17 Daniel 191
  Elizabeth B 19 Elizabeth H 19
  Hon Judge 200 Jane A 228
DUNN, Celeste 176 Edward 159
  Eliza W 266 Elizabeth 227 264
  J 19 James L 176 Milly 138
  Rev Dr 94 160 161 Robert L
  266 Sylvester 227 Thos 135
DUNNINGHAM, N S 27
DUNSCOMB, John H 66
DUNTON, Harriet J 44
DUPREE, James 77 Jerelene 77
  Zelena 28
DURANO, Elizabeth 244 Pierce N
  244
DURHAM, Thomas B 146
DUTCH, Ebenezer 132 Jeremiah
  131
DUTTON, Hon Judge 153
DUTY, G 179 Lavina 179
DUVALL, Algernon S 44 144
  Sarah Jane 262
DWIGHT, Charles W 205 E B 205
DYER, J M 49 Malissa 49 Martha
  Ann 117 Sarah 37
DYESS, John 49

EAGAN, Ann Eliza 258 Geo W 258
EARLY, H G 244 Mrs 244
EASLEY, Daniel 13
EASOM, Wm H 203
EASON, Martha J 104
EATON, C H 133 Mary 92 Mary Ann 133 Nancy Louisa 29 William H 40 William R 29
EBERER, Andrew 183
ECCLES, Benjamin 210 212 213 263 Jennette Ann 235 Wm 217
ECHOLS, Rutha P 250 Terry 250
ECKLES, E W 28 Mary A 28
EDMONDS, M A 29 R J 29
EDMONDSON, W H 97
EDMONSON, W H 96
EDSTROM, A G 14 Lauretta Antionette 14
EDWARD, N Elizabeth 258
EDWARDS, Anna E 85 B W 236 Charles 224 254 Charles A 252 Elizabeth 143 264 Elizabeth D 42 Emma M 224 Frances 135 J Erskine 108 J W 42 Jemima 264 Letitia 123 257 Nancy 57 Narcissa J 252 Rebecca 39 Samuel 138 139 142 146 153 164 Sarah 264
EDWIN, Henry 80
EGGLESTON, Dick H 237 William 142
ELAM, Thomas A 69
ELDER, Jordan 26 75 Rebecca Elizabeth 26 Susan 75
ELLESBERRY, William L 214
ELLIOT, Frances M 205 James 78
ELLIOTT, 60 Catherine 201 Daniel D 201 Henrietta 168 John 168 Minerva G 172 Nancy 139 Thomas D 139
ELLIS, Andrew 217 Ann Wilson 240 Eliza 27 90 Elizabeth 43 54 Ellen 252 Jane 217 John 162 M L 2 Margaret P 260 Maria 48 Martha 23 Mary 58 Robt 2 Susan 71 191 T W 59 Thomas 59 240 252 William 135
ELLISON, Elizabeth 107 Henry H 174 John A 101 Mary 101
ELLISON (continued) Nancy 78 Sarah Ann 174
ELLMORE, Orris 112
ELLONS, Rachel 46
ELLSBERRY, Tebitha 238
ELLWOOD, Patrick 191
ELLZY, Berry 58
ELSBERRY, Jacob 246
ELSBURY, Sarah Eveline 260
ELY, Sarah Ann 68
EMANUEL, Agatha A M 142 Bertha 142 Edith Brown 142 Martha 177 Mary Catharine 183 Morris 142 184 Samuel 177
EMBREE, Felix 246 250 252
EMERSON, Thomas 184
EMRY, Amanda 253 Wm 253
ENLOW, Eveline 233 Jesse 233
ENOCHS, John R 88 Louisa H 88
EPPERSON, Hasting 26 Mary 26
ERWIN, Caroline R 86 H B 109 Harriet W 46 Sidney S 86
ESTES, John 40 Maria Lucylle 114 Mary 172 Sarah A 114 Sarah Ann 179 W J 150 William 172 William J 10 11 114 152 179
ESTESS, Emeline 238 Syvester C 238
ESTIS, Frances Eliza 230 Samuel 230
EUBANK, Frances Ann 64 Margaret N 74 Richard N 74
EUELL, Annes 254 Turner B 254
EVANS, Adelaide 43 Assenith 55 Eliza Jane 71 Francis 225 Francis A 221 Francis A Jr 258 George 109 Jesse 6 Julia G 113 L S 71 Lesley 203 Robert P 55 Sarah 58 Thomas 128 Thomas L 40 Watson 49
EVERETT, Abner 179 John Abner 179 Lucinda S 179 William 171 172 175 176 180
EWING, Wm 19
EXLEY, Jane 134
FABEL, Thomas 109
FAIR, Eliza 234 Francis A 234
FAIRBANKS, Mary 55 W 55
FAIRCHILD, Sarah 239
FAIRFIELD, Sumner Lincoln 131
FAIRLY, Effy 55 James S 55

FALKNER, Nancy 36 Z 36
FALLIS, Susan 142 William 142
FALTON, Dennis V 145
FANEN, Thos 186
FANNER, James 213 Mary Ann 213
FARGUES, Armand 112
FARISH, C 260 Caroline S 251 Claiborne 260 Edward T 212 223 Eliza A 212
FARLEY, A L 96 Margaret 96
FARR, David Dickson 37 Rebecca H 34
FARRAR, Abram Scott 234 Dr 72 Eliza J 219 Frances 49 George H 82 Hon Mr 82 Preston W 219 234 Rosa M 72
FARRER, Ann Eliza 37
FAUST, Elizabeth 223 Peter 223
FAWCETT, Smith 168
FEA, John 128
FEAGAN, Emelia 198 Robt 198
FEAMSTER, Ann E 50 Samuel T 43
FEATE, Martin 105
FEBRODNAX, John 172 Mary E 172
FELDER, Charles 242
FELIGMAN, J 39 Jachiel 39
FELL, John A 244
FELTOS, A M 210
FELTUS, A M 208 257 Edward 219 Eliza Ann 208 257 Sarah W 232
FEND, Elizabeth 140
FENIMORE, Eliza 113 William 113
FENN, Green 80 82
FENNER, Esther Ann 240 Joseph 248 Mary Ann 233 Sarah J 247
FERGUSON, Benjamin 256 Catharine 93 Emily E 173 George Cochran 23 Harriet 256 Henry 220 James 98 Jane N 69 Mary 98 Rev 76
FERNANDIS, John H 216
FERNEY, Elizabeth 15
FERRALL, James 200
FERRAND, Michael 92
FERRELL, Samuel P 28 Zelena 28
FERRIDAY, Wm 16

FERRILL, Amanda 107
FERRIS, Ann M 40 138 Edmund W 40 138
FERRY, John 16 John C 77 Mary O 77
FEVERBAH, Valentine 114
FIELDS, E D 17
FINCHER, F 86
FINDLEY, Michael 71
FINLEY, Ann B 135 His Honor Judge 82 Isabella 51 James 146 John L 135
FINN, Harriet Eugenia Thompson 134 Philip 134
FINNEY, H H 162
FINUCANE, Ann 76 George 76
FISH, J F 242 244 John 242 John F 235 Julia 244 Rev Mr 235
FISHER, Andrew 121 Conrod 119 David 83 David M 139 Davis M 187 Eliza 139 187 M 146 Margaret 83 Penelope 22 Susan E 10
FITCH, Asel 102 Aurelia 102
FITHIAN, Geo H 19
FITZGERALD, R C 169 Rosina 137
FITZHUGH, Eliza 180
FITZPTRICK, David 206
FITZWILLIAM, Mary C 188 Mr 188
FLASBLY, Anthony 186
FLEMING, Lucinda 209 Margaret 133 Robert K 209
FLINN, Daniel L 253 Dinah T 253 Mathew 118
FLINT, Elizabeth 260
FLOWER, Elizabeth 91 George W 91 Martha Ann 131
FLOWERS, Benjamin 67 Col 167 Hannah 100 Ignatia 103 Richard 56 Sarahphina 103 Susan A 28 130 Uriah 50 148
FLOYD, Dr 223 Elizabeth 70 Samuel 70
FOAGEY, James H 102
FOGERTY, Patrick 127
FOGLEMAN, Priscilla 239
FOLEY, Alice 118 M P 221 Mary R 221 Michael 207
FOLKES, Adeline K 100 James 100 Levina R 36

FOLKES (continued)
  Louisa M 70 Lucilla 116 M C
  111 132 205 Miles C 185
  Raleigh 36 Rebecca A 185
  Samuel 111
FOLLER, Oliver W 196
FOLMAN, Frederick 129
FONDREN, Elizabeth 87
FORBES, Amanda 107 John 239
  Jonathan 107 Louisa 73 Louisa
  A 31 78 Lucinda C 239 Sarah
  Jane 73
FORD, Cornelia V 28 Ferdinand C
  29 Jane 8 29 140 Joice 30
  Joseph 220 Lavina 200 Mary
  228 Robin 200 Samuel 28 T 62
  63 Thomas 29 44 60 79 80 130
  150 163 207 228 Washington
  77
FOREMAN, Andrew 88 Ezekiel
  196
FORGET, William 196
FORRESTER, Delia Ann 32
  Elizabeth E 32 John B 32
FORSHEY, C C 127 Martha 127
FORSKS, James 29
FORSYTH, James L 61 John 15
  23 Mary 23
FORSYTHE, Augustus W 236
  Mary R 236
FORTS, Mrs 61
FORTSON, John T 161 William R
  116
FOSTER, Albert G 229 258 Charlotte 120 Eliza 183 Elizabeth
  197 Elizabeth E 175 Emily J
  255 H G 175 J 96 James D 109
  John 92 234 Joseph 183 Joseph
  A 226 Louisa 155 Samuel W
  255 Sara Jane 229 Sarah J 72
  Thomas 197 William Henry
  175 William P 211
FOURNIQUET, L 211
FOUSHTE, Jacob 18
FOUTE, Green P 84 J F 84 Jenny
  Cary 84 Martha Elizabeth 84
FOWLER, Alexander 198 Emily
  N 35 Gabriel 154 James 198
  Martha Ann 154 Sarah 42
FOWLETT, Elizabeth 47 John 47
FOWLS, Wm B 13

FOX, Arthur 40 56 Caroline M 61
  Edwin 61 Elizabeth 172
  Elizabeth Lark 56 Emma
  Louisa 92 Eve 114 Francis
  John 178 J A 212 James A 13
  92 131 178 211 263 265 John
  114 207 Lucy 128 Patience A
  40 Rev Mr 3 18 208 S S 108
  Samuel S 172 Sargent 196 T E
  148 Virginia E 46 William H
  46
FRAIL, Catharine 165
FRANCIS, Virginia 35
FRANKLIN, Elizabeth 55 J F P
  55
FRANKS, James 114
FRASER, Louise 241 Wm T 241
FRAYARD, Adaline 232 Hiram
  232
FRAZEE, Rev Mr 85 86
FRAZIER, Ann Eliza 245 Frances
  Eliza 230 George E 230 245
  John 214 Micajah 209
FRECKMAN, Mr 137
FREDERICK, John 184
FREEBORN, Malinda 128
FREELAND, Augustin 200 Eliza
  200
FREELOCK, James 57
FREEMAN, Eliza Ardine 74 253
  254 John D 74 253 Martha A 40
  Sarah Cornelia 48 Thos S 48
FRENCH, Mary Jane 115 Rev Dr
  178 Robert S 115
FRETWELL, Ann Eliza 205
  Elizabeth V 162 John R 205
  Mrs 159 Richard 172
FRIAR, Lovice 169
FRISBIE, Samuel Sr 86
FRISBY, Harriet 69 Theresa 66
FRITZ, James 119
FRONAGHU, Alexander 133
FROST, John E 98
FRY, Conrad H 129
FULKERSON, Charlotte B 42
  Horace 42
FULLER, Alfred 67
FUNCHES, Jacob R 29 Virginia A
  29
FUQUA, John W 256 Mary Y 256
FURR, Arena 51 Jepththa 51

GADBERRY, William P 216
GAGE, C 19 James A 44 Jno 19 Margaret E 147 Rosannah 44
GAHAN, Ann 83 Margaret 83 Wm 83
GAINES, Althea 90 E P 98 John 168 Margaret E 106 Myra 98 W W 106 168 Wm H 90
GALAGHER, Edward 120 Francis 119
GALE, Dr 59 Eliza Jane 59
GALIVANT, Mary 37
GALLAHER, Edward 5
GALLOWAY, Alfred 43 E E 12 81 Eugenia 12 81 Sophia Ann 43
GALTNEY, D K 67
GAMBLE, Andrew 5 122 165 Andrew Jackson 165 Batlett 17 Mary Elizabeth 165 Patience 5 122 165
GANIAL, Rev Mr 92
GANONG, Velina L 82
GARDNER, D B 25 Eliza Jane 139 James 146 Minerva 146 Phineas 139
GARLAND, Frances Ann 64 74 Jane Henry 74 William H 64 74
GARNETT, Henry 9 188 Henry A 29
GARRET, Louisa 101 Thomas 101
GARRETT, J G G 48
GARSON, Eliza 183 Sarah 183
GARTLEY, Elizabeth C 94 Julia 6 Louis Harrison 94 William 6 94 125
GASFORD, Jane 176
GASSELS, Henry Jr 201
GATEWOOD, R T 79
GAULDEN, Martha M 229
GAY, David Coopland 207 Sally N 207 Wm V 255
GAYDEN, Agrippa 196 Mary 259 Penelope 196
GAYLE, Emily S 254 Josiah 228 Rebecca M 228
GEAR, Danl Peer 192
GEE, Charles 126 Mary A 155 Mary Ann 126
GEISKER, Delia L 132 Henry 132
GEMMELL, Ann P 62 Jannett 62

GENELLA, A 129 Antonia 28 Joseph 143 Louisa 28 129 Lucinda 143 Mary Catharine 143
GEOFREY, Aaron 103
GEORGE, Mary Ann 171 Simeon L 93 Simson L 171
GERE, D G 7 G D 23 Gilbert D 29
GERIS, Evey 105
GERMANY, Washington 14
GERVAIS, Catherine Olivia 175 St Clair 175
GHERARD, Jane P 27
GIBBES, Sarah 36 Wilmet R 36
GIBBONS, Ann 74 T F 187 Thos K 80
GIBBS, Esther M 179 George W 75 94 J S 142 Mary 94 N B 176 Susan 75 94
GIBSON, Ann B 29 Elby 170 John 160 Louisiana 161 Martha Ann 160 Mary 160 Ophelia 251 Randal 20 161 180 211 Reuben 197 Samuel 200 William M 170
GIESKER, Henry 191
GILBERT, J P 219 Philip A 215 S B 121 Thomas Jefferson 37 138
GILCHRIST, Euphemia 42
GILDART, Caroline 255 Catharine 248 Eleanor W 208 F 249 255 256 257 Francis 195 208 212 217 248 249 252 258 Isaac D 255 John W 60 222 239 Judge 255 Judith 212 Mary F 235 Sophia 216 217 Susan T 222
GILES, G B 19
GILL, Catheirne 209 H M 209 Mary H T 252 Matthew 192 Samuel M 25 Sarah 44 188 Thomas M 252 William 105
GILLELAND, James 22
GILLESPIE, Harriet J 45 Mary Artimise 45
GILLESPY, Jane 117 Mary Jane 4
GILLETT, Ann E 70 Eliphalet 70
GILLIES, Charles 191
GILLILAND, Eliza E 160
GILLUM, Thos 130
GILMER, Mary Peachy 56
GIMP, John 190

GINN, Edmond 213 215 Eliza Ann 213
GIRAULT, Ann M 197 John 193
GIRTMAN, John M 48 Serenia L 48
GLANCY, Thos 112
GLASKINS, Thos 31
GLASS, Cornelia Herbert 261 Elizabeth 234 Eveline 168 Frances M 181 James 168 John 234 Joshua 261 Mary 180 Samuel 226 Sarah 233
GLASSCOCK, Ellen E 202 John 157
GLEICHSTEIN, Henry 101
GLENDENNEN, Nancy M J 75
GLENN, D C 83 Patience B 83
GLIDEWELL, I N 164
GLOVER, Caroline O 47 Eliza C 258 William 72 230
GOBLE, Ephraim 19
GODDEN, Amzi 32
GODFREY, E 129 Elenor 128 Frances Ann 175 William 175
GODLEY, Sarah 246
GODWIN, J H 162 W C 173
GOGGINS, Thomas 135
GOINS, Mr 58
GOLD, Sarah Ann 45 T E 111
GOOCH, George W 77 J S 77
GOODALL, Catherine 182 Thomas Henry 182
GOODE, Harriet E 63 James M 56 Mary Ann 56 Noble M 63
GOODIN, Elizabeth 128
GOODMAN, E B 205 Elizabeth B 3 139 Thomas J 3 139
GOODRICH, Eliza 228 Samuel 228
GOODRUM, Elizabeth 169 John 169 Martha R 137
GOODWIN, D G H 9 Leander S 9
GOODWYN, Lavinia 148 Sam 148
GOOSEY, Elizabeth 117 Ellen Green 117 Gabriel William 117 George Henry 117 Peter C 117
GORDON, Catherine 42 David 10 Ellen 231 George H 214 222 231 Julia 60 Lenora 222 Mary 214 Moses 215 Nancy M 36 Philadelphia 245 Susan E 10 Thomas 60

GORE, Mrs 194
GORMAN, T 82
GOULD, Gilbert 104 Theodore E 111
GOULDING, James 145
GOWAN, Elizabeth A F 176 John 17
GOWER, Elisha 211 Enoch 211
GRADDICK, Ann Jane 10 Joseph N 10
GRAFTON, A 10 Emma 10 George 10
GRAHAM, Biddy 215 Geo 215 Mrs A 25 Ransom 215
GRANBERRY, Jeremiah B 137 N R 80 148 Stephen 59
GRANDONNA, John 11
GRANT, H M 124 Nancy 77 Sarah Ann 124
GRAVES, Aurelay G 265 D F 48 E 90 Elijah 90 James J 240 Joseph 24 Margaret S A 256 Mary A A 240 Peyton S 265 Sarah Ann 24
GRAVIS, Frances Ann Virginia 236 Thos F 236
GRAY, A J 237 Augustus 205 David I 264 266 Elizabeth J 266 G H 62 63 J H 125 John 186 Loftus Henry 182 Lucy 62 63 Mary Ann 255 N 182 Rachael 258 Rev Mr 80 William 6 129 154
GRAYSON, A J 117 Beverly R 23 Frances J 117 Sarah 26 Spence M 63 T T 169
GREAVES, Charlotte C 62
GREEN, I A R 79 Abram 211 Abram A 38 Amanda 50 Ann 211 Caroline 89 90 D B 90 D V 39 Delia 162 Elizabeth 186 Elizabeth J 85 89 Emily 18 Ezra 144 Filmer W 18 Francis Girault 89 George W L 50 Henry 113 James 134 James S 76 Joseph 218 Joshua 85 89 Joshua Joseph 89 Mary Ann 137 Mary Ellen 121 Mary Hassan 38 Robert G 186 Rosanna E 47 Samuel C 70 Thomas Hughes 127 Thomas J 127 175 Thomas M 170 Thomas R 47

GREEN (continued)
 V D 40 Washington E 205
 William Lee 170 Willis M 126
GREENLEAF, D 197 Daniel 60 66
 177 David 194 Eliza R 66 177
 Emily 60 Eunice 197
GREGORIE, Edmund 180
GREGORY, Angelitha 75 Caroline
 73 Francis R 46 James H 166
GRESHAM, B 51 Benjamin 54
 John J 179 Norvill 59 Penelope
 179 Wm R 59
GREY, Leander 31 Rev Mr 130
GRICE, James M 29
GRIDLEY, Mr 208 Rev Mr 157
GRIFFIN, Ann C 225 B C 65
 Charles 19 Cyrus 185 David C
 66 Edward 189 Mary A 157
 Rebecca C 154 Sarah 65
 Theresa 66 Thomas 157 William D 154 William S 225 229
GRIFFING, Eunice 48 Harriet 69
 John J 69 M A 31
GRIFFITH, Eliza 15 John T 15
 Richard 121 191 Samuel A 41
 Sarah A E 191 Sarah B 121 125
 Theodosia L 13 William B 13
GRILLO, James 151
GRIMBALL, Eliza A 220 John A
 220
GRINES, Mildred Ann 100
GRISSAM, William C 12
GROCKFORD, Wm 109
GRONDONNA, Ellen 154 John 154
GROU, Caroline L 104
GROVES, Ann 51 81 James A 51
 81 Moses 66
GRUBBS, John W 16 17
GUFFY, Rebecca Jane 260
GUICE, Anne 199 Jonathan 199
GUIDRY, Felionise 263
GUINAN, Patrick 137
GUION, J L 185 John I 98 Judge
 218
GULHEIM, Rev Mr 89
GULLOCK, Jacob 5 127
GUSTAVUS, Rhoda 39
GUSTINE, James 15 Rebecca A
 15
GUTHRIE, Clarissa 10 Clarissa
 M 50 80 Samuel 10 50 80

GWIN, Caroline Isabella 158 Dr
 57 99 E 65 James 106 Samuel
 65 240 Thomas W 223
GWINN, 142
HACKETT, Mary Ann 159
HACKLER, Margaret 205 Martin
 205
HADLEY, B J 54 Benajmin Quitman 54 Thirsa Ann 212
HAGAMAN, Abraham 66
HAGAN, 1 Christian 128 James
 124
HAGERTY, John 118
HAILE, Nancy 263 William 234
 263
HAINES, Mary 192 W A 192
HAIR, Charlotte 207
HALCOMB, A H 103
HALE, Ann Eliza 3 Wm 3 Wm C
 49
HALEY, Eleanor Eliza 245
 Elizabeth 52 Francis Jr 245
 Oliver 52
HALFORD, Alexander 192 Martha
 Ann 61 77 R E 77 Robert E 61
 Virginia Caledonia 77 William
 Harrison 77
HALL, Alexander 21 Ann J 141
 Ann Jane 10 151 Catherine D
 23 David 151 Eliza 133 177
 234 Gertrude K 254 J J 10 141
 J W 23 James 177 James A
 133 Joem 116 John 103 John B
 102 John E 65 John R 37
 Joshua J 151 189 Julia 31
 Laura W 10 149 Levina 102
 Lucinda 73 Maranda 68 Margaret L 73 Mr 16 Nathan C 68
 Osman C 8 141 Osman Craddick 141 Sophia S 37 Virginia
 A 189 William H 23
HALSEY, C A 31 L J 36 80 81 90
 148 L S 41 Leroy J 31 M S 239
 Margaret 150 Mary 247 Mary
 Prudence 247 Rev Mr 27 William 239 247
HALSTEAD, Benjamin 24 Emily
 24
HAM, Julia Ann 48
HAMBLIN, Eliza W 27 John M A
 27 John Sidney 27

HAMER, W H 1
HAMILTON, Caroline 63 113 Charles West 228 Elizabeth C 245 Gertrude K 254 Isaac 116 James 2 255 Jno A J 254 John 63 65 185 Millberry 210 Mrs H C 17 Oscar 34 Sarah M 255 Sigismunda Mary 34 Thomas J 228 235 W S 256 William 82
HAMLIN, Isaac 72 Mary H 72
HAMMER, Mrs 8
HAMMET, Adeline 146 Laura C 11 Mrs 141 Rev Dr 177 Robert 11 Teresa 11
HAMMETT, A Teresa 152 Adeline A 48 Laura Cecelia 152 Mary 213 Robert 152 William 213
HAMMOND, Eliza Ann 31 R S 121
HAMPTON, Henry 213 221 John 247 John P 263 Margaret 247 Martha L 207 Mrs E 65 Susan 221 Wm H 207
HANCOCK, Richard 18
HANES, Catherine 175
HANHAM, James 259 Rebecca Tabitha 259
HANKINSON, A E 153 Rebecca J 153
HANN, Georgiana 39
HANNA, Aristipus White 113 Caledoria 163 G Washington 163 Laura 186 Laura Ann 113 Samuel M 162 Sarah W 89 T J 7 Thomas J 89 113 186
HANNAH, Samuel W 144
HANSEL, Elizabeth 30 John 30
HANSFORD, E 5 Malvina 5
HARBAUGH, Charles 115
HARDAWAY, Adaline W 158 David G 158
HARDEMAN, Anna G 156 Thomas 156
HARDING, Elizabeth 34 James N 34 Jane M 173 Stanford H 173
HARDIWAY, Adaline W 12 David G 12
HARDWICK, Amelia 218 Jane Elizabeth 36 John C 36 Thomas 90 William A 218
HARDY, James S 102

HARGIS, Aaron 54 Elizabeth 54 Elizabeth T 41
HARGROVE, Howel 95 Joseph Harmon 95 Kitsey 95 Mary 78 Mr 78
HARGROVES, Martha 30
HARLAN, Emma 10
HARMAN, Mary J 36
HARMANSON, Susan H 101
HARMER, Obedience W 169 William R 169 170 Wm B 172
HARMON, Christian 198 John 169 Margaret 169
HARNETT, Richard 115
HARPER, Ancyvilia 24 Ann 45 Edwin 82 Eugenia 164 Harriet 82 James E 24 John F 45 Miles 22 Mrs 164 Nancy Louisa 29 R W 140 T J 164 Thos J 125
HARRINGTON, Thomas 10 150
HARRIS, Adeline Louisa 52 Amanthus L 59 Benjamin 3 114 Buckner 43 55 Catharine S 192 Charlotte 165 Eliza S 231 Emily Jane 3 114 Francina 52 Hartwell 170 Henrietta 174 James R 52 Jemima G 263 John 58 John P 231 Letitia 60 Louisa 28 129 Lydia 10 Mary A E 123 124 Nancy E 43 Robert B 165 Robert P 123 Stephen 180 V N 231 232 233 234 Wiley P 59 143
HARRISON, Annie 158 Artalissa B 54 Benjamin 54 Charles E 134 Eliza Ann 171 213 Hannah Brown 70 Hiram 158 J P 168 John H 59 Maria Louisa 32 Patsey 196 Richard 70 175 Sydney Ann 168 William L 32
HARRISTON, D Peyton 83
HART, C M 74 Daniel 264 E T 81 Edward 111 112 George 118 James E 49 Mary 74
HARTFIELD, Anna 38
HARTFORD, George 73
HARVESTON, Rev Mr 55
HARVEY, Abraham A 52 Amanda 154 Eleanor W 190 Evan 4 Jas R 190 Mary 35 Narcissa 4

HARVY, Julia 26
HARWELL, Harriet W 46 Robert C 46
HARWOOD, 184 John C 150 Mary E 150 S B 11 12 137 151 156 165 Samuel B 10 11 138 147 148 149 150 152 154 161 167
HASELTINE, James W 178 Mary Francis 178
HASLET, Andrew 199 Ann A 199
HASSEL, Thos 132
HASTINGS, B F 139
HATCH, N W 40 121 125 Sarah B 121
HATCHER, Eliza J P 75 Rhesa 75
HATFIELD, Mary E H 252
HATHAWAY, Ephraim 131
HAUGHTON, Benj A 177 Benjamin 173 Benjamin A 174
HAVERSTRAW, Joseph 184
HAWK, Elizabeth 69
HAWKINS, Arra Ann 163 Benjamin K 84 Eliza 163 Eliza Ann 172 Evelina Jane 171 George 163 172 John M 171 Louisa Maria 86 Mary E 84 Mr 208 Richard 163 Sarah 134 Thomas J 86 William H H 163
HAWKS, Catharine N 147 Catharine Neville 119 Joseph P 119 147 202 M J Rebecca 202
HAWLEY, Samuel 173
HAWZEY, Harriet 55
HAY, Ann 48 Ann Maury 145 Isaac Hite 48 145 Isabella A 10 149 Isabella Annette 149 Margaret 149 162 Margaret A 43 William 149 162 William Henderson 162
HAYES, James 264 Louisa 238 Mary 264 Nancy 264
HAYNES, Bythall 220 Bythell 220 224 232 Elizabeth 223 William 223
HAYS, Andrew 77 219 Ann 219 Elizabeth 24 Ellen 252 Saray 255 Thomas W 252 Wm C 24
HAZARD, S H 72 Silas H 75 226
HAZELET, Caroline L 104 James 104

HAZELETT, J 126
HAZLETON, Charles 162
HEAD, E G 197 Elizabeth S 74 Maria 197
HEANY, Polly 14
HEARD, Ann 193 Joshua T 75 Martha Matilda 75
HEARLY, E 160
HEARSEY, Catherine 93
HEATH, Elizabeth J 207 Lawrence G 205
HEBRON, John 105 Julia 105
HEGEMAN, Dr 109 Sophia 109
HEIRSCH, Elizabeth 150 Jacob 150
HEISER, David 168
HEITING, Patrick 7
HELMER, Evilene 260 George 232 Mary Ann 232 Thomas 260
HEMINGWAY, Dr 75
HEMPHILL, L B 85 Marcus 85 Nancy 85
HENADIN, Dennis 185
HENDERSON, Duncan C 218 Elizabeth 260 Isabella A 200 John 194 200 John G 260 John L 12 155 Joseph 225 Mary 194 225 Mary Ann 218 Mary T 180 Miss 158 N M 66 Rev 158 Sarah Ann 138 Wm T 20
HENDRAY, Eliza 155
HENDREN, E C 4 Elizabeth Chapman 121 Elizabeth P 121 H 4 99 Hadry 121 Hardy 155 Washington 184
HENDRICH, Rowland 182
HENDRICK, David 173
HENDRICKS, Amelia 31 M J 29 Martha Jane 118 Mary 118 Richard E 118 Wm H 31
HENLEY, Elizabeth A 228 264 Joseph P 218 228 264
HENRY, Gabriel F 83 Misella A 156 O C 156 Olivia 156 Robert P 83 Robert W 74 Susan 74 Wm 185
HERBERT, Benj F 245 Cornelia 215 Eliz 238 Elizabeth C 245 Susan F 213 Thomas S 213 215
HERINGTON, Jeremiah 102
HERRING, Amanda H 37 David J 37 Mary A C 8 141 R B 125

HERRING (continued)
    Sarah 152 Willis 152
HERRN, 203
HERZOG, Xawerie 100
HESTER, Anne R 230 Augustus D 237 Caroline 79 Charles 227 Chas J 260 David 230 Eliza 30 31 Laura Ann 260 M M 262 Martha A 227 Theresa 78 William 78 79
HICKEY, Allice Colley 127 Elizabeth M 127 Thornton P 127
HICKMAN, Henry P 37 Mary 37
HICKS, Benj 194 Benjamin J 177 Eunice 194 George G 37 Henry Clay 26 Jamesy 227 John C 226 227 Jonathan 194 Joseph T 116 Martha 143 Martha M 177 W A 26
HICKSTON, David 133
HIGDON, Nancy J 189 Rebecca J 153
HIGGINS, Eunice W 231
HIGLEY, Charles 175
HILDERBRAND, Daniel 142 180 Eliza 180
HILL, Adomeline 259 Caleb 45 D 56 D J 56 Eliz 45 Eliz Lark 56 H 205 Henry 192 Philip 201 Solon 222 Thomas 259
HILLBURN, Emily 55 Samuel 55
HILLDERBRAND, Daniel 139
HILSON, Silas 106
HILZHEIM, H 89 Heyman 45 Martha 89 Martha M 45
HINCKLEY, O S 70
HINCKLY, O S 2
HINDS, Drusilla 92 Howell 92 Thomas 58
HINES, B M 141 B S 146 Bennet M 170 Frances E 141 John 140 187 Levenia 146 Minerva L 42 Minerva M L 140 Sarah C 170 Susan L 41 W B 41
HINMAN, Adeline 98 Samuel 98
HINTON, Annie S 87 C 87 N B 87
HITCH, J W 133 134
HOBBS, Elizabeth 43 Howell 43 Sarah 50 Wm H 50
HOBERTS, Anne M 153 Edward 153
HOBLITZELL, Anne M 153 Saml 153
HOBSON, R M 83 Richard M 83
HODGE, E 90 Fredk W 175 John 113 Margaret P 260 Mary L 113 Susan 90 W J 260 W T 65
HODGENS, Mattha B 97
HODGES, Elisha 230
HOGAN, Isabella 31 132 Samuel G 117 Sarah B 117 William 31 132
HOGERS, Charlotte R 127 Marsden 127
HOGG, Rosannah 44
HOGGATT, Agnes W 91 Charlotte S 249 Mary N 201 Nathaniel 91 249
HOLBROOK, Nancy 38
HOLCOMB, Gardner 73 Sophia M 73 Wilson 107
HOLDEN, James 262 Mary 262
HOLDER, Willis 96
HOLIDAY, John 13 Sarah 13
HOLLAND, Euriticity 89 Henry Dixon 233 Rachael 233 Wm Tucker 89
HOLLAWAY, Rev 50
HOLLEY, Adriann 46 Wm E 46
HOLLIDAY, John J 51 Sinah 27
HOLLINGSHEAD, Eliza Jane 158
HOLLINSHEAD, Charlotte 165
HOLLOWAY, L B 32 41 62 Rev Mr 72 79
HOLMAN, J L 70 Lucy M 70
HOLMES, Andrew Hunter 195 David 195 Dorcas 194 H J 29 James M 241 Mary 241 Wm 194
HOLT, Clara V 250 Dr 253 Gustave Adolphe 43 Maj 81 Mary Catharine 81
HONDON, E 31
HOOD, Harbird 170 Harbord 171 John Stanford 170 Nancy 170
HOOF, Isaac 56 Sarah 56
HOOK, Harriet 213
HOOKE, Margaret A 91 Wm Butler 236
HOOKER, Elizabeth 87 John 87
HOOTER, L J 121 M 121
HOOTSELL, Eliza Ann 233 Michael 233

HOOVER, C 53
HOPE, Martha 125 257 Orinda E 256 Rachael 233
HOPKINS, Alice Gertrude 35 Charlotte 158 David 262 E G 127 Enfield 34 F G 25 Henry 206 Jesse 192 Letitia Ann 262 M O 34
HORN, John S 199 Mrs 183
HORNSBY, Eliza H 240
HORRA, Jeremiah S 106 Martha 106
HORSLEY, J 136
HOSACK, Hamilton 2 184
HOSKINS, James W 84
HOSSLEY, Peter 157 202
HOTH, Eve 156
HOUESMAN, Tama 11
HOUGH, Andrew 185
HOUGHMAN, Henry 110
HOUGHTON, Benjamin 175 Jane C 114 L S 114 Rev Mr 73 100
HOUSEMAN, Turner 152
HOUSLEY, Anna 20
HOUSTON, Margaret M 247 Samuel 247
HOWARD, B D 90 Bainbridge D 93 Benjamin 195 Missouri 24 N G 223 Nicholas C 24 Stephen 106 Wm 99
HOWE, E P 39
HOWELL, Ambrose 33 Bynum 33 Matilda Adeline 237 Varia B 8 187 Varion B 42 Wm B 8 187
HOWLETT, Nicholas 133
HUBBARD, Asa 66 Benjamin M 246 Elizabeth 238 George B 186 Parthena 66 Susan 226
HUBBELL, P T 11 153 154
HUBBS, Sarah 201 Thomas 201
HUDDLESTON, Emily A 24
HUDSON, George 110 S P 259 Susan 169
HUFF, Holloway 242 Martha S 230 Mary Magdalene 242
HUGHES, Alexander 255 Elizabeth M 81 James 185 John 209 213 John B 150 Judge 82 Mrs 211 Robert 81 Sarah Ann 150 Susan F 213 Susan Halsey 150
HUGHLETT, Narcissa Jane 172

HUIE, James 146
HULETT, James M 57
HULEY, J 165
HULL, Anna M 48 Daniel 199 Hezekiah B 209 Isaac 199 John T 48
HUME, Ann M 44 Francis 44 51 Joseph Napoleon 58 Mary 51 Nancy C P 52 58 Robert 52 Robert C 58
HUMPHREYS, Balissa 29 78 Elizabeth 64 237 Geo W 20 George Wilson 29 78 John Cobun 29 Laura Ann 64 Margaret 20 S W 23 64 Sarah A G 29
HUMPHRIES, Martha E 49 Mary Ann 244
HUNT, Adeline 67 Angelina E 46 David 69 Martha J 104 Mary Ann 69 Thomas 104
HUNTER, 174 A 44 Ann M 197 G H 197 James 32 John A 41 Nancy 41 T W 144
HUNTINGTON, H W 39 Helen D 39
HUNTMAN, Frederick 207
HURBERT, Lewis 108
HURDUS, Adam 3
HURLEY, J 204
HURST, Elizabeth 138 Henry 106 Kemp 138 Nathaniel N 103 Sarah Ann 138 Solomon 86 Teresa 86 Wm H 106
HUSBANDS, Sebra 31 Wm J 31
HUSTIN, 92
HUSTON, Felix 13 Mary E 13
HUTCHCRAFT, Mary 100
HUTCHINS, Mary Ann 123 Telemachew 123
HUTCHINSON, J R 119 Jno R 104 John R 108 Matilda 190 Rev Mr 99 116 185
HUTCHISON, J R 3 113 John H 113 John R 103 Mr 17 Rev Mr 100 Thomas 1
HUTSON, Joseph H 41 Mary Ann 41
HYATT, Chas L 234
HYDE, Jesse 96 Sophronia E 96
HYLAND, Andrew G 164 Jacob 217 Martha Jane 164

HYLANDER, Levenia 146
HYNES, Bennet M 198 Ruth 198
ILER, Abram 228 Alexander S 229 Amanda 227 John 212 227 Mahala 230 Malissa 229 Mary 212 Thomas M 230
ILSLEY, Francis 125 Francis Jr 109 Francis Sr 121 Martha Ann 125 Mary B 109 Mary Belinda 125
IMPSON, Caleb 110 John 185
INDIAN, Puckshunnubbe 196 Thomas Jefferson 196
INGRAM, Anna 20 Oliver R 20 Priscilla 163 Thomas 26
INMAN, Christina 42
IRBY, Lovey 29 Milton 29 Nancy 125
IRION, George A 212 263 265 266
IRON, G A 13
IRVINE, Henry 196
IRWIN, James 122 198 John L 173 Margaret 122 Margaret A 220 Maria 198 Mary Philomelia 173 William 163 William C 220
IRWING, John L 59
IVES, Lorenzo Dow 261 R 261
IVEY, Nathaniel 198
JACK, 162 Hester 71 Robert 71
JACKSON, Andrew 44 Ann 94 Ann E 129 Ariann 225 Catharine 255 Cynthia 266 Eveline T 74 Evilene 260 James 74 Mariane 55 Robert 146 Sarah Ann 77 Stephen M 161 Thomas 212 Thomas M 129
JACOBS, Chas C 39 Elvira E 34 Lucinda M 39 Richard 34
JAMES, Ann 68 John G 68 Mary 28 130 Narcissa J 252
JANUARY, Derick P 197
JAY, Wm 134
JAYNE, Absalom H 37 Anselin H 38 Emily 37 38 William Jones 49
JEFFERSON, Mr 133
JEFFRIES, Matilda 120 Prescilla 35
JENKINS, Frederick O 241 H M 112 Harvey 2 105 Harvey M 184 Harvey N 105

JENKINS (continued) James 43 223 John 187 188 Lovicia M 181 M A 228 Mrs 119 Richard H 181 Roselie P 228 Sarah Ann 192 Virginia 2 184 Virginia P 105 123 William M 192
JENKS, Ariann 225 John 225
JENNINGS, Henry 127 Warren 126
JERNAGEN, Delila A 38
JETER, J W 266 Jane 29 Nancy 242 Susan 266
JEWELL, Jane Eliza 230 John M 152 Joseph 230 Lydia 164 Martha Jane 152 Mary 100 Thomas 23
JOHN, John W 32
JOHNSON, Caroline C 170 Caroline E 158 Emily S 254 George W 81 H G 28 H M 124 Henry 122 Horatio G 181 Isaac S 205 J A 98 J C 69 J H 90 J J Bulow 254 J Sr 97 Jno C 66 68 John M 192 Jordan 54 Joseph 33 Joseph E 93 Judge 219 Margaret 122 205 Mr 135 Mrs N N 43 R 57 Rachael N 33 Rev Mr 53 Richard 124 151 Robert 188 Roland 53 55 56 Rowland 56 S H 52 59 84 Sarah 54 Stephen 224 Thos C 128 Thos L 34 Wm 25 90 134 170
JOHNSOON, Allspey K 81
JOHNSTON, Agnes 97 Amos R 150 178 B W 34 Edward 112 Enfield 34 H G 127 Harriet A 178 Judge 10 80 Louisa U W 150 Mary Ann 126 Oscar D 150 R 64
JOINER, George 183
JONES, -- B 234 A P 65 Abby 154 Armsted 43 B 261 B F 67 Benjamin 250 Carter 94 102 116 145 D 265 Dodley 265 Eliza 122 139 187 Elizabeth 48 97 Elizabeth Ann 263 F C 188 Frances 246 Fredonia V 9 G P 104 Harriet 82 Hill 80 Isaac 263 Isaac B 29 J B 232 233 James 23 James M 48 Jeff 41 Jesse H 154 John 93 John B 240 John W 9 174

JONES (continued)
Julia P 213 Margaret W 65
Martha 41 104 Mary 26 67 265
Mary E 9 Mary Magdalene 242
Mr 98 Olivia 65 R B 140 Rev
Mr 29 61 250 Richard M 57
Sarah 23 Sarah Rebecca 50 80
Thomas L 12 Turman 65 William E 26 William R 9 122
William T 242 Wm 109
JONTE, George 229 Minerva 229
JOOR, Emily 218 Genl 209
George 218 John 218 263 Laura 218 Nancy 263 William Richardson 257
JOORS, Geo 262
JOST, John 102
JOURDAN, Charles H 91
JUDD, Elmira 73 Louisa C W 60 Saleb 73 Selah 60 75
JUNO, Zelia 260
KAIGLER, Catharine F 242
Easias 216 Eliza 246 Elizabeth H 247 Ellen Augusta 247 John 243 John D 242 Mary 218 Rebecca C 243 William 218 239 Wm W 238
KAISER, John 262 Mary Ann 262
KANE, John 103 Lucinda 38 Thomas 192
KANN, Joseph 246 Louise 246
KARY, Martha A 215 Mr 215
KAUFMAN, Fanny 131 Samuel 131
KEAGY, A L 223
KEAHEY, George J 79 Margaret M 79
KEALOFER, Ann C 180 John 180
KEARNEY, Elizabeth 116 G 117 Michael 118 Thomas 116
KEARSEY, John J 252 Julia H 252
KEARY, Ellen 225 Helen 249 Martha 18 Mr 18 Patrick F 249
KEATING, H 76 S C 76
KEEBLE, Frances H 28
KEEN, Dr 68 Hugh 110
KEENAN, James 11 152
KEENE, Helen E 28
KEIRAN, James 184
KEITH, James 200
KELLER, Louisa 210 Malinda 22

KELLEY, Anna M 125 Peter 240 Z 125
KELLOGG, C S 236 Chauncey S 227 Horace D 231 Laura Ann 260 Mary Ann 231 Rebecca B C 227
KELLY, 71 Euphemia 42 Hugh 42 James 32 132 Patrick 133
KEMP, Israel 199
KENDALL, Eliza Jane 140 Geo W 140 Marietta 94 Mary Philomelia 173 Wm G 173
KENEDY, James 132
KENNAN, Alexander M 237
KENNARD, Helen E 28 P S 28
KENNEDAY, Artalissa B 54 Lewis 54
KENNEDY, Eveline Sophronia 259 Mary C 40
KENNEY, Thomas C 1
KENNON, Robert W 253
KENNY, James 18
KENT, Henrietta 4 Luke 77 Sarah 245
KERCHEVAL, C G 130 Catharine 130 Charles G 158 J M 240
KERNS, John 85 Martha 85 Mary Ann Catharine 85
KERR, Cynthia 39 Joseph 178
KESSENGER, Anthony 138 Elizabeth 138
KETLET, Martha Ann 30
KEY, F 178 John A 245 Mr 178 Sarah 245
KEYS, Caroline 18
KIDD, A E 209 Richard 209 Sarah 6 133 Thomas 6 133
KIGER, Basil G 158 Caroline Isabella 158 George R 51 Margaret A 9
KILBOURN, Mary A E 246 Owen 246
KILLGORE, Hannah E 136
KILPATRICK, Andrew R 249 Caroline 35 J H 35 James 121 Martha 249 250 Mary Ellen 121
KIMBALL, Asa 215
KING, 262 A E 92 Alexander 57 Charles B 75 Dr 129 Edward 117 Eliza E 245 Esther 195 Esther E 153 Frances A 57 99 Isaac 126 Jane 11 152

KING (continued)
　Jemima G 263 John 10 11 150 156 183 263 John W 80 148 Joseph 198 Louisa 75 Lydia F 244 Martha L 232 Mary E 80 148 Mr 81 122 Nancy 12 57 156 Prosper 92 Prudence 81 Richard 195 Samuel 244 W P 108 William 183 William A 245 William R 76 Wm P 57 Wm T 99
KINGSBURY, Rev Mr 260
KINKEAD, James B 148 Martha A 148 Tunstella E A 170
KINNAN, Thos 119
KINNISON, Jane 36
KINSOLVING, N B L 123
KIRBY, Mrs 183
KIRK, John A 3 Mary 145 William 145
KIRKBY, Ann 229 Eliza Ann 229 Mark 229
KIRKLAND, Virginia 89 Wm H 89
KIRNEY, John 102
KLEIMANN, Catherine 113
KLEIN, Elizabeth B 5 John A 5
KLINE, Samuel 250
KNAPP, Adam 163 203 Wm 100
KNIGHT, E 249 Frances 30 Henry 225 Henry J 249 Isabella 225 Penelope 252 Susan 265
KNIGHTEN, John 233 Julina 233
KNOWLTON, Ann 237 E A 237
KNOX, Andrew 132 John 35 221
KOBLER, M 30 Nancy 30
KOGER, Joseph 75 Martha Matilda 75
KOONTZ, Michael 127
KORTZ, Michael 5
KRING, G C 2
KROES, Louisa 35 Martin 35
KROFF, John 126
KROPF, Julian 31
LACKEY, Amanda H 21 Archibald 21 Mary G 21
LACY, Mary Jane 264
LAFFY, James 128
LAIKER, Frederick 182
LAIRD, Nancy M 36 Robert H 36
LAKE, 92 Anne E 89 Jeannie P 89 W A 89
LAMAY, Lewis F 117
LAMAZE, John 166
LAMBERT, Augustus 157 Samuel 89
LAMBRIGHT, Sarah Ann D 56
LANCASTER, Charles 242 Rosena E 242
LANCHART, Abraham 241 Nancy A 239
LAND, Benjamin 147 Emily Lacy 257 Ezekiel 97 Louisa 50 Margaret E 147 Martha 97 Nancy 97 Sarah M 75 Thomas M 50
LANDFORD, Elizabeth 252
LANDRUM, James Jackson 241 Joel 231 Martha Scott 263 Thomas 245
LANDRY, Adomeline 259
LANE, Caroline 173 Edward W 167 Eliza 116 I 103 J 121 J A 135 John 8 64 80 104 105 123 137 140 148 153 157 167 168 170 172 176 179 187 246 John A 116 Laura 167 Simon T 173 Timothy 167
LANEHART, A C 259 Abraham 256 Abram 247 Catharine R 24 257 Jesse 260 Rebecca Jane 260 Sarah J 247
LANGFORD, Absalom 252 Martha 24 257 Susanna 233
LANGHAM, Wm 38
LANGLEY, Elizabeth A 41 Mary E 36 Matilda 209 Sophia D 62 74 W H 162 William Martin 74 William S 62 74 Willis W 41 Wm 209
LANGSTON, Amelia 31 Cornelia F 32 O D 32
LANIER, Ellen 229 Henrietta 95 Henrietta W 80 148 J C 44 144 Mary J 44 144 Mrs 95 137 Thomas I 229 W H 50 Margaret M J 163
LARIMERE, Charles V 198
LARKINS, M A 45
LATER, Franklin W 163
LATHAM, Harvey 178 Susan 178
LATTIMER, Martha B 53 Nathaniel W 53
LATTIMORE, Sarah Ann W 226 William 226
LAUDERDALE, Sarah 41

LAUGHLIN, Adriann 46 E C 190
　Florida 190 Jane 161 Mary 204
　Wm 161
LAURENCE, E M 61 Martha 61
LAUSETT, John A 49
LAVAL, Harriet Eugenia
　Thompson 134 Jacint 134
LAW, A 182
LAWRENCE, A 160 Minerva C
　141 Rev Mr 72 W P 141
LAWSON, Ann H P 57 99 Charles
　M 22 John H 57 99 Martha 22
LAWTON, Christopher F 120
　Sarah Jane 120
LEA, D Clay 258 David 37 Iveson
　G 210 Jesse 122 Lavinia 44
　Letitia 123 257 Margaret M
　247 Mary Ann H 92 Mary Ann
　Harriet 210 Minerva Ann 64 N
　Elizabeth 258 Pryor 44 64
　Robert M 123 257
LEAHY, Patrick 191
LEAKE, Amanda 253 Walter 212
LEAPARD, Green H 78
LEARNED, C D 72 Louisa C W
　60 Mary H 72
LEATHERBERRY, Elizabeth 13
LEATHERMAN, Charity 226 Cornelia Herbert 261 D 238 Daniel
　266 John H 260 John W 36 37
　Martha 256 266 Mary E 260
　Peter 226
LEATHERS, Asa 167
LEAVEL, H 51 81 166 204 Rev Dr
　162 167 Rev Mr 78 163
LEDBETTER, H 67 J H 71 Mary
　67 P M 75 Susan 71
LEE, Amanda 138 Catharine 37
　Charles L 18 Henry 138 Jesse
　30 John G 54 Mary M B 37
　Pryor 37 Sarah 30 Thos 216
LEECH, James 231 William B
　179
LEETON, Martha Ann 35
LEFLORE, Isabella 36
LEGGETT, Mary 47 Mary M 173
LEGRAND, Alexander 133 J W 57
　Margaret Ann 133 Mary W 57
　Matilda C 144
LEHMAN, David 134
LEIGH, B W 243 Thomas 243
LEITH, Parthena 197

LEIVER, Jas 113
LELAND, Lucinda 209
LELIEVRE, Jacques F 42
　Olympa F 42
LEMLEY, Ithel Town 34 Saml 34
LEMLY, Albert Gallatin 85 Laura
　85 Samuel Sr 85 T L 85
LEMON, Elisha B 32 Frances 32
　William 197 198
LEONARD, Edward 206 Eunice
　197 Joseph 91 197
LESLIE, Saml 235
LESSLEY, Mary 218 Miss 240
　Samuel 218
LESTER, Nathan 62
LEVIN, Ann 219 Lewis Charles
　219
LEVISTON, Wm 106
LEVOY, Susan Nephthali 24
LEVY, Thomas 129
LEWIS, Archibald 72 Benj H 225
　C W 82 Charles Ridgely 236
　Charles Ridgely 173 Col 6 D C
　248 David 192 E E C 231
　Elizabeth Jane 60 Eunice W
　231 Exum 60 Harriet Eliza 243
　Henry 55 Horace Keating 86 J I
　205 Jane Eliza 230 John 104
　121 John B 86 John G 87 John
　R Holliday 224 John S 221 231
　236 John Zachary Taylor 86
　Laura Lavinia 173 Mariane 55
　Martha N 248 Mary 96 Mary E
　256 Mary Y 256 Nancy 221
　Nancy J 86 Rebecca 224 Rev
　Mr 250 261 S W 173 224 236
　256 Samuel W 260 Thomas 66
　Vincent M 192 William 72 84
　William T 213 243 Wm Terrell 214
LIDDELL, Ann C 225 Bethia 209
　Bethia F 242 Moses 209 225
　229 242
LIEBE, Mrs 132
LIGHTCAP, Dr 7
LIGON, Louisa H 214
LILE, Catharine 46 Silas 46
LILLEY, Miles E 229 Virginia
　229
LILLY, Nancy 205
LIMERICK, George 189
LINCECUM, L L 41 Sarah 41

LINCOLN, Garret 207
LINDEN, John 136
LINDENBURGER, John D 3
LINDHEIM, Clara 41 John 41
LINDLEY, Rachael 258 Silas 258
LINDSAY, Susan 28 Wm 217
LINDSEY, Emily 60 John G 256 Landy 22 Martha 256 Mary F 251
LINSEY, John 172
LION, Edward T 17
LIPSCOMB, H P 229
LISLEBY, Sarah Ann 253
LITTLE, William P 107
LITTLEJOHN, Joseph 115 177 Olivia 115 Olivia E 177 Olivia F 115
LIVERMAN, B 149 Theresa 149
LLOYD, Caroline Matilda 54 W W 54
LOCK, Mary Ann 48 Thomas B 48
LOFTIN, Daniel 29 Rosanna 29
LOGAN, Harrison 25 Margaret S 67 Robert 25 Samuel 70 Sarah 70
LONDERGALE, John 110
LONG, Eliza J 48 Joshua B 68 Sarah 68 William B 22
LONGLEY, Mr 109
LONSBERRY, Joshua 166
LORCH, Fanny 131
LORTSON, Elizabeth A 161
LOTT, Hiram R 207 M A E 207
LOVE, Harriet E 50 80 Robert 80 Robert E 223
LOVELACE, Frances Matilda 243 G L 219 P E H 243 Thomas 219
LOVELESS, Delilah Delay 57 J R 57
LOVETT, Mr 135
LOVIE, Eliza 246 James 246
LOWE, Aaron 29 John J 160 203 Rosanna 29
LOWERY, Rebecca H 34 Thomas J 34
LOWRY, Robert Sr 193
LUBEN, W H 106
LUBER, Charles 95
LUCAS, Alexander M 49 Eliza H 25 Sarah Jane 49

LUCKETT, Ann C 220 C E 48 Noland M 220 P H 48
LUDLEY, Alexander 178 Louisa 178
LUDLOW, B A 60 Sarah L 60
LUM, Laura 167 Mary A 157 Samuel 180 William S 157 Wm 167
LUSE, Henry 13 Sarah 13
LUSK, Eveline 233 Myra E 74
LYLE, William 93
LYNCH, Daniel 129 Gov 75 Isaac 161 203
LYND, Ann 136
LYNE, James 247 Jas 242 Martha 247 Thomas 254
LYON, James B 48 James M 31 Matissa 31 Sarah 48
LYONS, David 169 Eliza Ann 171 John 241 Julia Ann 241 Lovice 169 R J 171 Richard J 37
M'ALEER, Caroline 73 Robert 73
M'ALLISTER, Elmira 73 John C 73 Maria J 82
M'ALPIN, Jesse 95
M'ALPINE, John 213 Susan H 213
M'BRIDE, Mary Ann 86
M'CLELAND, James 107
M'CLENDON, Annes 80 L B 80
M'CLUER, Dr 72 Sarah Ann 72
M'COMAS, Anne 194 J H 194
M'CONATHY, Elisha 199
M'CONNELL, Julius C 215
M'COOL, Eliza 45 J L 45
M'CORMACK, Wm 46
M'CORMICK, Jane P 69
M'CRAINE, Hugh 232
M'CUDDY, Andrew 104
M'DONALD, James 86 Mary Ann 86
M'GEHEE, E 214 William 214
M'GRAW, Catherine 93
M'HATTAN, Francis 185
M'INTOSH, James 199
M'KAY, Alexander A 96 Elizabeth 96
M'KENZIE, Chas 181
M'LANE, Margaret 169
M'LAUREN, Jane 36
M'LEOD, Clifton 87 George 87
M'MANUS, Rebecca 72
M'MORROUGH, John M 170

M'MULLEN, Jacob 99
M'NICKLE, Jno K 105 Mary Jane 105
M'ROBERTS, S S 168
MABEN, Joseph W 94 Lauretta 94
MABRY, George W 43 193 Jesse 29 John C B 29 Mary E 43 Mary Ellen 193 Nancy 29
MACKEY, Balzorah 180 Hugh M 185 James 20
MACKLEROY, T S 44
MACKLIN, J F 133
MACLENNAN, James 75 76 Lucy A F 85 Lucy Ann Frances 75
MACLEOD, Rev Dr 84
MACLIN, Augustine 174 I E 136 Imogene E 136 James F 136
MACNIS, James 7
MACOMB, Alexander 14 Martha K 14
MACQUILLEN, Cynthia Holland 178 197 Joseph 178 197
MACRERY, Andrew 26
MADDEN, Joseph 27
MADOX, Robt 109
MAGEE, David 54 E 262 Eugene 175 Felix W 51 Jacob 82 James 122 Martha C 51 Mary Jane 82 Mary Margaret 82 Nancey E 54 Rebecca 246 William 246
MAGOUN, B 245 C S 239 241 245 Calvin B 237 Calvin S 253 Celia Ann 245 Dr 253 Sarah B 239 241 Simon 245
MAGRUDER, Caroline E 191 Eliza 200 Thos 191
MAGUIR, Francis 130
MAHONEY, Elizabeth 149
MALADY, Bridget 135 Mary 125
MALONE, David 58 G C 203 Mary 58 S C 162
MALOY, John 117
MANAFEE, Rev Mr 200
MANCHESTER, Cyrus C 40
MANDEVILLE, Charlotte Augusta 37
MANGLEY, Mr 109
MANGUM, Elizabeth 53 Martha J 53

MANLOVE, Elizabeth B 3 Priscilla W 102 Rebecca A 185
MANN, Daniel 75 Martha Jane 88 T J 88 William 75
MANNING, Wm 104
MANSHIP, 77 Adeline 74 C H 87 Charles H 74 James D 74 Stephen 87
MARBLE, Abner 69 Eerra 217 Elizabeth 184 Frances 32 Hansey 217 Helen M 48 Hester Ann R 69 P 146 Percival 184
MARCY, Rev Mr 62
MARKS, Theresa 149
MARLEY, Ann 263
MARMON, Stephen 109
MARRERO, Elizabeth J 28
MARSCHALK, Andrew 20 90 193 196 Ann M 40 138 Elenora 20 Susanna 195
MARSH, Cyrus 18 Isabella 18 Peter 136
MARSHALL, Amanda 149 Amanda Vick 149 C K 5 57 71 74 98 100 103 106 120 143 149 154 161 253 Caroline 173 Charles Newet 149 Chas K 99 Letitia 78 Rev Mr 235 236 Thomas A 78 153
MARTIN, Abraham 201 Anne 201 Caroline E 108 Cornelius 166 David E 99 Egbert O 112 Emily 11 99 125 153 Emily M 134 G Earl 25 G T 66 George 241 257 Green T 67 Henrietta 118 Henry N 248 257 J H 108 John 107 108 118 John P 96 Lucy A 248 M W 257 Margaret 241 Margaret S 67 Mary A 245 Mary M 205 R M 11 125 153 Robert M 205 S 160 William B 108
MARY, Julina 128
MASALETTEXIA, Susan 16
MASEY, Nancy 78 W 78
MASON, Elizabeth 10 151 H M 149 Martha 30 Mary 168 Nancy 147 Samuel A 71 Thomas 10 Thomas B 151
MASSEY, Ann Eliza 62 Jackson 37 James H 62 Suletta 37

MASSIE, David Milton 51 Margaret 51
MASTERS, J H 93
MATHESON, Donald 171
MATHEWS, W E 256 257 Wm E 252 Wm F 219
MATHEWSON, William 92
MATINLY, Mary Ann 56
MATTHEWS, Charles 261 James E 31 35 78 81 131 Jos W 89 Lewis 32 Margaret 56 Penelope 261
MATTINGLY, A D 99 Mary 99 Rebecca E 259
MAURY, Ann 48 Caroline L 14 Elizabeth 34 John M 14
MAXEY, E H 1 2 180 184 E M 178
MAXWELL, Ann 211 E W 149 Eveline 59 J A 47 James A 207 211 John 59 Leonora 37 Sarah M 47
MAY, Jesse 191 Martha B 211 Sally 16
MAYES, Benjamin M 226 Cynthia 9 50 79 D 9 50 Daniel 79 Eliza Ann 233 Emily 222 265 Eveline R 226 F 225 J J 225 James 222 223 John 215 216 229 John Joor 222 S F 234 William T 222 265
MAYFIELD, Mark H 115
MAYO, George P 61
MAYS, F S 241 John 227 Martha C 241
MAYSON, Charles C 61 62 90 185 Louisa 61 Margaret E 62
MCADORA, Mr 18
MCAFEE, Abraham 47 Morgan 45 47
MCALEB, David 217 Florida A 217
MCALISTER, Elizabeth 200 John 200
MCALLISTER, Almyra J 81 John C 81 Selah J 81
MCALLUM, Anna 38 John 38
MCALPINE, Jennette Ann 235 Robt B 235
MCARTHUR, Caroline E 191 Catherine Jane 136 Duncan 191 Effie 143 Gov 143

MCARTHUR (continued) Sarah 136 Sarah Jane 33
MCAVOY, John 135
MCBEE, Caroline C 170
MCBRIDE, Ann E 50 William 50
MCBRYDE, Charlotte B 42
MCCALEB, David 35 Florida 190 Francis 175 Henrietta Matilda 175 Louisiana 161 175 Mary 66 Mrs A M 48
MCCALL, Amanda M 182 J R 181 182
MCCALLISTER, Margaret 56 William 56
MCCANTE, Catherine 248 Thomas 248
MCCARDLE, Emily Caroline 64 246 W H 98 William H 64 246
MCCARREY, Mrs 111
MCCARTER, Elizabeth 139
MCCARTY, Dennis 105 Ellen 191 James 114 Matinda 148 Pollard W 148
MCCAULEY, John 60 Mary 101
MCCILL, W 160
MCCLELLAN, Eliza S 167 John 167
MCCLENDON, Nancy 30
MCCOMB, Margaret 42 Margaret M 140
MCCONNELL, Amanda 154 Elizabeth 94 Robert 94 Thomas 154
MCCORMICK, Martha 39 Thomas 145
MCCOWN, Burr H 98
MCCOY, Helen 46 James H 46 Thomas 114
MCCRAINE, Elizabeth 253 Mary Ann 262 Robert A 253
MCCRAINEY, Mary 47 Philip 47
MCCRANE, Elizabeth 221 Hugh 221
MCCRARY, Thomas 104
MCCRATH, Michael 134
MCCRAY, Robt 216 S D 105
MCCREA, John 229
MCCREADY, John 235
MCCRON, John 237
MCCRUTCHEN, Jas 28
MCCURDY, James 195
MCCURRY, Neal 128

MCCUTCHEN, James 130 Mrs 157
MCDANIEL, C P 23 R H 258 Thomas Herbert 258
MCDERMONT, Thomas 129
MCDERMOTT, Anthony H 218 John 236
MCDONALD, D 238 Duncan 30 Emiline 30 John 30 Mary B 30 Michael 134 Thomas 238 Wm 53
MCDOUGALL, 38
MCDOWELL, James R 151 Jane M 169 Jas R 169 Robert 151
MCDUFFIE, George 216 Mary Rebecca 216
MCELRATH, E D Cutler 4 Geo W 4
MCELROY, Jno M D W 43 R 44 Susan 8 141 Zacheus S 44
MCELRUTH, Ann H 38
MCFARLAND, A B 155 H S 153 Henry 26 128 John 101 John Harvey 101 Julia 26 Julina 128 Lucy 101 Mary M 153
MCFERREN, Sarah 154
MCGARVIN, Margaret Ann 12
MCGARVIS, Margaret Ann 155
MCGAUGHERTY, Jno 184 Margaret Isabella 184
MCGEE, John 266 Martha Jane 35
MCGEHEE, Catherine J 32 Edward 27 258 266 Edward J 253 Francis William 27 258 Harriet 248 Harriet A R 266 Judge 14
MCGILL, Daniel 166 204 Elizabeth 251
MCGINNIS, Catherine 248
MCGINTY, R J 169 174 178
MCGRAIM, Bridget 12
MCGRAIN, Bridget 156
MCGRAW, Ann O 252 Catherine 17 Drusilla 220 Esther 234 John J 252 Margaret M 24 Matilda C 250 Thirsa Ann 263
MCGUFFIE, John 100
MCGUIRE, E C 2 Patrick 103
MCHENRY, Wm 110
MCINNIS, H 163 R 203
MCINTIRE, Hannah 134 M L 151

MCINTOSH, Daniel S 46 E 262 Mary 262
MCINTYRE, Peter 39
MCKAY, Catharine 181 Daniel 65 Daniel A 122 Maria Jane 34 Mary 122 Mrs 120
MCKEE, E G 44 Maria B 44
MCKEITH, Elizabeth 60 James 60
MCKENZIE, Mary Olivia 240
MCLAIN, Rob't 84
MCLANE, John 118
MCLAUREN, Cornelius 84 Martha Elizabeth 84
MCLAURIN, H C 50 80 Harriet E 50 80
MCLEAN, 108 Rev Mr 100
MCLEIM, 188
MCLENDON, Annes 50
MCLEOD, Alex 176 Daniel 36 Jane 36 Roderick 34
MCLIN, John 21
MCMACKIN, Martha M 45 T C 45
MCMAHON, Wm H 166
MCMAKIN, Martha 89 T C 89
MCMANNUS, Barney 133
MCMANUS, James 206 Thomas 205
MCMATH, M 30 Mr 30
MCMILLAN, A P 140
MCMILLIN, Thomas 135
MCMULLEN, Robert 133
MCMURDO, Eliza Rosana 233
MCMURRY, Jane 42 Wm S 42
MCMURTRIE, William 131
MCMURTRY, A T 17 Rebecca M 17
MCNAIR, Christian Priscilla 80 D 138 Harriet Jane 83 James 83 88 Martin 123 Mary Ann Catharine 123 R 80 Sarah 88
MCNAIRY, John A 142
MCNEELY, Mary A 225 Mary Ann 258 William 225 258
MCNEILL, Angus 13 Malcolm 96 Rebecca Jane 13
MCNULTY, E P 260 John 222 227 Mary Ann 260 Thomas D 222
MCNUTT, A G 39 177 Sarah A 177
MCPHILIPS, J S 101

MCRAE, Alexander Brooks 156 Caroline Matilda 54 Charles 32 David 220 Duncan 54 56 Eliza A 220 Elizabeth R 44 144 Indiana 156 James B 21 John H 144 John J 32 33 Mary A 32 33 Nancy J 56 William 156
MCRAVEN, James 122 Mary J 44 144
MCRAY, Indiana H 143 Virginia Rowlett 143 William 143
MCREA, John 241
MCREYNOLDS, Robert 142
MCROBERTS, Anthony 192 Rev Mr 168 170 S S 171 172 173 177
MCWILLIAMS, Francis A 263 Jennette S 263
MCWILLIE, A A 155
MEACHAM, H B 40 Mary 40
MEAD, Cowles 133 Gen 58 Sarah B 58
MEADE, Bishop 145 Cowles 88 Cowles G 160 Sallie 160
MEADERS, Margaret Caroline 47
MECREN, John 235
MEEK, James 236 Julina 233 Mary Ann 233
MEGHEE, Ann Beverly 253
MEIKLE, Virginia A 189
MELBOURNE, George 44 Mary Isabel 44
MELCY, Jonathan 154 Martha Ann 154
MELLON, Caroline 22 Wm 22
MELTON, B R 46 C E 48 Olevia 46
MELVEN, Mary 28 Stephen R 28
MELVIN, Awry M 104 Irma Louise Josephine 156 James W 156 Mahetabel 164 Mary 130 149 Stephen R 130
MEMARIAN, Hugh 140
MEMARIN, Hugh 8
MENG, Paulina 92
MENNEFEE, William B 169
MERCIEN, 205
MEREDETH, George 137
MERLIN, Abraham 200
MERRIFIELD, Alden S 145
MERRYMAN, Thomas T 169
MERSEILLES, Emily 265

MESSRSHMINT, Margaret 135
METCALF, Mary 96 McCullom 96
METCALFE, Alfred 64 Mrs E 1 Samuel 18
MEZELL, Ann 74 Augustin 74
MICHIE, A A 41 J J 41
MICKSON, Rev Mr 124
MICOUD, Louisa Henrietta 224
MIELKE, Edward C 151 Mrs 151
MILES, L 264 266 Lemuel 213 265 Rt Rev Bishop 159 202 Wm R 89
MILLER, Alexander 39 Anderson 78 Ann 176 Charles 183 Charles W 158 Christopher 15 Christopher E Hall 221 Daniel 230 David 17 191 Elizabeth 61 Ezekial 119 Frances 202 George 109 161 George R 27 Henry F 30 J W 176 James 239 Joanna 188 John 90 112 208 John W 44 144 Joseph E 61 Lackey T 238 Leath 238 Letitia 78 Livina Ann 158 Martha S 230 Mary 17 Mary A 30 Robert 175 Sarah A 90 Sidney G 202 Susan B 15 William 221
MILLIKEN, John 9
MILLS, A E 69 Isabella A 180 Jane M 169 Minerva G 172 Thornton A 127 William 168 169 172 Wm Jr 180
MILLSAP, Catharine 181 Emanuel 181
MILLSAPS, Martha 39 Thomas 39 William 95
MIMMS, Martha Massee 49
MINGO PUCKSHENUBEE (Indian chief), 21
MINIGAR, William 21
MINOR, Maria T 40 Rebecca A 15 Wm J 15
MINTZER, Maria Louisa 143 Peter 118
MITCHELL, A H 112 Alexander 244 Ann 51 81 B D 42 Betsy 201 Caroline P 166 204 Edward 169 Elinder 42 Eliza 7 139 G D 166 204 Geo H 123 Isaac N 87 Isabell 87 James 16

MITCHELL (continued)
  James C 25 90 James H 82
  Josephine 123 Lewis 114 M A
  29 Margaret 87 Mr 201 Robert
  C Jr 214 Velina L 82
MOCK, Elbert 233 Mary Ann 233
MOFFATT, R A 107 Ward 107
MOISE, E W 243 Priscilla 243
MOLES, Nancy 36 W A 36
MOLVANY, Thos 119
MONNAHAN, Thomas 159
MONROE, D D 120 John
  McKenzie 45 Mary 145 Mary
  Artimise 45 W R 69
MONTANDON, A 182
MONTGOMERY, Alexander K 36
  Amelia F 91 Daniel 205 Hugh
  78 James 207 Jane 36 Joseph
  91 Mary 67 Mary Eliza 163 203
  Rev 9 50 Rev Mr 79 153 159
  165 187 206 207 S 128 155 S H
  83 163 164 S M 8 140 148 150
  159 163 205 Samuel C 36
  Samuel M 188 Sarah 36
  Theresa 78 Thomas 49 William 38 Wm D 118
MOODY, A 50 Margaret 96
  Painela 50
MOON, Jas S 233 Mary Ann 233
MOONEY, John K 57 Mary W 57
MOORE, A T 243 Alfred T 256
  Allen 39 Caroline 47 E W 2
  Emma J 139 George 114 Harriet L 71 106 Henry T 139 John
  154 Julia 60 Lemuel C 62
  Mark 208 210 Mary 113 Mary
  O 2 Mary E 256 Mary L 243
  Miss 25 R L 166 R S 47 Robert
  16 Sophia D 62 Thos 124 William 46 74 106 115
MORANCY, H I 148 Martha A 148
MORANEY, Ann E 129 H P 129
MORAY, William 109
MORE, John T 59
MOREHEAD, Amanthus L 59 J 59
MORELAND, Catharine F 243
  Elisha F 243 256 Howell 210
  266 Orinda E 256
MORESE, Louise 246
MORGAN, A 73 Charles 82
  Charles R 31 Daniel 4 205
  David B 196 Eliza B 196

MORGAN (continued)
  J B 109 Mary Ann 16 Mary Ellen 205 Narcissa 4
MORHOUSE, Abraham 193
  Reuben 194
MORRIS, Ann E 86 Anna M 125
  Catharine 46 E W 159
  Florence C 159 George 247 262
  Henry 181 Isabella Virginia 50
  J J 86 J J H 64 Jefferson M
  245 Jno 108 John J 50 John P
  33 Lucinda 181 Mabry 230 248
  Mahala 230 Margaret E 64
  Martha 41 247 262 Mary A 245
  Minerva 159 Robt S 265
  Samuel 126 Sarah 50 Susan 265
  William 96
MORRISON, Jane 38 Lovica M
  260 Walter 260
MORROW, John 43
MORSE, Sarah 25
MORSSIE, Mrs 184
MORTIMER, Thomas H 182
MORTON, Catherine Jane 219
  Edward 219 Francis 102 G K
  82 J 108 Nancy Steel 82
MOSBACK, Jacob A 109
MOSBEY, E P 136
MOSBY, David 107 Fountain 107
  James C 107 James Wilson
  107
MOSEBY, Martha W 120
MOSELEY, Lewis 86
MOSLEY, Mary A 240
MOSS, H K 64 Joseph J 231
  Louisa H 133 Martha 231 Mary
  64 Rebecca M 17
MOUCHETTE, Capt 18
MOUGEAUN, Olympa F 42
MUDD, Lasthina 20 R M 138
  Walter 120 154
MUIR, Clarisa Ann 168 Frances
  Julia Ann 168 R D 168
MULADORE, Joseph 109
MULEGAN, L 203
MULLENS, James 21
MULLER, Rev Mr 13 92
MULLIN, Melinda M 21 Thos B
  21
MULVAHILL, Wm 162
MUMFORD, John I 244 Julia Antionette 244

MUNCE, Isabella 18 Mary 17
MUNGER, Mary C 183
MUNSON, Matilda Adeline 237 W
  W 237
MURDOCK, Alfred 81 Mary
  Catharine 81 Miss 102
MURPHREY, Daniel 223
MURPHY, Dennis 138 Emeline
  238 Eunice Ann 97 Hannah 92
  Hugh 128 James 160 John 103
  John S 97 Susan F 76 Timothy
  101 Vincent 76
MURRAY, Christopher 68 69 Jas
  H 216 Mr 15 Rev Mr 65 66 67
  Wm 23
MURRELL, Elizabeth H 38
  James 38 John A 174
MURREY, James P 247 Jane 247
MURRY, Martha 119
MURTHA, Henry 19
MUSE, Cassander 225 Eli 92
  James H 30 Martha Ann 30
  Western 225
MUSSENTINE, Rebecca 146 188
MYER, Amanda 95 Solomon 95
MYERS, A E 47 Barbette 89
  Emeline 161 Henrietta F A 134
  John 89 Noland 204 William
  134
MYGATT, Eliza M 144
MYRER, C W 111 Cornelia
  Sophia 111
NAFE, Charles 22
NAGHTON, Mary 138
NAGLE, Michae 115
NAGLLEY, Thos 183
NAIRNE, Elizabeth T 41 Wm 41
NALL, Patty 196
NANCE, Elijah W 135 Lucy Ann
  135
NASH, A B 49 T M 85
NEAL, John D 191
NEELY, Adaline W 12 158
  Caroline P 166 204 Wesley W
  166 204
NELSON, David 194 Dorcas 194
  Julia J 160 Margaret 191 Mary
  157 Newman J 157 Richard 191
  Samuel 160
NES, Rutha P 250
NESBIT, Richard 130
NESMITH, Jennette S 263

NETHERRY, Elizabeth 69 Preston W 69
NETTERVILLE, Ann 230
  Caroline 239 242 Catharine R
  24 257 Charles 243 Clarinda
  Catharine 257 Eliza E 245 Esther 250 Jesse M 24 257
  Josephine 227 Lavinia 261
  Susannah 243 Thos 227 Victor
  N H 239 242 257 William 223
NETTLES, Elvira E 34 Samantha
  Jane 34
NEWELL, Adaline 232 Cornelia
  H M 259 Geo B 266 Jane B 266
  Joseph 259 Mary B 227 Wm
  223
NEWMAN, Albert M 189
  Alexander F 184 Benjamin 198
  Charlotte 201 Delia L 132
  Eliza 7 139 Eugene 7 139
  Ezekiel 198 Fanny 196
  Frances A 38 George 42 201
  Isaac R 116 192 James C 100
  John 13 18 Joseph 229 Josiah
  155 Laura C 100 Louisa C 13
  Lucinda 214 Margaret Isabella
  184 Maria 198 Martha 18 Mary
  G 219 Minerva I 189 Reuben 44
  Ruth 198 Sara Jane 229 Sevella
  116 Thomas R 43 Virginia L
  155
NEWNINGHAM, Ruth Sophia 168
NEWSOM, Penelope 179
NEWTON, A 81 144 191 Rev 136
  Rev Mr 121
NEYLANS, Amanda 52 Eliza 53
  Joseph 52 Nancy 57 Wm 57
NICHOL, Sarah C 122 Wm H 122
NICHOLS, Anna 156 Elizabeth
  206 Hardin 149 Luther Jr 156 N
  194 Nancy 149
NICHOLSON, Calvin H 261
  Caroline C 261 Cornelia V 28
  Eliza W 266 I R 28 Isaac R 33
  Sally N 207 W R 28
NIEMAN, Henry 110
NILES, Ambrose B 206 Elizabeth
  206
NIMON, George 211 Martha B 211
NIXON, Beatina M 23 George A
  23 George H 20
NOBLE, Ann H P 57 99 Henry 49

NOBLE (continued)
  Seaborn Jones 218
NOLAN, Ann E 168
NOLAND, Ellen Ann 235 Jane 231
  Jeremiah 227 Jeremiah D 235
  Lydia 235 Philip 225 232 W P
  14 William F 207
NOONAN, John 50 Keziah M 50
NORCOM, Harriet J 115 Julia 115
  Wm R 115
NORMAN, C D 50 Delia Ann 50
NORRED, Samuel 61
NORRIS, Lewis F 69 Rebecca 23
  Sarah 69
NORSWORTHY, Caroline 96
  James N 96
NORTH, J H 30 Mary 78
NORTON, George F 12 Sarah 99
  Sydney Ann 168
NORWOOD, E E C 231 Jane 215
  Jas M 25 Levice 225 Robert
  215 225 231
NOWLAN, Ellen 190
NULL, Elizabeth 55
NUTT, Ann Eliza 141 Dr 141
  Harold Travis 189
NUTTING, Emily L 239
O'BRIEN, Bridget 166 Owen 10
  149 William 101 119
O'CONNER, Mrs 134 Esther E
  153 John 153 Patrick 191
  Susan 191
O'DONALD, Ann 266 Charles 266
  Patrick 119
O'HARA, T 129
O'HEYTOUR, Daniel 184
O'NEIL, James 185 Thomas 113
O'NEILL, James 44 188 John 136
  Sarah 44 188
O'REILLY, M D 140 144 Rev 148
O'REILY, M D 6 9 187 188 Rev
  Mr 121
O'RIELLY, John 11 Michael D 11
  153
ODOM, Sabra R 66
OGDEN, Amanda Caroline 241
  Caroline E 243 George 222
  Isabella Virginia 50 Jesse 243
  260 John 218 236 Martha 249
  Mary Ann 218 Mary S 225 P W
  244 Rebecca 241 Robert T 241
  249 Sarah Eveline 260

OGDEN (continued)
  Thomas E 50 William G 222
OGLESBY, Minerva 229
OLD, Ellen 229 Ellen M G 23
  William A 23
OLDCRAFT, James H 160
OLDCROFT, James A 202
OLDHAM, John P 45 71
OLDS, Mr 70
OLIVER, Francis M 141
ONEAL, James 239 Priscilla 239
ONIS, Sophia 190
OOTON, Margaret 45 Wm 45
ORR, Martha N 227 248 Wright B
  227
ORRICK, Barney 105 Elizabeth
  105 Mr 110
OSBORN, James 21 Mary G 21
OSTEEN, Gabriel 71
OSWALD, Ann Martha 248 Georgia Virginia 256 M M J G 254
  T H 248 256 Thos M 254
OTEY, Jos H 189 Rt Rev Bishop
  11 81 161
OTTO, Daniel H 36 72 76 Sarah
  Ann 72 76 Sophia 36
OVERMAN, Ellen 231 M 253 254
  258 Matthias 231 Sarah Ellen
  254
OVERSTREET, Sebra 31
OWEN, Clarissa 10 Clarissa M
  50 80 Eveline T 74 Levina R
  36 Minerva 146
OWENS, Ellen 96 James 96 97
OWIANGS, Rosana 94
OWINGS, Jonathan Lafayette 206
OZANNE, Beatrice Agnes 253
  Piere Martin 253
PACE, Ann 76
PADDLEFORD, Sarah M 24 T D
  24
PAGE, A C 83 D C 81 114 James
  169 Rev Dr 131 Rev Mr 8 53
  187 237 Susan 169
PALMER, Alva 252 Ann O 252
  David A 227 J D 35 Jeremiah
  253 John 80 Julia Ann 35 Julia
  D 86 Lawren 143 Maria Louisa
  143 Martha A 227 Mary 35 80
  Minerva 253 Thomas 86
  Thomas B 2 64
PANNELL, Joseph 201

PAQUINETT, Wm F 238
PARDEE, Luther 244
PARHAM, J G 190 John G 157 Mary E 157 Mr 189 William S 61
PARISH, Mary Ann 10
PARKER, Cath 40 Elizabeth 241 Fannie May 81 J P 9 Lewis L 72 Margaret 216 Margaret F 96 Mary H 38 Richard 255 Samuel 96
PARKISON, David 168
PARMER, Lackey T 238
PARROT, Emma L 149 Jas 149
PARSONS, George W 108 Talbot H 80
PASCO, Richard 112
PASCOE, Ann R 235 Charles 235 243 Emma Jane 243
PASSMORE, J C 142 Susan B 142
PATE, Eleanor E 247 James D 247 Sarah Jane 247 William 8 141
PATRICK, Eliza 223 Elizabeth 88 J C 223 Jane 52 Martha 224 Medora 89 Needham 52 Robert 89 Robert J 84 Sarah Ann 88
PATTEN, Thomas R 102
PATTERSON, Edward 122 213 George D 56 John 91 Joseph 218 220 226 Lovicia M 181 Rev 190 Rev Mr 79 92 154 158 161 189 202 Robert 210 S 152 Samuel 156 Stephen 162 165 202
PATTON, Alfred 163 Priscilla 163
PAU, Antonio 166
PAUL, Elijah R 46 Joel 6 132
PAXTON, A M 2 Alexander M 142 Andrew 84 Ann M 202 203 Eudora Anderson 142 Hannah 84 James G 202 Louisa 186 M L 2 Margaret V 8 141 Margaret Virginia 8 141 142 Rebecca Louisa 186 W H 4 8 142 186 Wm H 141
PAYNE, Catharine 60 Catharine W 76 Eliza S 98 Elvia K 60 John 69 98 Lucretia 69 Nathaniel W 60 76 Rev Mr 132 256 Susan 226 W C 133

PAYNE (continued) William 226 Wm C 11
PEABODY, Joseph Augustus 12
PEAL, Alexander 114
PEALE, Alexander 3 Ellen 153 Jacob 153
PEALER, Anderson J 101
PEARCE, Ann E 70 James 154 James Ann 154 Joshua L 229 Lavina 244 Myra 122 Rev Mr 164 William H 70
PEARSON, Martha Elizabeth 35
PEASE, Henry H 180 John B 180 Lewis S 181 Lydia 180
PECK, Daniel 214 Dr 152 Helen D 152 Louisa H 214
PEDRELI, Fideli 124
PEEBLES, J D 205 James Sterling 103 Martha 104 Mary F 103 Wm 52 53
PEEPLES, Allen 47 Elizabeth F 47
PEERS, W N 121
PEEVY, Archibald 56 Lanora 56
PEGUES, A H 36 Rebecca Ann 36
PELHAM, Ann B 135
PENDER, Celo 78 S S 78
PENDLETON, Delilah 58 Frances 30 J W 30
PENN, George 129
PENNINGTON, J J 144
PENNY, Elizabeth 227 William 227
PENROSE, Clement B 233 Clement Biddle 238
PERANO, Fronica 151 Louis 151
PERCYMAN, Elizabeth F 72
PERKENS, John 91 Zilpha 91
PERKINS, Cordelia 167 Elizabeth 56 John 56 132 Mary M B 37 R S G 167
PERRIN, Eliza W 94 Green R 94 S C 94
PERRY, Daniel 101 Elizabeth 60 John M 7
PERRYMAN, Laura M 79
PETERSON, Sydney 94
PETRIE, Lemuel M 72 Rosa M 72
PETTIWAY, I W 160 Julia J 160
PETTWAY, James E 180
PETTY, Caroline 175

PETTY (continued)
  Lucretia J 28 P H 175
PEUGH, Nancy A 37
PEYTON, Ann C 40 Balie 40 John B 145 Louisa U W 150 Major 72 Mary F 145
PHARES, Alacia Maria 46 D L 46 Lucetta A 258 M A 46
PHELPS, Alonzo 223 Elizabeth 24 Hannah Hoyt 253 Salmon Aretus 253 Samuel M 24
PHENNY, Catherine 182 Elias 182
PHILBRICK, John 226 Susan 226
PHILIPS, James 160
PHILLIPS, Benjamin 190 James T 63 Margaret 190 Mrs 19
PHIPPS, David 257 Mary 262 Mary E 257
PICKENS, Biddy 215
PICKERING, Isaac 136
PICKET, Jane Eliza 131 Micajah 131
PICKETT, Jas S 51 John K 250 Martha 250
PIERCE, Mary Ann 204 Phebe J 155 Thomas B 204 Thomas N 155
PIERSON, John F 105 Martha J 47 Saml 47
PIGEON, Lavinia 148
PIKE, James M 157 M W 101 Maria M 157
PILCHER, A E 76 77
PILMORE, Rev Mr 209
PINCHEN, Charlotte 261
PINCHING, Fanny 40 Guy R 107 Mrs 40 158
PINCKARD, 110 A M 141
PINCKNEY, Catharine 255 Cotesworth 255
PINDELL, Henry Clay 154 James Ann 154
PINNCHEN, Charlotte 86
PIPES, Abner 65 David 259
PIPKIN, B 264 Rev Mr 264
PITCHER, Lemuel 211 Mary 211
PITKIN, Catharine B 176 Walter 176
PLANT, Nancy 36
PLATNER, Stephen Jr 254
PLATT, Joseph B 97

PLEASANTS, Anna E 80 Warren E 89 Warren Eustace 80
PLUMB, Thos 130
PLUMMER, F E 82 Franklin 234 Mary C 82
POINDEXTER, George Jr 214 Henrietta 214 John G 238 246 John J 64 Mary 64 Thomas 211 William D 238
POLK, A J 152 Mary E 152 Virginia 28
POLLACK, Wm 129
POLLETT, E W 25
POLLOCK, D W 89 William 6
POOL, Mary 225 Moses 225
POOLE, Caroline E 243
POPE, Sophronia A 50
PORTER, C B 105 Catharine J 167 J P 167 John C 216 Rev Mr 61 63 261 Samuel H 12 Susan 266 Wm 94
PORTERFIELD, Margaret 202 W 139 William 7
POSEY, Carnot 87 Elizabeth 261 Jane 87 Jno B 261 John B 236 261 Maria 261 Maria E 236
POST, Mrs 211
POSTLETHWAITE, Samuel 18 23
POSTLEWAITE, Sophia T 240 Wm D 240
POTTER, Asa 53 Cynthia 9 50 79 G L 9 George L 50 79 Hatlett 224 Henry 54 Matilda 53 Rev Mr 68
POTTICARY, Elizabeth 105 155 John 98 155 Patience S 122
POTTS, George 15 18 91 214 219 229 Rev Mr 19 20
POURELL, Sarah 184
POURSH, Joseph 264 Sally 264
POWEL, Paul 184
POWELL, A 43
POWELL, Adelaide 43 Benjamin W 133 C L 49 Eliza Ann 31 George W 132 H J 31 Jackson 119 James 80 John 95 Mary 80 Olivia 133 Sarah W 232 T 242 247 248 T N 138 Truman 232 241 244 245
POWERS, Frances A 148 Martha Jane 152
POYNER, Ann 224 Stephen 224

PRATT, Helen M 48 John L 48 S 178 Seneca 73 75
PRENTICE, Horace 173 Louisa Ann 173 Minerva 173 R M 102
PRENTISS, Mary Jane 73 Sargeant S 73
PRESBURY, Mary E 229
PRESLER, Jael 243 Joshua 243 Lovica M 260 Peter 243
PREWETT, Celia 242 Celia Ann 245 Lemuel 242 Levi 210 Millberry 210
PRICE, D W 48 Elizabeth 165 Hugh J 51 J B 128 John 192 Martha 138 Martha Ann 51 Mary G 48 Peter 138 Samuel C 162 Sarah W 89
PRICHARD, Celia Ann 42 John 42
PRICKLES, Charles 160
PRIES, Elizabeth 140 John 140
PRIMER, John B 113
PRINCE, Balissa 29 78 Catherine 78 Cynthia Holland 178 197 Robert 178 197
PRITCHARD, Mrs 2
PROCTOR, J D 34 James 46 Rachel 46
PROPST, John 110
PROSSER, Thomas H 213 218 244
PRYOR, Eliza J 48 John P 48
PUCKET, Ann Matilda 169 Lawson 178 Mary Virginia 178 Walter R 169
PUCKETT, W R 151
PUCKLES, Charles 202
PUNCHARD, Eliza S 167 Mary C 183 Mary Francis 178 Samuel 178 Samuel W 183 Sophronia H 173
PURLEY, James 207
PURNELL, G W 27 Mary Ann 27 Micajah T 94
PURVIANCE, James 257
PURVIS, Elizabeth 61 Wm 3
PUTNAM, J R 122
QUARL, Feliciana 48 Reynold 48
QUEGLES, John B 24
QUIN, Elizabeth F 72 Irvine M 72 Maria Jane 34
QUINE, Jehu 235 Margaret 245 Mordecai 235
QUINLAN, Patrick 103

QUINN, W M 34
QUINNAN, John 118
QUITMAN, Albert J 50 149 Gen 149 John A 50
RABB, Daniel 93 Eliza 95 Sarah 161
RADFORD, Thomas W 121
RAFERTY, John 5 127
RAGAN, Amanda 61 Eliza A 177 Jesse B 61 177 Patrick 192
RAIL, John 51 Mary 51
RAILEY, James 131 Mary Eliza 131
RAINEY, Ann Eliza 62 Jas 62
RAINWATER, Nancy 43
RAIRDON, Sarah Jane 120
RALEY, Dr 165
RAMAGE, Thomas 206
RANALDSON, James A 212 220
RANDALL, Delia Ann 50
RANDELL, Eliza 218 Joel 218
RANDOLPH, A S 220 225 231 Cornelia V 242 Elizabeth 13 George F Jr 210 Harriet F 143 Joseph 153 Judge 211 Julia Ann 145 M J Rebecca 202 Mary A 145 Mary J R 176 Mary T 3 Peter 13 19 Rachel 210 Robert H 143 Sally 19 Sally Ann 211 T C 176 T J 121 Thomas C 114 Thos J 104
RANEY, James 2 Maranda 68 Margarett 1
RANNEY, Emma 157 Martin L 100 157 Ruth 100 157
RANNY, Martin L 189 R H 51
RAPAIDE, Frances M 115
RAPALJE, Frances M 181 George J 181
RAPELJE, Mary Allen 126
RAPPLEYE, 168
RARD, G F 155 Mary A 155
RATCLIFF, Ann 224 H M 3 Nancy 264 Saml N 264
RATLIFF, Ann 237 Ann Eliza 220 Cyrus 45 Emelia 198 Olivia Adaline 45
RAWLINS, Eleanor C 232 Emily 231 Sarah 245
RAWLS, Martha Caroline 24
RAY, Chasley 162 John Ellison 179 Martha Prissilla 180

RAY (continued)
  Martha S 143 Thomas Waitis 143 Valentine C 179 180 Wm R 143
RAYMOND, N E 262 265 Nathan E 229 R 265
RAZER, John B 22
RDWARDS, Richard 130 143 147
REA, George 51 52 53 54
READ, Charles W 152 Robert H 153 Sarah 152
READING, A B 152 173 Ellen G 108 Emma Elizabeth 11 152 Rosanna 101 Sophia 152 173
REAGAN, Ann E 200 Geo 200
REARDON, Michael 110
REAT, John F 146
REAVES, J 19
REDDITT, Sarah Ann 179 William 179
REDHEAD, Joseph 259 Mary 259
REDNEY, Jacob 186
REED, James 30 James L 219 John 186 L J 121 M 121
REES, Teresa 86
REESE, Ann B 50 79 J B 50 79 Mary L 48 Thos M 86
REEVES, John 203
REGAN, Mary Ann 157 William 157
REID, A P 229 Absolam 97 James 219 Jane 231 Margaret 215 Mary E 229 Mary Jane 115 William 231 251
REILY, Martha M 256
REIM, Moses 41 Sophia 41
REMBERT, John 51 Sarah 51
REMUS, John 158
RENEAU, Mary Jane 258
RENO, Lewis 77 Sarah Ann 77
RERWOOD, J R 162
RETTING, Tony 116
REVILE, Eliza Jane 59 Rankin R 59
REYNOLDS, John 113 Mary A 28 Sarah Ann 53
RHODES, Owen 223
RICE, Daniel 4 John B 124 John H 206 Mary A E 124 N L 156
RICHARDS, George 181 Hester Ann 181 J T 16 Lewis 109 Mary Ann 25 Mr 157

RICHARDSON, A A 186 Bethia F 242 C 239 Eliza Ann 253 Elizabeth 211 F R 225 246 Frances A 38 Frances Ann 175 Francis D 242 Francis M 253 Henry 210 J A 38 James B 227 John E 113 John G 265 Louisa 210 Margaret 215 Martha N 227 Mary 265 Mary E H 252 McAfee 246 Robert B 252 S M 246 Samuel 158 Susan 246 Wiley W 215 William 211 William Arthur 225 Wm A 208
RICHIE, James 120 Matilda 120
RIDDLE, Elizabeth McNeill 181 Jane 231 Joseph 171 Mary 40 Robert 171 181 250 Virginia A 181 Virginia E 171 Wm 80 83
RIDER, Catherine 42 Wm H 42
RIDLEY, R J 35
RIGGS, James R 188 Mary C 188
RILEY, Elizabeth D 42 Elizabeth G 19 Houghton 138 John 119 Mary Charlotte 261 Peter 119 184 Samuel W 261
RINEY, Benedict 178 Nancy 178
RINGGOLD, Chester 186
RITCHIE, Robt 108
RITTER, Flora Catharine 201
RIVES, William 199
ROACH, Jno 251 Louisa 50 Martha 264 Mary Ann 213 Rachael 251
ROACHE, Ellen 231
ROANE, Mary 43
ROBB, Louisa H 133 R B 133
ROBERTS, Catharine 114 Elizabeth 151 J J 169 Mary Ann 217 Thos 134
ROBERTSON, Albert G 176 Elizabeth A F 176 F H 131 John 218 Joseph 179 Joseph L 179 Lethy Ann 64 M A 64 Mary Leonora 131 S C 76 Wm T 179
ROBINS, Caroline 120 Thomas E 120
ROBINSON, Amos 191 Ann B 50 79 Caroline 63 Elizabeth 116 Emeline 260 Gordon 114 204 J W 129 John 128 187 260 L J 163 203 Margarett 1 Martha Ann 51 Martha P 114 204

ROBINSON (continued)
  Mary Louisa 235 Mrs 13
  Nathaniel 1 Raymond 116
  Robert B 64 S 235 Sarah Jane
  49 Sophia M 73 W H 175 William 51 William Gordon 204
ROBY, Augustus H 46 Mary C 46
ROCHESTER, Charles H 66 Mary 66
ROCK, Harrison 148
ROCKET, Eliza 5
ROCKMAN, Joseph 65
RODNEY, Thomas 201
ROFERTY, Timothy 206
ROGERS, E 182 George 109 M 145 Robert 157 Robina 242 Theo M 212
ROONEY, James 184
ROOT, Charles 101
ROPER, Benjamin E 76 78 Catharine W 76 78 Ella 78
ROSE, Mary Ann 128
ROSS, Andrew 18 Ann 147 Eliza 45 Elizabeth 47 Elmira 34 Isaac J 173 174 175 J 30 J D 77 J M 185 James 251 Jane 197 John 28 197 John F 147 157 Magdalena 34 137 Mahala Caroline 197 Martha 30 Mary 174 Minerva A 175 Rebecca Ann 230 Robert 45 47 80 Samuel 197 Sarah 175 Silviah C 174 175
ROSSMAN, Letitia A 177 W 100 Washington 177
ROURK, Jane M 159 Raymond Augustin 159
ROUSE, F W 206
ROUSSEAU, I F 192
ROUTH, John 187
ROUX, Abraham L 94 Marietta 94
ROW, George 246 Margaret 246
ROWAN, Elizabeth B 19 Sion G 19
ROWE, Eber 192 F H 133 Mary Ann 133
ROWLEN, Zenobia A 146
ROWLETT, Alfred H 123 Virginia 128 Virginia P 123
ROYALL, Virginia 2
ROZELL, Virginia 184
RUBICAN, Mrs 122

RUBY, Lucy Ann 135
RUCKER, W B 8
RUCKS, Elizabeth B 80 148 James 80 Jas 148
RUFF, Andrew 116 John A 116 Mary A 116
RUFFIN, Agnes 43 James 43
RUFFIN, Mary 43
RUNDELL, Eunice 48 J O 31 John 104 M A 31 Phoebe E 104 Wm S 48
RUNNELLS, Camilla 115 John P 217 Sarah 217
RUNNELS, Ex Gov 115
RUNYAN, Samuel 109
RUSH, Benjamin 193
RUSHING, Noel 178
RUSSELL, Ann 76 Arnold 94 B 94 D L 36 D R 31 Daniel L 42 140 Elizabeth 172 J T 167 James R 76 Joshua 140 Julia 31 Lauretta 94 Mr 16 Rev Mr 122 Sarah 42 140 Theodore M 145 W C 204 Wm C 172
RUTHERFORD, Benjamin 168 Emeline A 33 Ruth Sophia 168
RUTLEDGE, Dudley 212 232 Mary 212
S----, Caroline 90 Samuel E 90
SACKMAN, Paul 182
SADLER, Ethelwin 131 Isaac 20 Mary Leonora 131 Silenus O 20
SAFFOLD, Bird 152 190 Mrs 190 Sarah 152
SAINT CLAIR, Harriet L 63 Walter 63
SAINT JOHN, Ellen 26 John H 26
SALAN, Armissa 170
SALE, H E 261 Henry E 236 Maria 261 Maria E 236
SALLEY, John 192
SALTERS, Edward 18
SANBORN, J H 239 Jacob H 241 Sarah B 239 241
SANDERS, 244 Celo 78 Isaac 78 Israel 110 Martha 18 Nancy 78 Peter 84 Rev Mr 100
SANDERSON, Moses 191
SANFORD, Geo 190 Rev Mr 15
SAPE, Matilda 225
SAPP, Julia Ann 241
SARGEANT, C C 250

SARGENT, Turpin Kilby 16
SARTORIOUS, Clara 41 Jacob 34 Magdalena 34
SARTORIUS, Jacob 137 Magdalena 137
SATERFIELD, Jonathan 41 Mary Ann 41
SAUN, Mrs 135
SAUNDERS, A B 62 Augustus B 73 B F 85 H C 85 J 231 James 213 James Bailey 231 Jane 231 Jesse 208 248 249 Joseph Johnson 248 Lucretia 213 Margaret E 62 Maria 208 Maria L 248 249 Mason E 231 Rachel Johnson 249 William 174
SAWKINS, Sophia 36
SCALE, J M 45 James K Polk 45
SCANNEL, Matthew 127
SCANNELL, Honora 9 46 John 126 Owen 138
SCARBROUGH, Edward 107 Nancy 107 Wm Jr 107
SCHAEFFER, Michael 124
SCHEVANKE, Chas 100
SCHIERHOLZ, C 31 Julian 31
SCHMID, Herman 183
SCHMIT, Chistopher 113
SCHON, E 158
SCHRAMM, Catarine 124
SCHWARTZ, Barbette 89
SCISSON, James P 25
SCOBES, F 109
SCOGIN, L M 94
SCOTT, A M 219 Anne R 230 Arthur 53 Christopher C 94 Eliza 228 Eliza J 219 Eliza Jane 105 121 Elizabeth V 162 Fanny May 11 Hampton D 30 Harriet F 143 Isabella 154 J A 237 Jane 217 John F 228 L I 131 Letitia Ann 262 Mahalet 30 Martha Ann 26 77 Mary J R 176 R B 131 Rev Dr 190 Sarah Ann 53 Susan 226 Thomas 216 Thomas J 162 W J 17 William Parker 11 81 Wm P 105 111 112
SCRIBER, Mary Jane 40
SCRUGGS, A T 37 J W 27 Sarah 37

SCUDDER, M 238 N 225 226 227 233 234 235 237 238 239 240 241 242 243 Nathaniel 226
SCULL, Elizabeth 183 Ira 183 John H 183
SEARLS, C J 9 C R 9 W L 9
SEARS, A R 204 Albert R 205 John Jr 205
SEAY, Thomas M 132
SEDGWICK, J 15
SEEGER, 176
SEGUIN, Emma Louisa 92
SEIDES, Ambrose 186
SELBY, Jane 86 Lloyd 86
SELKIRK, Andrew 16
SELLERS, George W 41 Nancy A 41
SELOON, Zilpha 91
SELSER, Emily 99 Geo 154 Hester Ann 181 Isaac N 177 John M 161 Letitia A 177 Mary E 161 Rebecca C 154
SEMPLE, Francena R 251 John T 224 Leonora 229 240 Robert 229 240 251
SERDITH, James 16
SERVOSS, Elizabeth 198 Thomas L 198
SESSIONS, Anna G 156 Caroline L 14 Cornelia 14 Emily J 187 James P 156
SETTLE, John 73 Margaret 73
SEVIER, Julia 145
SEVIET, Julia 46
SEWELL, Laura Lavinia 173
SEXTON, Emily Jane 3 114 John M 3 114 S W 192
SEYMOUR, John W 225 Mary A 225
SHACKELFORD, A L 61 Addison L 60 H J 133
SHAFFER, Eliza C 255 Julia H 252 Mary Ann 245
SHAMBURGER, Susanna 11 Thomas 51
SHANE, Samuel 180
SHANNON, Ann C 180 Edward L 180 John 189 202 John M 5 Levina 5 Marmaduke 5 Pamela 220 Susannah 19 Thomas E 220 Wm 17

SHARKEY, Allen 171 Charles 183 James E 174 Mary Rhodes 174 Patrick R 171
SHARMAN, E L 96 Sophronia E 96
SHARP, John 115 Sumner M 24
SHARPE, Indiana Cordelia M 62 Richard 62
SHAW, Alexander G 78 B 231 233 243 245 246 Benjamin 231 236 246 Berry 18 Harriet 208 John F 209 Sarah H 209
SHEARMAN, Mr 178
SHEHAN, Jeremiah 109
SHELBY, Aaron 85 Love 52 Martha 52
SHELTON, Annes 80 Catherine V 165 David 44 George W 80 Jno 165 Lavinia 44 Virginia 89
SHEPARD, Thomas 149
SHEPHERD, Frances Ann 224
SHEPPARD, Charles 40 Charles M 91 James P 35 Margaret A 91 Rebecca 40
SHERMAN, Hiram 96 Mary 96
SHEROD, George 113
SHERRICK, 108
SHIELDS, John 63 John A 214 Mary R 236
SHILLINGS, Lavina 242 Wm W 242
SHIP, 172
SHIPLEY, J A 90
SHIPMAN, Jacob 48 Sarah Cornelia 48
SHIRLEY, Harriet J 44 James J 44
SHOCKNEY, David 129
SHORT, Clarinda 42 William D 183 184
SHOTARD, Sarah 197
SHRINER, Eve 114
SHRODES, Wm 10 148
SHROPSHIRE, George 233 Mary Jane 233 Sarah 253
SHULER, Chas W 134 Jacob 204
SHUMWAY, Edwin 63
SIBBLEY, Mariah Ann 30
SIBBY, Elizabeth 30
SIBLEY, Benjamin F 240 Eliza H 240
SILLERS, Katharine 68

SILVEY, Mary Ann 232
SIMMONS, A T 239 Annes 50 C W 50 Charles W 80 Eliza 251 H H 164 Martha E 79 Mary A 79 Morning 61 Robt 251 Tar--- 164 W W 79 Wm A 61
SIMONTON, Henry 216
SIMPSON, Ann 193 E M 3 George W 4 John 128 Josiah 193 Samuel H 190
SIMS, Chas 245 Ellen L 53 F 186 Ferdinand 177 Harriett A 55 James 82 John 53 55 220 Mary M 220 Philadelphia 245 S L J 26 Sarah A 177 Sarah M 168 Sarah N 224 Wm Henry 186
SINGLETON, David 153 Hiram 218 Laura 218 Mary Rebecca 216 Richard 216
SISSON, Mrs 136
SITLER, J M 74 Joseph M 254
SIZSE, A E 76 Henry E 76
SKATES, W D 103
SKINNER, Ann 68 Emeline R 77 Helen 46 John 202 Richard 46 68 Samuel 77
SKIPWORTH, George G 84 Jenny Cary 84
SLACK, Daniel 266 Harriet 266
SLADE, Elizabeth 46 John 238 Louisa 238
SLATER, John 192 Sarah Ann 192
SLAUGHTER, Arthur H 164 Madaline 164 Margeret 136 W H 143 W L F 164
SLEIGHT, Jacob 183
SLOCUMB, Joseph 16
SLYDON, Tar--- 164
SMALL, Jno 107 John B 1 111 Lavinia E 1 Levina E 120
SMITH, A F 100 Amanda J 262 Ann E 200 Anne W 72 Arthur 53 C P 231 252 C S 215 Calvin 215 Calvin Stephen 18 Caroline C 261 Charity 226 Charles 206 Charlotte 38 Daniel 200 Dr 199 Eleanor 36 Eliza 53 177 Eliza A 212 Eliza C 28 Elizabeth 234 Elizabeth Ann 55 Elizabeth B 257 Elizabeth H 218 Emily 37 38 Frances M 205 George 120 190

SMITH (continued)
George S 26 Henry Mason 190
Hester 71 Israel 194 J 174 J
Farris 153 J R 147 J W N 21
James 38 58 72 215 234 James
H 38 James Jr 72 Jane 38 194
Jedediah 209 Jefferson 26 John
20 22 John P 262 John W 183
John W N A 21 Joseph 65
Laura 252 Lawrence W 186
Leonard 37 Leonora 37 Louisa
147 186 Louisa M 70 Lucretia
209 Luther L 224 M Wm M
259 Malcolm 123 Malissa M
265 Martha 18 Martha A 215
Mary 22 168 Mary Ann 27 244
Mary Ann Catharine 123 Mary
E 176 Mary F 103 Mary J 190
Mary Jane 123 Mary O 76 126
Merrill 244 Myra 100 Nancy 57
P---wood 223 Peter 236
Prestwood 228 R 68 R D 169
188 R F 110 Reddick 170
Richard C 135 Robert 9 Robert
H 205 Russel 168 Russell 176
Samuel 57 Sarah 23 228 Sarah
C 170 Sarah Matilda 223
Thomas 218 254 W C 264
Walter 70 William B 8 141
William F 200 William H 142
Z 265
SMITHY, William 124
SMOOT, A E 32 Emily H 32
Laura Dade 32
SMYLIE, Amelia F 91 James 91
92 232 John A 259 Mary Ann H
92
SMYTH, Elizabeth J 26 W M 24
William Mortimer Jr 26 Wm
M 26
SNEATHEN, Virginia 28 Worthington G 28
SNEED, Geo J 45
SNELL, Hanson 49
SNETHEN, Nicholan 144
SNODGRASS, David 201
SNOW, Elizabeth 47 Ezra G 63
Mark 63
SNOWDON, Margaret 45
SNYDER, Adam J 207 Elizabeth J
207 Margaret Jane 32
SOHN, Francis 94

SOULE, Franklin 262 Mary Pierson 262
SOUSBY, Elizabeth 197 Samuel 197
SOUTH, Rev Mr 82
SOUTHERLAND, Amanda 25
George 25 Mary Ann 217 Peter 217
SPANN, C S 50 80 148 Caroline V
121 Charles S 95 Henrietta 95
Henrietta W 80 148 Indiana
Cordelia M 62 M 30 Martha W
120 Richard 120 S R 8 Susan
140 W H 50
SPARKE, Eliza W 94 Elizabeth B
131 Wm H 94
SPARKS, M 83 Richard 195
SPARROW, Elizabeth 24
SPEARS, Charlotte 170 John N 48
Julia Ann 48 Martha 214 Sarah
40 Wm R 170
SPEED, Flora Ann 30 Matissa 31
Napoleon Bonapart 30
SPEER, Matilda Jane 64 Rev Mr 64
SPEERS, Rev Mr 259
SPELL, Elijah 50 Sarah A 50
SPENCE, S S 110 Serenia L 48
SPIGHT, Jos C 48
SPITZER, Euphemia H 29
SPOHN, Maria 101 Samuel 101 129
SPRAGUE, Margaret G 154
Sturges 154
SPRINGER, B 101 Benjamin 164
D 100 Judge 140 145
SPROLES, Mary 38 Richard 141
SPURLOCK, Drury 246
SQUIRES, Norman 68
STACKHOUSE, Sarah 59 Wm 59
STAFFORD, Elizabeth 45
STAMPLY, Julian 70 Solomon B 70
STAMPS, Franky 88 Samuel 88 W
J 256 William 88 Wm 255
STANARD, Ann 193 H C 139
Robert 42 139 William 193
STANBROUGH, David 180 Zilpha 180
STANDRET, E 40
STANLEY, Catharine B 176 Rev Mr 62

STANTON, Aaron 16 Anna Maria 257 Betsy 209 F 16 P L 252 R L 250 253 256 258 Rev Mr 250 251 Robert Livingston 257 Varina 19
STAR, A M 241 Elizabeth 241
STARK, Mary 211 Robert 216 217 Sophia 216 217 Theodore 197
STARKE, Theodore 255
STARR, Caroline 113 Charles 113
STAUNTON, R L 254
STEARNS, Emeline A 33 William F 33
STEDMAN, B M 66 Balinda A 66
STEED, Caroline 79 Laura M 79 Wm 79
STEEL, E 245 248 Levina 102 Rev Mr 248
STEELE, Alex T 190 C 172 Elijah 242 245 251 Eliza 172 Maria L 190
STEEN, Robert 22
STEIGELMAN, Caroline 135 Conrad 163 203 F 135 M 135
STEMBRIDGE, John 233 Matilda 233
STENHENS, Minerva C 141
STEPHENS, Abednego 141 Elizabeth 24 F E 213 Henry 212
STEPHENSON, E M 3 Jos 99 L W 3 Mary E 257
STERDEVANT, Adaline 124
STERLING, John 15 Mr 235 Susan B 15 Thomas S 93
STERRETT, A M 4 117
STERRY, J L 38 Mary H 38
STEVENS, Edward 238 Elizabeth 238 J B 102 John B 4 William 6
STEVENSON, Mary 122
STEVETT, William 129
STEWART, Allan 63 Andrew 84 Catharine 255 Catharine A 83 84 Catharine J 238 Celia Ann 53 Charles 221 Duncan 222 Elenora 20 Elizabeth 63 227 252 Frances Adeline 8 Frances Matilda 257 Francis Matilda 125 G W 84 George W 61 Honora 9 10 46 149 Hugh C 84 J E 149 J P 25 J Philip 8

STEWART (continued) James 163 James E 9 46 Janette C 213 John 213 Lehonora 149 Margaret 84 Margaret N 74 Mary 242 Mary Ann 231 Mary C 8 Mary Jane 258 Miller 20 Moses 227 Nancey 53 Nancy 149 Nolan 255 Nolan D 258 Penelope 256 261 R A 241 R C 10 Rhoda L 25 Ruth 29 Sally Ann 211 Sarah A G 29 Thomas 53 Tugnal Jones 211 William 219 229 Wm H 74
STIDGER, H 153
STILES, Ed H 84 Mary Osborn 84
STILL, Elizabeth H 252 Nathaniel 252
STILLMAN, Elizabeth S 74 George 74
STINSON, Ann 126 John 126
STITE, H H 9
STITES, Girard 10 113 162 H H 188 Mary L 10 113 162 Phoebe A 142 Samuel 128 William F 10 William Folwell 10
STITH, Benjamin H 122 Capt 5 99 121 Julia Anna 99 Lawrence Washington 134 Thaddeus 5 Thadeus 121
STLENING, William 129
STOCKET, Sarah 264
STOCKETT, J J 240 Mary Olivia 240
STOCKTON, Ann H 38 Wm A 38
STOCKWELL, William 19
STOCUMB, A P 257 Clarinda Catharine 257
STOKES, Charlotte C 62 George 62
STONE, Amanda 61 Charles H 219 Mary G 219 William P 61
STOUT, Martha 138 Nancy 12 156
STOVALL, Caroline 22 Geo 146 Martha 117 Mary 100 127 Ralph 117 William W 100 117 William W R 127 Wm 127
STOWERS, John 39 138 Lewis 138
STRAMP, George 125
STRANSBURY, J 206
STRATTON, Jos B 143 Rev Mr 154 167

STRAUB, Catherine 193
STREET, Eliza 39 H 230 Henry G 232 Joseph H 229 230 Victorie Caroline 232 William 134
STRICKLAND, E R 10 149
STRICKLIN, Martin 22 Penelope 22
STRINGER, Celia Ann 42
STRONG, Eliza L 259 Henry 259 Priscilla G 159
STROTHER, Sarah 262
STUART, Benjamin C 241 Charlotte 170 Elizabeth Yates 27 128 J Philip 128 John Philip 128 Maria 101 Martha C 241 Martha E 68 Mary Eleanor 128 V M 68
STUBBLEFIELD, Jon L 127
STUBBS, Ann 53 Martha B 53
STUKY, John M 173 Mary M 173
SULIVAN, Mr 136
SULLIVAN, D D 202 Daniel 31 M 31 S A 35 Thomas 31
SULLY, John 190
SUMMERS, G W 139 John 139 M J 139 Mrs 136
SUMRALL, Drury 97
SUNGENATI, Joseph 205
SURGET, C 201 Catherine 201
SUTTON, D W 187 Sarah G 81
SWAIZE, Lucretia 213
SWANSON, Harriet E 63
SWARTWOUT, William 106
SWAYZE, Caleb 242 Nancy 242
SWEENEY, Peter 49
SWEET, Caroline 181 Daniel 43 181 Sarah 181 Sarah E 43
SWETT, Daniel 118 Sarah 118 Sarah E 118 Sarah Elizabeth 118
SWIGART, Lavina 242
SWINEY, J W 182
SWING, James 91
SWINGLE, Alfred 233 Laura E 233
SWINK, J 160
SWINNEY, Hampton 253 Sarah Ann 253
SWISHER, Samuel 188
SWORDS, Lorenzo D 112 Mary 161
SYDNOR, E A W 1 Thomas 1

TABB, Henry 178 Martha 178 Mary A O 2
TALBOT, 19
TALBOT, Caroline G W 108 Franklin 108
TALIAFERRO, Samuel L 121
TALLIFERRO, Catharine 25
TANKERSLEY, Benj F 41 Gertrude Eliza 41
TAPPAN, B S 157 Benjamin S 103 Gen 101 John Wood 101 Joseph W 103 M B 157 Margaret B 103 Virginius 157
TARBE, Ann 218 John 218
TARPLEY, Missouri 24
TATE, Charlotte 38 G B 176
TATOM, Leroy H 77
TAYLOR, Amanda E 132 B T 48 C 103 Catherine J 32 D V 39 E B 39 40 Eliza L 111 Isabella Norvelle 89 J M 34 76 149 J Theus 89 James W 68 John M 34 121 John P 159 Maria L 190 Martha P 114 Mary L 48 Mr 93 Nathaniel M 32 Sarah D 103 Sigismunda Mary 34 V D 40 W H 88 133 William H 89 124
TEER, James 185
TEKLE, Emeline 260 Robert 260
TEMONS, John H 266 Mary Dorothy 266
TEMPLETON, A M 171 James W 150 John 171 Martha E 128 150 Samuel 128 150
TENS, Lovey 29
TERRELL, Anne 201 Archibald 91 201 Courtney Ann 91 Diana 172 Elizabeth Lee 96 Samuel 172
TERRETT, Amanda 83 Amanda Olitipa 83 John Hunter 86 Julia D 86 Mary Amelia 83 William H 83
TERRY, Emeline R 77 Jno 56 John 56 Samuel D 77
THATCHER, J S B 149
THEILMAN, Catharine 260 Frederick 260
THERREL, Jane A 228 John B 228
THERRELL, Terresa Ann 264
THIGPEN, Jas Jr 59

THINKLER, John 202 John 159
THOM, Henry 248
THOMAS, Amanda 138 Andrew 150 Ann R 235 Caroline 150 Daniel 163 207 Danl 137 J P 113 James L 203 L M 174 M E 51 Maj 126 Martha L 207 Mary 37 Mary E 113 Mrs 203 Painela 50 Pitt 125 126 Priscilla 163 Rolly 21 Sarah W 26 William L 166 Wm 203
THOMPSON, Ann 176 Eliza C 255 Elizabeth 172 Emily F 189 George 132 Henry Nahum 55 Jacob 12 Mary 98 192 Mary B 55 Mr 17 Nancy H 52 Robert Wm 58 Robt 255 T J 55 Thomas J 58 W R 204 Wm H 3
THOMS, H T 257
THOMSON, Biddy 215 Delila 215 Littleberry 215 216
THORN, Henry T 209 M 209 T 127
THORNLEY, Thos 130
THORNTON, Charles A 242 Cornelia V 242
THRIFT, S B 136
THROCKMORTON, Maria 197 R L 249
THUM, Eliza E 160 William H 160
TICKELL, Edward 165 Elizabeth 165
TIDINGS, Mary E 154
TIEDEMAN, Margaret P H 168
TIFLE, Catlette 38 Prescilla 38
TIGNER, Amanda Caroline 241 Ann C 220 Wm 220
TILDEN, J W R 120 Levina E 120
TILL, Susan 129 Wm Henry 120
TILLBURN, Joseph 67 Theodosia 67
TILLERY, Martha L 232 William 232
TILLEY, Sophia 37
TILLMAN, Eliz 54 Thomas 54
TILLOTSON, Eliza Ann 228 Samuel 228
TILTON, Nehemiah 195
TIMBERLAKE, Henry A 45

TIMMONS, Frances J 117
TIMON, John 261
TIPTON, Emiline 30
TISDALE, Benjamin F 157 Maria M 157
TODD, Catharine 161 Joseph H 161 Susan 249
TOGET, John 135
TOMBS, William 54
TOMLINSON, Jacob Lafayette 55 W E 55
TOMPKINS, Catherine Jane 136 Elizabeth E 6 Lucy Ann 34 Mary Jane 99 Patk W 99 Sarah Jane 33 Thomas W 33 136
TOOL, Mary 232
TOOLE, Anne 219 Laura E 233
TOOLEY, Adam 194
TORRY, Miss 201
TOWER, Pliney 239
TOWNES, A T 100 Allen 151 Virginia A 100
TOWNSEND, Elizabeth 184 J 190 John 6 133 134 146 184 Matilda 146 William 135
TRACY, Dennis 111
TRAHERN, James Jr 20 Jesse 16 William 62
TRAINER, Mariah Ann 30 Torrence 30
TRARLL, Charles 186
TRASK, I E 230 J L 216 230 232 William P 263
TRAVIS, Edmund R 161 Elizabeth A 161 Joseph 182
TRAWACK, Dr 58 Margaret Matilda 58
TRAWEEK, George B 73
TREZVANT, G W C 151 Mary M 151
TRIBBLE, John F 106
TRIFORD, Martha 106 Mary Ann 184
TROTTER, Alexander 95 Ch 39 Elizabeth Lee 96 Faith 95 Rebecca 39 William B 96
TROWBRIDGE, Catherine 113 William 113 188
TRULY, B R 157
TRUMBULL, William 7
TUCKER, 199 Catharine A 83 Gray W 134 John 115

TUCKER (continued)
  M S 203 Robert 83 Sarah 134
TUELL, Ann 226 Samuel 211
TUFTS, Martha 178 William A
  178
TUNSTALL, Albert 127
TUOHY, John 127
TUOLEY, John 5
TURBERVILLE, Hannah 247
TURBEVILLE, Jane 249 Margaret
  B 221 Martha A 250 Samuel
  221
TURNBULL, Duncan 179 John
  175 181 Wm 101
TURNER, Amanda 227 E M 203
  Edward 13 Frances Ann 224
  Jane 176 John 135 John C 160
  Malissa 229 Martha Ann 160
  Robert 224 Theodosia L 13
  William 176
TURPIN, Delia S 30 Francis W
  30
TWICHELL, Rev Dr 192
TWO, L M 174 Wm 174
TWONEY, Bridget 54 John 54
TYLER, F 100 Virginia A 100
TYRON, Mary A E 246
ULMAN, Sophia 41
ULRICK, John 136
UNDERWOOD, Jas 15
UPSHAW, Edward W 81 Mary L
  81
URSERY, Mrs 93
VADEN, Harriet 256 Lodwick N
  256
VAIL, Richard H 108
VALENTINE, Adeline 67 Ann E
  177 Richard 67 Roswell 177
  Winfield S 156
VALLANDINGHAM, N W 81
VAN ALLEN, Miss 25
VAN METER, A 18
VANCE, Caroline 47
VANCOURT, Rev Mr 17
VANDORN, P A 91 Sarah Ross 91
VANGHEN, Ann Eliza 37 Chas N
  37
VANHOUTEN, C 217
VANNATTA, S W 132
VANSLIKE, Daniel 108
VANTINE, Mrs 108
VANTONE, John 186

VANZILE, Eliza 98
VARDAMAN, William 39
VARDEMAN, Rhoda 39
VARLEY, E 179
VARNELL, James 263 Marinda
  234 Thirsa Ann 263
VAUGHN, Charlotte 125 David W
  53 Mary R 55 Thomas 67
  Wiley B 55
VAUGHNS, Mrs 54
VEAZIE, J H 123 Mary Jane 123
VELVIN, Ann G 89 Anna E 80
VENPORT, Charles S 243
VENTRESS, Charlotte 86 261
  Eliza Ann 208 Elizabeth 210 J
  A 86 J Alexander 261 Lovick
  208 210
VERTNER, D 263
VETTER, J M 159 Joanna 145
VICK, Anne Marin 173 Asenith 56
  Eliz 180 H W 154 Hartwell 178
  Henry W 139 John 173 Martha
  Virginia 178 Mary E 172 Mary
  T 180 Newet 180 Wm 180
VICTOR, Peter L 265 T 179
VINCENT, William 149
VINSON, Nathan Lufbrough 119
VINTON, Charles H 158 Lavinia
  E 1
VIRDEN, Anne 85 Thomas 85
VOGH, Jacob 145 159 Leonora
  145 Margaret 109 145 Mar-
  guarett 97 Priscilla G 159
  Sevella 116 Valentine 192
VOGLE, Mrs 136
VOIGHT, John 87 Viola E 87
  William Augustus 87
VOSE, Anna 225 Eugenia
  Jamesella 122 Henry 70 225
  James 111 173 Mary Elizabeth
  225 Mrs 155 S P 122 Sophronia
  H 173
WADDEL, John N 152
WADDELL, J N 96
WADDILL, Charles D 250
  Matilda C 250
WADE, Ann 146 188 Francena R
  251 James D 179 Judge 248
  Maria Louisa 32 W A 55 Wil-
  liam A 55 56
WADSWORTH, Cytheria E 47 F
  C 47

WAGSTAFF, E T 136
WAHL, Gottleib 204
WAILES, Edmund H 266 Jane B 266
WALCOTT, E D 129 L I 131 Sarah Ann 161
WALDEN, Nancy 116 William 104
WALKER, 175 Amelia 218 Benjamin 227 Benson 53 Duncan S 176 Eliza 15 Emeline 227 Frances Minerva 66 Francis 79 Henry F 137 J B 35 84 James 227 Jefferson 88 John 222 John F 79 155 Jos N 232 Juliet T 222 Kinchen Holliman 224 Laurentina Ophelia 167 Lavina 232 Major 136 Martha Almedia 79 Mary B 227 Mary Fulton 179 Matilda 79 Peter 15 R J 35 Rev Mr 15 17 Samuel 95 Samuel D 66 Thomas F 107 179 W F 167 William 222 Willis 79 Z 224 Zachariah 261
WALL, Catharine S 192 Eliza B 37 John L 260 M H 192 Rev Mr 34 Spencer 232
WALLACE, 219 Caroline A 31 D M 191 Daniel 202 Suletta 37
WALLER, Rebecca B C 227
WALLS, Mary Ann 169
WALSH, Richard 16
WALTON, Daniel 73 Sarah 235 Thomas S 49
WALWORTH, John P 17 Sarah 17
WAND, James 41
WARD, Hester Elizabeth 96 John 132 Martha C 1 181 Mary 157 P W 1 2 181 W T 96 William H 124
WARDLOW, Talba L 124 Zachariah 124
WARE, G A 50 80 Gustavus A 89 Sarah M 75 Sarah Rebecca 50 80 William A 75
WARFIELD, Eliza W 27
WARREN, A N 6 113 173 E R 137 Edwd R 126 Emily E 173 Emma 126 Emma H 126 J B 68 John 33 John A 231 Mary Ann 231 Mary E 113 161 Mr 135 N 129 R H 109

WASHBURN, Alfred F 149 E W 149
WASHINGTON, Fairfax 63 Sarah 63
WATCHER, John 185
WATERS, Virginia 229
WATKINS, Flora Ann 30 Rebecca J 238 W H 260 Wm E 3
WATKINSON, R A 37 Sophia 37
WATROUS, John S 7
WATSON, Eliza R 66 Frances Minerva 66 James 67 James M Jr 69 James S 71 Jane M 173 Jeremiah 66 Martha Jane 69 Mary Jane 67 Nancy 27 Olivia 65 Sam 254
WATT, Hugh 128
WATTS, 130 Matinda 148 Rhoda L 25
WEAKLY, James C 254 Mary 254
WEASE, John 7
WEATHERSBY, Julia Ann 219 Solomon 219
WEAVER, Emeline Ann 35 Jesse 21 Melinda M 21 W Scott 191
WEBB, Catharine 260 John 164 Judith 58 Mary H 221 Noah 221 Susan 233 Wm R 58
WEBBER, Richard W 27
WEBSTER, Geo W 181 Isaac 100 Mary 100 Theodore 181
WECK, John 121
WEED, Reuben 45 William 259 William Jr 258
WEEKLEY, James C 241
WEEKS, A B 77 Andrew 48 Jane 42 John 130 Maria 48 Nancy 77
WEEMS, Jas I 251
WEIGART, B F 14
WEISSE, D 206
WEISSENGER, James M 143
WELCH, Margaret 118 Mary 115 Thomas 113
WELLER, Catharine 161 Dr 112 George 142 161 George Wells 112 Rev Dr 71 99 106 Rev Mr 104 219 Susan B 142
WELLS, Angelica Martense 104 Col 134 E 249 Henrietta F A 134 Isaac 61 J A 229 John 185 Martha L 13 Richard 104 Samuel 62 Thos J 13 Wm J 62

WELSH, John 130 Timothy 192
WEMPLE, James 28
WERLEIN, Margaret 150 Philip P 150
WERNER, Elizabeth 150
WESBROOK, Elizabeth A 264
WESLEY, Catharine Ann 147 John 147
WESSEL, Elizabeth Caroline 73 John 73
WEST, A M 47 Benjamin 92 C 244 C C 219 239 244 Caroline O 47 Charles C 240 James M 52 James R 173 Jane M 159 202 Martha Octavia 220 Nancy H 52 Paulina 92 Samuel H 92 Sara Olivia 237 Thomas W 220 Thos G 240 William Howard 237
WESTBERRY, Catharine 249
WHARTON, Henry 183 Rev Dr 14
WHATLEY, Martha 207 Olivia 133 Sarah 154 Tillman 154
WHEAT, J T 34
WHEATLY, Catharine B 127 R S 127
WHEATON, Rev Mr 249
WHEELER, 11 153 John 38 M W 38
WHELAGHAN, Walter 134
WHELAN, James K 64 Matilda Jane 64
WHELEES, Elizabeth Anne 6 Frederick W 6
WHETSTONE, Eleanor C 232 Jackson Carroll 232
WHIPPLE, William E 184
WHISTLER, John 92
WHITAKER, Ann B M 234 Anna 156 Charlotte L 159 J 156 J B 234 Mrs F 158 159 Robina E 246
WHITE, Ambrose J 17 Andrew 157 Ann M 202 203 Beatina M 23 Caroline 75 Chapman 210 Charles Henry 222 Elizabeth 227 Ellen 231 Harriet B 222 Harriet Jane 83 Isaac 30 J B 104 J M 82 James 222 Jane 87 John F 164 Joice 30 Joshua R 83 Julia E 80 Laura 186 Maria J 82 Mary 253 Mary G 9 148

WHITE (continued) Matthew 203 Nathan S 32 Rebecca Ann 230 Reuben 217 Right Rev Bishop 92 Samuel 23 Susannah Virginia 222 T S 75 Thomas 166 238 Thomas S 80 88 W V 44 William 7 Wm D 230
WHITEHEAD, Mrs F A 25 77
WHITESIDES, Lewis 71
WHITFIELD, B 113 Benjamin 191 Benjamin H 113 Julia A 32 Sarah A E 191
WHITIKER, James E 161 Sarah 161
WHITING, Elizabeth G 76 F A 76
WHITINGTON, L W 129
WHITMAN, Eliz Jane 103 Mary F 163 203 Roland M 103
WHITNEY, Elizabeth G 125 F A 125 John 36 Melissa Ann 36 Minor M 226 Myra Clark 98 Penelope 226 Sarah 183
WHITTAKER, John 242 Robina 242
WHITTEMORE, 16
WHITTINGTON, L W 6 Wm 130
WICK, Walter 160
WICKLIFFE, Aaron 148 Charles 153 Mary E 148 Nannie C 153
WICKLITTLE, Aaron 80 Mary E 80
WIER, Mr 162
WIGGINS, Mary R 55
WILCOX, Caleb 264 Ellen Hammond 35 Joseph M 194 Mr 16 P B 217
WILEY, Adeline 146 Adeline A 48 John 234 L 10 141 Lysander 48 146 R 10 Rev Mr 65
WILKERSON, Armissa 170 James 170
WILKINS, Caroline V 121 Charlotte 201 James Campbell 201 John 182 Robert 121 Talba L 124
WILKINSON, Amanda M 41 Ann 193 Benjamin R 28 Caledoria 163 Christian Priscilla 80 Cordelia 167 D W 41 84 Dr 83 Eliza 250 Eliza C 28 Geo B 167 James B 193 Jane M 84

316

WILKINSON (continued)
 Julia 46 145 Major Gen 193
 Mary F 235 Mrs S 28 Nancy 41
 Patience B 83 Robert A 235 S
 131 Stephen 25 Stephen D 250
 Thomas V 83 Vincent A 46 145
 Wm 191
WILLIAMS, Adalind 188 Adaline
 118 147 Agnes W 91 Alfred A
 255 B H 141 Balsora 156 Balzorah 180 Benjamin 50 Benjamin Baldwin 156 Benjamin H
 256 C C 207 Caroline 90 96
 Catharine 255 Charles S 202
 Charlotte 207 D O 90 Daniel O
 264 Ebenezer 237 Eli 128
 Eliza Jane 237 Elizabeth 194
 Elizabeth B 257 Elizabeth
 Caroline 73 Ellen 154 Ephm
 108 G B 180 G C 137 G W 79
 George B 156 Governor 194 H
 Elizabeth 108 Harriet 42 Henry
 124 J C 73 Jacob 127 James
 140 Jane 28 John O 234 Joseph
 W 118 Judge 213 Louisa 36 M
 A E 207 M C 32 Martha 127
 Martha M 256 Mary 208 Mary
 A 167 Mary Francis 118 Mary
 Jane 73 264 Maryann 42
 Matilda 79 Morning 61 Mrs E
 11 N T 93 167 Putnam T 68 R
 C 62 Richard S 91 Sophronia 46
 Sophronia A 50 U S 42 William
 96 Wm Harrison 247 Wm M 36
 257
WILLIAMSON, E A 155 Frances
 202 J B 202 Martha Almedia
 79 Mary Frrdonia 158 R M 79
 223 Rebecca 23 Russell M 43
 140 Sarah 94 Thomas 202
 Thomas G 159 Wiley W 23
WILLIFORD, Elizabeth 46 John
 H 97
WILLIS, Alexander 68 Assenith
 55 Katharine 68 Margaret 51
 Thomas A 51
WILLISTON, J P 155 156
WILLS, Eliza C 258 John F 258
WILMURTH, Catherine 204 Ralph
 P 204
WILSON, 13 Amanda 50 Caroline
 E 158 Charlotte A 36

WILSON (continued)
 Eliza Ann 172 Ellen 248 George
 W 158 Hamilton 25 Isaac 116
 J S 105 James 126 265 James
 F 37 John G 161 Joseph 185
 Joseph E 172 Margaret A 161
 Mary E 154 Mary F 163 203
 Miller 87 Nancy A 37 Rev Mr
 139 S H 163 203 Sarah 40 244
 William 36 248 William D 154
WILTSHIRE, Charles 171 Jordan
 171
WINANS, Cornelia Sophia 111
 John 111 Margaret L C 242
 Rev Dr 260 Rev Mr 238 246 W
 180 265 William 211 227 231
 232 240 242 245 251 253 255
 263 265
WINCHESTER, Josiah 154 Margaret G 154 Rev Mr 101
WINDHAM, Delila A 38 Jefferson
 38
WINDLEY, Susan 249
WININGHAM, Mary 265
WINKLER, Jacob 16
WINKLEY, Jno F 249
WINN, A M 8 Elizabeth 187
 James 108 John S 7 John W
 200 Margaret 42 Margaret M
 140 Penelope A 165 Peter 42
 140
WINNINGHAM, Mary L D 239
WINSLLOW, Minerva O 32
WINSLOW, 160 Martha 4 115
 Richard P 32
WINSTON, Fountain 66 171 Louis
 19
WINTER, A V 46 Isabella S 46
WIRT, William 225
WISE, Andrew 206 John J 56
 Sarah Ann D 56
WISNER, Emily 231 235 John 238
 260 Rebecca 246 Tebitha 238
 Thomas 231 235
WISSE, John 139
WONRIDER, 118
WOOD, Amanda M 182 B G 126
 Basil G 126 Benjamin F 131
 Eliza Jane 18 Ellinder 42 F 90
 Fleming 34 Fountain 165
 James G 44 Jas G 144 Julia
 156 Lucy Ann 34 Maryann 42

WOOD (continued)
  Mrs A C H 26 N N 125 132 133 134 135 139 150 187 Rev Mr 5 122 Sarah 56 Virginia E 152 William N 6 129 182
WOODARD, Elizabeth 234 Gilbert 250 J G 245 John G 250 Mary Ann 245
WOODBRIDGE, J 255
WOODBRIDLE, J 157
WOODBURN, Helen 163 Mary Ann 204
WOODFOLK, Elizabeth P 79
WOODLEY, William B 71
WOODMAN, Caroline 150 O O 150
WOODS, Ann B 29 Ann M 257 Ann Martha 248 David 29 Harriet 250 Isham 220 Isham F 250 258 Joseph 159 202 Mary A 240 Michael 213 Pamela 220 Sophronia 231 Susan H 213 William B 231 William F 257 William H 248 257 Wm 240
WOODSIDES, Emily Lacy 257 Thomas 257
WOODWARD, Olivia Adaline 45
WOODWARD, Roger D 45
WOOLDRIDGE, J 231
WOOLRODGE, A D 235
WOOLEY, Austin Bennett 41 Thomas R 41
WOOLFOLK, J P 190 Joseph 160 Sallie 160
WOOLS, Lasthina 120
WOOSTER, Nelson 220
WORD, Sarah 48
WORRAL, Mary C 97
WORSHAM, Susan C 259
WREN, John V 25 Sarah 17 W 17
WRIGHT, Ann Mariah 125 B W 238 Eliza 113 Ezekiel H 125 Geo B 113 J Gilbert 206 Marcellus L 206 Margt J 38 Mary N 201 Nancy 115 Rebecca J 238 William 191 201
WROTEN, Elizabeth 52 William C 52
WRY, Thomas F 207
WYATT, Joseph B S 227 Josephine 227 William 49
WYCH, Virginia A 29

WYCHE, G W 61
WYLEY, James W 128 Martha E 128
WYLLIS, Anne 194
YAGER, Edward 137 Mary Ann 137
YANCY, Charles 192
YARBROUGH, David 235 Elizabeth 237 Lewis A 237 Sarah 235
YARNELL, Isaac H 124
YATES, Daniel 33
YEISER, A L 142 E A 169 Eliza Lee 142 Eliza M 142 F Wm 169
YELVINGTON, Catharine 37 Henry 37
YERBY, B F 248 Catharine 248 Eleanor Eugenia 218 Elizabeth 243 Francis 212 Mrs 151 Thirsa Ann 212 William 21 210 212 243 William W 212 218
YERGER, Alexander 80 148 Elizabeth B 80 148 Geo S 189 J S 147 Mary 147 Mary Ann 189 Shalane 49 Shalline 147
YORK, James 105 Rosanna E 47
YOST, Jacob 185
YOUNG, Amanda H 21 Elizabeth 251 Henry 73 John G 88 John S 123 Letitia 60 Lewis 19 Louisa 73 Samuel 21 Sarah Ann 167 Thomas L 251 W H 60 Wm H 73
YULEE, David L 153 Nannie C 153
ZIMMER, James C 112
ZIMMERMAN, Hannah J 139 187 Solomon 139 187